Hong Kong in Transition

Also by Robert Ash

AGRICULTURAL DEVELOPMENT IN CHINA

ECONOMIC TRENDS IN CHINESE AGRICULTURE (*editor with Y. Y. Kueh*)

PERSPECTIVES OF CONTEMPORARY CHINA IN TRANSITION (*editor with Richard Edmonds and Yu-ming Shaw*)

THE CHINESE ECONOMY UNDER DENG XIAOPING (*editor with Y. Y. Kueh*)

Also by Peter Ferdinand

COMMUNIST REGIMES IN COMPARATIVE PERSPECTIVE

TAKE-OFF FOR TAIWAN

THE NEW CENTRAL ASIA AND ITS NEIGHBOURS

Also by Brian Hook

BEIJING AND TIANJIN: Towards a Millennial Megalopolis

CHINA'S 3000 YEARS (*with others*)

FUJIAN: Gateway to Taiwan

GUANGDONG: China's Promised Land

SHANGHAI AND THE YANGTZE DELTA: A City Reborn

THE CAMBRIDGE ENCYCLOPEDIA OF CHINA

THE INDIVIDUAL AND THE STATE IN CHINA

Also by Robin Porter

INDUSTRIAL REFORMERS IN REPUBLICAN CHINA

MANAGEMENT ISSUES IN CHINA: Volume 1: Domestic Enterprises (*editor with David Brown*)

REPORTING THE NEWS FROM CHINA (*editor*)

THE CHINA BUSINESS GUIDE (*with Mandi Robinson*)

Hong Kong in Transition
The Handover Years

Edited by

Robert Ash
Chiang Chin-kuo Professor of Taiwan Studies
School of Oriental and African Studies
University of London

Peter Ferdinand
Director
Centre for Studies in Democratisation
University of Warwick

Brian Hook
Emeritus Leverhulme Fellow
Visiting Professor, Centre for Southeast Asian Studies
University of Hull, and
Honorary Research Fellow
Centre of Asian Studies
University of Hong Kong

and

Robin Porter
Director
China Business and Policy Unit
University of Keele

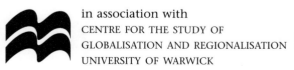

in association with
CENTRE FOR THE STUDY OF
GLOBALISATION AND REGIONALISATION
UNIVERSITY OF WARWICK

CENTRE FOR THE
STUDY OF
GLOBALISATION AND
REGIONALISATION

First published in Great Britain 2000 by
MACMILLAN PRESS LTD
Houndmills, Basingstoke, Hampshire RG21 6XS and London
Companies and representatives throughout the world

A catalogue record for this book is available from the British Library.

ISBN 0–333–77267–9

First published in the United States of America 2000 by
ST. MARTIN'S PRESS, INC.,
Scholarly and Reference Division,
175 Fifth Avenue, New York, N.Y. 10010

ISBN 0–312–23354–X

Library of Congress Cataloging-in-Publication Data
Hong Kong in transition : the handover years / edited by Robert Ash ... [et al.].
p.   cm.
Includes bibliographical references and index.
ISBN 0–312–23354–X (cloth)
1. Hong Kong (China)—Economic conditions. 2. Hong Kong (China)—Politics
and government—1997– 3. Hong Kong (China)—Social conditions. I. Ash,
Robert F.

HC470.3 .H668   2000
320.95125'09'049—dc21

00–023236

This book is printed on paper suitable for recycling and made from fully managed and sustained
forest sources.

10   9   8   7   6   5   4   3   2   1
09   08   07   06   05   04   03   02   01   00

Printed and bound in Great Britain by
Antony Rowe Ltd, Chippenham, Wiltshire

Contents

Preface and Acknowledgements

There may be no precedent in peacetime for the handing over of a whole society, functioning according to one set of rules, to another sovereign state which functions according to quite different rules and values. This, however, was the situation facing Hong Kong in recent years. Following discussions held in 1995, it was felt that an international academic gathering should be held in London to mark the passing of Hong Kong from British to Chinese sovereignty. This was achieved with the holding of the conference 'Hong Kong in Transition' at Chatham House in December 1997, jointly sponsored by four universities – the School of Oriental and African Studies, Warwick, Leeds and Keele – and Chatham House.

Following the conference, it was decided that the unique circumstances of Hong Kong at this time should be recognized in a significant publication. The transition throws up a range of pressing issues that call out for scholarly analysis, and it has been our aim to bring together the research of academics with different disciplinary perspectives on what was happening in Hong Kong, and from different part of the world, in a book that would cover with some degree of comprehensiveness the handover and the early period of Chinese rule.

It should be stressed, therefore, that the justification for the broad coverage attempted in this book lies in the particular circumstances of Hong Kong at this time. It seeks to raise issues that will be of fundamental importance for the survival of Hong Kong in its present form in the years to come. Through further conferences, and a further volume, it is hoped that it will be possible to follow Hong Kong's progress as it leaves behind the 'handover years' and stands ready to face a new century as part of China.

The editors wish to acknowledge the help of all who have made it possible to hold this series of conferences on Hong Kong and to produce this volume based on the first conference. In particular they would like to thank anonymous donors in Hong Kong, as well as the Centre for the Study of Globalization and Regionalization at the University of Warwick for contributing funding to the project, staff at Chatham House and at Warwick for their help with organization, Jan Keane at Keele for her patient work on the first draft of the text, and Keith Povey and staff at the publishers for the final version. To all we are most grateful.

SOAS	ROBERT ASH
Warwick	PETER FERDINAND
Leeds	BRIAN HOOK
Keele	ROBIN PORTER

Notes on the Contributors

The editors

Robert Ash is Chiang Ching-kuo Professor of Taiwan Studies at the School of Oriental and African Studies (SOAS), London, where he has taught in the Department of Economics since 1975. From 1986 to 1995 he was Director of the Contemporary China Institute at SOAS. In 1997, he became Director and Co-ordinator of the EU–China Academic Network, which is sponsored by the European Union. He has enjoyed a long association with *The China Quarterly*, for which, since 1982, he has compiled the 'Quarterly Chronicle and Documentation'. He has published widely on economic issues affecting China and Greater China. Recent books include *Economic Trends in Chinese Agriculture* and *The Chinese Economy under Deng Xiaoping* (both co-edited with Y. Y. Kueh), *Perspectives of Contemporary China in Transition* (co-edited with Richard Edmonds and Yu-ming Shaw) and *Agricultural Development in China, 1949–1989: the Collected Papers of Kenneth R. Walker*.

Peter Ferdinand has BA and DPhil degrees from Oxford and an MSc (Econ) from the London School of Economics. He has studied at Kiev University, held a Commonwealth Fund Fellowship at Harvard, and been a British Academy Exchange Fellow at the Chinese Academy of Social Sciences in Beijing. He taught in the Department of Politics at the University of Warwick between 1976 and 1989. From 1989 to 1993 he was Head of the Asia-Pacific Programme at the Royal Institute of International Affairs in London. Since 1993, he has been Director of the Centre for Studies in Democratisation at the University of Warwick. He teaches on the politics, economics and international relations of East Asia and the former communist world. Among his publications are *Communist Regimes in Comparative Perspective, The New Central Asia and its Neighbours* and *Take-off for Taiwan?*

Brian Hook is currently an Emeritus Leverhulme Fellow, Visiting Professor at the Centre for Southeast Asian Studies, University of Hull, and Honorary Research Fellow in the Centre of Asian Studies, University of Hong Kong. He was formerly a member of the administrative service in the Government of Hong Kong, a senior academic in the Department of East Asian Studies, University of Leeds and, from 1980–91, Editor of the *China Quarterly* at the Contemporary China Institute, School of Oriental and African Studies, University of London. He has published widely on China and Hong Kong.

Robin Porter holds BA and MA degrees in International Relations and in Chinese History from McGill University, Montreal, and a PhD in Modern

Chinese History from the School of Oriental and African Studies, University of London. Beginning in 1969, he taught Chinese and Pacific Asian History at Concordia University in Canada until leaving to spend a period working at New China News Agency in Beijing in 1979/80. He subsequently taught Chinese Politics in a visiting capacity at Murdoch and Melbourne Universities in Australia, and then became a full-time adviser on China to industry, based in London. Since 1989, he has been Director of the China Business and Policy Unit at Keele University. His publications include the books *Reporting the News from China* (editor) (Chatham House, 1992), *Industrial Reformers in Republican China, The China Business Guide* (with Mandi Robinson), and *Management Issues in China: Volume 1, Domestic Enterprises* (editor with David Brown).

The contributors

Beatrice Leung is Associate Professor in the Department of Politics and Sociology, Lingnan College, Hong Kong. She is the author of more than 30 scholarly articles on aspects of church–state relations, especially on Sino-Vatican relations, religious policy, and religious education in China, the Hong Kong SAR and Macao. She is author and editor of five books, of which the most recent is *Hong Kong SAR: in Pursuit of Domestic and International Order*.

Linda Chelan Li is Assistant Professor in the Department of Public and Social Administration, City University of Hong Kong, and author of *Centre and Provinces: China, 1978–1993. Power as Non-Zero Sum* (1998). Her current research interests include the politics of fiscal management in contemporary China, and a comparison of spatial politics in the European Union and China.

Teh-chang Lin is an Associate Research Fellow and Head of the Research Division of Economy and Society in Mainland China at the Institute of International Relations, National Chengchi University, Taipei. His recent publications include *Taiwan's Foreign Aid: an Instrument of Foreign Policy, Taiwan's Investment Policy in Mainland China: a Domestic Perspective*, and *Trade and Investment Patterns in Cross-Strait Relations: a Political and Economic Interaction*.

Tak-Wing Ngo is Lecturer in Chinese Politics at Leiden University, and currently a Fellow of the Netherlands Institute for Advanced Study of the Royal Netherlands Academy. He is the editor of *Hong Kong's History: State and Society under Colonial Rule* and co-editor of *The Cultural Construction of Politics in Asia*.

David J. Petersen is Vice-President, Distribution and Technical Services, for SMH (Hong Kong) Limited. He has lived and worked in Asia since 1989, travelling widely in the area. Prior to working for SMH he was employed by IBM.

Yin Qian graduated with her PhD from the Department of International Relations, Research School of Pacific and Asian Studies, the Australian National University. Her thesis was on Chinese foreign policy decision-making, with specific reference to the period between 1982 and 1997.

Elfed Vaughan Roberts lectured at the University of Hong Kong from 1978 until 1996. He is presently an honorary member of the Department of Politics and Public Administration, and Visiting Lecturer at the School of Business. He has published numerous books and articles on the Hong Kong business and political environment.

Janet Salaff received her PhD in Sociology at the University of California (Berkeley) in 1972, where she focused on the Chinese family and industrialization. She has studied Hong Kong since 1970, and especially Hong Kong factory workers. She is currently investigating decisions to emigrate from Hong Kong.

Miguel Santos Neves is Head of the Asia Programme at the Institute of International and Strategic Studies (IEEI) in Lisbon. He is a member of the Young Leaders Symposium of the Asia–Europe Forum (ASEM), and was on the advisory panel of experts to the Sino–Portugese Joint Liaison Group.

Ian Scott is Professor of Politics and Government at Murdoch University in Perth, Australia, having previously held the Chair in Politics and Public Administration at the University of Hong Kong. His most recent publication on the territory is the edited volume *Institutional Change and the Political Transition in Hong Kong*, published by Macmillan in 1998.

Susanne Weigelin-Schwiedrzik is Professor of Modern Sinology at the University of Heidelberg. She took her doctorate at Ruhr University in Bochum in 1982 with a thesis on the historiography of the Communist Party of China. Her publications include work on the history and historiography of twentieth century China, on the politics and political economy of China in the reform era, and on the transition process in Hong Kong.

Peter Wesley-Smith, the author of several books on the constitution and legal system of Hong Kong, was Professor of Constitutional Law at the University of Hong Kong. He recently resigned this post, and is now living in rural New South Wales.

Introduction

The Hong Kong Special Administrative Region: coping with uncertainty in the evolution of the second system

When the text of the Sino–British Joint Declaration was first published in September 1984, it launched Hong Kong into a new era. At that stage, the text still awaited formal ratification. But there was never any doubt it would be ratified and that this would occur on time. Despite the exclusion of Hong Kong as a formal party to the Anglo–Chinese talks, there was no possibility of re-negotiation to dispel local concerns about the detail, or lack of detail, in the text. In theory, there was a choice for Hong Kong: either accept or reject the agreement. In practice, there was no real choice: either accept the certainty conveyed in the terms of the agreement or face a prolongation of the current uncertainty about the future.

On paper the agreement looked good. There was a general consensus that the British negotiators had done a reasonable job. It is not surprising that they failed to persuade their Chinese counterparts of the advantages of their two preferred options: either extending the lease on the New Territories, the coming expiry of which had led to the negotiations, or of exchanging British sovereignty for continued British administration. Nor is it surprising the Chinese team failed to persuade their British counterparts of the bene-fits of a 'Macau-type solution'. The British options were well known negoti-ating positions. The Chinese option, formulated in the run-up to the negotiations, has only become widely known since the publication by Hong Kong Baptist University of the eponymous account by Wong Man Fong, a retired senior cadre, of China's resumption of sovereignty over Hong Kong.

The main benefit brought by the agreement lay in the promise of cer-tainty it conferred on Hong Kong. The main case for accepting it was not, however, the negative argument of the perils arising from the uncertainty of a unilaterally imposed solution. Although this consideration was ever present, the main case for acceptance was the argument that the agreement was reasonable and the best that could be achieved in the circumstances. There was no advantage to be gained from acting otherwise.

Once Hong Kong was launched into a new era, it would exchange the uncertainties of past decades for a more certain future. The precariousness of the post-war decades had been well captured in the title of Richard Hughes' book: *Hong Kong: Borrowed Place, Borrowed Time*. The aptness of this phrase is evident from the experience of the post-Second World War years. In the late 1940s, first the fear of Nationalist (Guomindang) interfer-ence, and then, as the tide of Civil War in China turned against that party, of Communist (Gongchandang) 'liberation', engendered sufficient uncertainty to impede progress on constitutional reform. In the 1950s, its raison d'être, entrepôt trade, having been undermined by the West's policy of containing China, Hong Kong was inundated by political and social refugees from the mainland. More migrants came in the 1960s, attracted now by Hong Kong's early economic success, which was due to immigrant entrepreneurs, local pragmatism and expatriate mercantilism. That respite was, however, short lived. The Cultural Revolution spilled over into Hong Kong and was a sharp reminder of the fundamental uncertainties in the colony's international position.

The 1970s was to be the most confident decade in an uncertain half century. By then the context had changed. Although the flaws in British administration had been exposed by indigenous rioting in the late 1960s, a clear majority of the people of Hong Kong emphatically rejected the ideology that had generated the anarchy of the Cultural Revolution. Attempts were made under Governor Maclehose to remedy the most conspicuous flaws affecting the administration, and the 1970s consequently became a decade of political consolidation and socio-economic progress.

The appointment of Sir Murray Maclehose, a British career diplomat, as Governor in 1971 was, however, a timely reminder that no matter how stable or prosperous Hong Kong might become, ultimately it would return to China. The appointment of a diplomat, in preference to a serving senior colonial administrator, signalled the advent of a new agenda. In retrospect, not only was the appointment exceptional, but so was the quality of the term in office. Hong Kong was well run and its prosperity increased significantly. By the end of the decade, such was the level of prosperity in, and the degree of identity of its people with, Hong Kong, that the horizons of planners and investors were increasingly projected forward to 1997.

For economic reasons, the question then arose as to what would be the constitutional position of Hong Kong at midnight on 30 June 1997, when the lease on the New Territories was due to expire. As the so-called New Territories had long since been fully integrated infrastructurally into the whole of the territory, the distinction between ceded and leased parts offered no obvious escape from uncertainty. This led to the Anglo–Chinese negotiations on the future of Hong Kong and, in turn, to the Joint Declaration. In this way Hong Kong was propelled into addressing the issues implicit in the impending transition from Dependent Territory under British sovereignty to Special Administrative Region under Chinese sovereignty. Once ratified, the agreement removed the uncertainty about constitutional status that, even while Hong Kong's prosperity increased and key international role developed, had hung like the sword of Damocles over the territory.

While the removal of such a major preoccupation was greeted with general relief, it was a particular relief for the local and resident international business communities. China had embarked on reform and had opened up to the outside world following the return to power of Deng Xiaoping. The Hong Kong economy was being rapidly restructured. Employers were taking advantage of abundant low-cost labour to relocate Hong Kong manufacturing facilities to the mainland. Outward processing and the growth of the service sector of the economy were to significantly characterize the first half of the 13-year transition period. At the same time, these developments were paralleled by new social forces engendered by the advances of the 1970s, epitomized by the growth of the Hong Kong middle class and ushered in by generational change. The negotiations had been deliberately shielded from the reality of these progressive forces, and it was inevitable, in retrospect, that they should come to play such an important part in the debates and controversies that were to characterize the transition period. Indeed, the influence of these social forces on the implementation of the agreement in the transition period would coincide with pressure from Leninist forces within the Communist Party of China seeking to influence the nation's path to modernization and to impede its fledgling democracy movement. Whereas in 1984 it seemed possible that the known imperfections in the agreement might be remedied through the liberal and market forces at work in China, within five years of the accord this seemed no longer likely to happen. The violent suppression of the democracy movement in 1989 was to have a profound effect on the remainder of the transition. The constitutional reform programme proposed under Governor Patten was opposed implacably by the Chinese government and much of the business community in Hong Kong. Its passage, with modifications, brought a decision of the National People's Congress to dismantle the three tiers of representative government elected in 1994–5, and to replace them with provisional bodies pending fresh elections under revised laws in 1998. In the interim, the Hong Kong Special Administrative Region would have a Provisional Legislative Council formed in early 1997 and sworn in after midnight on 30 June 1997.

With this provenance it was expected that the challenges facing the first Chief Executive, Tung Chee-hwa, and his Executive Council would primarily be political. To a limited extent this was initially to be true. The new administration promptly addressed the perceived need to set parameters for the emerging political culture. There followed controversial, yet not unexpected, amendments to the Electoral Laws, Bill of Rights, the Societies Ordinance, the Public Order Ordinance and the Adaptation of Laws Ordinance. Elections to the legislature were duly held in May 1998. Despite inclement weather, in an unexpectedly high turn-out and under a system of proportional representation less favourable to them than the former 'first past the post' system, most of the pro-democracy politicians summarily dismissed in 1997 were returned to the legislature.

Although this electoral response brought about a revival in the prospects for democratization, this central issue of the late 1980s and, early 1990s, was eclipsed by the sudden and unexpected regional economic crisis. Gathering momentum in 1998 the crisis had a severe impact on Hong Kong. The economy went into recession, property prices fell, unemployment rose. Pressure on the dollar peg culminated in an unprecedented intervention by the Hong Kong Monetary Authority into the local stock market in August 1998.

The challenges encountered during the years of transition, both before and since retrocession, set against the background of related issues over the preceding four decades, are the material for the studies in this book.

The chapters in this book on the Hong Kong business environment, government and politics, social discourse and external relations form the basis of an ongoing study of the unique and evolving practice of 'One Country – Two Systems' in the Hong Kong Special Administrative Region.

The Hong Kong business environment

Hong Kong is, par excellence, a centre for international business, so it is appropriate that in the first section of the book problems relating to the Hong Kong business environment should be addressed. Roberts and Petersen find, as they say, both 'opportunities and dangers' for business in the transfer of sovereignty. Optimists point to the smooth transition, an institutional framework favourable to business, congenial fiscal policies, the established civil service, the rule of law, the utility of Hong Kong as a platform for investment in China and other factors. Pessimists emphasize dangers to Hong Kong's administrative autonomy and legal system, structural problems in the economy, and Hong Kong's growing commercial vulnerability in Asia consequent on the financial crises in other states, as well as from south China's own economic emergence. The authors weigh the evidence, setting political stability against, in the short term anyway, hard times in the economy.

Ngo explores the relationship between business and government in Hong Kong. Looking back to government–business relations during the colonial period, he finds a situation that was neither complete government autonomy nor complete capture by business, a delicate balance that managed to prevent a decline into rent seeking, and helped Hong Kong business to focus on profit making. Since the transfer of sovereignty, however, with the marginalization of popular participation and enshrinement of sectional, and especially business interests in the government and legislature, he concludes that the collaborative relationship has turned 'into one of collusion'.

The chapter by Ferdinand examines the techniques of monetary management employed by Hong Kong during financial crises of the 1980s, and again in October 1997. Ferdinand argues that, while it was the crises of 1983 and 1987, and the government's response to them, that turned Hong Kong into a fully fledged participant in the international financial system, with developed management and regulatory mechanisms, the financial crisis of October 1997, when the Hong Kong dollar and its peg to the US dollar came under attack, actually may have consolidated Hong Kong's autonomy in financial matters. Ferdinand tentatively concludes that, while circumstances could occur that would cause the interests of Hong Kong and China to diverge, in this first test the Hong Kong Monetary Authority and the Chinese government complemented one another in their actions to preserve the credibility of Hong Kong's financial system.

The following two chapters look at dimensions of Hong Kong's role in the business of the region. Ash looks, for the years leading up to the transition, at the process of progressive economic integration of 'Greater China', the informal concept comprising Hong Kong and Taiwan, as well as Guangdong and Fujian – the provinces of China adjacent to Hong Kong. He goes on to detail and analyse the symbiotic relationship in trade and investment that has grown up in the 1980s and 1990s between Hong Kong and southern China in particular. Yet, by the mid-nineties, he finds evidence of some weakening of the Hong Kong–China trade axis, along with some decline in Hong Kong's share in foreign direct investment. Ash concludes, however, that Hong Kong 'remains a potent force, shaping China's trade and investment relations'.

For many years since the early days of reform, Hong Kong has served as the intermediary in developing economic relations between China and Taiwan, facilitating trade and investment. In his chapter, Lin, noting the interaction of politics and trade, investigates the nature of Taiwan–China economic relations conducted through Hong Kong. In his view, the political stalemate between China and Taiwan is likely to ensure that Hong Kong will continue to facilitate both economic and political contacts between China and Taiwan well into the future. The interim judgement, from the business point of view, therefore, a year and a half after the handover must be that compelling vested interests of a commercial nature both in Hong Kong and in China continue to ensure that the Hong Kong business environment remains viable in all essential respects. Set against this momentum, however, are certain destabilizing factors and trends, which, if they are not handled with great care, could damage Hong Kong's future economic success. Some of these are economic in the broad sense – structural problems in the Hong Kong economy, possible collusion between business and government, speculative attacks on financial institutions, the impact of the international crisis in Asia – but others are more strictly political, and it is to these that we now turn.

Government and politics

This section opens with Hook's consideration of the political balance sheet up to the beginning of 1999. Hook begins by examining the parameters established by the Basic Law, and in particular the four concepts that are key to the new arrangements – 'One Country – Two Systems', '50 years with no systemic change', 'Hong Kong people ruling Hong Kong', and 'a high degree of autonomy'. The provenance of these concepts, he argues, serves to shed light on the Chinese understanding of them, and degree of commitment to them. In practice, Hook notes a broadly positive record though with some imponderables and some clear instances of heavy-handedness on China's part; a process of 'acculturation between Hong Kong and China' is observed, and, overall, he finds that in the conflict over political culture, China has prevailed, though with some scope for Hong Kong players to take an active part in shaping China's second system. In a contribution that sheds new light on the political context of the transition, Yin documents the results of field work among the very many immigrants with Communist Party affiliation who moved to Hong Kong from China in the years leading up to the transfer of sovereignty. She argues, and is supported by the testimony of Party officials on the mainland, that China operated a policy of building up a 'fifth column' of Party loyalists in Hong Kong to help ease the transition. The rationale for this seemed to evolve over time, from the injunction to promote China's interests of the period when foreign policy formulation was still subject to the residual influence of Mao, through a period of Sino–British co-operation in the mid-to late-1980s, to the post-Tiananmen campaign against the Patten reforms and subsequently to win influence for China in democratic electoral contests. The fifth column was, in Yin's view, China's insurance policy in Hong Kong, conditioning the context for the transfer of power, and ultimately proving its worth.

Li analyses the prospects for central–local relations between Beijing and the HKSAR. The relationship offers scope, she argues, for something other than a simple tug of war in which one side gains and the other loses. In the context of 'One Country – Two Systems', the challenges posed by differing perspectives on issues offer an opportunity for learning that may well see China developing a more open culture with respect to the resolution of differences. Citing recent examples of conflict resolution, she asserts that much will depend on good political judgement on both sides, but particularly on the Hong Kong side, with Beijing best able in many instances to perform its part through inaction.

Administrative continuity is the subject of Scott's study. In particular he focuses on the values and culture that underlie the efficient functioning of the Hong Kong bureaucracy, the ability of the public service to sustain its capabilities despite personnel changes, and, finally, the possibility of corruption and a decline in political neutrality. Scott depicts a service whose largely positive record may stand as a bulwark against any attempt by China to exercise political control, reinforcing the belief that the impartiality and objectivity of its senior officials is critical to the continued stability and prosperity of Hong Kong.

Wesley-Smith in his contribution looks at constitutional dilemmas for the new SAR, especially continuity in the British legal system in Hong Kong, and the constitutional validity of the provisional legislature. He finds a Hong Kong legal profession unprepared for the transition. Using a notable legal case, that of HKSAR vs. David Ma, Wesley-Smith argues that the 'unimpeachable sovereignty' which the Court of Appeal held had been transferred from the colonial power to China, in fact denied the separate arrangements that were envisaged for Hong Kong through the Basic Law—coming firmly down instead on the side of 'One country', rather than 'Two Systems'. This runs contrary, he suggests, to the dominant purpose of the Basic Law, which was to preserve the HKSAR's autonomy and separate way of life.

In a final paper in this section, Porter raises the possibility of an ongoing democratic audit in Hong Kong, and by implication in China itself. Noting that Hong Kong at present is possibly the only case of a highly educated and developed society moving away from democracy, he suggests that a systematic audit over time of Hong Kong's political institutions and culture of the kind often used to assess the development of democracy could also be used to measure this change. Borrowing the principles and questions of David Beetham's qualitative democratic audit, he takes a snapshot of the Hong Kong political system at the end of the Patten governorship, sketches a comparison with the situation in China, and contemplates possible trends. He concludes that such an audit could help to pin down more precisely critical features of any change in the democratic culture of Hong Kong.

Social discourse

Any discussion of democracy naturally leads to a consideration of rights in a society. Weigelin-Schwiedrzik in her contribution traces the origins of widespread concern over human rights in Hong Kong to the Tiananmen massacre in Beijing in 1989, and outlines the developing positions of the various factions. She finds that the human rights discourse in Hong Kong has much in common with that in most highly industrialized, wealthy, western nations, but that, additionally, it exhibits the important particular characteristic that human rights are the central issue in a debate on the future identity of Hong Kong, and in Sino-Hong Kong relations.

The Christian church has more reason than most organizations to be anxious about the attitude of the HKSAR government towards its citizens, given the treatment of Christians over the years in mainland China. Leung focuses on the role in recent years as a contractor in the provision of education and social services of the Catholic Church in Hong Kong, and its adaptation to the new circumstances surrounding the transfer of sovereignty. The Catholic Church's heavy commitment to the provision of education of a certain kind, and the political support some Catholics have given the democratic movement in Hong Kong, together with Hong Kong's pivotal role in relations between China and the Vatican, in Leung's view suggest that church–state relations will continue to be problematic.

In the period between Tiananmen and the end of British rule, uncertainty over the consequences of the transfer of sovereignty caused many residents of Hong Kong to seek the means to emigrate, or at least to establish a family 'beach head' overseas. So marked was this trend that concern grew as to whether sufficient qualified people would remain to run Hong Kong' s complex economic and political institutions. Salaff, in her paper, explores the link between migration and identities among sample families from different strata of Hong Kong society. She identifies four distinct groups – the 'loyalists', the 'Hong Kong locals', the 'waverers', and the 'class enemies' of China – from those least likely, to those most likely, to emigrate. She finds that family experience on the mainland, location of kin, length of time in Hong Kong, and career opportunities combine to determine identity and the desire to remain in, or to leave, Hong Kong.

External relations

For a city with such an established and prominent international role, the conduct of international relations under the new circumstances of Chinese sovereignty is uncharted territory. Santos Neves points out that, under the new arrangements, external relations are an exception to the 'high degree of autonomy' granted in other respects to Hong Kong. Yet Hong Kong has been referred to as a 'quasi-state', and has been characterized by the possession of a real 'international legal personality'. Santos-Neves examines the framework established by China for decision making on various types of international issues, and the scope offered for local participation. He concludes that consolidation, rather than expansion, of Hong Kong's existing international status is the most likely outcome in the medium term, with the cultivation of Europe, as well as the US, necessary to guarantee Hong Kong's continued status in the longer term.

The Joint Declaration, an international treaty, dispelled one set of uncertainties, but through problems of implementation gave rise to another. A similar view may be taken of the Basic Law. It is both a reflection of the terms of the treaty, and a written constitution for the Hong Kong Special Administrative Region. The early years of governance of the Hong Kong Special Administrative Region under the Basic Law will perforce generate a range of new uncertainties different from, but no less challenging than, those that followed the Joint Declaration.

Abbreviations

ADB	Asian Development Bank
APEC	Asia Pacific Economic Cooperation
ASEAN	Association of South East Asian Nations
BL	Basic Law
BLCC, BLDC	Basic Law Consultative and Drafting Committees
BRO	Bill of Rights Ordinance
CCA	Chinese Customs Authority
CCF	Commander of Chinese Forces
CE	Chief Executive
CNAC	China National Aviation Corporation
CPC	Communist Party of China
CPG	Central People's Government
CPPCC	China People's Political Consultative Conference
DB	District Board
DP	Democratic Party
EC	Election Committee
FAO	Food and Agriculture Organisation
FC	Functional Constituency
FCO	Foreign and Commonwealth Office
FDI	Foreign Direct Investment
GATT	General Agreement on Tariffs and Trade
GDTJNJ	Guangdong Tongji Nianjian (Statistical Yearbook)
GNP	Gross National Product
HKCSD	Hong Kong Census and Statistics Department
HKGCC	Hong Kong General Chamber of Commerce
HKMA	Hong Kong Monetary Authority
HKMAO	Hong Kong and Macau Affairs Office
HKMDS	Hong Kong Monthly Digest of Statistics
HKMWC	Hong Kong and Macau Work Committee
HKP	Hong Kong Police
HKPRO	Hong Kong Public Records Office
HKSAR	Hong Kong Special Administrative Region
HKSARG	Government of the HKSAR
IAEA	International Atomic Energy Agency
ICAC	Independent Commission Against Corruption
ILO	International Labour Organisation
IMF	International Monetary Fund
JD	Joint Declaration
JLG	Joint Liaison Group

MFA	Ministry of Foreign Affairs
MFN	Most Favoured Nation
MPT	Ministry of Posts and Telecommunications
MSS	Ministry of State Security
NGO	Non-governmental Organisation
NIC	Newly Industrialised Country
NPC	National People's Congress
OECD	Organization of Economic Cooperation and Development
PADS	Port and Airport Development Strategy
PBOC	People's Bank of China
PC	Preparatory Committee
PL	Provisional Legislature
PLA	People's Liberation Army
POO	Public Order Ordinance
PR	Proportional Representation
PRC	People's Republic of China
PWC	Preliminary Working Committee
RMRB	Renmin Ribao (People's Daily)
RTHK	Radio Television Hong Kong
SCMP	South China Morning Post
SEZ	Special Economic Zone
SHTJNJ	Shanghai Tongji Nianjian (Statistical Yearbook)
SL	Selection Committee
SO	Societies Ordinance
SSB	State Statistical Bureau
SWB	Short Wave Broadcasts (monitored by the BBC, Caversham)
TJNJ	Tongji Nianjian (Statistical Yearbook)
UNCTAD	United Nations Conference on Trade and Development
WTO	World Trade Organisation
XHNA	Xinhua News Agency

Part I

The Hong Kong Business Environment

1
Hong Kong: The Business Environment in the New Special Administrative Region

Elfed Vaughan Roberts and David J. Petersen

Introduction

There are both opportunities and dangers facing business in Hong Kong as a function of the changeover of sovereignty which took place on 1 July 1997. On that date, over 150 years of British administration (with the exception of the Japanese occupation from 1941 to 1945) came to an end and the People's Republic of China (PRC) assumed power over the territory. The question that must be asked is whether or not the dynamic economic growth and favourable business environment of Hong Kong can be sustained under new management.

Hong Kong, of course, has been a highly successful economic entity for the last 30 years. Its Gross National Product (GNP) has grown at an annual rate of approximately 7 per cent in real terms during most of that time. Per capita GNP in the territory has overtaken that of the United Kingdom, Canada and Australia (by 1990 more investment was flowing from Hong Kong to Britain than from Britain to Hong Kong) (Cheah and Yu 1996, p 241). In the region, only Singapore and Japan enjoy a higher per capita GNP (as shown in Table 1.1). The growth rate of the PRC has been equally, if not more, spectacular over recent years, although its per capita GNP remains a fraction of that of Hong Kong. Of equal significance, Hong Kong is invariably ranked as the freest economy in the world (The Heritage Foundation 1998). In terms of national competitiveness, Hong Kong is consistently ranked in the top three in the world.[1]

Since the colony returned to the mainland there have been major developments that have brought into question the sustainability of Hong Kong as a major business centre. The upheavals in Indonesia, Malaysia, Thailand, and South Korea (as shown in Table 1.2), the economic inaction of Japan,[2] and fears of potential economic and banking crises in the PRC[3] have all rebounded on the Hong Kong Special Administrative Region (HKSAR). This turmoil in the external environment has exacerbated existing internal structural weaknesses, which had lain largely dormant, but which have

Table 1.1   Comparative GNP per capita

Economy	GNP per capita		PPP estimates of GNP per capita		
		Average annual growth	US = 100		PPP GNP
	1995 (Dollars)	1985–1995 (%)	1987	1995	
Switzerland	40,630	0.2	105.4	95.9	25 860
Japan	39,640	2.9	75.3	82.0	22 110
United States	26,980	1.3	100.0	100.0	26 980
Singapore	26,730	6.2	56.1	84.4	22 770
Hong Kong	**22,990**	**4.8**	**70.7**	**85.1**	**22 950**
Canada	19,380	0.4	84.6	78.3	21 130
Australia	18,720	1.4	70.1	70.2	18 940
U.K.	18,700	1.4	72.0	71.4	19 260
China	**620**	**8.3**	**6.3**	**10.8**	**2 920**

Note: PPP: Purchasing Power Parity.
Source: World Bank, 'Selected World Development Indicators', in *World Development Report* 1997, pp 214–215.

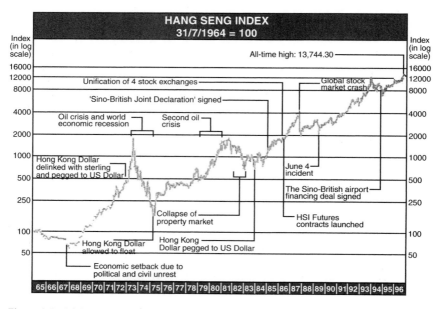

Figure 1.1   Major movements in the Hong Kong Stock Exchange Hang Seng Index
Source: Hang Seng Bank (1998) *Hang Seng Index Historical Performance [Online]*. Available from: http://www.hangseng.com/online/history/hsche.html [Accessed March 24, 1998].

Table 1.2 Impact of the regional economic upheaval on stock market valuations

City	Index	1997 Pre-crisis high		Post-crisis low			12 May 1998		
		Index	Date	Index	Date	% Decrease	Index	% Decrease on high	% Increase on low
Bangkok	SET	848.56	24 Jan. 1997	349.60	9 Jan. 1998	58.8	381.65	55.0	9.2
Hong Kong	Hang Seng	16,673.27	8 Aug. 1997	8,121.06	9 Jan. 1998	51.3	9,841.51	41.0	21.2
Jakarta	Composite	736.60	4 Jul. 1997	342.97	9 Jan. 1998	53.4	430.53	41.6	25.5
Kuala Lumpur	Composite	1,270.67	28 Feb. 1997	491.60	9 Jan. 1998	61.3	569.17	55.2	15.8
Manila	Composite	3,421.91	31 Jan. 1997	1,518.00	9 Jan. 1998	55.6	2,214.52	35.3	45.9
Seoul	Composite	791.97	14 Jun. 1997	351.86	13 May 1998	55.6	351.86	55.6	0.0
Shangai	B	94.13	9 May 1997	44.80	16 Jan. 1998	52.4	48.29	48.7	7.8
Singapore	Straits Times	2,252.46	14 Feb. 1997	1,176.35	9 Jan. 1998	47.8	1,400.05	37.8	19.0
Taipei	Weighted Price	10,116.00	26 Aug. 1997	7,375.14	12 Jan. 1998	27.1	8,278.43	18.2	12.2

Sources: The Asian World Street Journal, 1997–1998; The South China Morning Post, 1997–1998.

now awoken with a vengeance. It is not coincidental that the speech by the Financial Secretary, Donald Tsang, on the presentation of the 1998 budget was entitled 'Riding the Storm. Renewing Hong Kong's Strengths'.[4]

In the last 15 years, the colony has suffered major, if temporary, setbacks (as recorded in Figure 1.1). Two graphic examples illustrate this fact. The first was caused primarily by political factors: In September 1983, poor progress in British and Chinese negotiations on the future of Hong Kong, combined with an economic downturn, helped create a crisis in the stock and property markets and in the banking sector.[5] The second was led by global economic events, as the stock market collapse of 1987 was occasioned by factors largely beyond the control of the Hong Kong government and its regulatory authorities.[6] Both were temporary in nature and were followed by renewed and rapid economic growth.

The economy itself, however, was undergoing a major restructuring. Manufacturing, once the engine of growth for Hong Kong, began a rapid decline as factories relocated in the PRC, attracted by vastly cheaper land and labour. Increasingly, Hong Kong commerce began to rely on re-exports to and from the PRC, which was now fully engaged in its own economic miracle. This change was relatively painless and helped maintain a buoyant pattern of growth. In matters political there was a recognition that the handover of the colony to its new sovereign master would have ramifications for the business environment, but whether the effects would be benign or otherwise remained unknown. Could Hong Kong retain its business system based on the *laissez-faire* philosophy, or would forces within and without create a business environment less conducive to success?

There were, and still are, two main schools of thought relating to the continuing future of Hong Kong as a major business centre. They can be divided fairly neatly into two categories, namely the 'optimists' and the 'pessimists'. (Obviously, the two schools can be put on a spectrum relating to degrees of pessimism and optimism, but the dialectic will suffice for the time being.)

The optimists

The optimists point to a number of factors that they argue will be the key to the future success of the HKSAR. These factors begin with an analysis of the successful and smooth path towards transition of the territory from a British colony to a Chinese Special Administrative Region over the period 1984–1997. The Joint Declaration of 1984, which was the blueprint for the future political, economic and social arrangements for the period 1984–2047, guaranteed the 'Hong Kong way of life'. Its contents promised that an environment highly conducive to the *laissez-faire* philosophy would continue to apply in the future HKSAR. Socialism was quite simply forbidden, with the government and the economy guaranteed a high level of autonomy under the rubric of 'One Country – Two Systems'.[7] That guarantee was further underlined by the Basic Law, which, apart from a few minor economic amendments, also emphasised the desirability of not changing the successful business environment in the future SAR.[8] It was further argued by the optimists that even the political arguments on the nature of political reform between the new Governor Chris Patten and his opponents (both within Hong Kong and on the mainland) had remarkably little overall impact on business confidence.[9] Indeed, the interests of the business community are more than adequately safeguarded in the institutional framework of the SAR. The new Chief Executive was himself a businessman (whose family shipping business had once been 'bailed-out' by Chinese interests), his Executive Council was overwhelmingly made up of the business elite and the Legislative Council was so arranged as to guarantee a majority vote for those representing business. The cumbersome and labyrinthine arrangements for the May 1998 elections to the new Legislative Council were structured to ensure that the business community would triumph regardless of the voting pattern.[10]

The results of these arrangements are a set of fiscal and economic policies whose effects are largely favourable for the business community. Low taxation, prudent budgets with massive surpluses and restrained government expenditures,[11] and close cooperation between the government and the business elite help to sustain a mutually beneficial symbiotic relationship.

These factors are further reinforced by that pillar of stability, the Hong Kong civil service.[12] The civil service enjoys an enviable reputation for efficiency, honesty and continuity,[13] and is enmeshed in both the formal and informal decision-making processes. Members of the civil service sit on the highest decision-making bodies, including the Executive Council, thus ensuring constant bureaucratic input. The civil service is a supporter of the *laissez-faire* philosophy of Hong Kong,[14] and there is a considerable degree of communication between the civil service and the business community. The bureaucratic arm consults in depth with business over the feasibility of proposed policies, with both sides participating in advisory bodies that ensure that policies inimical to commercial interests are rarely produced. In turn, the powerful business elite has almost instant access to any government bureau should they require that their voice to be heard.

The optimists further argue that in the formal structure, the rule of law is still operative in the HKSAR. They point out that despite the change of sovereignty there is considerable evidence of a robust judicial branch operating within a clearly Westernised legal tradition, independent of internal or political interference.[15] Internationally, Hong Kong will retain its separate membership in bodies such as the World Bank, the International Monetary Fund and the Asian Development Bank (Ching 1998b, p 38).

In the larger community, much is made of the dynamic of the Hong Kong workforce. Optimists point to the fact that Hong Kong's greatest asset, which has allowed it to overcome its lack of any other major resources, is its people. Fully cognizant of the ethic of capitalism, they have shown an amazing capacity to take full advantage of opportunities as and when they arise. Entrepreneurial opportunism is seen as the byword for the tycoon in the SAR, where the ability to adapt quickly and efficiently to changes in the environment determines which ventures survive and prosper. In addition, this entrepreneurial responsiveness has been combined with the highly educated and largely non-unionised workforce to allow the rapid redeployment of those resources needed quickly to address potential new areas of growth. A glance at the manner in which Hong Kong's population has accommodated the change from entrepôt to manufacturing entity and now to tertiary service provider clearly illustrates this shared flexibility. Studies, such as that by Enright, Scott and Dodwell (1997), base their optimistic forecasts of Hong Kong's future largely on this history of adaptation.

It is further argued that the people of Hong Kong are firm supporters of the capitalist way of life. This can be partly explained by the movement of large sectors of the population up the social ladder from a predominantly working-class background into the middle classes, where they enjoy rapid improvements in wages and social provisions in areas such as housing, health and education.[16] The level of acceptance of capitalism in Hong Kong is perhaps best illustrated by the fact that there is not a single political party in Hong Kong, of those which have any electoral appeal whatsoever, that does not accept the broad principle of *laissez-faire*.

The optimists also point to the pivotal role of the PRC in the 20 years, since the 'Four Modernisations' – of agriculture, industry, science and technology, and national defence – began. The huge transformation of the Chinese economy has had enormous impacts on Hong Kong in a number of significant areas. Firstly, it allowed the reallocation of the resources of Hong Kong firms into Shenzhen, and beyond, into Guangdong, where lower land and wage costs and a sympathetic investment regime have combined to increase productivity. Secondly, Hong Kong has profited greatly by capitalizing on the tremendous increase in exports from the mainland, which are generally re-exported through Hong Kong to their destinations, primarily the US and Western Europe.[17] Thirdly, Hong Kong is by far the greatest conduit through which investment is channelled, either from local sources or from overseas, into Guangdong and the rest of China.[18] Hong Kong plays a particularly important role as the locus for many of the influential overseas-Chinese business networks that are major investors in the mainland. Fourthly, Hong Kong benefits from the entry of multinational companies, banks and other service industries that have begun operating in China. Fifthly, increasing numbers of Hong Kong people travel to Guangdong to provide managerial services, but remain located in Hong Kong.[19] At the same time the PRC is a major investor in Hong Kong, in such areas as banking, hotels, property and tourism.[20] Some optimists believe that Hong Kong's capitalist values, prosperity, and growing middle class, which have already contributed greatly to the success of China's modernization to date, will not only be maintained, but will ultimately triumph in China itself (Business Week 1997).

In the wider external environment there is considerable sympathy towards Hong Kong. The US, Europe and Japan, all major investors in the territory, continue to see Hong Kong as an excellent launching pad for the Chinese market, and recognize that maintaining the highly autonomous nature of the SAR is critical to perpetuating its fertile business environment.[21] It is also widely believed that China will act to ensure the success of its 'One Country – Two Systems' model in order to reassure Macau in preparation for its 1999 handover, and, particularly, to tempt Taiwan into closer consideration of reunification (China Daily 1998).[22]

The pessimists

In contrast to the optimists, there are those who are far less sanguine about Hong Kong's future business prospects. Indeed, some of the predictions, such as those of Marc Faber,[23] paint a very sombre picture, suggesting a retrogression of the territory to the status of a fishing village in the years to come. While Faber is probably exaggerating to a large extent (there are no longer fish to catch in Hong Kong's waters given the levels of pollution) there are worrying factors that it would be unwise to ignore.

Perhaps one of the most pressing concerns relates to the degree of autonomy that Hong Kong can retain under its new management. It is suggested that such levels of democracy currently possessed by Hong Kong will increasingly be diluted by interference from the political masters in Beijing and by certain local members of the elite who will initiate such action in order to please the PRC authorities.[24] Leaving aside the thorny question of whether full democracy is a prerequisite for a capitalist business environment, the thesis has been presented that levels of corruption imported from the mainland, interference in the government's freedom to regulate the economy, and preference for other provinces at Hong Kong's expense will reduce its competitiveness and leach its legendary dynamism.[25] Milton Friedman has said that he does not believe the link of the Hong Kong dollar to the US dollar will be maintained for long after the handover (Silverman 1997, p 79), while Bowring expects that the Hong Kong dollar will not long retain its relevancy under Chinese rule: 'the Hong Kong dollar will survive like the Scottish pound' (Bowring 1997).

Additionally, questions have been raised on the future of the Basic Law and the legal system. The continued status of the Basic Law, that document that defines the political, legal, social, cultural, economic and business environment of the HKSAR, has been questioned by those who express the concern that it is subordinate to the National People's Congress in the PRC (Roberts 1996, p 28). There is no entrenched means of safeguarding the autonomy of Hong Kong should forces on the mainland seek to make retrogressive changes. Pessimists point to examples of where they feel the Basic Law has been violated, albeit to date in the political-institutional field. Nossal (1997) predicts that the 'high degree of autonomy' promised for Hong Kong may become a 'high degree of ambiguity'.[26]

Internally, the fear has been expressed clearly that there are structural problems that have not been adequately addressed and that may well lead to a worsening business environment.[27] There are, indeed, some worrying economic indicators. Official unemployment figures showed a disturbing increase to 3.5 per cent in April 1998; they are predicted to rise significantly higher. On 19 April 1998, Financial Secretary Donald Tsang advised Hong Kong people to 'be psychologically prepared for a gloomy employment outlook amid the regional financial turmoil' (Choy 1998). The most important areas of the economy are experiencing major downturns. Prices on rented and private property have fallen over 15 per cent since the third quarter of 1997, and by almost 30 per cent from their pre-handover peak (Lo 1998). Receipts from tourism, a major foreign currency earner (generating approximately US$10 billion annually) dropped nearly 25 per cent in January and February 1998 compared with the same period in 1997 (Smith 1998). Domestic manufacturing has been declining at an accelerating rate since the early 1980s: in 1981 it comprised 24 per cent of GDP, but fell to 18 per cent of GDP in 1990, and 9 per cent in 1995 (Hong Kong 1997). In terms of exports, local manufactured goods represent only 15 per cent of the total, the remainder being made up of the re-exports that have been so vital in generating the great growth experienced by Hong Kong (Hong Kong 1997, Ching 1998a).

The pessimists argue that the cataclysmic decline in manufacturing and the over-reliance on property, re-exports and the service sector have left Hong Kong highly vulnerable to the vicissitudes of external forces. Such sensitivity was put to the test by the recent economic crises in South East and East Asia. Many of these nations experienced dramatic devaluations in their currencies (see Table 1.3), thus leaving the highly priced and pegged Hong Kong dollar in a precarious position. There are still fears that another lurch in these economies could markedly and adversely affect Hong Kong, particularly if the PRC was forced to devalue its currency in response to a renewed crisis (Economist 1998).

Suggestions of potential political instability have also been voiced. With rising economic uncertainty as a backdrop there have been suggestions that the legitimacy of the government of the HKSAR might increasingly come under question from certain quarters. The low turnout for elections, the format of the electoral system itself, and the undermining of confidence

Table 1.3 Impact of the regional economic upheaval on economic growth and currencies

| Country | GDP growth (%) | | | | | Currency units per USD | | |
| | Average annual | Actual | | Estimate | | | | % |
	1970–96	1996	1997	1998	1999	15 Apr. 1997	12 May 1998	Change
China	9.1	9.6	8.9	6.3	7.5	8.30	8.26	0
Hong Kong	7.5	5.0	5.1	1.8	3.8	7.75	7.75	0
Indonesia	6.8	7.8	5.4	–5.2	2.9	2,408	9,350	288
Malaysia	7.4	8.6	7.4	1.6	1.8	2.51	3.84	53
Philippines	3.6	5.7	4.8	1.9	4.0	26.40	39.15	48
Singapore	8.2	6.9	7.6	2.7	5.0	1.44	1.63	13
South Korea	8.4	7.1	5.6	–2.5	1.7	894	1,388	55
Taiwan	8.3	5.7	6.3	5.0	5.7	27.60	33.52	21
Thailand	7.5	6.7	–0.7	–4.0	3.7	26.10	38.56	48

Sources: Economist (1998) 'East Asian Economics Survey', March 7, 1998, p. 7; *Far Eastern Economic Review* (1998) 'Prices & Trends', March 26, 1998, p. 74; *The Asian Wall Street Journal* (1998), May 13, 1998, p. 24.

in the civil service's ability to effectively administer policy have sent alarm bells ringing for the pessimists.[28]

Regionally, the fear of Hong Kong losing out to rapidly emerging provinces in China has sent shivers through certain spines. With the modernization of Guangdong Province and Shanghai, many of the economic functions performed in Hong Kong have come under scrutiny. Guangdong has inherited Hong Kong's manufacturing mantle, is building its own shipping export structure and is seeking to reduce its dependency on Hong Kong for managerial skills and expertise.[29] In other words, it is gearing up to challenge in the very areas where Hong Kong had the competitive edge. The spectacular rise of Shanghai, its banking, insurance, financial institutions, and its increasingly sophisticated stock market, bodes ill for the future relevancy of the SAR according to the pessimists.[30]

In essence, the factors outlined above lead the pessimists, not surprisingly, to a very bleak view of the short-, medium-, and long-term future for Hong Kong. They are in direct opposition to the optimists, who either ignore or minimize the expected impact of these negative criteria. Which position should be taken?

Optimism or pessimism?

Politics and the business environment

When attempting to analyse the present situation and predict the future of the business environment in Hong Kong, it must be remembered that we are still broadly in the post-handover transition period. What is certain from the outset is that it would be both wrong and irresponsible to lay the blame for the hostile challenges facing the Hong Kong business environment solely at the feet of the new SAR government. Indeed, many of the problems now emerging are the function of a historical legacy handed down from the colonial period or are the consequence of external forces over which Hong Kong has little, if any, control.

To date, the political system has endured the handover far better than the pessimists would have dared hope. The Chief Executive, Mr Tung Chee-hwa, despite some early blunders,[31] has behaved reasonably prudently. Although not universally admired, he has avoided any greatly controversial policies, and has kept a low profile, emphasizing the theme of 'business as usual'. He retained the overwhelmingly popular Anson Chan as Chief Secretary and the soundly competent Donald Tsang as Financial Secretary, thus ensuring a high degree of continuity at the top levels of his administration. The elections, promised to replace the Provisional Legislature which held office from 1 July 1997 and whose legitimacy could be questioned, were held on 24 May 1998. Although the electoral system was unduly complicated[32] and elicited a high degree of political apathy, a fact reflected in a low turn out, there was no widespread opposition to its format, and even many of those opposed to the structure put up candidates for office. Indeed, not one of the candidates for any of the constituencies could be described as radical. All supported the broad theme of a capitalist system in Hong Kong and believed in the concept, if not the pure application, of *laissez-faire*. In any case, the election was so designed to ensure a majority for the business elite.[33] In addition, the business community retains the high ground of political influence within the institutional framework, dominating the Legislative Council and the Executive Council. On balance, and despite the bias towards the business elite in the institutional structures, it would nevertheless appear, that if political stability is a criterion for a successful business environment, then the optimists have the upper hand.

On the broader front, there is little evidence to suggest a radical cleavage in the body politic. Opinion polls on the question of confidence in the 'One Country – Two Systems' model and the form of government in Hong Kong after the transition are not discouraging.[34] Certainly, there has been no diminution in the number of peaceful demonstrations, some of which have led to a favourable response by the government.[35] The media remains robustly independent and critical of government policies where deemed relevant.[36] There are no indications whatsoever of political unrest in the general public, and disturbances are generally related to the democratization debate and are limited to a tiny minority, such as the 'April 5 Movement', which has consistently failed to gain support. (Of course, the pessimists argue that the government has not yet been tested by a sustained downturn in the economy, and warn that much of the political stability is based on the expectation of increasing affluence.)

Nevertheless, all sectors of the community, although not in the same proportions, have become more affluent over the last 20 years. As mentioned earlier, the social welfare system has rapidly improved during this time, and some of the worst effects of an economic downturn, should it be sustained, should be mitigated by the huge public housing provision (43 per cent), excellent and inexpensive hospital facilities, free education for all who need it under the age of 16, and a rapidly expanding and relatively cheap tertiary education sector.[37] At present, unemployment payments are virtually non-existent given the assumption that full employment makes them unnecessary. However, unemployment has begun to rise rather rapidly and the government will no doubt be forced to address this problem eventually. The best choice of policy option is currently a matter of debate, but the consensus view is that the government will prefer to seek job creation through investment in infrastructure, rather than make direct payments to the unemployed.[38] Whichever approach is followed, the majority of the population is unlikely to reject the broad framework in which the political system operates, although it can be expected to support incremental changes rather than major overhauls. Thus it may seem, in the absence of any further unanticipated crises, that a guardedly optimistic scenario for the business environment in the political arena is empirically more persuasive than the scenarios of the pessimists.

Economics and the business environment

On the question of the economic situation there is greater cause for concern, and there is the distinct possibility that here the pessimists are gaining the upper hand, at least in the short term. There can be no question that Hong Kong's economy has carried hidden structural weaknesses for some time, and that these are now being exposed. Hong Kong has lost virtually all of its manufacturing base to China, and there is little doubt that this pattern will continue into the future given the mainland's comparative advantage in land and labour factor costs.[39]

Internally, property prices in both the commercial and private sectors show no sign of imminent recovery, and little prospect of improvement in the medium term. The Hong Kong dollar is clearly overvalued, and may well be forced off its US dollar peg if the PRC devalues its currency in reaction to further lurches in the other East and South East Asian economies. Tourism continues to decline,[40] and retail sales are plummeting.[41] Unemployment is rising and the declining prices at government land sales give further indication of a lack of business confidence.[42]

Externally, the position of the pessimists also seems to be gaining ground. The large re-export component of the Hong Kong economy is highly vulnerable to external developments. The improvements in the standard of professionalism of Chinese producers make it less necessary to ship goods initially to Hong Kong, for quality inspection, packaging and overseas transportation, on the way to their final destination. It is reasonable, therefore, to assume that the lucrative margin earned on consumer goods by Hong Kong middleman (averaging 25 per cent) will certainly decrease over time. The likely eventual agreement for direct air and sea links between the mainland and Taiwan,[43] thus bypassing Hong Kong, will also have a significant negative impact on economic activity in Hong Kong. The effects of continued growth and success of Shanghai, and other mainland coastal areas, should also not be underestimated.

One question that begs an answer is whether the worrying economic indicators for the business environment can be addressed successfully, or whether Hong Kong is doomed to a slow decline in future years. To be fair, the territory still has considerable advantages that should not too readily be discounted. The government still possesses huge financial reserves that may be brought into play, the workforce is highly educated and highly adaptable, and the territory is a hub of modern communications with a highly developed infrastructure. The financial sector is effective, sophisticated, and subject to a well-regulated framework. Corruption in both the public and private sectors is low,[44] and the economy operates within a stable political environment.

The actual operation of *laissez-faire* principles in Hong Kong has been undergoing quite marked modification for some time, with the benefits clearly outweighing the costs. Government intervention, as mentioned previously, has been increasing in the field of social provision. Intervention has also been evident in the increasing regulation of business activity itself in such areas as securities and futures markets, safety and fire regulations, compulsory provident funds, bus franchises, pollution regulations, and consumer rights.

A major debate rages at present over the extent to which the government should become involved in leading industrial planning, or whether government should just leave the market to sort itself out entirely. Demands are coming from all directions for the government to take action, and for the Chief Executive to show decisive leadership. The reaction from the administration has been typically conservative, and the Financial Secretary (along with many in the powerful civil service) clearly believes that to increase government intervention dramatically, in the form of subsidies, tax breaks, or any further distortion of market mechanisms, would ultimately be damaging to the business environment.[45] If the unfavourable economic conditions continue to worsen, however, pressure for action will mount from labour, manufacturers, property developers, exporters and a host of other sectors. However, each group, hardly surprisingly, is pleading a special case according to perceived need. The Financial Secretary has made it quite clear that any further intervention, if it takes place, will be slow and 'prudent', and will be regarded as a temporary deviation from the levels of government expenditure now extant. On this question, once more, the likelihood of intervention levels approaching those of some Western economies is not entertained.

The pessimists' arguments, however, at least in the short term, have become more compelling. Although it would be entirely inappropriate to adopt the worst case 'fishing village' scenario, there are sufficient indicators to suggest that hard times have descended upon the business environment in the context of the economy.

The People's Republic of China

Perhaps the most crucial variable in the business environment is the role played by the PRC. Many of the fears articulated before 1 July 1997 have not been realized. The PRC has adopted a hands-off policy by allowing the territory considerable autonomy under the rubric of 'One County – Two Systems.' When necessary the PRC has also come to the aid of Hong Kong, as it did during the steep fall in the Hong Kong Stock market in late October 1997, when it pledged its resources to the defence of the dollar link. Also, as mentioned previously, Hong Kong is still the largest investor in China and remains a crucial point of inward investment and re-exports. Hong Kong is, without question, an integral part of the economy of China, with both parties enjoying benefits from the reciprocal relationship. In the longer term there is a fear that the successful coastal regions of China will overtake Hong Kong, and thus downgrade the importance of the territory. Although the concern that Hong Kong is becoming just 'another Chinese city' has been articulated by the pessimists, the indications of that are by no means conclusive.[46] In the meantime, the PRC allows Hong Kong a high degree of autonomy in the conduct of its own affairs and even allows the SAR to retain separate membership of international organizations.[47] In the sense that the business environment will be allowed to develop without external pressure or interference from the mainland, there is room for optimism.

The wider external environment

In the broader field of international trade, upon which Hong Kong is highly reliant, any downturn in the world economy hits Hong Kong fast and hard. It is in this area that considerable concern for the future business environment has been expressed. What, for instance, given the huge reliance of Hong Kong upon re-exports, would happen if the mainland, for whatever reason, suffered a contraction in its external trade? What are the costs to Hong Kong should a world or regional stock market crash take place? What would Hong Kong do if political instability in the region rebounded upon it? Events in Indonesia, Japan, Malaysia, the Philippines, South Korea and Thailand since mid-1997 have already had a marked knock-on effect upon Hong Kong. How would Hong Kong cope with a devalued Chinese currency should this occur? Indeed the external environment, certainly in Asia, is showing clear indications of marked political, social and economic volatility. If such volatility continues, and there is much to conclude that it might, then the pessimists' case once again becomes more persuasive at least in the foreseeable future.

Conclusion

A sober assessment of the Hong Kong business environment seems to point towards difficult times ahead. Internally, there are many structural economic problems to be addressed, in such areas as the over reliance of re-exports, the cataclysmic decline in manufacturing, the growing unemployment problem and the falling property market. Add to that the decline in tourism, retail sales and the stock market; factor in increased bankruptcies, high interest rates, and an overvalued dollar, and it is clear that business confidence cannot be high.

Externally, Hong Kong may well be losing its competitive edge, particularly in comparison with China. The territory is also a hostage to international forces over which it has little control. Recent events in Asia have demonstrated clearly the fragile business environments operating in many countries in the region. With respect to the PRC, upon which Hong Kong relies to an excessive degree, many suggest that its business environment may be entering a negative phase. In many ways Hong Kong's economic situation is new in the sense that an entire generation has grown up in the expectation of continued growth and increasing prosperity. Some might go so far as to suggest that a degree of complacency was built into the assumptions of the people (this is also true in most of the East and South East Asian countries where the shocks have been even more devastating). Perhaps a corrective was necessary to change the economic direction in which Hong Kong was moving.

There is little question that there is still much to commend Hong Kong's business environment as a force capable of overcoming those problems. It remains a politically stable system with a powerful government, wedded to the philosophy of capitalism and capable of acting decisively in difficult times. Government policies after the transition, remain directed towards retaining an attractive business environment. Hong Kong remains wedded to a sound legal system, an efficient civil service, low taxes, and control over corruption. It has huge accumulated financial reserves, and a well-regulated banking and financial sector. The population is well educated, adaptable, and able to respond to rapidly changing conditions. No internal forces seek to alter radically the broad consensual framework in which the business environment operates. Under such conditions, and given the proven adaptability of Hong Kong, many of the problems outlined by the pessimists, although causing a short-to-medium term decline in business confidence, may be surmounted by its more favourable holistic business environment.

Notes

1 IMD, *World Competitiveness Yearbook 1998*. Hong Kong is ranked as the third most competitive nation, behind Singapore (number two), and the USA (number one).
2 Japan has been described previously as Asia's locomotive, 'but these days the locomotive is pulling backwards.' See Cavallo (1998, p 19).
3 In order to keep its state-owned enterprises (SOEs) afloat and to maintain employment levels, the PRC government has directed banks continually to supply credit to loss-making SOEs. Such loans are unlikely to be paid back, and in effect represent a subsidy from the government to the SOEs. The effect on the financial health of the banks has been catastrophic: while the People's Bank of China (the PBOC, China's central bank) estimates that non-performing loans represent 18 per cent of GDP, Merrill Lynch estimates the figure at 40 per cent of GDP, and Standard & Poor's estimates that such bad loans represent 60 per cent of GDP – much worse than either Thailand or Korea (see Economist Intelligence Unit 1998, p 3). Using the PBOC's estimate that 20 per cent of outstanding loans are bad,

Rmb (Renminbi) 1.2 trillion (US$145 billion) in loans are non-performing. Since the combined capital base of the banks is only Rmb 448 billion (US$ 54 billion), the banks are 'technically bankrupt' (Economist Intelligence Unit 1998).

The World Bank has estimated that bad loans exceed US$ 200 billion, and confirm that these banks have 'negative net worth' (see Wonacott 1998, p 25). While the US$ 32.6 billion 'special treasury bond' announced by China's Ministry of Finance in early March 1998 is at least an initial step towards addressing the banking problem, it falls far short of the scale of solution required. Analysts also recognize the plan as partly 'accounting sleight of hand' (Wonacott 1998).

4   Financial Secretary Tsang's third Hong Kong budget (but his first wholly for the new Hong Kong Special Administrative Region of the People's Republic of China) was entitled 'Riding the Storm. Renewing Hong Kong's Strengths.' He described the reasons for this title, and his focus in preparing the budget, in point 5 of his budget speech: 'The main thought that has shaped this Budget is that in this time of economic uncertainty, when many people and businesses have experienced reduction of asset values or face gloomier prospects, the measures that I have set out must aim to provide comfort, bolster confidence, and strengthen competitiveness. Their object is to help us to ride out the present storm and to work to renew Hong Kong's distinctive strengths'.

5   The Hong Kong dollar to US dollar exchange rate was HK$ 5.69 = US$ 1 in September 1981, but by September 1983 it had fallen to HK$ 8 = US$ 1. When China made an announcement threatening unilateral action if agreement with the British was not reached, the Hong Kong dollar all but collapsed, reaching its lowest point on 24 September 1983 when it fell from HK$ 7.20 to HK$ 9.50 for US$ 1. The peg was announced on 15 October 1983 and fixed at the exchange rate of HK$ 7.8 to US$ 1, where it has remained ever since.

6   After the New York stock exchange's 'Black Monday' crash on 19 October 1987 – one week after the famous Wardley advice to 'buy, buy, buy' (see *South China Morning Post* 1997.) – the Hong Kong stock exchange closed its doors for 4 days, in an effort to protect its prices (Mulcahy 1997). When the Hong Kong stock exchange was re-opened on the following Monday, it plunged immediately, the Hang Seng Index falling 1120.7 points (thus losing over one-third of its value) on that single day (Lo, T. Wing 1993, p 115).

It might be added that although the root cause of this collapse lies with external forces, the crisis was very badly managed by the authorities in general, and by Ronald Li, the chairman of the Stock Exchange, in particular. The futile effort to protect prices by closing the exchange for 4 days significantly harmed Hong Kong's reputation for financial management. The Financial Secretary of the time, Piers Jacobs at first supported the closure ('the closure was necessary to protect the economy and that the government had been consulted beforehand'), however he later re-thought this position and said that 'he did not regard a single telephone call as consultation' (Lo, T. Wing 1993, p 115, p 117). It should be noted that Li was later to spend a sojourn in Stanley prison for certain stock transgressions, having been convicted of receiving shares in return for supporting applications for listing (see Heath 1993). Li was released on 16 June 1993, having served 973 days of his 4 year sentence.

7   The Joint Declaration guarantees that the Hong Kong Special Administrative Region will 'enjoy a high degree of autonomy', that 'the current social and economic systems in Hong Kong will remain unchanged and so will the

life-style', and that these basic policies of the Joint Declaration, and the later Basic Law, 'will remain unchanged for 50 years' (Miners 1995, p 261). Beijing coined the term 'Hong Kong people ruling Hong Kong' during the 1983–4 negotiations with Britain that led to the agreement. Chinese leaders – such as Lu Ping, when director of the Hong Kong and Macau Affairs Office – repeatedly specified that Hong Kong should be an economic city, not a political city (*South China Morning Post* 1994).

8   Article 5 of the Basic Law reproduces Annex I of the Joint Declaration, and provides that the 'previous capitalist system and way of life shall remain unchanged for 50 years. The key economic provisions in Articles 105 to 119 support this principle of independence, with virtually the only constraint appearing in Article 107, which obligates the HKSAR to strive to maintain a balanced budget, and ensure that the budget is 'commensurate with the growth rate of its gross domestic product' (see The Consultative Committee for the Basic Law of the Hong Kong Special Administrative Region of the People's Republic of China 1990, p 6).

9   Patten attempted to use the rubric of the Basic Law to maximize the democratic base of the Legislative Council. The PRC strongly objected to these reforms, and promised to void them if they were put into practice. This removal was performed very quickly indeed once the SAR was established and the new, hand-picked Provisional Legislative Council was inaugurated.

10   The May elections in Hong Kong were so complicated that the election commission themselves had difficulty explaining the finer points. For our purposes, the election arrangements were as follows: there were 60 seats in the new Legislative Council. Of these 60 seats, 20 were elected in a multi-seat constituency using proportional representation, 30 were reserved for functional constituencies that are overwhelmingly biased towards business representation, and the last 10 were chosen by an election committee who ensured that business interests were safeguarded as the 800 members of this election committee were either from the business community or closely allied to it.

11   There is one aspect of their respective performance that the British Chancellor of the Exchequer, Gordon Brown, and his counterpart in Hong Kong, Financial Secretary Donald Tsang, have in common: the imprudent use on all possible occasions of the word 'prudent'. On a more serious note, the Hong Kong Government's surpluses and accumulated reserves are the envy of any country: in point 52 of his 1998 budget speech, Tsang expected reserves at the end of March 1998 (including the Land Fund) to be almost HK$ 450 billion.

12   It should be noted that the localization of the civil service does not appear to have harmed its ability to administer, influence and even form public policy.

13   Harris has described Hong Kong as an 'Administrative State', whose civil service rulers are 'permanent, practiced, anonymous for the best part, and, at best, impartial', and whose ideology is a strict 'non-ideology; its basic credo is survival' (see Harris 1978, p 58).

14   Two major political characters in the post-1997 system are the Financial Secretary, Donald Tsang and the Chief Secretary, Anson Chan. Both are civil servants, but they do not conform to the British system of civil service silence. They are decision makers, in their respective fields, in every sense of the word.

15   In March and April 1998, concerns arouse over judicial independence in relation to Bureau of Justice actions in two high profile cases. The first involved the failure of the New China News Agency to release information within the statutory

period of 40 days to describe any files they held on Emily Lau, an eminent local dissident. The second related to the allegation of fraud against a Ms Aw, the proprietor of the newspaper *The Hong Kong Standard*, and a person known to have links to the Chinese leadership. In both cases the Secretary for Justice refused to lay charges, in the first case on the grounds that the breach was a mere technicality, and the second case since it was not in the 'public interest' to do so. This begs the question of what criteria the Justice Secretary believes can be used to define the public interest (see Ching 1998b, p 38).

16   Some of the figures are most impressive. The overall monthly average wage for craftsmen is HK$ 7,853 and supervisors HK$ 10,804. Public housing, which houses over 40 per cent of the total population, costs an average of 18.5 per cent of monthly income. Life expectancy is 76 for a male and 81.5 for females – higher than in the United Kingdom and the USA. Over 18 per cent of the peer group now enter universities within Hong Kong and another 10 per cent are thought to be studying abroad. Add to this over 87,000 students studying for further qualifications, mostly in the areas of law, accounting and business, and the scale of the transformation becomes clearer (Cheah & Yu 1996, p 251).

17   The margin earned by Hong Kong middlemen on re-exports is estimated at approximately 25 per cent on consumer goods (see Mok 1996, p 84).

18   Between 1979 and 1997, Hong Kong accounted for approximately 56 per cent (US$ 280 billion of a total of US$ 470 billion) of contracted foreign direct investment in China (Hong Kong Trade Development Corporation 1998a).

19   Overseas companies are well aware of the advantage of using Hong Kong people in Guangdong because of their language skills and knowledge of local conditions. The Hong Kong government estimates that over 97,300 Hong Kong residents were working in mainland China by the end of 1995 (see Hong Kong Trade Development Corporation 1998a).

20   Mainland China is the third largest source of foreign direct investment in Hong Kong (after Japan and the UK), accounting for over 28 per cent of the total. Chinese government estimates put the number of mainland-backed ventures registered in Hong Kong at over 1,850, representing a net asset value of US$183 billion at the end of 1996 (see Hong Kong Trade Development Corporation 1998a).

21   The 'Hong Kong: The United States – Hong Kong Policy Act' of 1992 was reaffirmed in 1996, and although non-binding, it would be used to pressure the presidency to initiate punitive actions through bilateral agreements (such as Most Favoured Nations certification) with the HKSAR if it is found that China has violated the terms of the handover treaty with Britain, and that Hong Kong is thus not sufficiently autonomous (see Szulc 1997).

22   It should be remembered that Deng Xiaoping originally created the 'One Country – Two Systems' construct for the purposes of re-integrating Taiwan into the mainland.

23   Marc Faber, the 'Dr. Doom' of the Hong Kong financial community, has repeatedly expressed his 'ultra-negative' view of Hong Kong's economic prospects. Faber bases his pessimism on China's lessening need for Hong Kong as it progresses along the road of reform. Faber also gives the example of the fall to insignificance of Salzburg after it was absorbed into Austria in 1803 (*South China Morning Post* 1996).

24   Lam argues that the essence of China's policy towards Hong Kong is to prevent the 'peaceful evolution' that the Chinese leadership sees as the result of Western

political, economic, and cultural efforts to change political attitudes and beliefs, and which they blame for the termination of socialism in Eastern Europe (see Lam 1998). Guyot reports on widespread fears of interference both from Beijing, and from within Hong Kong, on Beijing's presumed behalf (Guyot 1998, p 8).

25 *Fortune* editor Louis Kraar in 1995 predicted that interference from Beijing would jeopardize Hong Kong's special capabilities, and would thus lead to the 'Death of Hong Kong' (Kraar 1995). Szulc considered it likely that the handover would be the 'beginning of the end' of most political freedoms enjoyed in Hong Kong, and expressed the common contention that the Chief Executive would be 'largely irrelevant' since major decision making would be controlled by the central party leadership (Szulc 1997). Roberti also shared the belief that power would be exercised through a senior cadre sent from Beijing, nominally responsible only for Foreign Affairs (Roberti 1996).

26 It should be remembered that Deng Xiaoping was quoted telling the drafters of the Basic Law that they 'should not think Hong Kong affairs should all be handled by Hong Kong people', since 'this is impossible, and such an idea is unrealistic' (see Nossal 1997, p 84).

27 In a contrast to the 'Hong Kong Advantage' study by Enright *et al.* mentioned previously, the 'Made by Hong Kong' competitiveness study by Berger and Lester argues that Hong Kong is facing serious problems and must reach beyond its middleman role to develop its industry (Berger & Lester 1997).

28 Civil servants have been blamed for a series of embarrassments, such as mismanagement of the mass chicken slaughter to counter the HV51n virus, confusion over land supply and housing policies, resentment over the 'high-handed' approach to mother-tongue education, and perceived favouritism in decisions not to prosecute entities aligned with China. Calls have grown for reforms to make it easier for such officials to be replaced if they commit such blunders (Yeung 1998, p 11).

29 Guangdong Governor Lu Ruihua said in June 1997 that the 'shop front, factory back' symbiotic relationship between Hong Kong and Guangdong had to change. 'The relationship', he added, 'must be on equal terms' (see Gilley 1997).

30 Although Shanghai has recently toned down its boasts of its plans to overtake Hong Kong as the financial capital of China – for political reasons, so as to 'welcome' Hong Kong back to the motherland – it is increasing its efforts to attract international business. Citibank and Standard Chartered Bank have moved their China headquarters from Hong Kong to Shanghai, and other multinationals – particularly banks and consumer-goods firms – are expected to follow, prompting a certain feeling of unease in Hong Kong (Yatsko 1997).

31 On 30 October 1997, Chief Executive Tung Chee-hwa said that 'I do not think property prices will drop dramatically because there are real demands'. The Asian crisis soon worsened, however, and proved him wrong (see No 1997).

32 A university survey in April 1998 found that 'more than 80 per cent of Hong Kong people do not understand' the electoral system used in the May 1998 elections (see Kwong 1998).

33 The interests of the Hong Kong business elite will certainly be protected under Chief Executive Tung Chee-hwa, who, as a fellow business person, appears to share their views, which *The Economist* has described as an 'almost 18-century view of oligarchic right' (*The Economist* 1997).

34 Polls conducted by the University of Hong Kong Social Sciences Research Centre indicated that a sound majority of respondents maintained confidence in the

'One Country – Two Systems' model for Hong Kong: 59 per cent of respondents in December 1997, and 66 per cent in February 1998. The polls also found that a high percentage of respondents were confident of the future of Hong Kong itself: 68 per cent of respondents in December 1997, 65 per cent in February 1998, and 70 per cent in March 1998.

35   Protests from poultry farmers, vendors, politicians, and union officials led the government to pay HK$ 760 million in compensation to the poultry industry for the 1.4 million birds killed at the start of 1998 to prevent the spread of the 'bird-flu'. (Ku & Li 1998, *South China Morning Post* 1998a). Protests from fish farmers led the government to pay HK$ 17 million in grants and HK$200 million in unsecured, low-interest loans to the aquaculture industry in compensation for the 'red tides' that killed their stocks in April 1998 (Lee 1998 Pang 1998).

36   In March 1998, Chief Secretary Anson Chan was quick to admonish local Chinese People's Political Consultative Conference deputy Xu Simin for criticizing the editorial freedom of RTHK, the government radio and television media entity (Choy & Yeung 1998). It should also be noted that the Beijing government showed admirable restraint by refusing to support Xu's call, particularly when it is remembered that less than two years previously, Zhang Junsheng, the deputy director of Xinhua, called on the Hong Kong government to 'discipline' RTHK and called on the government to 'tell its subordinate how to cooperate with the Preparatory Committee' (Lee & Fung 1996).

37   There are, of course, areas in social provision that are in need of dire attention in an affluent society such as Hong Kong and they should not be ignored. A Hong Kong Social Security survey released in September 1997 found that the number of people living below the poverty line had almost tripled in the 25 years to 1997 (Kwok 1997). The survey found that the top 10 per cent of households accounted for 42 per cent of total income while the bottom 50 per cent accounted for only 19 per cent (*South China Morning Post* 1997b).

38   Chief Executive Tung Chee-hwa has repeatedly ruled out the introduction of the 'dole' as compensation to the rising number of unemployed in Hong Kong (see *South China Morning Post* 1998b).

39   Guangdong has become the hinterland and labour source for Hong Kong business. Hong Kong has de-industrialized at an extremely rapid rate, with the manufacturing workforce contracting by 50 per cent between 1984 and 1994 (see Lau 1997, p 428).

40   Kraar points out that consumer items, hotel rooms, and other goods/services are often 50 per cent to 100 per cent more expensive in Hong Kong than in other centres, such as New York City (Kraar 1997).

41   Retail sales for the peak months of January and February (which include the Chinese New Year festival) were down 15 per cent in 1998 from 1997 (adjusting for inflation). This included a decrease in department store sales of 28 per cent over this same comparison period (Tsang 1998).

42   Polls conducted by the Hong Kong University Social Sciences Research Centre indicate that the number of respondents who had confidence in Hong Kong's future fell from 71.8 per cent in November 1997 to 50.1 per cent in January 1998 alone. Compared to the pre-handover period, by February 1998 93.1 per cent of respondents felt that the economic condition was worse.

43   Currently the political impasse between China and Taiwan requires bilateral traffic to pass through Hong Kong.

44 Transparency International's 1997 index of corruption ranks Hong Kong as the fourth 'cleanest' nation in Asia – less corrupt than Japan and Taiwan, and only slightly more corrupt than New Zealand, Australia, and Singapore (*Far Eastern Economic Review* 1998, p 70).

45 Financial Secretary Donald Tsang ridiculed the idea of Hong Kong adopting a Singapore-style interventionist industrial policy in an April 1998 speech (see Gittings 1998).

46 If Hong Kong were to become 'just another Chinese city', then, unfortunately, international financial institutions could be expected to assign Hong Kong the same level of risk as other mainland cities.

47 Thus, after 1997 Hong Kong retains its membership in international bodies such as the World Trade Organization (WTO), International Monetary Fund (IMF), Asia Pacific Economic Cooperation (APEC), and Pacific Economic Cooperation Council (PECC), and continues to negotiate and operate its own Investment Promotion and Protection Agreements with over 20 major trading partners (Husain 1997, p 5; Hong Kong Trade Development Corporation 1998b).

Bibliography

Berger, S., Lester, R. K. 1997 *Made by Hong Kong*. Hong Kong: Oxford University Press.

Bowring, P. 1997 'Red–and–Yellow Flag the Symbol of What is to Come'. *South China Morning Post*, 23 June.

Business Week 1997 'We're Betting on Hong Kong', 9 June.

Cavallo, D. 1998 'Asian Dominoes'. *Forbes Global Business and Finance*, 20 April.

Cheah, Hong Beng and Yu, F. L. Tony 1996 'Adaptive Response: Entrepreneurship and Competitiveness in the Economic Development of Hong Kong', *Journal of Enterprising Culture*, September.

China Daily 1998 'Reunification Confidence Felt by Lawmakers', Hong Kong edition, 3 March.

China Quarterly 1997, issue 151, September.

Ching, F. 1998a 'Hong Kong: Are Basics Sound?'. *Far Eastern Economic Review*, 12 March.

Ching, F. 1998b 'Protecting the Public Interest'. *Far Eastern Economic Review*, 9 April.

Choy, L. 1998 'Financial Secretary Warns of Jobs Gloom'. *South China Morning Post*, 20 April.

Choy, L., Yeung, C. 1998 'RTHK Row Invites Mainland Meddling'. *South China Morning Post*, 6 March.

Consultative Committee for the Basic Law of the Hong Kong Special Administrative Region of the People's Republic of China 1990. *The Basic Law of the Hong Kong Special Administrative Region of the People's Republic of China*.

Economist 1997 'All Eyes on China', 28 June.

Economist 1998 'East Asian Economics Survey: Chinese Whispers', 7 March.

Economist Intelligence Unit 1998 'China's Rickety Financial System', *Business China*, 19 January 1998.

Enright, M. J., Scott, E. E., Dodwell, D. 1997 *The Hong Kong Advantage*. Hong Kong: Oxford University Press.

Far Eastern Economic Review 1998 'Scandal Inc.', 7 May.

Gilley, B. 1997 'Loosening Bonds'. *Far Eastern Economic Review*, 3 July.

Gittings, D. 1998 'Industry Debate Changes Course'. *South China Morning Post*, 12 April.

Guyot, E. 1998 'Some Fear Hong Kong Could Face Loss of Autonomy'. *Asian Wall Street Journal*, 1 April.

Hang Seng Bank 1998 Hang Seng Index Historical Performance: http://www. hangseng.com/online/history/hsche.html (accessed 24 March 1998).

Harris, P. 1978 *Hong Kong: A Study in Bureaucratic Politics*. Hong Kong: Heinemann Asia.

Heath, R. 1993 'Crash Ended Day of Shame'. *South China Morning Post*, 5 November.

Heritage Foundation 1998 *1998 Index of Economic Freedom Rankings*: http://www.tdc. org.hk/hktstat/97index.htm.

Hong Kong Government, Hong Kong 1997 (Annual Report). Hong Kong: Government Printer.

Hong Kong Trade Development Corporation 1998a *Market Profile on Mainland China*: http://www.tdc.org.hk/main/china.htm (accessed on 14 May 1998).

Hong Kong Trade Development Corporation 1998b *Hong Kong's Economic System After 1997*: http://www.tdc.org.hk/beyond97/after.htm.

Husain, A. M. 1997 *Hong Kong, China in Transition*. World Bank, September.

Kraar, L. 1995 'The Death of Hong Kong'. *Fortune*, 26 July.

Kraar, L. 1997 'The Real Threat to China's Hong Kong'. *Fortune*, 26 May.

Ku, G., Li, A. 1998 'Slaughter Payouts Dismissed as Inadequate'. *South China Morning Post*, 6 January.

Kwok, S. 1997 'One in 7 Survive on Less than $90 a Day'. *South China Morning Post*, 8 September.

Kwong, K. 1998 'Without the Fanfare'. *South China Morning Post*, 3 May.

Lam, J. T. M. 1998 'Chinese Policy Towards Hong Kong: Prevention of Peaceful Evolution'. *Journal of East Asian Affairs*, Winter/Spring.

Lau, Siu-Kai 1997 'The Fraying of the Socio-Economic Fabric of Hong Kong'. *Pacific Review*, no. 3.

Lee, N. 1998 'Fish Farmers' Red Tide Demands Thrown Out'. *South China Morning Post*, 23 April.

Lee, V., Fung Wai-kong 1996 'I Don't Care about Editorial Policy…it is a Government Department'. *South China Morning Post*, 20 April.

Lo, J. 1998 'Older Buildings will Suffer Most as New Space Comes on to the Market'. *South China Morning Post*, 22 April.

Lo, T. Wing 1993 *Corruption and Politics in Hong Kong and China*, Buckingham: Open University Press.

Miners, N. 1995 *The Government and Politics of Hong Kong* (Fifth Edition). Hong Kong: Oxford University Press.

Mok, Wai-kwong V. 1996 'Hong Kong's Post-1979 Trade with China: The Impact of China's Trade Liberalization'. *China Information*, Summer.

Mulcahy, J. 1997 'Black Monday: 10 Years On'. *South China Morning Post*, 20 October.

No, Kwai-yan 1997 'Tung Soothes Fears of Falling Property Prices'. *South China Morning Post*, 31 October.

Nossal, K. R. 1997 'A High Degree of Ambiguity: Hong Kong as an International Actor after 1997'. *Pacific Review*, no. 1.

Pang, J. 1998 'Reluctant Nod for 'Deficient' Red Tide Aid'. *South China Morning Post*, 24 April.

Patten, C. 1998 *East and West: The Last Governor of Hong Kong on Power, Freedom and the Future*. London: Macmillan.

Roberti, M. 1996 *The Fall of Hong Kong: China's Triumph and Britain's Betrayal*. Chichester: John Wiley & Sons.

Roberts, E. V. 1996 'Political Developments in Hong Kong: Implications for 1997', in Skidmore, Max J. (ed.) *The Annals of The American Academy of Political and Social Science: The Future of Hong Kong*, September.

Silverman, G. 1997 'The Price of Success', in Ching, F. (ed.) *Hong Kong: 1997 and Beyond*. Hong Kong: Review Publishing.

Smith, A. 1998 'Prices Not to Blame for Tourism Slump, Says Survey'. *South China Morning Post*, 26 April.

South China Morning Post 1994 'Set on a Political Course', 10 May.

South China Morning Post 1996 'Dr. Doom Sees Change will Bring Gloom', 11 November.

South China Morning Post 1997a 'Market Shake-up Instilled Some Pride after the Fall', 20 October.

South China Morning Post 1997b 'Making a Billion the Wrong Way', 24 October.

South China Morning Post 1998a 'Time to Clean Up our Act', 17 April.

South China Morning Post 1998b 'Job Creation', 23 April.

Szulc, T. 1997 'A Looming Greek Tragedy in Hong Kong'. *Foreign Policy*, Spring.

Tsang, D. 1998 'Retail Woes Deepen with Lunar New Year Slump'. *South China Morning Post*, 25 April.

Wonacott, P. 1998 'Is China's New Bond Deal a Loan Trick or Bank Treat?'. *Asian Wall Street Journal*, 9 March.

World Bank 1997 'Selected World Development Indicators', *World Development Report 1997*. Washington, D.C.: World Bank.

Yatsko, P. 1997 'A Hearty Welcome: Shanghai and Xiamen Play Down Hong Kong Rivalry'. *Far Eastern Economic Review*, 3 July.

Yeung, C. 1998 'Searching for a Civil Solution'. *South China Morning Post*, 28 March.

2

Changing Government–Business Relations and the Governance of Hong Kong

Tak-Wing Ngo

The dominance of business interests in the Hong Kong Special Administrative Region (HKSAR) government is obvious. Even before the formal inauguration of the HKSAR, sceptics were quick to point out that 'Hong Kong people governing Hong Kong' was becoming 'business people governing Hong Kong'. Without doubt, the voice of business has been loud during the entire transition period: from the drafting of the Basic Law, the setting up of the Preliminary Working Committee, the Preparatory Committee and the Selection Committee, to the selection of a shipping magnate as the Chief Executive and the creation of a Provisional Legislative Council, business interests have been well represented. This leads some observers to suggest that the supposed new era of rule is, in fact, a continuation/reproduction of the 'colonial pact': a strategy of wooing the business élite by co-opting their representatives into policy making and law making (Beja 1997).

The purpose of this chapter is not to reiterate the dominance of business in HKSAR politics. Lindblom's seminal work on *Politics and Markets* (1977) has already reminded us that in a market-orientated system, not only does the government have to collaborate with business, but it must also often defer to business leadership to make the system work. While agreeing with this proposition, this paper argues that government–business relations under the HKSAR are not simply a continuation or reproduction of the colonial situation, as some observers have suggested. This is so firstly because government–business relations under colonial rule were never simply a matter of business capture or government–business collusion, and secondly, because the institutional setting under which government–business interaction takes place changed entirely after the handover, resulting in the search for a new relationship.

Government autonomy *versus* business capture

To understand government–business relations under the HKSAR, we first have to look at such relations under colonial rule so as to identify continuities

and changes. Existing scholarship is polarized on this question of government–business relations. One view sees the Hong Kong government during
the colonial period as insulated from business influence, similar to other
East Asian countries (Haggard 1990, pp 115–116). According to this view,
colonial rule in Hong Kong is characterized by indirect rule carried out by a
politically neutral 'administrative state', which imposed an almost complete monopoly of power on an atomistic society (Harris 1988, p 1). This
administrative state disengaged itself from societal affairs, notably by its
policy of *laissez-faire*, resulting in a separation of the state from society (Lau
1982). The only link between state and society was institutional co-option
of a social élite into advisory bodies for the sake of information exchange
and public opinion testing (King 1981).

The opposing view maintains that while Hong Kong society in general
was separated from the state, big business was not. Those who maintain
such a view argue that the colonial regime secured its basis of support
through a coalition of bureaucrats and big businesses. They argue that it
was either a colonial state captured by business interests, or that it was a
collusion of bureaucratic and business interests (Rear 1971, Davies 1977,
Leung 1990). The colonial government is thus not regarded as politically
neutral, since its economic policy of free markets and low taxation was
aimed at protecting business interests. The situation is figuratively described
by the old joke: power in Hong Kong resided in the Royal Hong Kong
Jockey Club, Jardine, Matheson & Co., the Hongkong and Shanghai Banking
Corporation, and the Governor – in that order (Hughes 1976, p 23).

These polarized views of an administrative co-option of a social élite and
a business capture of state power have over-simplified the complexity of
state–society relations in Hong Kong. Recent studies have highlighted the
agency of different actors (government bureaucrats, business élite, rural
interests, social activities, marginalized groups, etc.) in shaping colonial
rule in Hong Kong (Ngo 1997a). This chapter further argues that the stability of the colonial system and its policies was in fact maintained by
painstakingly upholding a delicate policy consent among the ruling élite.
This consent was undermined during the transition period when different
economic interests competed for domination after 1997. A new consent
has yet to be worked out after the handover. Tentatively, this chapter points
to the difficulties of reaching such a consent because of the institutional
impasse of the HKSAR political structure.

The institutionalization of business in politics

Before we look at the nature of the above-mentioned policy consent, we
need to understand the origin and institutionalization of business participation in politics. This began shortly after Britain acquired the island of
Hong Kong, whose purpose was defined from the outset to be a place for

commercial and trade activities (Endacott 1964a, p 255). The colonial administration was set up with a view to serving the interests of the British merchants. It was to encourage, but not to interfere with, the conduct of trading and related businesses.

Thus, the British merchants had little difficulty in dominating the economy and the polity during the first hundred years of colonial rule. They acquired large plots of land on which they built their empires: offices, warehouses, residential quarters, junior and senior messes, and stables. Some operated their own fleets of clippers, trading in opium and tea and dominating the entrepôt trade. To protect their interests, these princely *hongs* (as the British merchant houses came to be called) built up an extensive social and political network. They formed the Hong Kong General Chamber of Commerce (HKGCC) in 1861, which claimed to represent the entire business community in Hong Kong, because it 'embodies in its membership all the leading business houses in the Colony' (HKGCC 1949, p 10). From its inception until the 1980s, the Chamber was firmly controlled by the big British *hongs*. During its first hundred years, half of the period was under the chairmanship of four merchant houses: Jardine (19 years), P&O Steam Navigation Co. (12 years), Swire (10 years), and Turner & Co. (10 years).

With unchallenged dominance, the *hongs* became the main power interlocutors of the colonial administration. Yet Hong Kong's government–business relations before the Japanese War were characterized by mutual hostility between the colonial administration and the British merchants. This hostile relationship reminds us of Lindblom's insight that 'disputes between government and business are intense because of – not in spite of – their sharing the major leadership roles in the politico-economic order' (Lindblom 1977, p 179).

The major source of conflict was taxation. Being the main taxpayers until the 1900s, the *hongs* saw the colonial government as predatory whenever the latter tried to raise revenue to sustain the administration. Serious conflicts occurred frequently over the introduction and increase of tax, rates, stamp duties and land rent. The *hongs* saw the colonial government as an over-staffed and over-manned administration responsible for eating up the revenue collected from them (Endacott 1964a, Scott 1989, pp 54–60).

To ensure that the government ran according to their interests, the *hongs* demanded control over legislation, policy making, and government finance. Whenever their demands were rejected by the Hong Kong government, the *hongs* petitioned the Colonial Office and the Parliament, arguing that it was 'the common right of Englishmen to manage their local affairs and control the expenditure of the Colony' (Endacott 1964b, p 120). Eventually, the government yielded to the pressure. Unofficial members were included in the Legislative Council from 1850, although the government still kept an official majority in the Council. Beginning in 1885, the practice of allowing one unofficial member to be nominated by the HKGCC and another by the Justices of the Peace was institutionalized. This practice lasted until 1974. The Executive Council, the top policy-making body, was opened to the *hongs* in 1896, when Bell-Irving of Jardine, and Paul Chater, a financier and property developer, were appointed as unofficial members (Crisswell 1991, pp 179–180).

The co-option of business representatives into the legislative and policy-making bodies represented a compromise between the colonial authorities and the *hongs* over the framework of governance. Nevertheless, even when the *hongs* and the government became mutual power interlocutors, they saw each other more as a necessary evil than a close partner. The long period of conflict between the *hongs* and the government resulted in a deep sense of mutual suspicion in the otherwise mutually dependent political relations. The *hongs* were, at the same time, the major opposition and the supporters of the colonial regime. The government agreed to constrain revenue extraction, minimize public expenditure, maintain a free trade policy, and share the policy-making power in exchange for the political support of the merchants.

Oligarchical interests

Business participation in politics during the first hundred years of British rule means in essence the *hongs'* participation. Other business interests, notably manufacturing, were marginalised by the overwhelming dominance of the *hongs* (Ngo 1997b). This began to change after the Japanese War when rapid population growth and industrialization brought new economic actors into the political arena. The Shanghainese spinners were among the first to emerge as an organized economic interest (Wong 1988). The Chinese Manufacturers' Association, which had been established early in 1934 to represent mainly the interests of Cantonese manufacturers, also became more active than before. Overt conflicts of interest existed between different groups of capitalists, cutting across economic, ethnic, regional, and even dialectal lines. For the colonial administration, their alliance with the British *hongs* was thus no longer an adequate way of gauging public support.

However, the colonial status of Hong Kong prevented the development of any forms of representative government. It was believed that China's tolerance for British rule in Hong Kong would end if the colony made any move towards self-government (Miners 1981, p 32). In the 40 years between 1945 and 1985, Hong Kong was governed by a system in which even political institutions that could be found in authoritarian regimes were absent. Not only was there no popular form of political representation, but there was also no political party, no general election, and no elected assembly.

The absence of popular representation may constitute a problem for a modern republic, but not for a colony. The question of regime support for a colony depended not on any abstract principles of political legitimacy, but on the assent of the powerful. As Stinchcombe (1968, p 150) puts it, 'the person *over whom power is exercised* is not usually as important as *other power-holders'*. To gauge the political support of the other power-holders, the colonial government co-opted old and new business interests into the power networks, especially into the Executive and the Legislative Councils. The appointment system allowed the government to expand political representation by co-opting newly emerged groups and sectors into the existing system, without changing the constitutional structure. The number of advisory bodies and the number of unofficial members in these bodies gradually increased over the years. These co-opted interests supported, or even defended, government policies in exchange for privileges in using public goods, inclusion in the policy process, and access to insider information.

A number of studies have documented 'an unholy alliance of businessmen and bureaucrats' under co-optive politics (Harris 1988, p 57). Rear (1971, p 73) describes the unofficial members of the Legislative and the Executive Councils during the early 1970s as forming a 'fairly tight-knit group' directly representing the interests of big business. He finds a high degree of inter-marriage and interlocking directorship among the councillors. In another extensive survey of the major advisory bodies, Davies (1977) tracked down their overlapping membership and finds that they were controlled by a relatively small élite group. There were some 100–200 people who could be found in all parts of the advisory networks. Among the 775 places in the various government councils, boards, and committees in 1975, he found that 21 per cent of the membership controlled 46 per cent of the total committee votes. Of this 21 per cent, 38.9 per cent were directors in 56 large companies and they held 24 per cent of the directorships. These companies, in Davies' words, were 'the richest, the oldest, and the most all-embracing, and they own more property in Hong Kong than any other equivalent group' (1977, p 65). Likewise, in a similar study, Leung (1990) finds that interlocking relationships among large business groups, and the dominance of these business groups in governmental bodies, were still in place in the 1980s.

The problem of rent seeking

Although the above-mentioned system of political co-option helped to cope with the problem of interest representation by sharing ruling power with the economic and socially powerful, it did not resolve the problem of policy deliberation. The oligarchy – composed mainly of dominant business interests – did not constitute a homogeneous group. Rather they met as 'hostile brothers' in the political system. As Longstreth (1979, p 160) puts it, although they are capable of combining to meet an external threat to 'bourgeois class relations', they are more characteristically divided among themselves by their market position, policy goals, ideological orientations, etc. While they did not dispute the fundamentals – that is, the creation of wealth – they argued over an ever-shifting category of secondary issues, such as trade policy, tax rates, and regulation and promotion of business.

The policy dilemma facing the government was how to give more say to the powerful and yet keep the underdog happy. This problem arose when the oligarchical interests sought to use their political privilege to obtain preferential treatment in the deployment of public resources. If the government allowed a specific group of business élite to undertake rent-seeking activities repeatedly over time, those excluded from, or marginalized in, the power structure would turn their attention from policy conflicts to the question of who controlled the policy agenda. This might lead to demands for political reform to redistribute power, or even to challenges to colonial rule.

In this regard, the government was torn between several contradictory tasks. In the first place, it had to favour selectively the interests of the business élite to gain their support. At the same time, it had to assume the role of an arbiter of sectional interests within the ruling élite when policy conflicts arose. Worse still, it had to convince the wider public that it was a gatekeeper against rent seeking, in order to prevent widespread discontent about the unfair political system. Arguably, this dilemma was not unique to Hong Kong. O'Donnell (1979, p 290) suggests that the 'tension between the underlying reality of the state as guarantor and organiser of social domination on the one hand, and as agent of a general interest which, though particularised and limited, is not fictitious, on the other, is characteristic of any state'. What was unique for Hong Kong was that there were only very limited political devices to tackle or to conceal the tension.

Substantive consent

The government tackled the above dilemma by forging a 'substantive consent' among the ruling élite. Consent is not to be understood here as the absence of disagreement or simply élite collusion. As Kavanagh and Morris (1989, p 13) put it, it is more useful to think of consent as 'a set of parameters which bounded the set of policy options regarded by senior politicians and civil servants as administratively practicable, economically affordable and politically acceptable'. By setting a boundary on the policy options, this consent set a limit on both the bureaucratic and the business élite about their privilege and relative power. The consent is 'substantive' because it was not based on electoral or procedural arrangements, but by policy outcomes. Arguably, this matched the deep-rooted Chinese concept of a good government, which judges a government more by its policy outcomes than by its procedural mandate (Yee, Liu and Ngo 1993, p 137; Lau and Kuan 1988, p 75).

This substantive consent involved the inseparable components of allowing business domination in the power oligarchy while upholding a policy against preferential treatment for selected business interests. Under this consent, besides the privilege of sharing policy-making power, the oligarchical interests were guaranteed that their profit making would be protected and facilitated by the government. This was realized by a range of pro-business policy measures, including low profits tax, limited social welfare provisions, minimal labour protection, free enterprise, and free capital inflow and outflow. All worked to facilitate profit maximization – a policy goal that was proudly admitted by the government.

At the same time, the ruling élite agreed to constrain their privileges by accepting a policy of non-selective intervention. This meant that the government refrained from using public resources to assist or protect individual business sectors and enterprises. This avoided rent-seeking by individual élite groups, ensuring that policy outcomes were acceptable to the less powerful and to the wider population of players. It represented the solution offered by Wildavsky to Lindblom's problem of business capture of the government: reducing the abuse of public power by business through reducing government intervention (Wildavsky 1978, p 227).

The policy of non-selective intervention, together with the above-mentioned policy of low taxation, limited welfare, minimal labour protection, free enterprises, etc., was commonly labelled as constituting a policy of *laissez-faire*. Hong Kong has been well known for supposedly being the modern economy that came closest to the *laissez-faire* ideal, when in fact the nineteenth-century economic doctrine was ingeniously appropriated and articulated here to serve as a political mechanism for consensus building (Ngo, forthcoming).

With a few exceptions, the government adhered strictly to this principle with 'an almost religious fervour' (Harris 1988, p 159). Demands for preferential allocation of resources to particular business interests and market protection for specific enterprises were all rejected. And despite futile demands from time to time for preferential treatment, the business élite were willing to restrain their conflicts in order not to undermine the whole system. The existing system allowed them privileged access to information, deliberation in policy actions, and prestige in the community. By upholding the *laissez-faire* policy, they shared the common interests of having low taxation, free flow of capital, absence of government interference, and low labour welfare. Whenever a conflict arose over the deployment of resources, it was settled with reference to the principle of non-selective intervention.

As result, although the majority of the population was deprived of any chance of obtaining ruling power, the colonial regime remained stable and effective because of such a substantive consent. This is opposite to the principle of 'contingent consent', under which the political élite agree among themselves to compete in such a way that those who win electoral support in a modern democracy can exercise political authority and make binding decisions until the next round of contest (O'Donnell and Schmitter 1986, p 59). In contrast to this procedural consent that produces contingent policy outcomes, Hong Kong's substantive consent guaranteed a certainty of policy outcomes. It guaranteed the adoption of pro-business policies while at the same time preventing the use of public resources to subsidize selected interests. Although running contrary to the principles of modern democracy, this substantive consent ensured a fairer and more acceptable politico-economic system. Given the fact that the introduction of any electoral arrangements into the system was prevented by constitutional constraints, political representation could only be achieved through oligarchical politics. In such a context, the substantive consent prevented any ruthless rent seeking by the ruling élite, and allowed a higher degree of competition in the social and economic spheres.

The struggle for domination

Once we understand the delicate consent maintained by bureaucratic and business interests under colonial rule, we can analyse the politics of transition in this light. Here, we find several intertwining processes taking place during the transition period, which are far from resolved even now after the handover. These processes include the determination of who should be the new power interlocutors in the HKSAR government, and the struggle to set the rules of governance. According to Kuan (1997, p 6) the political transition is marked by processes in which conflicting interests, competing jurisdictions and fragile legitimacies are being negotiated at various levels. The major difficulty in the transition is to create either a contingent consent or a substantive consent for the new rule under Chinese sovereignty.

The problem begins with the emergence of new players and their struggle for domination in HKSAR politics. The promise of 'Hong Kong people ruling Hong Kong' created an aspiration for more political participation in the new regime, especially among those who had been excluded from the power stratum under colonial administration. When experimental political reforms were introduced in the early 1980s, social interests began competing to register their voice in the future system. They were represented in the drafting of the Basic Law, the mini-constitution that was originally envisaged to be a pact of alliance among various social interests concerning the governance of Hong Kong under Chinese sovereignty.

Among the first to organize and participate in the limited elections introduced since 1982 were middle-class professionals. They formed political parties, mobilized popular support by articulating a pro-welfare platform, and won landslide victories in District Board, Municipal Councils and Legislative Council elections (So 1997). With popular support and organizational power, they demanded a democratic HKSAR government that was constituted by universal suffrage, returned by direct election, and ruled according to a contingent consent based on electoral outcomes.

This demand was opposed by business leaders. They included not only the traditional British *hongs*, but also a new generation of Chinese tycoons. These Chinese tycoons began to take over the economic dominance of British business in the late 1970s (Wong 1991). As latecomers to politics, they were eager to preserve the existing system that guaranteed business influence. They believed that the development of representative government would increase labour power, abandon pro-business policy measures, and turn Hong Kong into a kind of welfare society. They complained that the business community was losing its political voice and influence in the policy process as a result of the political reform.

The reason for the business élite's opposition to the democratization of the political system also came from the poor political organization of business interests. Wong (1994) argues that inherent features of the Hong Kong business community, including diversity of ownership patterns and internal segmentation, prevent the diffused economic power from being organized into a cohesive political force. Despite efforts by the Beijing government and the local Xinhua Office – the *de facto* representative of the Chinese government in colonial Hong Kong – to assist in organizing business interests into a united political grouping, these 'hostile brothers' expressed little interest in co-operating and participating in electoral politics (Xu 1993, p 190). Because of that, they were destined to be the losers in a popularly elected political system.

Alarmed by the threat of being excluded from a system constituted by popular elections, business interests sought patronage from Beijing. Beijing's moves against the development of a fully representative government in Hong Kong coincided with those of the business élite. On the one hand, Chinese leaders believed that Hong Kong's capitalist system should be run by the bourgeoisie; on the other hand, Beijing was suspicious that a fully elected government would serve to insulate the HKSAR government from central government influence, and would allow colonial interests to be continued by popularly elected pro-British and anti-Chinese politicians (Xu 1993, Ch. 6).

As a result, the transition turned gradually from a process of pact negotiation to one of political exclusion. The reformists sought a popularly elected system that could exclude pro-business and pro-Beijing interests. The latter sought a system that could exclude anti-business and anti-Beijing candidates, by avoiding popular elections as much as possible. Business interests eventually won the struggle for domination: business leaders and pro-Beijing activists were increasingly drawn to the forefront of the political stage – they became the new power interlocutors through their appointment as members of the Basic Law Consultation Committee, Hong Kong Affairs Advisers, District Affairs Advisers, Preliminary Working Committee, and Preparatory Committee. At the same time, middle-class professionals and activists who advocated democratic reform were increasingly marginalized. They became the targets of political exclusion.

The politics of exclusion

The possibility of creating a contingent consent to future governance was further eroded when the Basic Law adopted a political system that was angrily rejected by the reform-minded activists and professionals. The system limits the proportion of direct, territory-wide election in the HKSAR legislature. Half of the seats are reserved for functional constituencies, which include mainly economic sectors such as banking, trading, manufacturing, etc. The franchise in these designated economic sectors is, in general, limited to employers only, thereby guaranteeing business domination. Another portion of seats is to be returned by an Election Committee, which is subject to manipulation. Furthermore, business interests are also well represented in the selection of the Chief Executive by the Selection Committee.

Seeing the Basic Law provisions as trying to exclude their participation in HKSAR politics, the reformists supported the reforms introduced by the last Governor, Chris Patten. Despite stern warnings from Beijing and strong condemnation by the business community, Patten carried out his reforms. He expanded the number of electorates in the 1995 Legislative Council election fivefold, by extending the eligibility of functional constituency voters to the entire working population, and by abolishing the appointed membership of District Boards and Municipal Councils. Although the reformists won a landslide victory in both direct and functional constituency elections, the Legislative Council was abolished by Beijing after the handover. It was replaced, on 1 July 1997, by an appointed Provisional Legislative Council. The transition period thus officially ended with little compromise among the conflicting interests.

The politics of exclusion continued after the handover, when the HKSAR government and the Provisional Legislative Council were charged with the responsibility of drawing up new electoral arrangements to replace those created by the Patten reforms. In fact, the manoeuvring of electoral rules had already begun even before the handover, under the work of the Preparatory Committee. Being completely dominated by pro-Beijing celebrities and business interests, the Preparatory Committee and the Provisional Legislative Council had little reservation about designing a system that could further marginalize the reformists in future elections. The reformists, headed by the Democratic Party, saw the setting up of the Provisional

Legislative Council as unconstitutional and took the case to court. Although the Court of Appeal upheld the appointment of the Council as lawful, the reformists did succeed in undermining the credibility of the Council. This also undermined the credibility of the electoral arrangements passed by the Council under the Legislative Council Bill. The Bill, containing arrangements for the first HKSAR Legislative Council election in the May 1998 election, was approved, on 28 September 1997, by 29 votes to nine with 11 abstentions, after a marathon 20-hour debate.

Under the new arrangements, the popular vote introduced by Patten for functional constituencies was replaced by the corporate vote for a new list of functional constituencies. The number of eligible electors was reduced dramatically from 2.5 million to 180,000. The majority of the newly added functional constituencies for the 1998 election belonged to the business sector, including import and export, textile and garment, wholesale and retail, shipping and transport, and insurance. These were added to the existing constituencies, such as banking and finance, industry, commerce, real estate and construction, and tourism. Altogether, the functional constituencies occupied half of the total 60 seats in the Legislative Council.

The May 1998 election result showed that the functional constituency election had succeeded in ensuring the dominance of the business voice in the legislature. One-third of the candidates in the functional constituency election were uncontested; all but two of them were businessmen. Over half of the elected functional constituency councillors were connected with business interests. In terms of party affiliation, the Liberal Party – backed by big business – won more seats than any other party, obtaining nine out of the total 30 seats.

Another area of electoral change endorsed by the Provisional Legislative Council was the composition of the Election Committee. According to the Basic Law, 10 seats of the first HKSAR Legislative Council should be returned by an Election Committee. Under Chris Patten, this Election Committee was composed of elected District Board members. The new law replaced it with an 800-member Election Committee coming from four functional groups and returned by consultation and corporate voting. The Committee eventually (s)elected 10 pro-Beijing loyalists during the May 1988 election. Among them, one was affiliated to the Liberal Party and three to the Hong Kong Progressive Alliance, who represented the interests of small, pro-Beijing businessmen.

The arrangement for direct election was even trickier. According to the Basic Law, 20 seats of the first HKSAR legislature should be returned by popular votes in geographical constituencies. Past records of direct elections showed that the reformists won by a big margin. To prevent landslide victories of the reformists in future elections, the Preparatory Committee abandoned the existing single seat–single vote system in 20 geographical constituencies. The system was believed to have benefited the Democratic

Party and its allies during the 1995 election (Choi 1998, pp 20–34). After long deliberation, the HKSAR government and the Provisional Legislative Council adopted a proportional representation system in five geographical constituencies. The new system was seen as favouring 'minority groups', hence allowing the less organized and less popular parties, such as the pro-Beijing Democratic Alliance for the Betterment of Hong Kong and the pro-business Liberal Party, to obtain seats.

During the May 1998 election, the new electoral system did prevent the reformists – led by the Democratic Party and its allies – from gaining an overwhelming victory, although they still won 14 out of the total 20 directly elected seats. The Liberal Party was totally defeated in the direct election. Despite the victory in the direct election, the reformists are still in a minority position in the Legislative Council. This is essentially what the Basic Law and the electoral law were intended to achieve. However, with popular backing and electoral mandate, the Democratic Party has already vowed to keep pressing for reform. The issue is unlikely to be settled without general consent over the rules of the game.

Difficulties in reaching a new consent

One may wonder why, in failing to reach a contingent consent, the HKSAR cannot achieve some kind of substantive consent like that experienced under colonial rule. To do so, it requires the power-holders to restrain their privileges, and the peripheral players to believe that, in view of such volunteered restraints, they will not be disadvantaged intolerably. Such a consent, however, seems to be rather difficult to achieve because of changing government–business relations.

From the outset, the functional constituency election encourages rather than discourages rent seeking. When legislative power is divided into the hands of economic and social groupings, the different interests fight hard to be included as a functional constituency. Representatives of the functional constituencies, mostly businessmen-cum-politicians, are meant to protect the interests of their own sectors rather than to constrain the pursuit of sectoral interests. Elected councillors run the risk of losing their electoral support in the next election if they are not seen as advancing the interests of their functional constituencies. In essence, conflicts of interest are institutionalized in the legislative system, making any general policy consent difficult.

Then there is doubt whether the HKSAR government can maintain an impartial role in arbitrating conflicts among the ruling élite (Ngo 1997c). Unlike the colonial Governor, whose appointment was entirely controlled by London, the Chief Executive of the HKSAR government is elected by a Selection Committee comprising of people with vested interests. They chose Tung Chee-hwa, a shipping magnate with close connections with the

Beijing authorities, as the first Chief Executive. Besides the pro-democracy parties, even business tycoons such as Li Ka-shing have expressed reservations over the selection of a businessman as the Chief Executive. They are concerned about the impartiality of the Chief Executive when policy decisions involving business conflicts are taken.

An outstanding example of their concerns can be found in the controversy over the appointment of an interested party to review housing and land policies. An out-pouring of scepticism and criticism appeared when Tung Chee-hwa appointed Executive Council member Leung Chun-ying to look into housing policy. Leung was in charge of investigating and making policy recommendations concerning the provision of residential housing units, with a view to finding a solution to the over speculation in real estate prices that deprived many people, including high-income professionals, from buying a residential flat. The appointment was widely criticized as inappropriate because of conflicts of interests between Leung's public responsibility and his private business – Leung is the owner of a surveying firm in the property market, and is strongly connected with property developers.

The criticism of Leung's appointment as a kind of government–business collusion is rather surprising at first sight. This is so because, as mentioned earlier, business interests had always been well represented in Hong Kong's policy-making and law-making processes. The existence of conflicts of interest were more than obvious when big *hongs*, such as Hongkong and Shanghai Banking Corporation, Jardine, Swire, etc., were making decisions on financial, land or labour policies. Yet no similar uproar in public opinion arose because of the substantive consent found under colonial rule. Putting this into perspective, severe criticism is understandable given the absence of a new consent under the HKSAR government.

The worry about the HKSAR government's impartiality is further aggravated by the fact that the Hong Kong business élite have intricate business relations with the mainland government (Ngo 1997d). The majority of the business conglomerates in Hong Kong has established joint ventures with various levels of government, party, or even military authorities and enterprises in the mainland. Many mainland enterprises, including direct subsidiary companies of central and provincial governments, are also operating and co-operating with local businesses in Hong Kong. There have been discussions about the problem of corruption with these ventures. The question, however, hinges not only on whether the HKSAR government is able to combat unlawful corruption, but also whether it can prevent rent-seeking of the powerful who want preferential treatment in exchange for political support.

All these issues have led to a general feeling of suspicion and scepticism towards the businessmen-cum-politicians. Opinion surveys have long revealed popular distrust towards business interests (Lau and Kuan 1990, p 773; Lau, Kuan and Wan 1991, p 202; Wong and Lui 1992, pp 28–30; Wong 1994, pp 230–232). The general public is sceptical about the integrity of businessmen and believes that business interests have excessive political influence in Hong Kong. Ordinary people see business leaders as dishonest and not dependable, and do not have a high regard for, or confidence in, the political leadership of business interests. In such circumstances, as one observer points out, it becomes more difficult to take up public positions on issues without being accused of acting in bad faith or of pursuing private gain (Yahuda 1996, p 107).

Perhaps the most telling sign of this distrust towards businessmen-cum-politicians was the result of the May 1998 election. None of 12 Liberal Party members who contested the 20 directly elected seats was elected. The losers included Lee Peng-fei, leader of the Party, who has been a legislator for 20 years. Out of the total 1.48 million votes cast in the five geographical constituencies, the Liberal Party received only 50 335 votes.

The above-mentioned factors undermine the basis for reaching a substantive consent based on policy outcomes rather than electoral results. Under the present system, the power-holders pursue (and need to be seen to be pursuing) sectional interests on behalf of their constituencies; there is uncertainty even among the ruling élite that the government can continue to be a gatekeeper against rent-seeking; and the marginalized players, as well as the general public, have little confidence in the integrity of the dominant players. The result of the absence of either a contingent or a substantive consent will be an ongoing struggle to change the rules of the game.

Conclusion

The foregoing discussion explains why government–business collaboration under colonial rule did not degenerate into the kind of collusion and rent seeking described by Krueger (1974). It shows that the orthodox view that sees government–business relations as characterized by either government autonomy or business capture is inadequate to describe the governance of Hong Kong. Effective governance during the colonial era depended upon the painstaking maintenance of a substantive consent that restricted any distributional policies for private gain. It was this delicate consent that drove Hong Kong business into profit seeking instead of rent seeking.

This delicate consent has been undermined during the transition to Chinese sovereignty. The marginalization of popular participation and the institutionalization of sectional interests' representation in the HKSAR government and legislature turn an originally collaborative relationship into one of collusion. Although the actual performance of the HKSAR government has yet to be seen, one is alarmed by Olson's (1982) prediction that capitalists and their allies tend to form 'distributional coalitions' that pressure governments to divert resources to them and away from societal use.

Acknowledgement

The author would like to thank the Netherlands Organization for Scientific Research (NWO) for supporting the research of this article.

Bibliography

Beja, J. P. 1997 'Hong Kong Two Months Before the Handover: One Territory, Two Systems?. *China News Analysis* 15 April: 3–10.

Choi, C. 1998 *Insight into the Hong Kong Electoral System*. Hong Kong: Ming Pao Publishing Co. (*in Chinese*).

Crisswell, C. N. 1991 *The Taipans: Hong Kong's Merchant Princes*. Hong Kong: Oxford University Press.

Davies, S. N. G. 1977 'One Brand of Politics Rekindled'. *Hong Kong Law Journal*, 7(1): 44–84.

Endacott, G. B. 1964a *A History of Hong Kong*, 2nd edn. Hong Kong: Oxford University Press.

Endacott, G. B. (ed.) 1964b *An Eastern Entrepôt: A Collection of Documents Illustrating the History of Hong Kong*. London: Her Majesty's Stationery Office.

Haggard, S. 1990 *Pathways from the Periphery: The Politics of Growth in the Newly Industrializing Countries*. Ithaca: Cornell University Press.

Harris, P. 1988 *Hong Kong: A Study in Bureaucracy and Politics*. Hong Kong: Macmillan.

Hong Kong General Chamber of Commerce 1949 *Hong Kong General Chamber of Commerce Report*. Hong Kong: Hong Kong General Chamber of Commerce.

Hughes, R. 1976 *Borrowed Place, Borrowed Time: Hong Kong and Its Many Faces*. London: André Deutsch.

Kavanagh, D. and Morris, P. 1989 *Consensus Politics from Attlee to Thatcher*. Oxford: Basil Blackwell.

King, A. Y. 1981 'Administrative Absorption of Politics in Hong Kong: Emphasis on the Grass Roots Level', in King, A. Y., Lee, R. P. L. (eds) *Social Life and Development in Hong Kong*. Hong Kong: Chinese University Press.

Krueger, A. O. 1974 'The Political Economy of Rent-Seeking Society'. *American Economic Review*, 64 (June): 291–303.

Kuan, H. 1997 'Hong Kong after the Handover'. *China News Analysis* 1–15, August: 1–15.

Lau, S. 1982 *Society and Politics in Hong Kong*. Hong Kong: Chinese University Press.

Lau, S., Kuan, H. 1988 *The Ethos of the Hong Kong Chinese*. Hong Kong: Chinese University Press.

Lau, S., Kuan, H. 1990 'Public Attitude Toward Laissez Faire in Hong Kong'. *Asian Survey*, 30(8): 766–81.

Lau, S., Kuan, H., Wan, P. 1991 'Political Attitudes', in Lau, S., Lee, M., Wan, P., Wong, S. (eds) *Indicators of Social Development: Hong Kong 1988*. Hong Kong: Hong Kong Institute of Asia-Pacific Studies, Chinese University of Hong Kong.

Leung, B. K. P. 1990 'Power and Politics: A Critical Analysis', in Leung, B. K. P. (ed.) *Social Issues in Hong Kong*. Hong Kong: Oxford University Press.

Lindblom, C. E. 1977 *Politics and Markets: The World's Political-Economic Systems*. New York: Basic Books.

Longstreth, F. 1979 'The City, Industry and the State', in Crouch, C. (ed.) *State and Economy in Contemporary Capitalism*. London: Croom Helm.

Miners, N. J. 1981 *The Government and Politics of Hong Kong*, 3rd edn, Hong Kong: Oxford University Press.

Ngo, T. 1997a 'Hong Kong under Colonial Rule: An Introduction'. *China Information*, 12(1/2): 1–11.

Ngo, T. 1997b 'The Legend of a Colony: Political Rule and Historiography in Hong Kong'. *China Information*, 12(1/2): 135–156.

Ngo, T. 1997c 'Hong kong onder Chinees Bestuur: Het Dilemma van Verandering en Continuïteit'. *Internationale Spectator*, 51(5): 274–78.

Ngo, T. 1997d *Global Market, Regional Networks, and State Intervention in the East Asian Cases*. Paper presented to the International Colloquium on 'Globalisation, the Formation of Economic Blocs, Nation States, and Regional Response', Utrecht, 12–13 June.

Ngo, T. (forthcoming) 'Social Values and Consensual Politics in Hong Kong', in Antlöv, H., Ngo, T. (eds), *The Cultural Construction of Politics in Asia*. London: Curzon Press.

O'Donnell, G. 1979 'Tensions in the Bureaucratic-Authoritarian State and the Question of Democracy', in Collier, D. (ed.), *The New Authoritarianism in Latin America*. Princeton: Princeton University Press.

O'Donnell, G., Schmitter, P. C. 1986 *Transition from Authoritarian Rule: Tentative Conclusions about Uncertain Democracies*. Baltimore: Johns Hopkins University Press.

Olson, M. 1982 *The Rise and Decline of Nations: Economic Growth, Stagflation, and Social Rigidities*. New Haven: Yale University Press.

Rear, J. 1971 'One Brand of Politics', in Hopkins, K. (ed.) *Hong Kong: The Industrial Colony*. Hong Kong: Oxford University Press.

Scott, I. 1989 *Political Change and the Crisis of Legitimacy in Hong Kong*. Hong Kong: Oxford University Press.

So, A. Y. 1997 'Hong Kong's Embattled Democracy: Perspectives from East Asian NIEs'. *Issues and Studies*, 33(8): 63–80.

Stinchcombe, L. A. 1968 *Constructing Social Theories*. New York: Harcourt, Brace & World.

Wildavsky, A. 1978 'Changing Forward Versus Changing Back'. *Yale Law Journal*, 88: 217–234.

Wong, G. 1991 'Business Groups in a Dynamic Environment: Hong Kong 1976–1986', in Hamilton, G. (ed.) *Business Networks and Economic Development in East and Southeast Asia*. Hong Kong: Centre of Asian Studies, University of Hong Kong.

Wong, S. 1988 *Emigrant Entrepreneurs: Shanghai Industrialists in Hong Kong*. Hong Kong: Oxford University Press.

Wong, S. 1994 'Business and Politics in Hong Kong During the Transition', in Leung, B. V. P., Wong, T. Y. C. (eds) *25 Years of Social and Economic Development in Hong Kong*. Hong Kong: University of Hong Kong.

Wong, T. W. P., Lui, T. 1992 'From One Brand of Politics to One Brand of Political Culture'. *Hong Kong Institute of Asia-Pacific Studies Occasional Paper* no. 10. Hong Kong: Chinese University of Hong Kong.

Xu, J. 1993 *Xu Jiatun's Memoir of Hong Kong*. Hong Kong: United Press (*in Chinese*).

Yahuda, M. 1996 *Hong Kong: China's Challenge*. London: Routledge.

Yee, H. L. B., Ngo, T. 1993 *The Political Culture of the Macau Chinese*. Macau: Macau Foundation (*in Chinese*).

3
Hong Kong, China and the Handling of the Financial Crises: Monetary Management in 1983, 1987, 1997 and 1998

Peter Ferdinand

The main purpose of this chapter is to assess the impact of the transition to Chinese sovereignty upon the ability of the Hong Kong government to exercise effective control over its economy. It will compare the ways in which the authorities handled the currency crisis of 1983 and the stock exchange crisis of 1987, when Hong Kong was a British colony, and the financial crises of autumn 1997 and 1998, when it had become a Special Administrative Region of China.

This chapter argues that it was the crises of 1983 and 1987, as well as the official responses to them, that turned Hong Kong into a genuinely international financial centre in its own right. Before that Hong Kong's financial system had been more a kind of cosy club, where everyone knew everyone else and where regulation relied upon trust. The government applied 'positive non-intervention' to this branch of the economy, as it did to all others. Afterwards, as the government devised measures to cope with the crises, it sought to exert a greater influence upon the financial world, and in so doing it developed a greater capacity for institutional autonomy, first from London, and later from Beijing. The intervening 14 years proved crucial for Hong Kong, enabling it to develop the institutional capacity to run its own monetary system and to maintain the exchange rate, even in the face of immense external pressures from global finance. Without that, Hong Kong would not long have been able to practise any meaningful version of 'One Country – Two Systems' as far as monetary management was concerned.

First of all, it is important to recall the background. Hong Kong's institutions for macroeconomic management are quite different from those of both London and Beijing. Hong Kong does not have a central bank, unlike both the UK and China. Since 1983, the Hong Kong dollar has been managed by a currency board. The key difference is that the currency board does not directly control the money supply within the territory over which it has authority. Instead its main function is to maintain the stability of the foreign exchange value of the currency. Indeed, according to Joseph Yam, the current Chief Executive of the Hong Kong Monetary Authority, it may well be *ultra vires* for the Authority to conduct money market operations or any other market activities that are contrary to the objective of maintaining exchange rate stability (Yam 1998a). Money supply within the territory depends upon the inflows and outflows of other currencies and in Hong Kong it was the responsibility of two commercial banks – the Hongkong and Shanghai Banking Corporation (HSBC) and the Standard Chartered Bank (the Bank of China has now been added to the list) – to issue bank notes, under the supervision of the Hong Kong government.

Until 1988, management of the Exchange Fund was supervized from the Treasury of the Hong Kong government. The Governor was always responsible for consulting with the authorities in Britain over any policy or policy change that might affect the stability of the currency, but, in practice, neither the British government nor the Bank of England interfered much in the running of the Hong Kong economy. There was no guarantee on the part of Britain to support the HK dollar if it ran into difficulties, although the Bank of England was always ready to supply sympathetic advice. Already, therefore, Hong Kong did to a significant extent practise 'One Country – Two Systems' in terms of financial institutions.

Until 1973, the Hong Kong dollar was tied to the pound sterling, but the decision in that year to allow the pound to float against other currencies led the Hong Kong authorities to do the same for their currency. The next 10 years saw the value of the HK dollar fluctuate quite widely. Initially, Hong Kong prospered, but then the difficulties grew. In effect, since there was no exchange rate anchor, monetary policy became discretionary and unpredictable. There was no monetary authority that could impose effective monetary targets or foreign exchange controls. There were no reserve requirements on banks.

Hong Kong was heavily buffeted by international economic turbulence: oil 'shocks', increasing uncertainty over relations with the mainland, and speculation against the US dollar. In 1974, the Hang Seng Index fell 60.5 per cent but rose 104.5 per cent the following year. Real GDP growth dropped to 0.3 per cent in 1975 and climbed to 16.2 per cent in 1976. Inflation fell to 2.7 per cent in 1975, but rose to 15.5 per cent in 1980 (HKMA 1995, p 57).

The crisis of 1983

These problems came together in 1983. Volatility, which spread from international markets, was compounded by extreme uncertainty over the progress of Sino-British negotiations about the future of Hong Kong. Already, by the end of 1982, the HK dollar had fallen 12 per cent to HK$6.48 against the US dollar compared with the previous 12 months. Then, in 1983, the turbulence pushed the HK dollar down further. By mid-September it had fallen to HK$7.89 to the US dollar. The then Financial Secretary,

Sir John Bembridge, attempted to prop-up confidence by declaring that the authorities had no intention of pegging the HK dollar to the US dollar. This failed to reassure the markets and within two days the HK dollar dropped further to HKUS$9.60 to the US dollar, despite intervention from the Exchange Fund. The effect of this lack of confidence upon Hong Kong's economy, which was so heavily dependent upon foreign trade for its prosperity, was serious. No manufacturer or trader could have any confidence about the prices of imported raw materials, or profitable prices for exports.

Thus, on 16 October 1983, the Hong Kong government announced that it would henceforth fix the value of the HK dollar at HK$7.8 to the US dollar for all its dealings with licensed banks. With this, it set up a Currency Board to manage the currency on the advice of outside economists and the Bank of England. At the time, several economists in Hong Kong argued that this rate understated the value of the HK dollar, but a lower rate was chosen because of the political uncertainty over the colony's future relationship with mainland China. This commitment was not, however, extended to individual holders of HK dollar notes, who could only convert them into foreign currency, including the US dollar, at rates fixed by the foreign exchange markets. Thus, for individuals, actual exchange rates fluctuated around the equivalent of the US$1:HK$7.8 figure.

The 'peg' and the currency board

According to Joseph Yam, the current Chief Executive of the Hong Kong Monetary Authority, 'essential to the Currency Board system is a Monetary Rule that requires any change in the Monetary Base to be brought about only by a corresponding change in Foreign Reserves in a specified foreign currency at a fixed exchange rate' (HKMA 1998, p 8). He describes this rule as 'almost sacrosanct'.

The intention of the reform was to reintroduce stability into Hong Kong's economy and, by and large, it worked. Although there were some early attempts by speculators to force changes in the value of the HK dollar, these failed. There was a moderate banking crisis in 1985–1986, which led to the restructuring of five more banks, but Hong Kong's sustained prosperity, coupled with growing confidence about the future of its relationship with the mainland, combined to ensure that the 'pegged' relationship with the US dollar was not broken.

It is no exaggeration to say that the 'peg' has now become the cornerstone of macroeconomic monetary management in Hong Kong. It has come to be regarded as the foundation of price and economic stability. Thus, defending it has become the number one economic priority of the Hong Kong government.

One key consequence should be noted. The introduction of the peg in Hong Kong implied that, if the authorities were consistent, then they would have to be prepared to accept the pain caused by interest rates rising to whatever levels were necessary to maintain the stability of the exchange rate. Potentially, this could lead to extreme deflation whenever the exchange rate was under threat – as we have seen since autumn 1997.

Nevertheless the 'peg' laid the foundation for the remarkable resurgence in Hong Kong's prosperity in the second half of the 1980s and in the 1990s, which was in part, but only in part, due to the signing of the Joint Declaration between Britain and China in 1984. The 'peg' encouraged foreign investors to believe that the economy would stay open to capital movements with the rest of the world. This was particularly important for an economy like Hong Kong's that is so heavily orientated towards foreign trade and investment – by the late 1990s the total value of Hong Kong's external trade in goods and services was equivalent to over 250 per cent of GDP. So money poured into Hong Kong. Yet this kind of growth also facilitated financial virtue. It enabled the Hong Kong authorities to exercise genuine control over the Hong Kong money supply for the first time (Lui 1991, p 206). The result was that, despite all the growth, inflation was reduced.

This influx of foreign capital turned Hong Kong into a much broader-based international financial centre. Over the next few years, Hong Kong's economy grew significantly. Exports surged by 27 per cent after 1983, to a point where the US government hinted that it wished to see a revaluation of the HK dollar. Foreign currency deposits in licensed banks and deposit-taking companies soared from HK$10.6 billion in 1980, when they represented 12 per cent of total deposits, to HK$363.2 billion in 1987, when they represented 57 per cent. Unemployment was 1.8 per cent. If anything, there was a chronic labour shortage rather than a surplus. Annual inflation was below 10 per cent.

In turn, however, this influx of capital caused the next major economic crisis – the stock market collapse of 1987.

The crisis of 1987

While macroeconomic financial management in Hong Kong had become more professional in the 1980s, the Stock Market had lagged behind. It remained a relatively small closed club, even though its activities had grown enormously over the period. Average daily turnover had risen from HK$250 million in 1983 to over HK$4 billion in 1987, largely because of a massive expansion of futures and options trading. Market capitalization on the Exchange had risen to HK$84 billion, though partly because it had been merged with three private stock exchanges. Between July 1986 and September 1987, the Hang Seng Index had risen by nearly 50 per cent, with some estimates that between 5 and 10 per cent of US pension fund money was invested there, as a result of the declining attraction of the Japanese market (Financial Times, 15 October 1987). Many were also attracted by the opening of the mainland China market. The economy seemed to be growing healthily, possibly even too healthily. In 1986, it grew by 11 per cent, instead of the government's earlier predictions of 8.7 per cent. Exports in the first seven months of 1987 grew by 40 per cent. In September 1987, the Hong Kong Financial Secretary, Piers Jacobs, remarked: 'The economy is obviously a little overheated at the moment, but it will correct itself' (Financial Times, 11 September 1987).

Only one month later came the big crash on world stock markets. The effect was greatest in Hong Kong. 19th October saw an 11 per cent fall in the value of equities on the Stock Exchange and this sparked a rush to sell, which caused serious liquidity problems. The most serious effect, however, was on the recently created Futures Exchange. There, the crisis focused upon the Hang Seng Index futures contract. It had been intended to insulate investors from risk, but now it had the reverse effect of jeopardizing the whole equity market. In the absence of adequate information and surrounded by swirling rumours, there seemed a serious danger of major defaults by companies.

As a result, the Chairman of the Stock Exchange, Ronald Li, decided to close the Stock Exchange for four days while a recovery operation could be mounted, even though it put a serious question mark over the Exchange's ability to compete with top exchanges in other parts of the world. Hambros was asked by the Hong Kong government to organize a 'lifeboat' of support for potential losers so as to prevent a complete loss of confidence. Initially, it raised HK$2 billion, with half contributed by leading stockbrokers and half by the government's Exchange Fund. The overall potential liabilities at that time were pure guesswork, but everyone knew that the existing compensation fund of only HK$22 million would be inadequate. Subsequently a further HK$2 billion was raised, including, most intriguingly, HK$1 billion from the Bank of China on the mainland, although in the event it was not actually needed.

At that time, this assistance from the mainland created a great deal of speculation, because it was the first occasion on which the mainland had so obviously come to the assistance of the Hong Kong economy. Initially, they had not been asked for a contribution, because it was feared that China would take too long to make a decision. In any case, the Bank of China did not want to appear too eager, in case it led to suspicions about 'the mainland' taking over well before 1997. Nevertheless there was no doubt that the assistance could be attributed to the efforts of the head of the Xinhua office in Hong Kong at that time, Xu Jiatun. Not only did it help with the immediate crisis, it also influenced expectations about the future. It created the impression that Hong Kong would be able to appeal to the mainland for assistance again even before 1997. It also contrasted with the British government's approach to the crisis, which was limited to advice and moral support.

When the Stock Exchange reopened on 26 October, the Hang Seng Index took a further dive of 33 per cent. After that, however, the market and the economy gradually stabilized. The Chairman of the Stock Exchange, Ronald Li, was dismissed and later arrested for illegal profiteering. The economy resumed its growth and already by the end of the year the US government was again hinting that it wanted to see a revaluation of the HK dollar because of the latter's mounting export surplus.

The reforms – the Hong Kong currency board becomes more professional

The successful resolution of the crises of 1983 and 1987 was a testament to the growing skill of the Hong Kong authorities in managing their own affairs. Yet both had been quite close-run things – there was no room for complacency. The crises had been reminders of the economy's vulnerability to international financial flows, especially as the latter were swelling. The willingness of the authorities to accept the offer of the Bank of China to support the 'lifeboat', indeed the warmth with which it was welcomed, also suggested nervousness, since in other respects the authorities were trying to prevent premature interference from the mainland. Given the speed with which Hong Kong's economy was changing, as previously unheard-of sums of money flooded into the colony, there was clearly a need to draw lessons. The fact that Hong Kong's had been the only stock exchange in the world to close at all during the October 1987 crisis, even though vast sums of money were being taken out of markets elsewhere, drew adverse comment. People openly asked whether Hong Kong was seriously interested in becoming a major international player.

In the aftermath, various enquiries were conducted to improve the colony's ability to respond to crises. The best-known of these was the Hay-Davison enquiry into the workings of the Stock Exchange. It concluded that self-regulation had failed – a group of insiders had run it as their own club and had failed to allow an adequate say to the rapidly increasing numbers of international members. Equally, the Securities Commission, which had supposedly been regulating the Exchange, had been starved of resources. The report made five groups of recommendations to professionalize management in both.

The raising of the Futures Exchange's margin requirements to ultra-conservative levels did later play an important part in preventing defaults in 1997 (South China Morning Post, 25 October 1997). On that occasion there would not be any temptation to close the Stock Exchange, with all the renewed damage that this would have done to international confidence in the openness and stability of the market.

Equally important, however, were the reforms of the monetary system, which were introduced in the years following 1987. To defend the new pegged rate, the authorities initially needed repeated intervention. Gradually, the government came to the conclusion that it needed additional levers to exercise more effective influence over liquidity and interest rates in the inter-bank market, so as to reduce the reliance upon direct and ad hoc intervention.

Till then the Currency Board had observed the 'Monetary Rule', but had applied it only to changes in the number of bank notes in circulation, not the aggregate total of balances in the clearing accounts that the licensed banks maintained with the Hong Kong authorities. Since the latter represented the total sum of inter-bank liquidity in Hong Kong, and since during the 1980s this amount had swelled enormously as compared with the number of notes in circulation, it meant that the base figure relating the aggregate balance to foreign currency holdings was smaller than it needed to be, and also therefore potentially much more easily destabilized. The exchange rate could only be kept stable by intervention in the foreign exchange market. But since the Currency Board could not trade there on its own account and had to rely upon the HSBC to act for it, it was difficult for those actions to be separated from the HSBC's own commercial activities. Confusion encouraged rumour and speculation, so the success of intervention was not guaranteed.

In July 1988, the authorities changed the basis of the Monetary Rule. Instead of it just being limited to the amount of bank notes in circulation, it was expanded to include the Aggregate Balance of all inter-bank clearing funds. This reduced the dangers of currency rate volatility.

Also in 1988, they introduced new accounting arrangements, which required that the HSBC open an account with the Exchange Fund as Managing Bank of the Clearing House of the Hong Kong Association of Banks. All the other banks would then have dependent accounts with the HSBC. Through this measure the Exchange Fund was able for the first time to regulate the amount of liquidity in the banking system. The government also abolished the statutory 60 per cent ceiling on interest rates, thus adding to its ability to penalize banks that funded speculators.

The government followed this with other innovations to enhance its ability to influence banking liquidity, culminating in the establishment in 1993 of the Hong Kong Monetary Authority, which combined responsibilities for both the Exchange Fund and banking supervision. All these measures marked a significant professionalization of the Currency Board.

On the other hand, the Hong Kong Monetary Authority (HKMA) also sought to increase transparency in the financial system, in part so that it could stimulate international confidence and predictability in the way the currency was being managed, and in part so that it too could have a better idea of any speculation. They began to publish the accounts of the Exchange Fund for the first time in 50 years. In 1996 they introduced an automated Real Time Gross Settlement system (RTGS), which speeded up the processing of deals within the banking system, despite the extremely rapid increase in daily banking transactions in the 1990s – average daily transactions on the inter-bank market (excluding swaps) rose from HK$38 billion in November 1991 to HK$81.2 billion in July 1994. This also required that all banks, including the HSBC, had their own account with the HKMA. This ended the HSBC managing the banking system on behalf of the HKMA. Henceforth it was possible to distinguish between commercial dealing by the HSBC and interventions of the HKMA in the foreign exchange markets to stabilize the currency. This also meant that the authorities could form a picture of the activities of individual banks much more rapidly than before – particularly useful if any of them were funding currency speculation.

During this period of running-in the new arrangements, the authorities were assisted by two things. First, there was no major speculative attack on the HK dollar, and second, the renewed dash for growth on the mainland so obsessed investors in the rest of the world that the general confidence washed over Hong Kong and submerged worries over the colony's reversion to China in 1997. It also hid the lack of experience of the monetary authorities (HKMA 1998, p 35).

The crises of 1997 and 1998

As Hong Kong approached 1997, its monetary authorities had acquired greater ability to manage the currency and money in circulation than they had ever had before. None of this was driven by the events of 1997 as such. Yet it was not difficult to predict that speculators might attempt to test the nerve of the new HKSAR authorities, as well as those in Beijing, by organizing a run on the HK dollar after 1 July. So the HKMA ran several simulations to try to anticipate moves against them, and to try out counter-measures. They were also helped by the experience of 1994, when they had had to minimize the effects upon Hong Kong of the Mexican currency crisis, but, just in case, the People's Bank of China offered additional liquidity if it was needed, though it would have to be paid for on commercial terms.

By the time of the handover, the Hong Kong economy was very strong. Growth remained around 6 per cent per annum, and unemployment was low. The only significant problem was the property market, which had clearly been bubbling up for the previous few months. All of this suggested that the economy ought to be fairly well protected against speculation. Foreign currency reserves at the disposal of the HKMA reached around US$80 billion, though this included US$16 billion of strictly fiscal foreign currency reserves from the Land Fund (Asian Wall Street Journal, 24–25 October 1997). In addition, the People's Bank of China had accumulated around US$120 billion, some of which could be pledged to Hong Kong if necessary. The HKMA was able to see problems emerging around East Asia well before they began to have a serious impact upon Hong Kong. Sir Donald Tsang, the Financial Secretary of the HKSAR government, felt able to offer US$1 billion from Hong Kong's reserves to help Thailand stabilize its economy.

This comfortable situation changed with the sudden decision of the Taiwanese government to devalue their currency in mid-October. Given that Taiwanese foreign currency reserves had been roughly equal to those of Hong Kong, i.e. around US$80 billion, this suggested that the famed 'war chest' that Hong Kong had built up might not be as much of a deterrent as had been assumed. In trying to shore up its currency, the Taiwanese government apparently lost US$5 billion (Asian Wall Street Journal, 20 October 1997) – a relatively small sum given its US$80 billion reserves. Yet it had still given way.

Once this had happened, Hong Kong stood out as the only open economy in the region that had not suffered devaluation. Suddenly, its own US$80 billion reserves did not look so impregnable and even though the obstacles for speculators were large, the very challenge encouraged some of them because the HK dollar would have to settle at a much lower level against the US dollar if the peg to the US dollar were broken. The profits for speculators would then be correspondingly greater and it might easily lead to a further round of devaluations in the region, with renewed opportunities for speculative profits.

The storm broke on 23 October, with massive selling of the HK dollar. According to Joseph Yam, throughout this crisis speculators sold short about US$3.8 billion of Hong Kong dollars (South China Morning Post, 25 June 1998). The Hang Seng Index dropped 14 per cent in one day. The HKMA responded by allowing overnight interest rates to rise to 300 per cent for an hour, which ironically had the effect of raising the HK dollar slightly above its pegged value to the US dollar on exchange markets.

The response proved sufficiently vigorous to discourage further direct assaults on the currency itself. Nevertheless, some uncertainty still persisted. On 24 October two of Hong Kong's largest banks, HSBC and Standard Chartered, announced that they would refuse to allow the holders of time-deposits to make early withdrawals. Clearly, this would inhibit speculation by local citizens. Yet, it also suggested a nervousness akin to the 1987 decision to close the Stock Exchange for four days. In addition, having raised overnight inter-bank interest rates to astronomical levels on 24 October, the HKMA then moved to increase liquidity on 25 October. According to dealers, this again suggested uncertainty (Asian Wall Street Journal, 24–25 October 1997). This was compounded when prominent figures in the financial community, such as David Li, Chairman and Chief Executive of the Bank of East Asia, remarked that the peg should be removed at some point in the future, although he emphasized that this should certainly not happen immediately (Asian Wall Street Journal, 23 October 1997).

Speculators then turned their attention to the stock market. It was a way of testing whether the authorities really had the resolve to accept falls in share and property values as a consequence of keeping the fixed exchange rate. Would institutions on the mainland that had been buying up property pressure Beijing to intervene on their behalf? Weaker banks might collapse, especially those over-exposed in the property market. This could lead to a more general crisis of confidence in the banking system. Whether the currency depreciated, or stock market values appreciated, speculators still stood to gain.

Fairly rapidly, however, the speculation subsided. The HKMA maintained with some credibility its single-minded defence of its currency. The People's Republic was not called upon to offer any assistance to Hong Kong, nor did it offer any. According to Sir Donald Tsang, there was not one phone call, fax or instruction from Beijing during the crisis week (Financial Times, 19 November 1997). The mainland authorities remained silent over the falls on the HK stock market, even though several mainland companies were due to launch issues there (Far Eastern Economic Review, 6 November 1997, pp 73–74).

That, however, was not the end of the story. Spring and summer 1998 saw apparent probes by speculators against the HK dollar. The real assault was renewed in August. This was a time when general trading on the Stock Exchange was only one-third of what it had been earlier in the year, so the Hang Seng Index could be moved more easily. It coincided with news that the Hong Kong economy had been in recession in the first quarter of 1998, while there were plenty of rumours of Chinese devaluation. More importantly, however, the speculators had learned the lessons of previous failures. This time they tried to play off the currency board system against the stock and futures market. First, they acquired large quantities of Hong Kong dollars in the debt market, swapping US dollars for Hong Kong dollars with multilateral institutions that had raised Hong Kong dollars by issuing debt. Next, they took out major short positions in the stock index futures market. Then, they sought to create turmoil in the money market by dumping huge amounts of Hong Kong dollars. This was aimed at causing a sharp rise in interest rates, which in turn would have sent the stock market plummeting. They would then have reaped a handsome profit from the futures contracts that they had taken out.

The HKMA estimated that the hedge funds involved had amassed roughly the same amount as the previous October, i.e. US$4 billion in currency borrowings, costing them some US$500000 per day. They also held roughly 80000 short contracts. So, for every fall of 1000 points in the Hang Seng index they stood to make a profit of roughly US$500 million. They would have broken even if they had achieved that fall within 1000 days. If they had achieved it in 100 days, their profit would have been around US$470 million (Yam 1998b).

The response of the HKMA took everyone by surprise. It shored up the stock market by buying US$15 billion of shares in all the blue chip stocks quoted on the Hong Kong Stock Exchange. It was a massive intervention, amounting to roughly 10 per cent of the total capitalization of the stock market, and it lasted for two weeks. The effect was dramatic. The speculators were forced to abandon their short positions, in many cases with heavy losses.

Of course, this action also constrained the freedom of manoeuvre of the HKMA afterwards, since it could not afford to sell the stocks for a while, and certainly not all at once, in case this caused the stock market to plummet. It took several months before off-loading could begin, although there was consolation in that the value of the shares appreciated in the meantime.

The action of the HKMA was highly controversial. It suggested that the Authority was abandoning its traditional policy of non-intervention in markets. Subsequently, it led the Freedom Foundation in the US to downgrade Hong Kong from first to second most free economy in the world, with Singapore moving above it. Nobel prize-winner for Economics, Milton Friedman, condemned it as unwise. Businessmen, and especially bankers, around the world expressed misgivings in case it marked an abandonment of Hong Kong's traditional policy of 'positive non-intervention' in financial markets.

Yet, official figures suggest that Hong Kong's foreign reserves have continued to grow despite the costs of the defence. At the end of 1996 they amounted to US$87 billion, at the end of 1997, US$93 billion, and at the end of 1998, US$95 billion (International Monetary Fund 1999) and within Hong Kong there was fairly general support for the government's action. Most crucially, slightly more Hong Kong savings were being held in HK dollars than in foreign currency – the average was 70 per cent at the end of 1996, 68 per cent at the end of 1997 and 71 per cent at the end of 1998 (Hong Kong Monthly Digest of Statistics, April 1999). Since the pressure for devaluation becomes overwhelming when a territory's own citizens start moving out of their own currency, this was reassuring.

In the aftermath of these events, the HKMA introduced further changes to enhance its ability to defend the peg. Some of these were mainly technical, but it also published a report, *Review of Currency Board Arrangements in Hong Kong*, with an introduction by Joseph Yam. This was intended both to clarify the workings of the Currency Board, since the HKMA believed that widespread misunderstandings about the system had contributed to pressure to change the peg, and also to propose further reforms to increase its effectiveness.

The chief of the latter was a Currency Board Committee to oversee its operations. This would have four members from the HKMA, including the Chairman, and four from outside – one academic economist, one accountant, and two bankers (one of whom would represent the Chairman Bank of the Hong Kong Association of Banks). These arrangements would resemble the monetary policy committees of central banks in other countries, e.g. the US and the UK, but there would be one crucial difference – where elsewhere such committees were expected to exercise discretion in setting interest rates, etc., the chief function of the Hong Kong committee would be to ensure that discretion was *not* exercised, since this would undermine the automatic operation of the rule that changes in foreign currency reserves should automatically lead to changes in the domestic money supply.

Overall, the HKMA has sought to strengthen the effectiveness of the Currency Board in two ways: first, by increasing both the transparency of its operations, as some experts had recommended (Hanke 1997); and second, by extending the range of options for defence of the currency. In other words, it is trying simultaneously to increase the transparency of its operations, and the ambiguity over the range of actions available to it. As an example of the first type of change, the HKMA will, in future, publish the Monetary Base on an hourly basis, with predictions for the next two days. Previously, these figures were either not available at all or produced infrequently, which allowed speculation about changes to build up and encouraged investors to dive for cover. As an example of the second type of changes, the Currency Board has tried to increase the Monetary Base that can be exchanged for US dollars, so as to increase the amounts that speculators would have to put up to try to break the peg. The budget speech of March 1999 announced that, in future, the Currency Board will hold part of its assets in HK stocks and shares, thus increasing its ability to block speculators' attempts to drive down the Hang Seng Index as a prelude to an attack on the peg. This means that it will hold on to roughly one-third of the shares that it scooped up in August 1998. Lastly, the HKMA also decided to extend the principle of the fixed exchange rate between HK and US dollars to coins in circulation as well as HK bank notes. This would add about US$775 million to the Monetary Base. The HKMA has also established an affiliated monetary institute to carry out research into policy-related issues, so further changes may follow.

Conclusion

There have been three main points in the argument presented above. The first is that during the last 14 years of colonial rule, the Hong Kong government evolved a system for managing its finances that gave it the institutional capacity to cope with the many new pressures of global financial markets. This is embodied in the currency board system and the maintenance of the US dollar 'peg' as the core of the territory's monetary policy. These were not explicitly introduced so as to enable Hong Kong to implement the principle of 'One Country – Two Systems', yet they have become its financial embodiment. Its key features distinguish it from the institutions and the practices of both London and Beijing. Without those changes, it is difficult to see how Hong Kong would have been able to withstand the speculation against its currency in 1997 and 1998 without significant assistance from Beijing, as in 1987.

The second point is that, as a result, the Beijing authorities have allowed Hong Kong to run its own financial affairs with a freedom that many doubted before the handover. In fact, as Joseph Yam pointed out, in formal terms the PRC has less authority to intervene in the internal financial affairs of Hong Kong than did the British government before it. Under the old Royal Instructions to the Governor of Hong Kong, the Governor should not assent 'to any Bill affecting the Currency of the Colony or relating to the issue of Bank notes', or 'any Bill establishing any Banking Association or amending or altering the constitution, powers, or privileges of any Banking Association', without previously obtaining the approval of the Secretary of State. Under the Basic Law, however, there is only the corresponding general requirement that 'laws enacted by the legislature of the Hong Kong Special Administrative Region must be reported to the Standing Committee of the National People's Conference for the record', and 'the reporting for record shall not affect the entry into force of such laws.'

The third point is that the chief challenge to Hong Kong's autonomy has not come from inside China, as most had feared, but rather from outside. It has been the concerted attacks of speculators in the West that have posed the greatest challenges to Hong Kong's financial autonomy.

At least for the time being, the speculators have been thwarted, but the Hong Kong authorities are only too aware of the fact that pressures could reappear at any time. The economy is only slowly recovering from the effects of the Asian financial crisis. Falling land prices, increasing unemployment and government deficits all continue to raise question marks. In any case, pressures might not necessarily arise for reasons associated with the performance of Hong Kong's own economy. Reverses for other currency boards – and there are very few of them – can revive speculation over Hong Kong's, even though, according to Joseph Yam, four fundamental strengths of the Hong Kong economy underpin its currency board system:

- ample foreign currency reserves
- a prudent fiscal policy, with small government and no external debt
- a sound financial system, with a strong and solvent banking system, well able to cope with frequent interest rate adjustments and world-class standards of banking supervision
- a flexible and responsive economy (Yam 1998b).

These ought to reassure investors, yet the speculation in spring 1999 about Argentina contemplating 'dollarisation' of their economy if the fall-out from Brazil's economic difficulties became too contagious, again raised the spectre of Hong Kong's problems if the Rmb were to be devalued.

Though the Chinese authorities continue to assert their absolute unwillingness to contemplate devaluation, the Chinese economy has been slowing down, in part as a result of the devaluations by other countries in the region. A devaluation of the Rmb need not necessarily affect the HK dollar – indeed in some respects it might be beneficial for China if Hong Kong did *not* devalue. This could encourage Hong Kong investors to put more money into China, where Hong Kong is still by far the largest investor, with nearly 50 per cent of all contracted and utilized foreign direct investment stock (Sung 1998, pp 42–43). Nevertheless, that kind of speculation will inevitably recur.

Of course, it may turn out that hedge funds themselves become more cautious after losing large sums in 1998. The collapse of the Long-Term Capital Management fund in the US has certainly made banks more wary of allowing them massive credit. Furthermore, international debate about the desirability of introducing institutional curbs on hedge funds may have an effect.

Yet, if the institutions have remained unchanged, it is undeniable that Hong Kong has already substantially revised its practices of economic management. In some respects this has meant a further systematization and professionalization of existing institutions, but commentators have also pointed to a possible change in the way in which the authorities regard intervention in the economy, for example, the intervention in the stock market in August 1998.

According to the Chairman of the Economics Department at Hong Kong University, Professor Richard Wong, Financial Secretaries in the past were predictable because of their fiscal conservatism. This helped entrepreneurs to calculate risks and make investments. Now, however, positive non-interventionism has begun to give way to a new paradigm: 'maximal support and minimal interference'. According to Wong, this approach is much less clear for outsiders to fathom, for it crucially obscures the point at which support ends and interference begins, or vice versa (South China Morning Post, 24 February 1999). By practising 'creative ambiguity' to fox foreign speculators, the authorities are also in danger of confusing their own businessmen.

We may be witnessing a change in the paradigm of economic management in Hong Kong. If that is the case, then the cause is more likely to be increased international pressure rather than the reversion to the mainland, though the emergence of a much more technocratically orientated civil service leadership may also be a factor. In any case, the maintenance of the peg and its crucial importance in managing the currency will ensure that these issues will continue to be a subject of serious interest and speculation.

Given all the recent turbulence in the world's, and especially the region's, financial markets in recent years, it is impossible to guarantee that the peg will survive forever at its current rate. Apart from the current uncertainties over its relationship with the exchange value of the Rmb, it is not difficult to think of longer-term issues that may still feed speculation. For example, would the PRC be prepared to tolerate a US dollar aligned zone within its borders if the US economy was at a different stage of the business cycle, and where US monetary policy was causing unnecessary pain in Hong Kong? Some can certainly envisage the pegging of the HK dollar to a basket of currencies rather than the US dollar (Huang 1996, pp 69–71). At present, though, the HKMA will not hear of the idea, and there is no doubt that this could be an administrative nightmare when trying to determine and publish the Monetary Balance with complete accuracy every hour.

Nevertheless, the peg and the Currency Board have survived in far better shape than seemed likely in the autumn of 1997 or 1998. And the HKMA has shown itself absolutely committed to its preservation. As Joseph Yam put it:

> 'The most sturdy small boat cannot realistically ride and float in the rough seas for long. It will be tossed around until it cracks and sinks. It is a lot better for it to be welded inseparably on to the biggest ship in sight and sail along in its wake. Sometimes it may be under water or above, but it will not sink.'
>
> (HKMA 1998, p 6)

But if the peg were to sink, so too would most of Hong Kong's financial autonomy. It would bring financial chaos. It seems unlikely that the HKMA has any serious plan for coping with such an eventuality. So, in a real emergency the mainland would be called upon to provide far more assistance and far more direct intervention than it displayed in 1987. Where in 1987 the People's Republic was a late addition to the crew of the 'lifeboat' that saved Hong Kong's financial system, in such a crisis in the future it would direct the rescue operations and determine what happened to the survivors. It could be the biggest challenge to the principle of 'One Country – Two Systems'.

Bibliography

Asian Wall Street Journal, various.
Enright, M. J., Scott, E. E., Dodwell, D. 1997 *The Hong Kong Advantage*. Oxford: Oxford University Press.
Far Eastern Economic Review, various.
Financial Times, various.
Hanke, S. H. 1997 'The Solution: Autopilot for Hong Kong'. *Asian Wall Street Journal*, 30 November, p 8.
Ho, R. Y.-K. (ed.) 1991 *The Hong Kong Financial System*. Oxford: Oxford University Press.
Hong Kong Monthly Digest of Statistics, various.
Hong Kong Monetary Authority (HKMA) 1995 *Money and Banking in Hong Kong*. Hong Kong: HKMA.

Hong Kong Monetary Authority (HKMA) *Quarterly Bulletin*, various.

Hong Kong Monetary Authority (HKMA) 1998 *Review of Currency Board Arrangements in Hong Kong*. Hong Kong: HKMA.

Huang Guobo 1996 'The Linked Exchange Rate and Macroeconomic Policy', in Mole, D. (ed.) *Managing the New Hong Kong Economy*. Oxford: Oxford University Press.

International Monetary Fund 1999 *International Financial Statistics*. Washington: IMF, April.

International Herald Tribune, various.

Lui, Y. H. 1991 'Money and Capital Markets', in Ho, R. Y.-K. (ed.) *The Hong Kong Financial System*. Oxford: Oxford University Press.

South China Morning Post, various.

Sung Yun-wing 1998 *Hong Kong and South China: the Economic Synergy*. Hong Kong: City University of Hong Kong Press.

Yam, J. 1998a 'The Hong Kong Dollar Link'. Speech in Tokyo, 3 March 1998, from http://www.info.gov.hk/hkma/pub/speeches/y980303e.htm.

Yam, J. 1998b 'Coping with Financial Turmoil'. Speech in Sydney, 23 November 1998, from http://www.info.gov.hk/hkma/pub/speeches/y981123e.htm.

4

'Like Fish Finding Water': Economic Relations between Hong Kong and China

Robert F. Ash

Hong Kong's transformation from a tiny, dependent colonial enclave into one of the most successful economies in the world is one of the most remarkable stories in post-war economic history. With real GDP rising, on average, by almost 10 per cent per annum in the 1960s and 1970s, Hong Kong's growth record during this period was unmatched anywhere else in the world (Howe 1983). But by the early 1980s, high land rents and spiralling wages began to erode the international competitiveness that had been the basis of this success.[1] By a happy coincidence, the emergence of such pressures coincided with the opening of the Chinese People's Republic to the outside world. This initiative unexpectedly made available to Hong Kong entrepreneurs a huge, hitherto untapped reservoir of cheap labour and gave them access to inexpensive factory sites across the border in Guangdong. It was a lifeline to which they responded 'like fish finding water' (*Renmin ribao*, 31 March 1997) and in the following years Hong Kong manufacturers found a new lease of life through cross-border relocation of their factories out of the British Crown Colony.

The proliferation of such activities not only facilitated the regeneration of Hong Kong manufacturing industry, but also became the basis of a process of integration between the economies of Hong Kong and the Pearl River Delta in Guangdong. This process was the key element in the emergence of a new regional economic grouping, known as 'Greater China' – an informal triangular partnership between Hong Kong, Taiwan and two southeastern Chinese provinces (Guangdong and Fujian). Its success, demonstrated by buoyant growth in both Guangdong and Hong Kong,[2] owed most to the impact of inflows of Hong Kong capital for purposes of outward-processing operations (Ash & Kueh 1995, Kueh & Ash 1996, Taylor 1996, Cheung 1997).

Inherent in the evolution of the cross-border economic symbiosis was a profound qualitative change for Hong Kong, as its economic dependence shifted from the West (above all, the United States) to China. The changing pattern of bilateral trade and investment flows was the most striking outward manifestation of this process. In particular, an important watershed was reached in 1985, when, for the first time, the value of Hong Kong's trade with China exceeded that with the United States.[3]

This chapter examines the development of trade and investment relations between Hong Kong and China prior to the retrocession of British sovereignty over the former Crown Colony. In order to place this development into perspective, initial consideration is given to the meaning and relevance of the economic concept of 'Greater China' – that informal triangular association whose economic success owed most to Hong Kong's cross-border activities. There follow quantitative analyses of Hong Kong's trade and investment relations with China, supplemented by an examination of the narrower, but critical economic relationship between the former colony and Guangdong. The use of mainland Chinese, as well as Hong Kong statistical sources highlights serious discrepancies between these major sources and throws into relief the difficulties of interpreting recent trends in bilateral trade. Concluding remarks summarize the main findings and speculate briefly about the likely course of Hong Kong's economic relations with China in the foreseeable future.

Hong Kong, China and Greater China: economic themes

The evolution in recent decades of a new typology of formal transnational, regional entities[4] is not coincidental. It largely reflects the operation of economic forces and highlights the processes of integration and globalization that have increasingly characterized economic activity in much of the world – especially in the Northern Hemisphere.

In the 1980s, Hong Kong was the pivotal actor in the creation of a different kind of identity – that of Greater China. Its emergence was largely a geographical convenience, lacking any formal institutional framework. It was also an inherently ambiguous concept, for which it proved difficult to find a universally acceptable definition (Harding 1995). As an economic entity, however, the significance of Greater China seemed clearly enough to derive from the development of that triangular economic relationship between Hong Kong, Taiwan and southeast China and the integrative impact associated with the expansion of trade and capital flows within these three regions.

Accelerated trade and investment were also, of course, the hallmarks of China's 'open door' strategy. But even allowing for the role of the Special Economic Zones (SEZs) in Guangdong and Fujian, it would be misleading to suggest that Greater China was a model to which the rest of the country could realistically aspire. Not least, the southern China economic triangle benefited from the inestimable advantages of ethnic homogeneity – its 'Chineseness' – and the geographical propinquity of its elements. These are advantages that have been denied to other emerging economic axes involving China, whether they have embraced other geographical neigh-bours (for example, South Korea) or assumed more complex transnational forms (for example, those involving the United States and Western Europe).

Indeed, there is an irony that the broader analytical value of 'Greater China' in its original economic formulation may ultimately prove to have been undermined by the very factors that contributed to the success of that triangular relationship – its ethnic homogeneity and geographical narrow-ness. In any case, since the late 1980s, internal and external initiatives have changed the parameters of China's economic transnationalism.[5] Entrepreneurs from Hong Kong have themselves been part of this process, as the geographical destination of capital inflows from the former British colony has become increasingly diversified beyond the boundaries of Guangdong and Fujian towards other coastal regions in central and north-ern China. As early as 1990, Hong Kong was the single most important source of overseas capital not only to Guangdong, where it contributed 82 per cent of provincial foreign direct investment (FDI), but also to Shandong, Liaoning and Beijing, where the corresponding figures were 53, 50 and 44 per cent (Yabuki 1995, p 182). By 1995, inflows from Hong Kong were responsible for 58 per cent of Shanghai's annual utilized foreign investment (Shanghai Statistical Bureau (SHTJNJ) 1992, p 127).[6]

The broadening of China's external economic relations and their greater complexity contained an even more fundamental challenge to the original, narrow interpretation of Greater China. It derived from the overwhelming debt that the creation of the Hong Kong–Taiwan–South China economic triangle owed to the *sui generis* character of trade and investment relations between Hong Kong and China. The unique quality of this relationship was captured in the contribution made by Hong Kong-funded outward processing activities to the emerging economic symbiosis.[7] Following a period in which the mainland's economic role in Hong Kong's rapid growth had been peripheral, by the end of the 1970s the two regions had, quite coincidentally, reached separate and distinctive watersheds in their development paths, the nature of which encouraged the forging of much closer economic relations. In Hong Kong, bottlenecks caused by shortages of land, labour and technical skills threatened to undermine the growth momentum. Meanwhile, across the border and under the impact of reform initiatives by the central authorities, Guangdong – the site of three of China's four SEZs – was uniquely placed to benefit from capital inflows, which simultaneously promised to serve the profit-maximizing interests of Hong Kong manufacturers. The logical outcome of this mutuality of self-interest was an integrated, regional economy. Once China was set on its reformist path, such mutuality of interests readily found an outlet in increasing cross-border flows of Hong Kong capital and expertise, embod-ied, above all, in the re-siting of Hong Kong industrial activities, designed to capture the advantages of cheap land and labour.

By 1989 – the first year for which relevant data are available – the value of Hong Kong's imports from China related to outward processing was HK$ 113.6 billion, and already accounted for 58 per cent of the value of all imports originating in China. Some five years later, the corresponding figures had risen to HK$354.9 billion and 75 per cent. During the same period, the value of outward processing-related shipments from Hong Kong to China increased from HK$145 billion to HK$181.2 billion. Concealed in these figures is the finding that by 1994, 71 per cent of Hong Kong's domestic exports and 43 per cent of re-exports derived from outward processing activities (*HKMDS* various; Cheung 1997, pp 89–92).[8] Such transactions were, of course, dominated by shipments of goods to and from Hong Kong-invested enterprises in Guangdong province.[9]

The success with which cross-border relocation enabled Hong Kong manufacturers to maintain the competitiveness of their labour-intensive industries was also reflected in the increasingly important role played by outward processing in shipments from (to) Hong Kong to (from) China of associated raw materials, intermediate goods and finished products. By the early 1990s, for example, over 80 per cent of Hong Kong's imports from China of clothing, plastic products, and machinery and electrical appliances were related to outward processing activities. For electrical appliances, electronic products, watches and clocks, and toys, games and sports goods, the figure was in excess of 90 per cent (Cheung 1997, p 88).

A major theme in the post-war economic history of the Asia-Pacific Region has been the outward thrust of the growth strategies adopted by newly-industrializing countries. In particular, the 'four Asian tigers' (alternatively, 'dragons') all experienced rapid rates of export expansion.[10] A strong export orientation may be regarded as highly desirable for countries like South Korea and Taiwan, and essential for 'economic city-states',[11] such as Singapore and Hong Kong, whose economic growth would otherwise have been constrained by the smallness of their domestic markets.

On the surface, the same cannot be said of China, whose continental size has shaped virtually every aspect of its economic development.[12] China remains, however, a low-income country and its market is still an insufficient basis on which to build sustained growth. The Chinese government has, in any case, been reluctant to sanction unimpeded access to its domestic market. Unlike its Maoist predecessor, the Dengist government did, however, recognize the force of conventional international trade theory and advocated the development of foreign trade relations as a means of securing familiar static and dynamic gains. This policy thrust underlined the mutuality of self-interest between Hong Kong and China.

There are interesting parallels between China's post-1978 and Hong Kong's earlier experience. It is a commonplace that since 1978, China's has been the fastest-growing economy in the world (World Bank 1997, pp 2–3), just as Hong Kong's had been in the previous two decades. Trade expansion made a notable contribution to Hong Kong's earlier performance, with exports registering an average growth of 11.4 per cent per annum between 1966 and 1981, and outstripping GDP growth of 9.5 per cent during the same period (Howe 1983, p 516).[13] At first, textiles were instrumental in driving the export expansion,[14] although by the end of the 1970s the shift towards a more diversified export structure was already apparent.

It is noteworthy that on the eve of China's reforms, Hong Kong's merchandise trade was dominated by countries other than China. In 1978, the United States, the UK and Germany accounted for 58 per cent of all exports – purchases by the US alone contributing some 37 per cent of the total (HKMDS December 1983, p 24). By contrast, exports to China were non-existent. The United States was also an important source of Hong Kong's imports, although less important than Japan *and China,* these latter accounting, respectively, for 22.8 and 16.8 per cent of all such imports.

Subsequent changes in the geographical distribution of Hong Kong's foreign trade reflect the process of economic integration within Greater China to which reference has already been made. However, *domestic* exports from Hong Kong to China did not exceed those to the American market until 1992, even though China had in the meantime long since overtaken all countries other than the US as a destination for Hong Kong-produced goods.[15] The revival of entrepôt activity was another notable feature of Hong Kong's foreign trade in the late 1970s and one which, with hindsight, proved to be the most telling precursor of subsequent developments. During the previous two decades, the importance of such trade had fallen markedly, but in the second half of the 1970s it experienced a spectacular recovery.[16]

The re-siting, in the 1980s, of Hong Kong manufacturing activities in the Pearl River Delta marked the beginning of a process of de-industrialization in favour of the development of a service economy – described by some as 'Manhattanization' (Cheng & Tsang 1997, p 74) – in the former British colony. Between 1986 and 1996, employment in Hong Kong's manufacturing sector fell by 577 000 – a reduction in the manufacturing workforce of 94 per cent. This decline was offset by new job opportunities emerging in commerce, finance and real estate, transport and telecommunications, and social and associated service activities (Ohashi 1997).

That the deepening economic symbiosis between Hong Kong and the Pearl River Delta benefited both the British Crown Colony and Guangdong – and by extension, the rest of China – is not in doubt. Whether those benefits were unqualified is, however, more questionable. For example, it has been argued that the superficially buoyant economic performances of Guangdong and Hong Kong since the mid-1980s (at least, until the onset of the Asian financial crisis)[17] derived primarily from static gains consequent upon the relocation of regional industries, rather than from growth-enhancing dynamic effects attendant on improvements in productivity.

In particular, genuine technological upgrading has – to a greater or lesser extent – been absent in the two regions (Cheng & Tsang 1997, Howe 1998, pp 1, 5). The result in Hong Kong has been falling growth with high inflation, as well as a deterioration in income distribution. Meanwhile, quite serious regional imbalances have emerged in Guangdong, side-by-side with structural imbalances attendant upon the absence and weakness of internal economic linkages.[18]

Merchandize trade flows – a Hong Kong perspective

An analysis of trends in Hong Kong's global trade and bilateral trade with China during the 1980s highlights the critical contribution that China made to Hong Kong's overall trade performance.[19] In 1978, on the eve of China's economic reforms, Hong Kong's trade with China was entirely one-sided, imports, to Hong Kong, of HK$10.5 billion comparing with exports, to China, valued at a mere HK$ 81.2 million (*HKMDS* December 1983, p 23). Only two years later, the beginning of what was to become a massive expansion in trade during the rest of the 1980s was already apparent.[20] Domestic exports to China admittedly accounted for only 2.4 per cent of the global figure, while the import share was two per centage points lower than in 1978. But a telling harbinger of future developments is revealed in the finding that Hong Kong's re-exports to China already exceeded its domestic exports by a factor of three to one and constituted over 15 per cent of its re-exports worldwide.

During the rest of the decade, both domestic exports and re-exports to China grew rapidly and roughly in tandem.[21] Imports from the mainland also underwent buoyant expansion, although the growth of *re-exports* of Chinese imports markedly outstripped that of retained imports.[22] Indeed, by the mid-1980s, the shares of domestically produced goods and re-exports in Hong Kong's total exports had already risen to 11.7 and 44.1 per cent – China's involvement in Hong Kong's total merchandize trade (exports plus imports) having meanwhile more than doubled (from 13.4 to 25.7 per cent, 1980–85) (*HKMDS* various). Table 4.1 shows the extent to which such trends were further strengthened in the second half of the 1980s and first half of the 1990s.

The estimates in Table 4.1 point to the continued and dramatic resurgence in the importance of Hong Kong's trade with mainland China.[23] The most notable feature of all however, is the continuing pre-eminence of Hong Kong's entrepôt role, the data suggesting that the first half of the 1990s saw a break from the previous pattern of export behaviour, as re-exports accelerated alongside more sluggish domestic export growth.[24] They also indicate that Hong Kong suffered a chronic deficit on its merchandize trade account,[25] although a comparison of export and import growth from bilateral and global perspectives shows why China's contribution to this

Table 4.1   Hong Kong's merchandize trade *vis-à-vis* China and the rest of the world (1990 and 1995)

	1990	1995	Average growth (% per annum)
I Hong Kong's global trade			
Total exports (X_W)	639 874	1 344 127	16.0
Domestic exports (DX_W)	225 875	231 657	0.5
Re-exports (RX_W)	413 999	1 112 470	21.9
Total imports (M_W)	642 530	1 491 121	18.3
Total trade ($X_W + M_W$)	1 282 404	2 835 248	17.2
Balance ($X_W - M_W$)	−2 656	−146 984	
II Hong Kong's trade *vis-à-vis* **China**			
Total exports (X_C)	158 378	447 598	23.1
Domestic exports (DX_C)	47 470	63 555	6.0
Re-exports (RX_C)	110 908	384 043	28.2
Total imports (M_C)	236 134	539 480	18.0
Total trade ($X_C + M_C$)	394 512	987 078	20.1
Balance ($X_C - M_C$)	−77 756	−91 882	

Notes: All figures in HK$ million, unless otherwise stated.
Sources: *HKMDS*, January 1994, pp 19, 21, 22; and December 1996, pp 29, 31, 32.

deficit was smaller in the mid-1990s than it had been at the beginning of the decade (Table 4.2).

Concealed in the figures shown in Table 4.2 is the debt that Hong Kong's overall export expansion in the 1980s and 1990s owed to the opening of China.[26] Nor do the figures do proper justice to Hong Kong's *import* profile. In particular, they make no allowance for the distinction between retained imports and the re-export of shipments from third countries. Estimates of Hong Kong's bilateral trade with China, which take account of re-export margins, suggest that retained imports may have fallen, on average, by as much as 7 per cent per annum in the first half of the 1990s (re-exports of shipments from Chinese sources meanwhile having grown by almost 20 per cent annually).

The most striking finding from an examination of Hong Kong's bilateral trade relationship with China since the early 1980s is its emerging pre-eminence as a channel for the re-export of goods originating from (or des-tined for) China. In analysing this phenomenon, careful consideration must be given to the critical contribution made by outward processing activities, managed by Hong Kong entrepreneurs but sited in Guangdong.

The growing importance of such activities and their role in shaping the emergence of Greater China have already been noted. Statistics published by

Table 4.2 Changes in the structure of Hong Kong's merchandize trade *vis-à-vis* China and the rest of the world (1990–1995)

	1990	1995
I Hong Kong's global trade		
DX_W/X_W	35.3%	17.2%
RX_W/X_W	64.7%	82.8%
RX_W/DX_W	183.3%	480.2%
II Hong Kong's trade *vis-à-vis* China		
DX_C/X_C	30.0%	14.2%
RX_C/X_C	70.0%	85.8%
RX_C/DX_C	233.6%	604.3%
III Hong Kong's trade *vis-à-vis* China relative to its global trade		
DX_C/DX_W	21.0%	27.4%
RX_C/RX_W	26.8%	34.5%
M_C/M_W	36.8%	36.2%

Note: 'W' refers to Hong Kong's trade with the world; 'C' refers to its trade with China.
Source: as for Table 4.1.

Hong Kong's Census and Statistics Department (HKCSD) show that by the first half of 1996, 80 per cent or more of all imports from China were related to outward processing – 85 per cent, if re-exports of China origin were considered on their own (HKMDS December 1996, p 39). Almost half of all exports to China were similarly related (45 per cent for re-exported goods passing through Hong Kong, but 72 per cent for domestic shipments).

Merchandize trade flows – a Chinese perspective

The data presented in the previous section leave no room for doubt about the critical role that the opening of China has played in supporting Hong Kong's trade expansion in the 1980s and 1990s. In this section, consideration is given to the complementary effect of Hong Kong on China's merchandize trade performance during the same period, as revealed by official Chinese statistics.

Accordingly, Table 4.3 gives a Chinese perspective on Hong Kong's bilateral trade with China during the 1990s, as revealed by statistics published by the Chinese Customs Authority (CCA).

Literal interpretation of the data in Table 4.3 indicates that having reached an historical peak in 1992, China's imports from Hong Kong fell

Table 4.3   Chinese exports (imports) to (from) Hong Kong (US billion)

Year	Exports	Imports
1990	26.65	14.25
1991	32.14	17.46
1992	37.51	20.54
1993	22.05	10.45
1994	32.36	9.46
1995	35.98	8.59
1996	32.91	7.83
1997	43.78	6.99

Sources: TJNJ 1992: 632–634; 1995: 543–545; 1997: 594–596; 1998: 626.

sharply in 1993 and thereafter maintained a consistently downward trend. Indeed, if the figures are to be believed, by 1997 the value of such imports was almost 40 per cent below the level of 1990 and lower than in any year since 1986. A *negative* average annual rate of growth (−9.6 per cent, 1990–1995) is implied – a finding that contrasts sharply with the strong, positive growth rate of 16 per cent per annum revealed in Hong Kong government statistics (see Table 4.1). The latter source also points to a much more buoyant Chinese export performance, annual growth of shipments to Hong Kong being some 12 per centage points higher than that shown by the CCA (18.3 per cent (Table 4.1) and 6.2 per cent (Table 4.3)).

There is little doubt that the estimates of Hong Kong's Census and Statistics Department (HKCSD) offer the more accurate picture of emerging trends. The most likely source of inconsistency in the CCA series are statistical adjustments made in and after 1993, when Chinese trade officials sought to exclude outward processing from aggregate merchandize trade data in the apparent belief that such activities had seriously distorted China's trade profile. For reasons that are obvious, these adjustments particularly affected statistics relating to China's bilateral trade relationship with Hong Kong. We return to this point in a subsequent section.

In support of the HKCSD estimates, reference should be made to Deng Xiaoping's tour of southern China in January and February 1992. One commentator has referred to the 'euphoria … [and] … consequent nation-wide scramble for foreign capital' generated by this event and by Deng's demand that the door to the Chinese economy should be opened even more widely to the western world (Kueh 1996, pp 166–167). For purposes of the analysis here, Deng's visit to Guangdong (where he inspected Shenzhen and Zhuhai SEZs) is of particular significance, for it was here that he not only praised Guangdong's role as an engine of China's previous economic growth, but also urged the province to catch up with the 'four [East Asian] dragons' and become the fifth dragon. Against this background, it is surely impossible to believe that the rapid trade expansion that characterized the rest of China in the immediate wake of Deng's southern tour should not equally – indeed, even more strongly – have affected Hong Kong.[27]

In short, credence cannot be given to the figures shown in Table 4.3. The reported sharp falls in export and import trade with Hong Kong during 1993 almost certainly reflect statistical manipulation rather than a genuine 41 per cent decline in such shipments. In the light of developments taking place at this time, the findings of HKCSD, which reveal that between 1992 and 1993 both domestic exports and re-exports to China increased (by some 23 per cent in the aggregate), with imports meanwhile rising by 13 per cent (HKMDS January 1994, pp 21–22) are more acceptable.

Table 4.4 examines the wider significance of the estimates in Table 4.3 by setting them in the context of China's trade with other parts of the world. For comparative purposes, estimates for the first and second halves of the 1980s are also provided.

In the broadest terms, and allowing for the complicating role of Hong Kong as a centre for entrepôt trade, the picture that emerges in Table 4.4 is not in doubt. The estimates show China's merchandize trade since 1980 to have been consistently dominated by its Asian partners. For the time being, these circumstances remain unchanged, although it is significant that the 1990s have witnessed a weakening in the degree of dependence.[28] The counterpoint to these developments lies in the changing roles of North America and Europe, especially as markets for Chinese goods.

Even taking them at face value, the figures in Table 4.4 leave no room for doubt that Hong Kong has been and remains the single most important of China's trading partners. In speculating about likely future trends, care is

Table 4.4 China's export and import profiles: some regional dimensions

	Share in total PRC exports/imports			
	1981–1985	**1986–1990**	**1991–1995**	**1996–1997**
Asia	X 67.7	X 69.0	X 64.1	X 60.0
	M 46.0	M 51.2	M 61.5	M 61.1
Hong Kong	X 25.5	X 38.9	X 30.9	X 23.0
	M 9.1	M 20.8	M 13.8	M 5.3
North America	X 9.1	X 8.9	X 16.1	X 18.8
	M 20.7	M 14.8	M 15.8	M 13.2
Europe	X 15.9	X 17.5	X 15.2	X 15.8
	M 22.1	M 25.8	M 20.1	M 19.0

Notes: X: exports; M: imports.
Sources: Table 4.3 (1991–1995 and 1996–1997). Data for earlier years are taken from Ash (1995, pp 1–8).

needed not to exaggerate the weakening of the China–Hong Kong trade axis, as it emerges from the figures. Between the second half of the 1980s and first half of the 1990s, CCA data suggest that the share of all Chinese exports shipped to Hong Kong declined by nine percentage points, and the import share by eight points. But if, as argued above, allowance is made for distortions associated with the exclusion of outward processing trade, this deterioration is likely to be more apparent than real. In the end, the most important finding – one that is supported by even a literal acceptance of the estimates shown in Tables 4.2 and 4.3 – is that Hong Kong has maintained its dominant position as an export destination[29] during the 1990s. The problems of statistical interpretation, to which reference has been made, make it difficult to know precisely to what extent North America and Europe have encroached on this dominance, although it does seem likely that some erosion of Hong Kong's position has taken place. If this is so, we may suppose that the economic role of Greater [south] China has also declined.

The role of foreign investment

The separation of foreign trade from foreign investment is ultimately an analytical convenience. The dominance of outward processing in Hong Kong's relations with China (above all, with Guangdong) has made the role of cross-border supplies of supporting capital critically important. In the end, the changing pattern of China's trade with Hong Kong cannot be viewed in isolation, but must be considered side by side with an analysis of developments affecting foreign investment on the mainland – above all, foreign direct investment (FDI).

Table 4.5 shows the extent to which foreign investment in the PRC has been driven by Hong Kong since the mid-1980s.

The source from which the figures in Table 4.5 are derived shows that for the entire period under consideration, capital flows from Hong Kong to China have been dominated by FDI. In the second half of the 1980s, inflows of FDI grew steadily – in nominal terms, by some 25 per cent per annum – until temporarily levelling off in the wake of the 'Tiananmen massacre'. The most spectacular expansion took place from 1992 to 1994, when utilized FDI grew by 95 per cent annually. Since 1994, there has been a marked slowing in capital inflows, FDI growing by a mere 2.8 per cent per annum (1994–1997).

Once again, there is room for scepticism in interpreting these figures and it would be interesting to compare them with Hong Kong-based statistics. Even so, there is no doubt that the former British colony has faced new challenges in its investment relations with China in recent years. In 1994, for example, attempts by Beijing to exclude simple assembly processes from preferential foreign investment incentives and to limit foreign investment

Table 4.5 The changing contribution of Hong Kong to China's foreign investment

	Hong Kong's share in AFI in China (%)	Hong Kong's share in FDI in China (%)
1985	22.9	49.0
1986	21.6	58.9
1987	24.7	68.3
1988	30.4	65.0
1989	28.9	62.1
1990	23.6	50.9
1986–1990 average	26.2	60.7
1991	25.3	57.0
1992	43.9	68.3
1993	48.5	62.8
1994	45.9	58.4
1995	42.4	53.4
1991–1995 average	43.8	58.7
1996	38.1	49.5
1997	33.6	41.1
1996–1997 average	35.7	45.7

Notes: The figures reflect utilized investment. FDI: foreign direct investment, AFI: all foreign investment.
Sources: Except for 1986, the figures are from *TJNJ* 1986: 582; 1988: 734; 1990: 654; 1992: 642; 1994: 528; 1996: 598; 1997: 606; 1998: 639. The figures for 1986 are from SSB (*ZGSYWJTJZL* 1952–1988) 1992: 544 and 548.

in real estate – activities that had hitherto attracted a major share of Hong Kong capital flowing across the border – had a deterrent effect on Hong Kong entrepreneurial investment across the Chinese border. This is likely to have contributed to the decline in Hong Kong's share of FDI flows from well over 60 per cent (1993–1994) to less than half (1996–1997). The decline in Hong Kong FDI during these years contrasts with continued expansion – by 27 per cent per annum – of inflows from the rest of the world.

The Hong Kong–Guangdong connection

It is misleading to assess the impact of Hong Kong's increasing involvement in the Chinese economy since the mid-1980s without reference to the core of that relationship – the Hong Kong–Guangdong connection. This section seeks briefly to review the main trends in merchandize trade between Hong Kong and Guangdong, as well as in Hong Kong's investment in the cross-border hinterland.

Table 4.6 highlights Hong Kong's role in the foreign trade of Guangdong between the mid-1980s and mid-1990s.

Table 4.6   Hong Kong and Guangdong: foreign trade

	Exports to Hong Kong (US$100 million)			Imports from Hong Kong (US$100 million)		
	China–nation wide	Guangdong	Ratio (%)	National	Guangdong	Ratio (%)
1985	72.0	21.3	29.5	47.97	21.4	44.7
1986	97.9	29.6	30.2	56.0	18.7	33.5
1987	137.8	37.5	27.2	84.4	29.0	34.3
1988	182.7	57.3	31.3	119.7	40.9	34.2
1989	219.2	63.7	29.1	125.4	35.0	27.9
1990	266.5	85.4	32.1	142.6	41.2	28.9
1986–1990 average	180.8	54.7	30.2	105.6	33.0	31.3
1991	321.4	113.7	35.4	174.6	62.3	35.7
1992	375.1	155.6	41.5	205.3	82.7	40.3
1993	220.5	229.5	104.1	104.5	155.4	148.7
1994	323.7	391.6	121.0	94.4	254.4	269.5
1995	359.8	484.5	134.7	85.9	303.5	353.3
1991–1995 average	320.1	275.0	85.9	132.9	171.7	129.2

Sources: Data for 1985–1992 from Kueh & Ash (1996, pp 182–183, Table 5.15). Remaining data from *TJNJ*, 1995, 543; 1996, 586; 1997, 594; *GDTJNJ*, 1994, 306; 1996, 350.

The national and provincial trade contributions of Hong Kong implied by these figures are summarized in Table 4.7. The estimates suggest a significant acceleration of trade growth between Hong Kong and Guangdong between the second half of the 1980s and first half of the 1990s. The rate of export expansion was already extremely rapid in the former period (rising on average by 32 per cent per annum), but such was the impact of Deng Xiaoping's southern tour (*nanxun*) in 1992 that it increased to more than 40 per cent (1991–1995). The growth of imports from Hong Kong was even more spectacular, the annual rate of expansion accelerating from 14 to almost 50 per cent per annum between 1986–1990 and 1991–1995. Hidden in such figures are significant rises in Hong Kong's share of Guangdong's total imports and exports after the mid-1980s (Table 4.7).

Reference was made earlier to problems of interpreting recent estimates of CCA bilateral merchandize trade involving Hong Kong. Such difficulties are dramatically highlighted in the estimates shown in Table 4.6, which improbably suggest that in and after 1993, the value of Guangdong's imports from Hong Kong, as well as the reverse flow of provincial exports to the former British colony exceeded the corresponding *national* figures!

Table 4.7 The contribution of trade with Hong Kong: national and provincial perspectives

	Exports: percentage share			Imports: percentage share		
	National	Guangdong	Ratio	National	Guangdong	Ratio
1985	26.3	72.0	273.5	11.4	88.3	778.0
1986	31.6	69.5	219.8	13.1	73.3	561.2
1987	34.9	68.9	197.2	19.5	79.8	408.8
1988	38.4	76.5	199.0	21.7	80.0	369.5
1989	41.7	77.8	186.4	21.2	72.4	341.4
1990	42.9	80.9	188.5	26.7	71.6	267.9
1986–1990 average	(37.9)	(74.7)	197.1	(20.4)	(75.4)	369.6
1991	44.7	83.1	185.7	27.4	73.2	267.4
1992	44.1	84.4	191.2	25.5	74.0	290.3
1993	24.0	84.9	353.8	10.0	78.1	781.0
1994	26.7	83.3	312.0	8.2	74.2	904.9
1995	24.2	87.0	359.5	6.5	79.5	1223.1
1991–1995 average	(32.7)	(84.5)	258.4	(15.5)	(75.8)	489.0

Notes: 'National' and 'Guangdong' columns show Hong Kong's percentage share in total exports (imports) of China and Guangdong. 'Ratio' means the Guangdong percentage share divided by the national percentage share.
Source: Table 4.6; GDTJNJ, 1994, 307; 1995, 351.

The inconsistency is likely to have its origins in the adjustment of national trade data in order to exclude trade related to outward-processing activities (see above). To have excluded such activities from trade between Guangdong and Hong Kong would have been to remove the dominant element in cross-border trade and to introduce an absurd degree of bias into the statistics. Hence, the fundamental lack of consistency between estimates of bilateral trade with Hong Kong published by the Guangdong provincial authorities and the corresponding national trade estimates compiled in Beijing.

The use of official statistics published in Hong Kong is one way of checking the veracity of the conflicting estimates. Such figures do in fact confirm the trend revealed by the figures in Table 4.6 and show that far from there being a sharp break in the expansion of export and import trade between Hong Kong and China after 1992, the forward momentum was sustained. Recourse to Hong Kong data cannot, however, provide a full reconciliation of the statistical inconsistencies for the simple reason that Guangdong was not the only region of China that was involved in outward processing-related trade.

In the end, even if the estimates in Table 4.7 do not wholly reflect the changing relative importance of Hong Kong's merchandize trade *vis-à-vis* the whole of China, there is no reason to suppose that they do not accurately represent the changing level of trade between Hong Kong and Guangdong. From this perspective, the estimates confirm the continuing dominant role of Hong Kong *vis-à-vis* its neighbour. They suggest that by the mid-1990s, exports to Hong Kong accounted for almost 90 per cent of Guangdong's total exports – some 20 per centage points more than a decade earlier. Although less marked, import trends also demonstrate an increasing degree of dependence on the former British Crown Colony.

Because so much of Hong Kong's economic involvement in Guangdong has reflected the cross-border relocation of its manufacturing enterprises, a large part of two-way trade has been driven by cross-border flows of Hong Kong capital – above all, FDI. We conclude this section by briefly considering trends in this investment (Table 4.8). It is again useful to express these figures in terms of the implied contribution of Hong Kong to national and provincial investment inflows (Table 4.9). Quite detailed consideration has been given elsewhere to trends in Guangdong's investment relations with Hong Kong up to the point at which Deng Xiaoping undertook his visit to southern China (Ash & Kueh 1995, pp 178–184). Two principal findings

Table 4.8   Hong Kong's share in utilized foreign investment

	FDI from Hong Kong (US$100 million)			AFI from Hong Kong (US$100 million)		
	National	Guangdong	Ratio (%)	National	Guangdong	Ratio (%)
1985	9.6	4.5	47.1	10.2	8.5	83.2
1986	13.3	6.0	45.4	15.7	11.0	69.7
1987	18.1	5.0	27.8	20.9	8.8	42.3
1988	24.3	8.4	34.5	31.1	15.4	49.5
1989	23.4	9.5	40.7	29.1	15.4	53.4
1990	21.2	10.2	48.1	24.3	13.0	53.4
1986–1990 average	20.1	7.8	38.8	24.2	12.7	53.7
1991	25.8	13.6	52.7	28.3	16.2	57.2
1992	77.1	30.4	49.4	84.2	34.5	41.0
1993	174.4	65.3	37.4	188.9	73.7	39.0
1994	198.2	77.7	39.2	198.4	87.0	43.9
1995	201.9	79.7	39.5	204.0	89.9	44.1
1991–1995 average	135.5	53.3	39.3	140.8	60.3	42.8

Sources: Data for 1985–1990 from Kueh & Ash (1996, pp 180–181, Table 5.14). Remaining data from *TJNJ*, 1993, 648; 1995, 555; 1996, 606; 1997, 598; *GDTJNJ*, 1996, 366 and 370.

Table 4.9 Hong Kong's shares in FDI and AFI intakes

	Hong Kong's share in FDI (%)			Hong Kong's share in AFI (%)		
	National	Guangdong	Ratio	National	Guangdong	Ratio
1985	48.9	87.4	178.8	21.9	92.0	420.7
1986	59.2	93.7	158.2	21.7	76.8	354.0
1987	68.4	84.6	123.8	24.7	72.7	293.6
1988	64.9	91.0	140.2	30.4	63.0	207.3
1989	62.1	82.4	132.7	29.0	64.4	222.4
1990	56.4	69.8	123.7	23.6	64.2	271.6
1986–1990 average	(62.2)	(84.3)	135.5	(25.9)	(68.2)	263.3
1991	55.3	74.4	134.5	24.5	62.8	256.3
1992	68.2	85.6	125.5	43.8	71.0	162.1
1993	62.8	87.1	138.7	48.5	76.4	157.5
1994	58.4	82.7	141.6	45.9	76.0	165.5
1995	53.4	78.3	146.6	42.4	74.3	175.2
1991–1995 average	(59.6)	(81.6)	136.9	(41.0)	(72.1)	175.9

Source: Table 4.8.

emerged from that analysis. The first is that between 1985 and 1992, some 42 per cent of cumulative FDI from Hong Kong to China was destined for Guangdong. The second is that Hong Kong was the immediate origin of 84 per cent of the province's total FDI intake during the same period.

The more recent estimates confirm a major acceleration in inflows of capital from Hong Kong to Guangdong (especially as FDI) in the 1990s. Between the second half of the 1980s and first half of the 1990s, the rate of growth of FDI increased from 18 to 51 per cent per annum, while in cumulative terms, inflows rose from US$39 billion to US$267 billion (US$222.7 billion being transferred in just three years – 1993–1995).

Spectacular though such figures are, it is interesting that the growth of national FDI inflows from Hong Kong was even more rapid. The outcome is that Guangdong's share in the total fell from a high of 48.1 per cent (1990) to 39.5 per cent (1995). The estimates in Table 4.9 also show that the importance of Hong Kong as a source of FDI funds for Guangdong has fallen slightly since the mid-1980s, although its dominant position has not altered. The inference is that the pattern of Hong Kong's trade *vis-à-vis* China has become more diversified since the mid-1980s. But the implications of such changes should not be exaggerated. For the time being and into the foreseeable future, Hong Kong's links will remain orientated towards its neighbour.

Concluding remarks

The changing profile of China's foreign trade and inward foreign investment underlines the much more varied and complex pattern that has character- ized its foreign economic relations in the 1990s. There is, however, one respect in which conditions today remain unchanged from those of the 1980s. It is that the coastal provinces remain the dominant force in China's external economic relations, far outstripping the interior in terms of both their absorption of foreign capital and contribution to foreign trade earnings.

The emergence of 'Greater China' was the earliest manifestation of this coastal bias and the triangular economic nexus between Hong Kong, Taiwan and south China (Guangdong and Fujian) remains an important dimension of China's external economic relations. More recent develop- ments have, however, challenged the traditional identification of Greater China with this narrow triangle through the growing importance of new trade and investment partners for China, not all of which are Chinese – nor even, some of them, located in Asia. At the end of the 1990s, Guangdong and Fujian no longer constitute the only regions that are being subsumed into a transnational entity.

Meanwhile, Hong Kong's own role as a trade and investment partner of China has changed in the face of the new challenges that have emerged in the 1990s. The territory's share of total exports and imports peaked in the early 1990s, since when its relative position has been in decline. If capital inflows (especially FDI) have continued to increase annually since 1990, an even more rapid rate of expansion in inflows from other countries has, since the early 1990s, caused Hong Kong's *share* of overseas investment to decline.[30] In particular, northwards along the Chinese coast Hong Kong's dominant trade position has been seriously threatened. For the Yangtze Delta region, for example, Japan has emerged as a more important export market.[31] The US's position for exports from this region has also been enhanced. In the Bohai Rim, the export market roles of Japan and the United States, as well as of the UK, South Korea and Singapore have mean- while also been enhanced.

Such developments notwithstanding, at the end of the 1990s, Hong Kong remains a potent force, shaping China's trade and investment rela- tions. If its economic status elsewhere in the country has become more sus- ceptible to competitive forces from other countries, in southern China its position is still unchallenged. As a market for exports from this region, Hong Kong remains well ahead of its competitors, its share of such ship- ments not only from Guangdong, but also Fujian, Guangxi and Hainan continuing to rise. Meanwhile, by the very nature of the cross-border sym- biosis that has developed with Guangdong (above all in the Pearl River Delta), Hong Kong's economic dominance in the immediate cross-border hinterland seems destined to endure for many years to come.

Notes

1 Nominal wages in Hong Kong rose fourfold during the 1980s and doubled again in the first half of the 1990s (Ohashi 1997, p 17).

2 Hong Kong's real GDP grew, on average, by 6.9 per cent per annum (1981–1990) and 5.2 per cent (1991–1997). The corresponding figures for Guangdong are 12.2 per cent and 16.7 per cent (*TJNJ*, 1995 and 1998; and ADB, 1995).

3 In 1994, Hong Kong–US trade was HK$94.3 billion, compared with Hong Kong–PRC trade of HK$120.2 billion (*RMRB*, 31 March 1997).

4 To date, the EU, NAFTA and ASEAN are probably the most important embodiments of economic transnationalism in Europe, North America and Asia.

5 One inference of such developments is that the triangular 'Greater Southern China' grouping has been complemented by the emergence of parallel groupings among northern, central and north-eastern (perhaps in time, even western) provinces, and foreign partner countries or regions.

6 Cumulatively, as of the end of 1995, Hong Kong had contributed almost 49 per cent of Shanghai's utilized foreign investment (*SHTJNJ* 1996: 127).

7 The Hong Kong Census and Statistics Department's definition of outward processing trade embraces three elements: exports to China for purposes of outward processing; imports from China derived from outward processing; and the re-export through Hong Kong of goods produced in China through outward processing (Kui Yin Cheung 1997, p 84).

8 Implied are the following average annual rates of growth of outward processing-related activities (1989–1994): imports, 25.8 per cent; total exports, 18.8 per cent (domestic exports, 5.7 per cent, re-exports, 25.5 per cent).

9 Partly associated with outward-processing activities, Hong Kong's role as a channel for the redistribution of goods and capital originating from, or destined for mainland China (sometimes both), many PRC investors having established 'front companies' in Hong Kong in order to benefit from preferential treatment accorded to foreign investors. This is a factor which further highlights and distorts the uniqueness of Hong Kong's contribution to China's economic development.

10 Between 1965 and 1990, the share of the 'four tigers' (Republic of Korea, Hong Kong, Taiwan and Singapore) in global manufactured exports rose from 1.5 to 7.9 per cent. These four countries' share of manufactured exports originating in *all* 'developing' countries increased from 7.9 to 44.9 per cent (World Bank 1993, p 38).

11 *RMRB*, 31 March 1997, characterises Hong Kong as an 'international economic city' (*guijixing de jingji chengshi*).

12 As per capita incomes have risen in the wake of post-1978 reforms, the widening domestic market has undoubtedly facilitated China's own industrial expansion – witness, for example, the rapid growth of so many consumer goods industries during the last decade. It has also driven the investment activities of overseas investors, anxious to fulfil that perennial, but frequently chimerical goal of penetrating the huge Chinese market.

13 By 1980, the export-GDP ratio was about 72 per cent; the import-GDP ratio was 82 per cent (Ho and Kueh 1993, p 338).

14 Even in the early 1980s, clothing and textiles accounted for more than 40 per cent of the total value of Hong Kong's exports.

15 At the end of the 1980s, the value of domestic exports to China (HK$43.27 billion) exceeded the combined value of exports to Hong Kong's 4 most important

European markets (HK$38.78 billion to Germany, the UK, Netherlands and France) (*HKMDS* January 1994: 20). In 1995, domestic exports to China were valued at HK$63.56 billion, compared with HK$61.25 billion to the USA (*HKMDS* December 1996: 31).

16 During 1975–1982, domestic export growth averaged around 20 per cent per annum, compared with around 30 per cent for re-exports (Howe 1983, p 517).

17 Preliminary official estimates suggested that Hong Kong's GDP would decline by 4 per cent in 1998. GDP growth in Guangdong meanwhile rose by 10.1 per cent – only marginally lower than in 1996 and 1997 (10.7 and 10.6 per cent) (*SWB*, FEW/0574, 3 February 1999). For consideration of the impact on Hong Kong of the regional financial crisis, see Chapter 3 by Peter Ferdinand in this volume.

18 Thus Cheng and Tsang's conclusion that, '... while the mutually beneficial mechanisms should be maintained and improved, there is a strong need to develop long-term competitiveness and dynamic advantage, a task which is likely to call for more independent efforts on the part of Hong Kong and Guangdong than in the past decade. Hence, a certain distancing in relations is healthy' (1997, p 81).

19 This brief summary derives from Ash and Kueh (1995, p 61).

20 The following estimates of Hong Kong's trade with China in 1978 and 1980 (all in HK$ million) indicate the swiftness of the impact of the open door strategy on bilateral economic relations (*HKMDS* December 1983, p 23; December 1985, pp 21–22.):

	(HK$ million)	
	1978	1980
Total exports		6246.94
Domestic exports	81.17	1605.18
Re-exports		4641.76
Total imports	10549.77	21948.23

21 For example, average annual rates of growth were 32 per cent for both domestic exports and re-exports to China (1980–1991) (Ash & Kueh 1995, p 62, Table 4.1). Interestingly, there was a significant acceleration of the growth of domestic exports relative to that of re-exports in the second half of the 1980s.

22 For example, growth rates were 33 per cent per annum (re-exports) and 9 per cent per annum (retained imports) (1980–1991) (Ash & Kueh 1995).

23 The calculation of growth rates of bilateral trade flows is bedevilled by the role of Hong Kong as a channel for the re-export of goods from (to) Hong Kong to (from) China and the consequent need to allow for a 're-export margin,' added to goods which have passed through the Crown Colony (HKSAR). The estimates in Table 4.1 ignore this problem. For reference purposes it may be useful to point out that in an earlier paper, the convention was adopted of assuming a re-export margin of 25 per cent for re-exported Chinese imports into Hong Kong, and a rate of 14 per cent for goods deriving from other countries (Ash & Kueh 1995, p 61, footnote 5).

24 In absolute value terms, the gap between re-exports (undiscounted) and domestic exports to China rose from 133 per cent to 504 per cent between 1990 and 1995. Note, however, that between January-October 1995 and the same period of 1996, domestic exports *grew* by 4.4 per cent, compared with an 8.3 per cent expansion for re-exports (*HKMDS* December 1996).

25 The deficit in merchandize trade has generally been more than offset by net inflows of income derived from trade in services.

26 In 1978, on the eve of the Dengist reforms, domestic exports to China accounted for less than 1 per cent of Hong Kong's total exports.

27 Official Chinese data show China's total foreign trade to have risen by 18 per cent and 21 per cent in 1993 and 1994, respectively (*TJNJ* 1995, p 512; *TJNJ* 1993, p 543).

28 In fact, figures for 1991–1992 show that the share of Asia (including Hong Kong) in China's exports and imports strengthened (Ash 1995, p 8 note 17).

29 But not as a source of imports into China. The fact that since the mid-1980s, the combined share of North America and Europe in total imports has also declined, as has that of all Asia, highlights the more complex and diverse pattern that has characterized import behaviour.

30 In 1997, its contribution to FDI in China was lower than at any time since the middle of the previous decade.

31 As early as the first half of the 1990s, Japan's share of exports from Shanghai rose from 14 to over 25 per cent, so that Japan replaced Hong Kong as the most important export destination.

Bibliography

Ash, R. F. 1995 'Mainland China's Emerging Role in the World Economy: Implications and Future Prospects', in *Issues and Studies*, Vol. 31 no. 1.

Ash, R. F., Kueh, Y. Y. 1995 'Economic Integration within Greater China: Trade and Investment Flows between China, Hong Kong and Taiwan', in Shambaugh, D. (ed.) *Greater China: The Next Superpower?* Oxford: Oxford University Press.

British Broadcasting Corporation (BBC) *Summary of World Broadcasts* (*SWB*), Part 3: Asia-Pacific, Caversham Park, Reading: BBC Monitoring, various issues.

Cheng, Yuk-shing, Tsang, Shu-ki 1997 'The Economic Link-Up of Hong Kong and Guangdong: Structural and Developmental Problems', in Chai, J. C. H., Kueh, Y. Y., Tisdell, C. A. (eds) *China and the Asian Pacific Economy*. Brisbane: Department of Economics, University of Queensland.

GDTJNJ (various years) *Guangdong Tongji Nianjian* (*Guangdong Statistics Yearbook*), Beijing: Statistics Publishing House.

Harding, H. 1995 'The Concept of Greater China: Themes, Variations and Reservations', in Shambaugh, D. (ed.) *Greater China: The Next Superpower?*, Oxford: Oxford University Press.

Ho, Y. P., Kueh, Y. Y. 1993 'Whither Hong Kong in an Open-Door, Reforming Chinese Economy?'. *Pacific Review*: 6(4): 333–351.

Hong Kong Census and Statistics Department, *Monthly Digest of Statistics*, various issues. Hong Kong: Government Printer.

Howe, C. 1983 'Growth, Public Policy and Hong Kong's Economic Relationship with China'. *China Quarterly* 95 (September): 512–533.

Howe, C. 1998 *The Political Economy of Hong Kong since Reversion to China*. Cardiff, California: Japan Policy Research Institute (JPRI), Working Paper no 52.

Kueh, Y. Y. 1996 'Foreign Investment and Economic Change in China', in Ash, R. F., Kueh, Y. Y. (eds) *The Chinese Economy Under Deng Xiaoping*. Oxford: Clarendon Press.

Kueh, Y. Y., Ash, R. 1996 'The Fifth Dragon: Economic Development', in Hook, B. (ed.) *Guangdong: China's Promised Land*. Hong Kong: Oxford University Press.

Kui, Yin Cheung 1997 'Hong Kong's Outward Processing Investment in China: Implications for the Hong Kong Economy' in Chai, J. C. H., Kueh, Y. Y., Tisdell, C. A. (eds) *China and the Asian Pacific Economy*. Brisbane: Department of Economics, University of Queensland.

Ohashi, Hideo 1997 'The Hong Kong Economy under the 'One Country, Two Systems', in *China Newsletter* 5(130). Tokyo: Japan External Trade Organization.

Renmin ribao (People's Daily) 1997 'Luoshi "yiguo liangzhi" fanrong Xianggang jingji' (Implement 'One Country, Two Systems' for a Prosperous Hong Kong Economy), 31 March.

SHTJNJ 1992, *Shanghai Tongji Nianjian (Shanghai Statistical Yearbook)*, Beijing: Statistics Publishing House.

State Statistical Bureau, *Guangdong tongji nianjian (Guangdong Statistical Yearbook)*, various issues, Beijing: Tongji chubanshe.

State Statistical Bureau 1996 *Shanghai tongji nianjian (Shanghai Statistical Yearbook)*, Beijing: Tongji chubanshe.

State Statistical Bureau 1992 *Zhongguo shangye waijing tongji ziliao, 1952–1988 (Statistical Materials on China's Internal and External Trade)*, Beijing: Tongji chubanshe.

State Statistical Bureau, *Zhongguo tongji nianjian (Chinese Statistical Yearbook)*, various issues, Beijing: Tongji chubanshe.

Taylor, R. 1996 *Greater China and Japan: Prospects for an Economic Partnership in East Asia*, London and New York: Routledge.

TJNJ (various Years) *Tongji Nianjian (Statistics Yearbook)*, State Statistical Bureau, Beijing: Statistics Publishing House.

World Bank 1993 *The East Asian Miracle: Economic Growth and Public Policy*. New York: Oxford University Press.

World Bank 1997 *China 2020: Development Challenges in the New Century*. Washington, D.C.: World Bank.

Yabuki, Susumu 1995 *China's New Political Economy: the Giant Awakes*. Boulder, Colorado: Westview Press.

5
Hong Kong and its Intermediate Role in Cross-Strait Economic Relations

Teh-chang Lin

Introduction

The political antagonism between Taiwan and mainland China over the years, but especially since 1987, has made the movement of people, goods and investment across the Taiwan Strait reliant on a 'third place' – Hong Kong. The policy of openess and economic reform in mainland China since 1978, and the ability of Taiwanese residents to visit their relatives in mainland China, have induced and enhanced economic communication across the Strait. However, because 'three direct links' (trade, postal and shipping) are still impossible between Taiwan and mainland China, trade and investment from Taiwan to mainland China need to be channeled by way of Hong Kong. Thus, Hong Kong becomes an important entrepôt in the development of cross-Strait economic relations.

In addition, with the impetus of mainland China's open door and economic reform policy, and with a potentially large market in mainland China, Hong Kong's trans-shipment status for the whole world has thus been underlined. In 1991, 34.6 per cent of the total value of Hong Kong's foreign trade was the value of trade to mainland China. This caused Hong Kong's foreign trade figures to move it into the top ten world trading countries. In 1995, Hong Kong's total foreign trade reached a value of US$2835 billion, an increase of 83.5 per cent over the 1991 figure (The Hong Kong Economic Yearbook 1996, Ch. II, p 56). Thus, the significance of Hong Kong's role as an economic connection within the region can be appreciated.

This chapter attempts to discuss Hong Kong's intermediate role in the cross-Strait economic relations from a political and economic perspective. First, it endeavours to analyse the economic relations between Hong Kong and mainland China, and between mainland China and Taiwan, and to examine if economic connections, such as trade and direct foreign investment, could be factors contributing to the maintenance and the enhancement of Hong Kong's intermediate role in cross-Strait economic relations. This paper also attempts to explore some possible economic and political factors that may influence Hong Kong's intermediate role in the future.

Political and economic relations

Theoretically, the interaction of politics and economics in international economy can be illustrated through two different perspectives; the liberal perspective and the economic nationalist perspective. Liberal economic theory is dedicated to free markets and minimal state intervention. It assumes that politics and economics exist, ideally, in separate spheres. It also argues that markets should be free from political interference. In essence, liberals believe that trade and economic intercourse are sources of peaceful relations among nations because the mutual benefits of trade and expanding interdependence among national economies tend to foster cooperative relations (Gilpin 1987, pp 26–31).

Economic nationalism advocates the primacy of politics over economics. It asserts that economic activities should be subordinate to the interests of the state. Benjamin Cohen thus views foreign economic policy as part of a country's total foreign policy (Cohen 1968, p 32). Economic nationalism also focuses on the state as the predominant actor in international relations and as an instrument of economic development. This perspective stresses the importance of security and national interest in a country in conducting its foreign economic relations. In this sense, states tend to influence markets for their own interests (Gilpin 1987, pp 46–47). As a result, the economic relations can only be understood by viewing political and economic analysis in the same light.

For economic liberals and nationalists, the effect of trade on international politics is a controversial issue. Liberals consider trade a force for peace because they believe that economic interdependence creates positive bonds among peoples and promotes a harmony of interest among societies. However, economic nationalists regard trade as pernicious, since economic specialization and interdependence make states insecure, dependent, and vulnerable to external developments. Thus, according to David Baldwin, regulation of foreign trade has been used as a technique of statecraft throughout history (Baldwin 1985, pp 206–207). Albert O. Hirschman asserts that economic pressure on a country consists mainly of the threat of severance and ultimately of actual interruption of external economic relations with that country. He further contends that this sovereign right to interrupt commercial relations is the cause of the politicization of international economic relations (Hirschman 1980, pp 14–16).

Internationally, whereas market forces in the form of trade and direct foreign investment tend to jump out of national boundaries and escape political control, the tendency of a government is to restrict and make economic activities serve the perceived national interests of the state. As a result, although the logic of the market is to locate economic activities where they are most productive and profitable, the logic of the state is to control the process of economic growth and capital accumulation, or to regulate those economic activities that might endanger a country's national interests. The political economy thus represents a dynamic interaction in international economic relations.

The increasing role of the state in economic affairs is a key component in the study of domestic and international political economy. All the successful East Asian countries, such as Japan, the 'four little dragons' (South Korea, Taiwan, Hong Kong and Singapore) and the PRC, have been marked by strong states committed to developmentalist policies. According to Alexander Gerschenkron's study, the state generally has to play a much stronger role in late-developing countries (e.g. the East Asian nations) (Gerschenkron 1962, Ch. 1). Additionally, in his analysis of statism, Edwin A. Winckler focuses on the autonomy and activism of state institutions and the extent to which they influence socioeconomic processes. He then concludes that national development requires state intervention in both market processes and mass mobilization (Winckler 1988, pp 275–276). As a result, no state allows the full and unregulated development of market forces. States tend to direct market forces to benefit their own citizens and to serve their own national interests.

Economic growth in Taiwan has been rapid and continuous over the past four decades. Domestically and internationally, the role of the government of Taiwan has contributed to its economy's extraordinary growth rates and the emergence of its economic miracles. Taiwan is clearly a society in which state control of the economy is extensive and entrenched. Several structural transformations in Taiwan's society, without which sustained growth would have been impossible, have been the direct result of government decisions and policies. This chapter thus argues for the importance of the coexistence and mutual interaction of state and market. Neither state nor market is primary, and their relationships are interactive. There can be few cases where this can be seen more clearly than in the economic relations between mainland China and Taiwan, conducted through Hong Kong.

The economic relations between Hong Kong and mainland China

Hong Kong's continued stability and prosperity is indispensable to the successful implementation of the historic task of China's reunification and the modernization programme. Beijing's interest lies in the maintenance of Hong Kong's dynamic economy, from which mainland China receives significant amounts of its foreign exchange as well as managerial and technical know-how for the modernization effort. Since the founding of the PRC in 1949, Hong Kong has been mainland China's major source of foreign exchange. From 1950 to 1982, mainland China earned US$33.4 billion of foreign exchange by trading with Hong Kong. Since mainland China's new opening to the West in 1978, Hong Kong has served as a school for mainland China to learn about foreign banking and international trade practices.

When Beijing started to encourage foreign direct investment in mainland China, Hong Kong always played a key role in it. Since 1978, Hong Kong's foreign direct investment in mainland China has been the largest one. According to Beijing's official data, until 1995 the accumulated amount of foreign capital actually used by mainland China was US$48 billion, the Hong Kong share of this being US$20 billion. By 1996, the amount of foreign capital actually used in mainland China reached US$55 billion, with the Hong Kong share at US$21 billion. The second largest foreign investor in mainland China, the United States, had invested only US$5 billion by 1996 (China Statistical Yearbook 1997). The importance of Hong Kong's foreign direct investment to mainland China's economic development can thus be illustrated.

For the past several years, Hong Kong's investment in mainland China was mainly in small and medium-sized enterprises. However, recently, there is a tendency to move up to medium and larger-sized enterprises. The geographical distribution of Hong Kong's investment in mainland China in the 1980s and the beginning of the 1990s was concentrated on coastal provinces, such as Guangdong and Fujian. The pattern of this geographical distribution has been broadened recently from the South to the interior of mainland China. The industries in which Hong Kong invested in mainland China also changed gradually from manufacturing to service industries. All of these indications illustrate the deeper involvement of Hong Kong in the process of mainland China's economic development.

In Guangdong province, the Shenzhen special economic zone across the border from Hong Kong, and increasingly the vast Pearl River delta around Guangzhou, are becoming economic extensions of Hong Kong. Four-fifths of foreign investment in Guangdong, which amounted to almost $3 billion in 1991, originated in Hong Kong. In 1995, 76 per cent of the foreign capital utilized in Guangdong was from Hong Kong, a total of US$20 billion (Lin 1997, p 41). Hong Kong is not only the key to economic growth for Guangdong but also mainland China's most important window on the international marketplace. Owing to an excellent geographical location and to it being a centre for finance, international trade, and shipping, Hong Kong has been historically an important partner to mainland China. Since 1989, over 60 per cent of the substantial increase in total Chinese foreign trade has moved through Hong Kong. According to statistics from Hong Kong Customs, in 1994 the total foreign trade value between Hong Kong and mainland China reached US$110 billion. This then increased to US$135 billion in 1996 (Mainland Affairs Council 1997, p 60). In 1987, for the first time, Hong Kong replaced Japan as mainland China's largest trade partner. Although Japan recovered its position in 1993, Hong Kong remains the recipient of the greater part of mainland China's exports.

If Hong Kong is a goose that lays golden eggs, it would be an error to slay that goose. It is not in Beijing's interests to change the Hong Kong economic system. However, it will not be possible to maintain the integrity of Hong Kong as a powerful economic tool of mainland China without allowing the social system to remain substantially intact. Additionally, since the early 1980's, mainland China has made huge investments in Hong Kong. The Bank of China Building, for a time Asia's tallest structure, symbolizes mainland China's investments in Hong Kong real estate, construction and business. Mainland China has large holdings in Hong Kong companies, such as HK Telecom and Cathay Pacific Airways. Continued prosperity in Hong Kong's market economy requires Beijing to allow the full practice of all individual, political, economic, legal, and social rights. Hong Kong's open economy is extremely sensitive to the slightest loss of international business confidence. This is why mainland China is allowing Hong Kong to sustain its capitalist economy for 50 years after 1997.

Whether Hong Kong will continue to play its intermediate role in cross-Strait trade and economic relations is an issue which especially concerns the people of Taiwan. Because of Beijing's great political interest in gaining the Taiwanese people's support for its goal of national unification, and for its experiment of 'One Country – Two Systems', optimism seems reasonable. It is very unlikely that Beijing will abruptly slow down cross-Strait economic communication through Hong Kong after its return to mainland China.

The economic relations between Taiwan and mainland China

Before the 1980s, because of political and military antagonism across the Taiwan Strait, the trade flow between the Taiwan and mainland China was quite limited. In 1979, Beijing began to ask Taipei for economic communication. Since the 1980s, Beijing has sought to utilize Taiwan's capital, technology and its management skill for its own economic reconstruction and development. In the 1990s, the main objectives of Beijing's economic policy toward Taiwan were to enhance economic communications across the Strait, to attract investment to mainland China from Taiwan's larger enterprises, and to foster 'three direct links' across the Strait. It is clear that for Beijing, economic communication across the Strait is also an instrument to pursue political ends. For Beijing, the achievement of the 'three direct links' would not only help to foster economic development, but would also promote national unification and thus deter claims for Taiwan's independence (Chen 1994, pp 53–56).

For Taipei, the main motivation for investment in mainland China was economic. In cross-Strait relations, Taipei consistently took the position of no contact, no negotiation and no compromise toward Beijing in earlier years. However, in recent years, Taiwan has gradually allowed its people to visit mainland China, and the economic ties across the Strait have thus developed rapidly.

Faced with the transformation of Taiwan's economic structure, and the pressures arising from developments in the international economy, a number of small and medium-sized enterprises in Taiwan, which have been the driving force behind Taiwan's economic development, have had no choice but to move their operations to mainland China. The main purpose behind the move has been to take advantage of the lower wages and cheaper land on the mainland. Other considerations have been to assure supplies of raw materials, promote export opportunities, and transfer sunset industries (Lin 1995, pp 5–6). On average, these firms each probably invested less than US$1 million on the mainland; they are largely engaged in labour-intensive manufacturing (Kao Chang 1994, p 6).

Other contributing factors in Taiwan's investment in mainland China are its geographical proximity and cultural and linguistic links. Taiwanese investors frequently put money into Guangdong and Fujian provinces because of geographical convenience and proximity to Hong Kong. This in turn highlights the importance of the geographical location of Hong Kong. In 1992, for the first time, mainland China became the top destination in attracting foreign investment from Taiwan. After 1996, Taiwan became the second largest investor in mainland China, next to Hong Kong. Moreover, 80 per cent of Taiwan businessmen who invest in mainland China have chosen Hong Kong as their intermediate channel (The Hong Kong Economic Yearbook 1996).

Economic relations in the form of trade and mutual investment between Hong Kong and Taiwan existed long before the launching of mainland China's economic reforms and open-door policy in 1979. However, these bilateral economic relations experienced fundamental changes after the adoption of the open-door policy and economic reforms by the mainland. Hong Kong then acted as the indispensable mediator between mainland China and Taiwan, helping to resolve political conflicts and promoting their increasingly important economic ties. Since 1979, Hong Kong has been very successful in playing an intermediate role by serving as a shipping, trading, financial, and information centre, or simply as the 'third place' in cross-Strait economic exchanges stipulated by Taipei.[1]

From 1979 to 1995, the growth rate of trade flow across the Strait was amazingly high, with an annual average of 40.6 per cent. The total trade amount also increased 231 times in that period (Central Daily News, 4 November 1996, p 10). There is no parallel for this between any two other trading countries. In addition, for the past 10 years exports from Taiwan to mainland China via Hong Kong have increased 703 times, with an average annual growth rate of 50.7 per cent. Between 1990 and 1995, exports from mainland China to Taiwan also increased 54 times, with an annual growth rate of 58.5 per cent.

Several high points are visible in this trade. From 1979 to 1981, indirect trade through Hong Kong increased by 146.7 per cent per year. As shown in Table 5.1, the value increased from US$78 million in 1979 to US$459 million in 1981. Within the same period, the volume of Taiwan's exports to mainland China increased 17.5 times, with an annual growth rate of 330 per cent. In 1985, indirect trade across the Taiwan Strait reached US$1.1 billion in value. A further boom occurred in 1987. That year, Taiwan allowed its people to visit their relatives in mainland China for the first time. This helped trade flows. In 1987, the indirect trade across the Strait was US$1.5 billion, and in 1988 US$2.7 billion, an increase of 79.5 per cent. Between 1989 and 1992, indirect trade across the Strait grew steadily, with an annual rate of 28.8 per cent. Taiwan's exports to Hong Kong again increased in 1995, growing by 16 per cent over the previous year, for an aggregate value

Table 5.1 Trade volume across the Taiwan Strait via Hong Kong (US$ million)

Year	Total value		Taiwan's exports to mainland China		Taiwan's imports from mainland China		Balance
	Amount	Growth rate (%)	Amount	Growth rate (%)	Amount	Growth rate (%)	Amount
1979	77.8	–	21.5	–	56.3	–	−34.8
1980	311.2	300.2	235.0	994.4	76.2	35.4	158.8
1981	459.3	47.6	384.2	63.5	75.2	−1.4	309.0
1982	278.5	−39.4	194.5	−49.4	84.0	11.8	110.4
1983	247.7	−11.1	157.9	−18.8	89.9	6.9	68.0
1984	553.2	123.3	425.5	169.6	127.8	42.2	297.7
1985	1102.7	99.3	986.9	132.0	115.9	−9.3	870.9
1986	955.6	−13.4	811.3	−17.8	144.2	24.4	667.1
1987	1515.5	58.6	1226.5	51.2	288.9	100.4	937.6
1988	2720.9	79.5	2242.2	82.9	478.7	65.7	1763.5
1989	3483.4	28.0	2896.5	29.9	586.9	22.6	2309.6
1990	4043.6	16.1	3278.3	13.2	765.4	30.4	2512.9
1991	5793.1	43.3	4667.2	42.4	1126.0	47.1	3541.2
1992	7406.9	27.9	6287.9	34.7	1119.0	−0.6	5169.0
1993	8689.0	17.3	7585.4	20.6	1103.6	−1.4	6481.8
1994	9809.5	12.9	8517.2	12.3	1292.3	17.1	7224.9
1995	11457.0	16.8	9882.8	16.0	1574.2	21.8	8308.6
1996	11300.0	−1.4	9717.6	−1.7	1582.4	0.5	8135.2

Source: Mainland Affairs Council 1997 *Cross-Strait Economic Statistics Monthly*, no. 53, (January), p 20.

of US$11 billion. Hong Kong has, since 1990, supplanted Japan to become the second-largest export destination for Taiwan products. The large amount of trade flow across the Strait, along with political antagonism between Taipei and Beijing, further consolidates Hong Kong's intermediate role.

Economic factors influencing Hong Kong's intermediate role

With regard to the Hong Kong economy, there is a clear commitment from Beijing in the Basic Law to maintain after 1997 the capitalist economic and trade systems practised in Hong Kong, and to retain Hong Kong's free port status and free trade policy, which includes the free movement of goods and capital. Further, the Hong Kong Special Administrative Region (HKSAR) government will be committed to safeguard the free operation of financial business and the free flow of capital within, into and out of Hong Kong. Hong Kong will be allowed to raise its own taxes and control revenue. The Hong Kong dollar will continue to circulate and remain freely convertible to the US dollar and other hard currencies. The HKSAR will have independent financial institutions. Beijing will not levy taxes on the Region. Within this framework, decisions on economic, trade, monetary and fiscal policies are to be taken by the HKSAR without any necessity for these policies to be adjusted in line with those in operation in the rest of mainland China.

Beijing's commitment to Hong Kong's stability and prosperity will very probably facilitate continuity in Hong Kong's intermediate role in cross-Strait economic relations. It is assumed that no drastic changes in foreign direct investment policy will be implemented by Beijing. Taiwan will continue to be a major source of investment for the mainland, and Taiwan's small and medium-sized enterprises will continue to use Hong Kong to facilitate their investment.

Regarding the trade relationship between Hong Kong and Taiwan, the indirect trade between Taiwan and the mainland is mostly investment-induced, with Taiwan businessmen shipping their older machinery and equipment from their Taiwan plants to the mainland location, along with parts and partially finished components manufactured in Taiwan. Mainland exports to Taiwan in the past have been constrained by Taiwan's administrative regulations. Since the early 1990s, though, Taipei has adopted a more open policy toward the importation of mainland products, probably under pressure from the business sector.

However, since June 1997 direct navigation across the Strait has become a fact. As a result, the so-called 'three direct links' may materialize in the future, which could have a great impact on Hong Kong's intermediate role in cross-Strait economic relations. On the trade side, considerations of cost of transportation may affect the pattern of trade via Hong Kong. Direct navigation between Fujian and Taiwan, and between Kaosiung, Xiamen and Fuzhou, has signalled an important step in this process.

While the 'three direct links' are intertwined with the political stalemate in cross-Strait relations, which has resulted in Taipei's reluctance to develop its trade and investment relations with mainland China directly, as market forces might normally dictate, political compromise may be reached in the foreseeable future. Even now, Beijing claims that it will open other harbours, such as Shanghai, Guangzhou, Dalian and Tianjin, if Taipei shows its intention to improve cross-Strait relations. If this situation materializes, the pattern of trade flow between Taiwan and mainland China by way of Hong Kong will be influenced dramatically, and Hong Kong's intermediate role will gradually lose its importance. Taiwan businessmen will conduct their export or import to or from mainland China on the basis of market and cost considerations, choosing one of these harbours as the most convenient destination.

On the investment side, investment in mainland China via Hong Kong cannot be easily displaced by other third places due to Hong Kong's historical importance as a financial and service centre in the region. Given any increase in tensions across the Strait, Taiwan might reduce the amount of its investment in mainland China, but the use of Hong Kong as a 'third place' will remain.

Political factors influencing Hong Kong's intermediate role

In recent years, political tensions between Taiwan and the PRC have complicated economic communications across the Strait. Mainland China's insistence on the separation of political and economic factors in dealing with cross-Strait affairs has pushed Taiwan into a dilemma. Taiwan's overdependence on trade and investment in mainland China has made it vulnerable to Beijing's economic sanctions and military threats. Additionally, the increase in Taiwan's investment in mainland China is resulting in greater amounts of trade flowing across the Strait, especially in respect of Taiwan's exports to mainland China, further increasing Taiwan's dependence. In this sense, trade and investment are becoming issues that cannot be separated by the decision makers in Taiwan. As a result, whenever cross-Strait relations deteriorate, Taipei must always worry about Beijing's utilization of economic sanctions to endanger Taiwan's economic development. In particular, Beijing's tough position in its insistence on the 'One China Policy' and its refusal to relinquish the possibility of using force to attack Taiwan have impeded the progress of economic relations. By the same token, Taipei, in its trade and investment policies toward mainland China, must also take into account both national security and economic considerations.

The deterioration of cross-Strait relations in June 1995, when Lee Tenghui visited the United States, and again in March 1996, when Lee became Taiwan's first elected president, is a case in point. Although the PRC's military exercises did not influence Taiwan's international trade in general, they did have an impact on the indirect trade flow across the Strait via Hong Kong. In May 1995, Taiwan's exports to mainland China were in decline. From January to May 1995, the growth rate of indirect trade still maintained a rate of 24.4 per cent. However, from June to December of 1995, the growth rate of cross-Strait trade fell to an average of only 10.6 per cent. In November, growth declined to its lowest point since 1992.

In March 1996, under the impact of Taiwan's presidential election and Beijing's military exercises and missile tests, Taiwan's indirect trade with mainland China declined again. Although Taiwan's exports to mainland China achieved a growth rate of 33.9 per cent in January 1996, the rate became negative in February and March (−20.4 per cent and −10.3 per cent respectively). In May and June 1996, Taiwan's exports to mainland China once again dipped to a negative growth rate of −10.7 per cent and 13.3 per cent respectively.

Not only trade, but investment was also affected. For instance, only US$63.4 million of Taiwan business investment in mainland China was approved by the Chinese mainland Ministry of Economic Affairs in August 1995. This was much less than the average monthly amount of US$100 million from January to July. Ratification of Taiwan's proposals for investment in mainland China had occurred in an average of 54 cases. However, immediately after the PRC's military exercises in June, the approved cases of investment across the Strait declined to only 29, a decrease of 46 per cent. Although the cases increased to 44 in August, they fell to only 31 for both September and October. The impact of political tension on cross-Strait investment can thus clearly be demonstrated.

With regard to the overall amount of investment, it reached US$193 million in June 1995. However, the amount declined from July to October. In July, the amount of Taiwan's indirect investment in mainland China decreased to US$86 million; it was further reduced to US$63 million in the following month. By observing the amount from July to October 1995, it can be seen that the average monthly amount was far below that of June. Thus, Beijing's military exercises played their role in influencing Taiwan's investment in mainland China. Similar effects can be seen following the tensions of 1996. This clearly impacted on Hong Kong. The Taiwan government became increasingly aware of the vulnerability of its dependence on China for trade and as an outlet for investment, and initiated the 'Jie Je Yong Ren' policy in September 1996 to slow the process down.

Since the return of Hong Kong to mainland China, the issue of Taiwan has received increased attention on both sides of the Taiwan Strait. With Hong Kong being an SAR of mainland China, Hong Kong–Taiwan relations naturally constitute a special component of cross-Strait relations. Hong Kong's Chief Executive Tung Chee-hwa has expressed a strong desire to improve cross-Strait relations and is willing to facilitate mainland China – Taiwan exchanges through Hong Kong. It is expected that the interaction of the mainland, Taiwan, and Hong Kong will create better understanding, promote mutual benefits, and reduce misconceptions, thus reducing the scope for conflict.

For its part, Taipei has recently passed the Statute Governing Relations between the Taiwan area and the Hong Kong and Macao area, reflecting its intention to maintain normal investment, visits, trade and emigration flows with Hong Kong (and with Macao). According to the Statute, as long as the two territories retain a high degree of autonomy, the Taiwan government will regard them as special regions separate from the rest of the Chinese mainland.

In the light of the close and comprehensive links described, it is to be expected that policy concerning Hong Kong is a high priority of the Taiwan government. The goals are to preserve democracy, freedom, stability, and prosperity in Hong Kong and Macao, to promote understanding and cooperation between the peoples of Taiwan, Hong Kong and Macao, to expand reciprocal bilateral exchanges and co-operation, and to respect the wishes of the people of Hong Kong and Macao.

Additionally, the declaration of the Seven Basic Points and Policies in Hong Kong–Taiwan Relations by the mainland's vice premier Qian Qichen in June 1995 gives two important signals. First, mainland China's policy toward Hong Kong–Taiwan ties under the new circumstances will be based upon the principle of separating politics from economics such that economic and civilian exchanges between the two 'regions' are encouraged, while Taipei's political activities in Hong Kong will be highly restricted, if not totally banned. Second, Beijing, as the 'central government' for Hong Kong, will take positive action in dealing with Hong Kong's relations with Taiwan.

According to the above analysis, the requirement for indirect trade and investment by Taipei, and Beijing's stipulation that it should pass through Hong Kong, has helped to determine Hong Kong's role as the pivotal point in economic ties between the two sides. Additionally, because of the change of Hong Kong's political status in July 1997, Taipei thus has the opportunity also to pursue government-to-government contact with Beijing through Hong Kong. In this sense, Hong Kong may play another crucial role in cross-Strait political contacts.

Conclusion

Since the 1980's, trade and investment across the Strait between Taiwan and China have been conducted largely by way of Hong Kong. It is therefore possible to predict that the role of Hong Kong as a bridge between Taiwan and mainland China will not only be maintained, but also enhanced in the years to come. Moreover, while the normalization of cross-Strait relations is still unattainable, Hong Kong's role will also be to diminish the political antagonism between Taipei and Beijing. As a result, Taiwan is unlikely to withdraw from Hong Kong abruptly, but on the contrary, should continue to utilize Hong Kong to influence mainland China's economic and political development.

In this sense, Hong Kong's return to mainland China in July 1997 can be seen as an opportunity for both Taiwan and China to develop their ways of interacting, with Hong Kong as intermediary. Pending establishment of the 'three direct links' across the Strait, or the final unification of Taiwan and mainland China, it may be expected that Hong Kong's role will continue well into the future.

Note

1   The 'PRC's' Guidelines for National Unification outline the principles and positive steps that both sides can take to expedite China's reunification. According to this gradual, sequential plan, China's reunification is imperative not only for the sake of territorial unity, but also for the political freedom and equitable distribution of wealth for all Chinese. The Statute Governing Relations, implemented in September 1992, covers administrative, civil and criminal affairs, and recognizes the rights of the people living under the control of the authorities in the mainland. Thus, with certain exceptions necessary to maintain the economic and social stability of Taiwan, in the eyes of the law the people living on the Chinese mainland are basically the same as those living in the Taiwan.

Bibliography

Baldwin, D. A. 1985 *Economic Statecraft*. Princeton: Princeton University Press.
Central Daily News 1996, 4 November.
Chen Teh-Sheng 1994 *Political and Economic Interaction across the Strait*. Taipei: Hung Yeh Publishing Co..
China Statistical Yearbook 1997.
Cohen, B. J. (ed) 1968 *American Foreign Economic Policy: Essays and Comments*. New York: Harper and Row.
Gerschenkron, A. 1962 *Economic Backwardness in Historical Perspective: A Book of Essays*. Cambridge: Harvard University Press.
Gilpin, R. 1987 *The Political Economy of International Relations*. Princeton: Princeton University Press.
Hirschman, A. O. 1980 *National Power and the Structure of Foreign Trade*. Berkeley: University of California Press.
The Hong Kong Economic Yearbook 1996.
Kao Chang 1994 *An Investigational Study of Taiwan and Foreign Countries Investment in Mainland China*. Taipei: Ministry of Economic Affairs.
Lin Teh-chang 1995 'The ROC's Foreign Aid and the Southward Policy'. *Issues and Studies*, 31(10).
Lin, Teh-chang 1997 *The Investment of the ROC's Small and Medium-sized Enterprises in Guangdong and its Relations to a Political and Economic Interaction across the Strait*. Taipei: Ministry of Economic Affairs.

Mainland Affairs Council 1997 *Cross-Strait Economic Statistics Monthly* 53 (January), 58 (June).

Winckler, E. A. 1988 'Globalist, Statist and Network Paradigms in East Asia', in Winckler, E. A., Greenhalgh, S. (eds) *Contending Approaches to the Political Economy of Taiwan.* New York: An East Gate Book.

Part II
Government and Politics

6
Hong Kong under Chinese Sovereignty: A Preliminary Assessment

Brian Hook

Introduction: Retrospect and prospect

In 1984, after protracted negotiations, the UK and China initialled an agreement on the future of Hong Kong.[1] In the context of the agreement, the future was distinguished from the past by specific references to what would happen to Hong Kong after the expiry of the 99-year lease on the New Territories on 30 June 1997.[2] During the negotiations, the UK had reluctantly conceded the inevitability of returning both ceded and leased territory to Chinese sovereignty.[3] Accordingly, the past was separated from the future by a transition period of some 13 years. This transition period was, in practice, to be divided into two sub-periods. The difference between the two was to be reflected in the intensity of the interaction between the sovereigns and by the increasing level of consultation and co-operation as the date for the handover approached.

Although the transition occurred over 13 years, the period located between the past (pre-1984) and the future (post-1997) took the form of a long and, at times, rather uncertain present. From the point of view of the existing sovereign, the social, political and economic progress of Hong Kong should continue. From the point of view of the future sovereign, political progress could not proceed beyond the limits set by its interpretation of the agreement when it was signed (Hook 1993, pp 840–863). The actual events in the period of transition are well documented and now a matter of history. The analysis of these events, recently predominantly a preserve of journalists, has already passed to the historians.[4]

In accordance with the treaty, Hong Kong embarked on its future on 1 July 1997.[5] Under the terms of the agreement, the constitutional future is determined for 50 years; that is, to the year 2047. During the 50 years following the retrocession and the establishing of the Hong Kong Special Administrative Region (HKSAR), there is the guarantee of systemic continuity, defined in terms of capitalist economics and life-style, the enjoyment of a high degree of autonomy and the practice of governance characterized by Hong Kong people ruling Hong Kong. The guarantee is underpinned by the Basic Law (BL) of the HKSAR which came into effect at the point of retrocession.

The specific aims of this chapter are set against this general background. The first, to which the main part of the chapter is devoted, is to examine the steps leading to, and the early development of, the HKSAR in relation to the parameters established by the letter and spirit of the agreement. The parameters are the achievement of 'One Country – Two Systems' and '50 years with no systemic change', 'Hong Kong people ruling Hong Kong' and 'a high degree of autonomy'. The second, is to assess the evidence from the process of this development and identify what it actually reveals of the exercise of Chinese sovereignty over Hong Kong. The third, is to make some very tentative predictions about future trends in the development of the HKSAR. The second and third parts of the chapter are in the form of preliminary assessments, relying for their evidence on the main part of the paper. They are therefore tentative conclusions.

Before examining the evidence so far of the operation of 'One Country – Two Systems' and '50 years with no systemic change', 'Hong Kong people ruling Hong Kong' and 'a high degree of autonomy' it will be helpful to consider the provenance and functional interdependence of these vital parameters. The concept of 'Hong Kong people ruling Hong Kong' has been described as the greatest 'invention' among the special policies formulated for Hong Kong (Wong 1997, pp 35–56). The reasons for this view are, first, its implicit message that the Chinese government has confidence in the people of Hong Kong, and second, its generation, provenance, and implementation demonstrate considerable courage on the part of the then leadership of the Communist Party of China (CPC) (Wong 1997, pp 35–56). The origins of this concept, and indeed the other key concept of 'a high degree of autonomy' together with the fundamental premise of 'One Country – Two Systems' and '50 years with no systemic change' can be traced to the work of the veteran leader Liao Chengzhi. Liao Chengzhi was the son of Liao Zhongkai, a close associate of Sun Yat-sen. There are branches of the Liao family in Hong Kong and, therefore, Liao probably had the best network for understanding the needs of Hong Kong of all the senior party members in the post-1949 period. He is said to have once remarked at a meeting of the central authorities in Beijing that there were over 400 members of his extended family in Hong Kong.

Towards the end of the 1970s, at the time of the initial British pressure on China to reach a resolution of what Britain perceived to be the 1997 issue, Liao was centrally involved in work to resolve the Taiwan issue. Following the fundamental adjustment in US policy towards China, the concern had been to explore ways to achieve constitutional reunification between Taiwan and the mainland. While recognizing the need eventually to take back Hong Kong, China at the time, preferred to maintain the status quo. Indeed, a Chinese view is that only after Britain declined to adopt the Macau model (Wong 1997, pp 1–28), leaving China with no realistic choice, was a decision to enforce retrocession reached. Deng Xiaoping emphasized that historical sensitivities precluded Britain's preferred solutions of either extending the lease on the New Territories or exchanging British sovereignty for continued British administration (Wong 1997, pp 1–28). Consequently, Liao Chengzhi was asked to focus his attention on the arrangements for the future of Hong Kong (Wong 1997, pp 1–28).

In the circumstances, Liao was the ideal man for the job. Moreover, the shift in focus was not inopportune, since aspirations that a solution to the Taiwan problem was imminent were not realised following the accession of President Reagan. Liao Chengzhi had all the qualifications: impeccable revolutionary provenance, family links, local knowledge and experience. Before the Cultural Revolution, together with Zhou Enlai and Chen Yi, he had been a member of the Hong Kong and Macau Affairs Office group, known as the Zhou-Chen-Liao group, under the Central Committee of the CPC. Latterly, he was a key member of the Deng-Deng-Liao group (Deng Xiaoping, Deng Yingchao and Liao Chengzhi) on Taiwan.

Once the Hong Kong issue was placed on the agenda (Wong 1997, pp 1–56), Liao Chengzhi became an architect of policies towards both Hong Kong and Taiwan. Policies towards Hong Kong were derived from those formulated for Taiwan. The most important policy was 'One Country – Two Systems'. The development of the other two main policies, namely 'Hong Kong people ruling Hong Kong', and 'a high degree of autonomy' emerged as essential concomitants to the basic policy of 'One Country – Two Systems'. The essence of the latter was to maintain the prosperity and stability of Hong Kong so that it would never be a burden on, and could continue to play its unique economic role for China. A time frame of 50 years during which there would be no systemic change was applied to generate public confidence.

The rationale for 'Hong Kong people ruling Hong Kong' was that practising communists could, by definition, never run a capitalist economy and the social system linked to it. Thus, for 'One Country – Two Systems' to succeed, Hong Kong people had to rule Hong Kong. This presupposed that by 1997 they would be sufficiently expert, experienced and, indeed, confident to undertake the task. Furthermore, for 'One Country – Two Systems' to succeed, as Liao Chengzhi envisaged it, not only should Hong Kong people rule Hong Kong but, in so doing, they would have to enjoy 'a high degree of autonomy'. Unless that were achieved, or conversely, were there to be undue intervention from China, the stability and prosperity of the second system in Hong Kong could be placed in jeopardy.

One Country – Two Systems

> The essence of 'One Country – Two Systems' is to maintain prosperity and stability in Hong Kong so that the territory can remain useful instead of becoming a burden to China.
>
> (Wong 1997, p 40)

The evidence of the initial period of the HKSAR testifies to the success of the implementation of this policy by China. Although the banking crisis and the fall in the levels of stock markets in the region that began in Autumn 1997 had local repercussions, as Peter Ferdinand shows in Chapter 3, the main adverse element found elsewhere, namely weak bank supervision, was notably absent in Hong Kong. Moreover, the specific challenge to the monetary peg linking the Hong Kong and the US dollars was defeated by the response of the Hong Kong Monetary Authority, whose Chief Executive, Joseph Yam, echoed the statement of the Financial Secretary of the HKSAR, Sir Donald Tsang, that at no time did the authorities in Beijing seek to influence the local handling of the crisis.[6]

The regional economic crisis cannot fail, for a time, to influence the level of economic activity within the HKSAR and on the mainland of China. With weaker currencies, imports by other countries will fall while competition from their exports will increase. The reform, restructuring and corporatization of state-owned enterprises in China will be retarded. There is also the probability of a protracted recession in tourism. Each has affected the HKSAR economy.[7]

Despite these economic challenges, there was no evidence in the early period of the existence of the HKSAR to suggest that the essential features of 'One Country – Two Systems' were in any sense permanently threatened. Regarding economic continuity, even in the periods of extreme volatility in the local stock market, the credibility of the long-term economic fundamentals of the HKSAR and southern China was seldom questioned. Regarding political continuity, although, predictably, the expanded democratization introduced in the Patten years was reversed, the operation of the political economy remained unchanged. Although the ratings of the Chief Executive, Tung Chee-hwa (Dong Jianhua), and the Provisional Legislature (PL) fell, confidence in the ability of the executive-led government ultimately to meet the challenges of the regional economic crisis remained high.[8]

Hong Kong people ruling Hong Kong

The regional economic crisis was the first major test for the HKSAR government (HKSARG) under the Chief Executive, Tung Chee-hwa. The administration, in particular the Finance Branch and the Hong Kong Monetary

Authority, emerged well from the crisis. This appeared to confirm both the high standards achieved in the civil service, and the success of the localization policy. Localization had come relatively late in the history of British Hong Kong but it was clearly soundly based. Moreover, in the shaping of 'Hong Kong people ruling Hong Kong', those involved, while predictably negating the results of the Patten constitutional reforms, confirmed in office the principal civil servants. They were equally prudent in appointments to head the Independent Commission Against Corruption (ICAC), the Department of Justice, and the Judiciary.

The major appointment, that of the Chief Executive, was made by the Central People's Government (CPG) in Beijing on the recommendation of a 400 member Selection Committee (SC) formed for that purpose by the Preparatory Committee (PC) for the HKSAR.[9] There were, in the event, three main candidates, two businessmen Tung Chee-hwa and Peter Woo and the former Chief Justice T.L. Yang. A fourth contender, a distinguished retired judge, Simon Li, was eliminated at the penultimate stage. It was, however, reasonably clear from the outset that Tung Chee-hwa, who had been singled out at a reception by President Jiang Zemin earlier in the year for the benefit of media, was a clear favourite for the post.

The PC, which played a crucial role from its inception at the end of 1995 until the resumption of the exercise of sovereignty, had been preceded by a Preliminary Working Committee (PWC). The first plenary session of the PWC had been held on 16 July 1993 as the UK pressed ahead with the programme for constitutional reform under the last Governor. The formation of the PWC was, in practice, the first step along the path towards carrying out the threat to set up a 'second stove'.[10] The PWC comprised a number of sub-groups whose task it was to prepare policy options for the PC and, on its formation, the Provisional Legislature (PL), which epitomized the 'second stove'. Ultimately, this led to the defenestration of many of those elected in the 1994 and 1995 elections to the three tiers of representative government and the appointment of replacements on provisional representative bodies. The authority for these arrangements was conferred by the National People's Congress (NPC).[11]

When the PC was formed in December 1995, the role of the PWC ceased. The PC itself comprised 56 mainland members and 94 Hong Kong members. At the beginning of November 1996, it had arranged for the convening in Beijing of the 400 member Selection Committee (SC) to recommend a candidate for the post of Chief Executive. In the special circumstances in the approach to 1997, the SC was also used to select the members of the PL. There had been 5,791 public nominees in Hong Kong for the SC. These had been reduced by two voting stages, to 340 members. The 60 local delegates to the NPC and the Chinese People's Political Consultative Conference (CPPCC) were then added (South China Morning Post, 19 November 1996) to bring the total to 400.

On 11 December 1996, the SC recommended Tung Chee-hwa as the first Chief Executive of the HKSAR. On 21 December 1996, it named the members of the PL it had elected to replace the Legislative Council (Legco) elected in 1995 under the Patten constitutional reform programme. Among them, 33 were members of the existing Legco. The principal losers were the members of the Democratic Party and independent politicians similarly ideologically and politically aligned. They would have to await a review of the electoral system before being given an opportunity to contest the decision in fresh elections promised for 1998.

On 25 January 1997, the Chief Executive named the members of his Executive Council (Exco). The appointment of 15 members to form the first Exco of the HKSAR provided the clearest evidence so far of the composition of the leadership elite after 1997. It was this group that, with the Chief Executive, interacted with the senior civil servants on policy formation on the one hand, and the PL in legislating on the other. The Exco team included, besides the Secretary for the Administration, the Secretary for Justice, the Financial Secretary, a partner from the accounting firm Arthur Andersen, a pre-eminent property surveyor, a Vice-Chairman of the Hong Kong Federation of Trade Unions, a senior researcher at the Xinhua News Agency (XHNA) currently Chief Executive of the SAR Government Land Fund, a former Chairman of the HK Stock Exchange, a former Chairman of the Federation of Hong Kong Industries, the Chairman of the HK Housing Authority, the Managing Director of Chase Manhattan Bank, the Chairman of the Federation of HK Industries, a former Chief Justice and a former senior member of Exco and Legco who was also designated as convenor.

The business community regarded the composition of the Exco as reassuring. In fact, its pattern resembled that of pre-Patten equivalents, save for the shift away from the pro-British elites towards professionals drawn largely from the pro-China business community. For this reason, concern was expressed about the lack of political diversity and consequently, the narrow range of political views available to the Chief Executive from his inner cabinet. It was evident, however, that while the new Exco was identifiably drawn from the pro-China business community, as individuals they were arguably more firmly based in Hong Kong than any of the pre-Patten equivalents.

The task of appointing those Hong Kong people who would rule Hong Kong after the handover, was completed in just over a year following the appointment of the PC (South China Morning Post, 22 December 1996). The stages in the process were, as expected, accompanied by controversy, mainly because, pending the 1998 elections, democratically elected legislators were the principal losers. The UK government, itself preoccupied by the increasing likelihood of electoral demise in May 1997, expressed concern. It was self-evident, however, that legal action by the UK was a non-starter. Even if it had been tried and had succeeded, the judgement would have been unenforceable, the handover could have been destabilized, Sino–British relations would have been fatally poisoned, and British business interests in Hong Kong, capitalized at £70 billion, would have suffered a potentially devastating blow.[12]

While these procedures did not conform to those of a democratic political culture, it could be argued, as indeed it was, that both the intention and the spirit of the agreement, and their embodiment in the law, regarding the principle of 'Hong Kong people ruling Hong Kong', had been observed. The PRC argued this legality to have been so from the outset with the Basic Law Consultative and Drafting Committees (BLCC, BLDC) in the mid-1980s, the groups of Hong Kong advisors in the early 1990s, the PWC, the PC, the SC, the PL and Exco in the run-up to retrocession. It was arguably so in the selection of the first Chief Executive. The process of appointing Hong Kong people to rule Hong Kong in the SAR Government continued with the confirmation of the key appointments in the civil service on 20 February 1997. In the event, Tung Chee-hwa, whose visit to Beijing for the ratification of nominees coincided with the death of Deng Xiaoping, announced the appointment of 21 incumbent officials at the level of policy branch secretary or equivalent. The two new appointees at this level were the Secretary for Justice, a local solicitor and NPC delegate, and the Commissioner of the ICAC, who was appointed from the Administrative Service (South China Morning Post, 21 February 1997).

The confirmation of the nominations, which had obviously been the subject of discussions with the central authorities, ended speculation about CPG interference that would preclude certain candidates. The decision represented the best possible boost, as regards local governance, for systemic continuity and the principle of Hong Kong people ruling Hong Kong. Among the appointees, the confirmation of Anson Chan as Secretary for Administration and Donald Tsang as Financial Secretary were regarded as particularly reassuring as senior figures among a group of policy level secretaries, whose average age, owing to the delayed localization and early retirements, was relatively young (South China Morning Post International Weekly, 1 March 1997).

It does not of course follow automatically that the *appointment* of Hong Kong people to positions of power in the governance of the HKSAR would ensure, in practice, that Hong Kong people actually *ruled* Hong Kong. For that to be so there has to be clear evidence not only of the appointment of Hong Kong people, but also of non-interference in their exercising power in areas designated by the treaty in which Hong Kong, as part of the PRC, would enjoy a high degree of autonomy. This is the subject to which we will turn in the next section. Suffice to say, however, that had the appointments gone to other candidates, or, indeed, in the worst-case scenario had the appointments included one or more officials of mainland origin, the impact would have been entirely different. Local confidence in the standard of future governance would have fallen. In all likelihood, this would have been reflected in a corresponding fall in international confidence in Hong Kong both as a financial centre and as a key player in the modernization of China.

The developments reviewed so far show that in the area of representative government, while one set of political elites was summarily supplanted by another, the new incumbents were all Hong Kong people (South China Morning Post, 22 December 1996). Although regrettable for its thwarting of the democratic will, it did not represent an abandonment of the concept and practice of local people running the HKSAR. The appointment of the Chief Executive and the appointments at senior level in the civil service and the judiciary ensured continuity in those areas. The extent to which Hong Kong people were actually ruling the HKSAR depended, however, on their ability to exercise a high degree of autonomy. It is to this area we now turn our attention.

A high degree of autonomy

During the transition period, the extent to which the UK Hong Kong administration sought to exercise autonomy in political and economic matters frequently became a source of Sino-British controversy. It is conceivable that the Chinese side was either not fully aware of, or aware of but unwilling to acknowledge, the level of independence from Britain enjoyed by Hong Kong in the 1980s. This could be explained by the role played by the Foreign and Commonwealth Office (FCO) in the negotiations. The Chinese negotiators could have gained the impression that the Hong Kong administration was, in practice, answerable to the FCO in the matter of the governance of Hong Kong. It was, of course, a fact that the Governor of Hong Kong was answerable to the Secretary of State for Foreign Affairs. Moreover, from the appointment of Murray Maclehose in the 1970s, until the arrival of Christopher Patten, the governors, unlike their predecessors from the former Colonial Office, were all FCO diplomats.

The incumbents did, however, differ in their approach to the exercise of levels of autonomy while in office. The differences were determined by personality and political context. Murray Maclehose had a distinguished governorship, characterized by his successfully meeting and surmounting the twin challenges of syndicated corruption and a lack of adequate housing and other amenities for the population. He was a dominant figure not only in Hong Kong, but also in London. Consequently, the Hong Kong that Edward Youde and David Wilson inherited and administered had established precedents, both material and psychic, for the exercise of a high degree of autonomy. These would not have been readily comprehensible to those who, perforce, or for convenience, drew conclusions from appearances rather than reality.

In practice, the effect of the Chinese interpretation of the treaty was to place limits on the level of autonomy to which Hong Kong aspired in the 1980s. This was evident in China's successfully retarding the pace of constitutional reform, the case for which had existed since the late 1970s (Hook 1993, pp 840–863). China sought to limit the degree of autonomy to that commensurate with its perception of the dependent territory status of Hong Kong. It did so with a view subsequently to transpose that degree of autonomy to, and avoid any dilution of its sovereignty in, the post-handover period.

This was achieved under the David Wilson governorship for both the political and economic development of Hong Kong. The direct elections to the Legco, which could have enhanced the level of autonomy of Hong Kong, were postponed until 1991. By then, the handling of the crisis in China had ensured a maximum anti-communist politicization of Hong Kong, which generated a hostile reaction by the CPC.[13] Unfortunately, the well-intentioned initiatives in Hong Kong, designed to restore confidence, the Port and Airport Development Strategy (PADS), the Bill of Rights Ordinance (BRO) and the British Nationality Selection Scheme (BNSS), were regarded as threatening extensions of the degree of autonomy enjoyed by Hong Kong. Consequently, the CPC sought to impose strict limits on the relative freedom of action enjoyed by the Hong Kong Government. It was not surprising, in those circumstances, that the Patten constitutional reform programme was adopted by reform-minded politicians in Hong Kong. Nor was it surprising that the threat to dismantle its achievements was duly carried out by the new sovereign. It was consistent with the parameters within which Hong Kong could practise a high level of autonomy having been systematically narrowed to correspond to China's selective perception of the level of autonomy exercised by Hong Kong at the time of the signing of the agreement.

The process of limiting the level of autonomy temporarily achieved in Hong Kong under the Patten reform programme began with a decision taken by the NPC on 31 August 1994. This stated that the terms of office of the three tiers of representative government generated under the 1994/ 1995 reform provisions would end on 30 June 1997. This meant there would be no 'through train'. It further stated that the PC would be responsible not only for preparing the establishment of the HKSAR under the 1990 decision, but also for prescribing the methods for forming, and actually constituting, the PL of the HKSAR. Under a 1990 decision, the PC duly arranged for the formation of the SC for the Chief Executive (CE) and first government of the HKSAR. On 24 March 1996, the PC announced it would set up a PL. The PL would be formed and come into operation after the appointment of the CE. In addition, the PL would be elected by the SC in accordance with a method prescribed by the PC. Accordingly, by early 1997, despite the protestations of the British side, a shadow government existed: the PL met at regular intervals in adjoining Shenzhen to avoid any legal challenge.

On 23 February 1997, following the appointments of the CE, the PL and the Exco, the Standing Committee of the NPC decided on the handling of Hong Kong's existing laws under article 160 of the BL. This decision specified which laws contravened the BL.[14] The list was based on the recommendations of the PWC, the legal panel of which, assisted by the Hong Kong and Macau Affairs Office (HKMAO) of the State Council, had scrutinized the legislation. Among the laws that would not be adopted were three sections of the BRO and amendments to the Societies and Public Order Ordinances (SO, POO) introduced in 1992 and 1995.[15] Thus, among the significant examples of the delimitation of the degree of political autonomy to be enjoyed by the HKSAR were adjustments to the composition of its tiers of representative government and to human rights provisions and personal freedoms. The latter, in effect, sought to restore the legal provisions formerly deemed anachronistically colonial and unnecessarily restrictive by the British authorities and reformist politicians. The adjustments were the subject of a consultation document issued by the CE's office in April 1997 (Chief Executive's Office 1997).

Other significant examples of China's delimiting the degree of political autonomy enjoyed by the HKSAR are in the preparations for the elections for the first Legco of the HKSAR, and in the election of the Hong Kong delegates for the NPC. Regarding the Legco elections, it was clear that the 1995 system would not survive. The single seat constituency, single vote, first-past-the-post system had enabled the Democratic Party (DP) to dominate the contest for the 20 directly elected seats. The DP was known for its criticism of China's policies for Hong Kong. A system of proportional representation (PR), based on list-voting in five large multi-seat constituencies was adopted as being politically more appropriate for Hong Kong.

In addition to the political reasons for revising the Legco election arrangements, there were also practical reasons for the changes. Those have to be weighed against the contention, implicit in the foregoing section, that the SAR government did not enjoy a high degree of autonomy in deciding on the new arrangements. The practical reasons included the need to construct a system in which the administration could enjoy an efficient relationship with Legco. The system was prescriptively executive-led; the executive had to be accountable to the Legco; it had been seriously dysfunctional when the dominant political party in Legco was excluded from Exco. This had been the case in 1991 and 1995. To function with optimal efficiency, the administration needed majority support in Legco. Other practical reasons for revising the system included the need to provide a system of geographical constituencies that would be able to accommodate both the chosen system of PR and the evolution of the democratic process of direct elections set out in the BL. The adoption of five large multi-seat constituencies would avoid the need for radical change as the system evolves.

The systems for generating the Functional Constituency (FC) and Election Committee (EC) were also revised. The trend towards universal suffrage in FC voting was reversed. The role of the FC as an interim arrangement to give professional and grassroots sectors a say in governance, to maintain balance and continuity while the democratic process evolved, was restated. The rule limiting the proportion of foreign nationals in the Legco to 20%[16] was imposed by requiring such candidates to contest 12 pre-designated FC seats. Consequently, all candidates had to declare their nationality and right of abode. Regarding the EC, instead of an electorate of some 300, based on the former District Boards (DB), it would comprise 800 electors, mostly formally elected from 38 EC sub-sectors. This followed the arrangement stipulated for the second-term Legco.[17] Not all the seats on the EC were to be filled by election. The PL members were ex-officio members, as were 36 NPC and 41 CPPCC members. Significantly, the total of ex-officio members exceeded the number of seats for the DBs and the Heung Yee Kuk (HYK). The NPC members included the head of the Hong Kong branch of the XHNA. Separate arrangements were also made for the religious sub-sector, whose representatives were returned through nominations. Along with the revised provisions for the direct elections, these changes guaranteed a pro-HKSARG and pro-CPG majority in the 1998 Legco elections, eliminating any risk of dysfunctionalism.

The arrangements for electing the Hong Kong delegates to the Ninth NPC generated much debate. There were no suitable precedents for this procedure, former delegates from the British territory having been invited. With the NPC meeting scheduled for early 1998, the HKSAR had the constitutional right to send 36 delegates (an increase from the existing 28 appointees). In this instance, the Standing Committee of the NPC decided that the SC, the local CPPCC members and the members of the PL – altogether 424 members – would form an ad hoc EC for the Ninth NPC. The use, once more, of the SC concept for this purpose was criticized by those favouring direct elections.[18] Other objections concerned the advisability of PL members seeking elections as delegates to the NPC, on the grounds of divided loyalties and time constraints.[19] The main reaction, however, came when it was revealed that the current director of the XHNA, former ambassador and vice-foreign minister Jiang Enzhu, was seeking election as a Hong Kong delegate. The view was that his election could lead to interference in the affairs of the HKSAR and be inconsistent with the principle of 'Hong Kong people ruling Hong Kong' (Yeung 1997, Hong Kong Standard, 14 November 1997); in the event he won more votes than any other candidate.

The exercise of sovereignty over the HKSAR

The resumption of sovereignty over Hong Kong by China is, by treaty and law, to be moderated (in the sense of its being rendered 'less intense' or 'less vigorous') by the application of the concepts of 'One Country – Two Systems', 'Hong Kong people ruling Hong Kong' and a 'high degree of autonomy', for at least the first 50 years of the HKSARG. In the preceding sections, an attempt has been made to examine the practice of the resumption of the exercise of sovereignty by addressing salient evidence under each of those three criteria. The evidence is, of course, by no means complete. There is, for example, no examination of the commercial challenges by Chinese state agencies in the fields of aviation and telecommunications, of the presence and role of the People's Liberation Army (PLA) garrison, of the changing role of the XHNA, of the social and cultural issues such as the effect of legal and illegal immigration, and the challenge of mainland-induced corruption.

The potential for commercial challenges to the practice of 'One Country – Two Systems' is evident from the interest of the China National Aviation Corporation (CNAC) and of the Ministry of Posts and Telecommunications (MPT) in HKSAR *hongs*. This may or may not develop into a challenge to the 'high degree of autonomy' promised for the HKSAR. The potential for direct political interference has not been overtly exploited. The conduct of the PLA garrison has, so far, been exemplary. The fears of uniformed soldiers on the streets have proved unfounded. General Liu Zhenwu has been a model Commander of the Chinese Forces (CCF).[20] The XHNA has a much lower profile than it did in the approach to 1997. Its new Director, Jiang Enzhu, despite being at the centre of a controversy over his election as a HKSAR delegate to the Ninth NPC, is generally regarded as being moderate, experienced and much less interventionist than his predecessor, Zhou Nan. There is evidence that the XHNA, home of the Hong Kong and Macau Work Committee of the CPC, is indeed developing a new role in post-handover Hong Kong, the aims of which will gradually emerge.[21]

Similarly, the other state agencies with a direct political interest in and influence on the HKSAR, the HKMAO of the State Council, the Ministry of Foreign Affairs (MFA) and the Office of the PRC representative to the Joint Liaison Group (JLG), have each managed to maintain a good image and keep a very low profile in the HKSAR. Both the HKMAO and the local MFA Commissioner were carefully selected appointees. Liao Hui, who replaced Lu Ping as the head of the HKMAO, is a son of Liao Chengzhi, the architect of Chinese policies towards Hong Kong. He therefore inherited an extended family in the HKSAR. Ma Yuzhen, the Commissioner for Foreign Affairs, is a former PRC ambassador to London, a distinction he shares with Jiang Enzhu. General Liu Zhenwu is an alumnus of the Royal College of Defence Studies. At first glance, nobody could cavil at these appointments. Individually and collectively they represent probably the best expertise and experience the CPG could muster to ensure a smooth passage from UK to Chinese sovereignty. All three are familiar with the concepts of

'One Country – Two Systems', a 'high degree of autonomy' and 'Hong Kong people ruling Hong Kong'.

In these circumstances, it was difficult to understand why the XHNA director sought to be a Hong Kong delegate to the Ninth NPC. Allowing for the precedent before 1997, when Zhou Nan enjoyed a similar but unelected status, it appears that an opportunity may have been lost at that juncture to allow all 36 vacancies to be filled by Hong Kong people. Similarly, it was disturbing that despite an early draft of the Adaptation of Laws Ordinance confining the equivalent to the privilege of crown immunity to HKSARG organs, the final version actually extended it to state organs in the HKSAR. This appeared to place the XHNA, the PLA and the MFA organs above the HKSAR law, contrary to the popular interpretation of an express provision in the BL.[22]

The twin challenges of immigration and mainland-induced corruption must await the accumulation of more evidence before they can be satisfactorily factored into assessments of the application of 'One Country – Two Systems', 'Hong Kong people ruling Hong Kong, and a 'high degree of autonomy'. Suffice to say there is a perceptible trend towards acculturation between Hong Kong and China. This is promoted not only by the change in sovereignty, but also by immigration from the mainland. Much of the immigration is legal, reflecting the symbosis between the mainland and Hong Kong economies, and the arrival of relatives from the mainland. Among the latter will be, in a phased manner, at least 60 000 children. Although the HKSARG has successfully argued in a controversial legal case for a phased entry of qualified children from the mainland, over time the distinctive social and cultural autonomy of Hong Kong may be affected by such immigration.[23] Inevitably, the local culture will become more sinicized. In practical terms, this raises the question as to whether the distinctive social and political culture will survive more or less intact, or in a recognizably evolved form, characterized by the prevalence of the Cantonese dialect. Alternatively, will the social and political culture undergo a fairly rapid and fundamental change characterized by the prevalence of Putonghua (standard mainland Chinese) on account of southward migration? These complex issues of identity will, eventually, be reflected in the way the HKSAR implements its right to a high degree of autonomy.

Lastly, there remained public concern about the danger of increased corruption and the erosion of the rule of law. The official view was that corruption, though present, was under control. A successful investigation into allegations of corruption in the police promotion system was cited as evidence of this. But sceptics cited what appeared to be a negative example in a case involving the *Hong Kong Standard*, whose proprietor Ms Sally Aw was excluded from prosecution. They implied political considerations could have been a factor in reaching the decision. Some contended this could lead to a two-track legal system. Such a contention had already surfaced as a result of a decision not to prosecute the XHNA for an alleged breach of the Data Protection (Privacy) Ordinance following a complaint by the politician Emily Lau.[24]

Trends in the development of the HKSAR

Among the trends on which predictions about the future development of the HKSAR can be based, the first is a natural outcome of the retrocession. With the resumption of Chinese sovereignty there has been an inevitable initial decline in British influence, extending beyond the confines of the administration. The number of British expatriates is falling, reflecting the departure of expatriate civil servants, as the number of American, Australian and Japanese expatriates is rising, reflecting a growth in the interests of those countries in regional affairs. There remain a large number of British Hong Kong citizens, but their status under British immigration does not give them the right of abode in the UK. With the change in sovereignty and a reduced presence, it is likely that British influence will decline until it finds a new level which will reflect the British legacy for Hong Kong. This should be a durable presence. In the twenty-first century it could also be a more comfortable presence than that of a twentieth century sovereign in a borrowed place on borrowed time.

The new British Consulate-General, with the staff of a major embassy, together with the British Council Offices, symbolize the official view of the importance of the residual relationship with Hong Kong. The appointment of two former PRC ambassadors to London, Jiang Enzhu and Ma Yuzhen, to important posts in Hong Kong is an indication that the new sovereign acknowledges the importance of the legacy of the past and the future link with Britain. This link is underpinned, not only in business and the profes-sions, but also in education, the arts and religion. The British expatriate community is indeed reducing but, thanks to Commonwealth support, not to the extent that a cricket league will be impossible to organize. Moreover, in qualitative respects, many of the British expatriates are well prepared to pursue their careers in a part of China. On this basis, although Britain's influence will decline before it restabilizes at a new level, having done so, it will remain important and support substantial HKSAR–UK busi-ness and cultural links in the twenty-first century.

As this readjustment occurs, the influence of China as the sovereign power will grow rapidly. It is in this context that both the CPG and the HKSARG will have jointly to put down the essential markers to delineate with some precision what, in practice, is meant by 'One Country – Two Systems', 'Hong Kong people ruling Hong Kong' and a 'high degree of autonomy'. It will be evident to the CPG that the integrity of the HKSAR is as vulnerable to uninvited interference from the mainland, if not more so, as was the former British colony to unwelcome liberation at any time after

17 October 1949, when the PLA halted at the border. For this reason, more should be read into Jiang Zemin's reiteration of the saying 'jingshui bu fan heshui' (literally, the well water does not intrude into the river water) than is usually the case in the west. It contains important messages both for Hong Kong and the mainland authorities that Hong Kong should not become a base for subverting the CPC, and for the mainland that it should respect the integrity of the second system in Hong Kong. In the ongoing readjustment, the use of this particular saying suggests it is for the leadership in the HKSAR actively to convince the leadership in the CPG of the mutually acceptable parameters for exercising a high degree of autonomy in the second system.

This has become of particular interest following the elections to the first Legco. The new arrangements, based on proportional representation (PR), as expected, delivered a more even distribution of seats among parties contesting geographical constituencies than in 1991 and 1995. This was a consequence of the reframing of the electoral laws according to the wishes of the new sovereign. Discomforting though it has been, this must be seen on the one hand in the context of the political challenge to the CPC, supported in Hong Kong, before and after 4 June 1989 (Wong 1997, pp 35–56).[25] On the other hand, the CPG cannot ignore the results of the Legco elections: despite the careful restructuring that had occurred, the Democratic Party and those allied to or aligned with it, did remarkably well in a record turnout during bad weather.[26] With the first Legco in place, the second system became properly operational and the development of its systemic characteristics open to scrutiny.

Between 1998 and 2000 when the next Legco elections take place, Hong Kong politicians and administrators must rise to the challenge of shaping them. With the return of 18 of the 24 defenestrated legislative councillors, including some of the most charismatic politicians in Hong Kong, it would be tempting to conclude that there could be a resumption of the political contention of the 1995–1997 Legco. Although the PL, whose legality was challenged in and upheld by the Court of Appeal,[27] is extinct, a complex and apparently potentially negative legacy remains. The three judgements were significant not only because they avoided stasis and political confrontation in the short term, but also because they transposed the concept of parliamentary supremacy to NPC decisions in the long term. This precedent may yet have a vital bearing on the degree of autonomy enjoyed by the Legco.

Looking back, in the controversy over political culture, China has prevailed. The structure of the first Legco reflects China's political preferences. Looking forward, the future arrangements for municipal and local government will similarly reflect the new sovereign's political preferences. Allowing for the effects of the imposition of Chinese political preferences, it does not necessarily follow that those involved will not attempt to shape and maintain a genuine second system, incorporating the principles of 'Hong Kong people ruling Hong Kong', and the practice of 'a high degree of autonomy'. While the destruction of the old system and the construction of the new were taking place, new priorities emerged to eclipse the questions of constitutional reform. The HKSAR became a sufferer from the regional economic crisis, and its population, in varying degrees, faced serious economic challenges. It was against that background that the new Legco took office and within that context that the HKSAR system began to take shape. Although there is no surviving institutional legacy attributable to the last governor, his contribution to the practice of debate, open government and public accountability could yet play a part in optimizing the second system within the PRC state structure and preparing the HKSAR for the twenty-first century.

Acknowledgement

The author would like to express his thanks to the Leverhulme Trust for its support in the research conducted in the preparation of this chapter.

Notes

1   The Sino-British Joint Declaration on the Question of Hong Kong initialled on 26 September 1984, signed 19 December 1984, ratified 27 May 1985.

2   The agreement, an international treaty comprised a declaration, 3 annexes and 2 memoranda. Annex 1 is an elaboration of PRC policies regarding Hong Kong. The agreement makes no explicit reference to the lease, but its effect is implicit in a reference in Annex 3 on land leases.

3   Introduction to *A Draft Agreement on the Future of Hong Kong*, a Hong Kong White Paper reproducing the text of the White Paper published by the government in London, 26 September 1984.

4   Hong Kong studies now occupy a place in the lists of many publishers reflecting interest in the subject and its elevation to university curricula.

5   See notes 1 and 2.

6   Joseph Yam, speech to the Hong Kong Association, London, 2 June 1998.

7   Ibid. Government Statistics show that the economy was in recession in early 1998.

8   The government announced 7 measures to counter the economic difficulties on 29 May 1998. On 4 June, it announced 12 measures to boost employment and training. Official statements did not underestimate the difficulties but expressed confidence they could be overcome.

9   The Chief Executive was elected by the SC on 11 December 1996 (*South China Morning Post International Weekly*, 14 Dec. 1996).

10   Lu Ping, Head of the Hong Kong and Macau Office of the State Council, gave a press conference on 17 July at which he said the PWC was not a second stove, it would not interfere in the work of the Joint Liaison Group nor decide on the objective criteria for upholding the BL. The latter would be done by the future PC. This reflected Zhou Nan's statement at the Second Meeting of the Standing

Committee of the Eighth NPC on 1 July. (PWC database, Hong Kong Government).

11 Ibid. The Standing Committee of the Eighth NPC approved the establishment of the PWC and its membership on 2 July 1993.

12 The measure of British investment in Hong Kong was given in a speech there by the Prime Minister, John Major, on 4 March 1996 (Source: Hong Kong Government Information Services).

13 The CPC view of the role of Hong Kong in the crisis appears in the official report by Chen Xitong in *Renmin Ribao (Waiban)*, 10 July 1989. It was the basis for much of the attitude adopted subsequently by the CPG on Hong Kong issues and engendered a hostile reaction there among critics that affected the outcome of the 1991 elections.

14 Decision of the 24th Meeting of the Standing Committee of the Eighth NPC, 23 February 1997 (*Renmin Ribao (Waiban)*, 24 Feb. 1997).

15 Ibid.

16 See 'Electoral arrangements for the first Legislative Council of the HKSAR', (Hong Kong Government, 8 July 1997).

17 See the BL, Annex 1 and 2.

18 See *Qianxian dui Gangqu Renda Xuanju de Lichang*, issued by the Frontier, 5 Nov. 1997.

19 Ibid.

20 The CCF is highly regarded by qualified observers for the low profile of the PLA in the first year of the HKSAR.

21 XHNA was described as an empowered organ of the CPG, which appeared to suggest a shift away from its CPC role and an enhancement of its role vis-à-vis the supervision of state enterprises and investments in the HKSAR.

22 Article 22 of the BL requires all mainland government offices and their personnel in the HKSAR to abide by its laws.

23 See judgment delivered in the High Court of Hong Kong, Court of the First Instance, *Administrative Law List*, 9 Oct. 1997, by the Hon. Mr Justice Keith in the case between Cheung Lai-wah et al., applicants, and the Director of Immigration, respondent (1997 A.L. No.s 68, 70, 17 and 73).

24 For comment on the complaint by Emily Lau against the XHNA see the *South China Morning Post* 28 Feb. and 3 March. The basis for the decision regarding the newspaper case was outlined by the Secretary for Justice at a special meeting of the PL panel on the Administration of Justice and Legal Services on 23 March. For earlier commentary see *Pingguo Ribao* and *Xin Bao*, 18 March.

25 See Chen Xitong, op. cit., note 13.

26 The turnout in the direct election was 53 per cent compared to 35 per cent in 1995. The DP and its allies secured 60 per cent of the votes cast. They remain in a minority because of the results of the indirect elections from FCs and the EC.

27 High Court, Court of Appeal, Reservation of Question of Law No. 1 of 1997 between HKSAR, applicant and Ma Wai-Kwan, David et al., respondents; *coram* Judges Chan, Nazareth and Mortimer, 29 July 1997.

Bibliography

Chief Executive's Office 1997 *Civil Liberties and Social Order* (Gongmin Ziyou he Shehui HKSAR). Hong Kong: Hong Kong Government, 8 July.

Hong Kong Standard 1997, 'Baby Sung, Diplomatic Xinhua chief to stand 'for sake of HK', 14 November.
Hook, B. 1993 'Political change in Hong Kong'. *China Quarterly*, 136 (December).
South China Morning Post, various.
South China Morning Post International Weekly, 1 March 1997.
Wong Man-fong 1997 *China's Resumption of Sovereignty over Hong Kong*. Hong Kong: David C. Lam Institute for East-West Studies, Hong Kong Baptist University.
Yeung, C. 1997 'Two systems face to face'. *South China Morning Post*, 15 November.

7
Beijing's Fifth Column and the Transfer of Power in Hong Kong: 1983–1997

Yin Qian

Introduction

This chapter shows that over 83 000 mainland Chinese officials with changed names and false identities have entered Hong Kong from 1983 to 1997 as part of a covert scheme by the PRC government to groom a political force *extraordinaire* – a fifth column – in Hong Kong. The fifth column, by definition of this study, refers exclusively to those Chinese Communist Party (CCP) cadres with one-way exit permits and Territory residential status who were dispatched to Hong Kong under the false pretence of the 'family reunion' category in the transitional period. Although these people are from truly diverse backgrounds in terms of age, education, profession, origin of work locations and sponsoring organizations, they usually had one important thing in common: they were well-connected within the Chinese party–state system and enjoyed prominent patronage within the party. These fifth columnists appear to be ordinary immigrants, but they carry the Chinese government's official blessing. Ultimately, they were the winners in China's domestic political contest, and beneficiaries of economic reform.

On the surface, these fifth columnists, residing alongside the other 6 million Hong Kong people, were not under direct CCP control, as were those cadres who worked in the Chinese official representative bodies, corporations and other business outlets. But, in substance, the fifth columnists were used to complete the CCP's political mapping of future Hong Kong. In addition to Beijing's well-established control network, e.g. Xinhua News Agency (XHNA), People's Liberation Army (PLA) Garrison, intelligence units and business enterprises, the fifth column was obliged to function as an invisible hand for Beijing to level the political playing field, to boost its popular support and to consolidate its power from within. In putting in the fifth column, Beijing hoped that its future interests in the Hong Kong Special Administrative Region (HKSAR) would be accommodated and its long-term political goals catered for.

Although the logic of Beijing's fifth column policy has emanated from underlying fears, suspicion and distrust, the policy itself has not been operated with a single and strictly defined goal. The evolution of the policy objectives of the fifth column has demonstrated the vulnerability, volatility and dynamics of the policy process in general. This chapter finds that there was an enormous discrepancy between the expectation of the policy makers in Beijing and the actual implementation of the operational standards and effectiveness of the fifth columnists in Hong Kong's capitalist reality. Notably, the transformation of the fifth columnists themselves and the fluctuation in the perceived need for continuing such a policy among the policy-making bureaucracy were accompanied by two parallel events: the institutionalization of a more open, flexible Chinese foreign policy regime characterized by strong performance of the official representative bodies in the territory; and the development of domestic politics shaped by weakening central control *vis-à-vis* ascendancy of local, sectoral and group bargaining power. The trends in the operation's scale, and in the intensity of fifth column activity in Hong Kong, have reflected changes in Chinese foreign policy from 1983 to 1997 – from a rigid, enclosed and vertically controlled revolutionary policy to a more open, flexible and pragmatic one, which steers a middle course to balance rival forces within the party and to respond to new circumstances. However, although the operational preparedness of the fifth column may have been temporarily weakened, the underlying rationale of the policy has persisted, as demonstrated by the revival of fifth column activity since the early 1990s.

The first section of this chapter summarizes the scope and scale of the fifth column operation, including recruitment procedures, missions and loyalty control issues. This section is based on interviews with high Chinese officials and with dozens of fifth columnists currently working in Hong Kong. The second part analyses the political sources of fifth column policy from the perspective of China's revolutionary historiography, principles of sovereignty and dynamic discourse on domestic and international politics. The final part assesses the fifth column policy implications for Beijing's Hong Kong political agenda, and the likely impact of the policy on power structures of the future HKSAR.

The operation of a fifth column – a hijacked agenda

Fifth column strategy, as an old art of war and politics, can be dated at least to the Peloponnesian War in the fifth century BC. The survival of the fifth column strategy lies in its ability to accomplish what a state could not otherwise achieve by conventional military or political means. The circumstances for deploying fifth columns differed from case to case, but they share the common motivation: to infiltrate and weaken from within.

The Chinese government is a very skilful fifth column operator in its domestic politics. For example, in Tibet and other autonomous regions, the CCP has been systemically dispatching its cadres to penetrate the local border areas and to control the local governments.

The acceleration of the fifth column operation as an auxiliary policy in Hong Kong completed the CCP's organizational programme in Hong Kong. While the CCP's official penetration attracted much public scrutiny, the fifth column activities were quietly going on with little notice. The secretive and almost elusive existence of the fifth column enabled it to evade public interest.

Beijing's political penetration into Hong Kong's social fibre has been all encompassing. The fifth column policy was intended to expand the CCP's power base into the marginal areas and to shore up its support from below. These fifth columnists were nominally detached from any official Chinese organizations in Hong Kong and they exercised substantial economic freedom and autonomy, which differentiated them from those employees with official status working for the Chinese government establishments.

Due to the secrecy of the overall CCP cadre establishment in Hong Kong, the exact number of them is very difficult to confirm.[1] According to Xu Jiatun, former head of XHNA Hong Kong, in 1983 there were only about 6000–7000 CCP members in Hong Kong and Macao, among whom those of mainland origin numbered about 3000, with more than half being local CCP members (Xu 1993, p 69). Although China is now the legitimate sovereign of Hong Kong, the communist party system still cannot operate as it does in mainland China due to Beijing's international commitment in the two basic documents.[2] These constraints have been the critical factors in forcing Beijing to adopt a different approach to the operation of its party system in Hong Kong.

One distinctive characteristic of Hong Kong's immigration is that 95 per cent of current Hong Kong residents have their roots in mainland China (Hong Kong Annual Report 1995). Family reunion, with its humanitarian connotations, tends to arouse sympathy from others. It can, therefore easily be exploited to advance a hidden agenda. That was exactly what Beijing did, hijacking the immigration agreements between Hong Kong and China to serve its own political aspirations.

Beijing has always put great emphasis on enhancing its strength and power in Hong Kong. Immigration to Hong Kong has long represented a convenient and legal avenue for Beijing to further explore power consolidation in the Territory. The initiation of Sino-British negotiations on Hong Kong greatly increased the political imperative, and the sensitivity of immigration to Hong Kong. Ever since then, questions of who would stay in Hong Kong and what they would do before and after 1997 have become matters of considerable importance to the leaders in Beijing. There is little doubt that, left to its own devices, Beijing would almost certainly have flooded Hong Kong with larger numbers of mainland cadres. But under the watchful eyes of countries and parties who had a high stake in Hong Kong, Beijing's choices were circumscribed. Under such circumstances, to hijack the existing immigration programme became an attractive option.

Organizing the fifth column[3]

In early 1983, the Central Organization Department of the CCP was instructed to oversee a programme, in consultation with relevant ministries and government agencies, to dispatch officials to Hong Kong with one-way exit permits as immigrants for 'family reunion'. These immigrants were different from those people who had working visa status in Hong Kong Chinese establishments, who were to return to mainland on completion of their work assignment.

At the central government level, five major sponsoring bodies – the Office of Hong Kong and Macao Affairs (HKMAO), the Ministry of State Security (MSS), the Department of United Front, the Office of Overseas Chinese and the Office of Taiwan Affairs – were responsible for organizing, supervising and coordinating the recruitment and management of the 'outpost' cadres at the central level. All these five bodies, except HKMAO, have affiliations at most provincial (or equivalent) levels. The governments of the eastern coastal provinces and autonomous municipalities enjoyed some privileges and were actively involved in the programme.

Recruitment

The recruitment of the fifth columnists started as early as 1983 and steadily increased in subsequent years. It peaked twice in the 13 years: in 1986–1987 and 1991–1993. An annual centrally controlled quota system was adopted at the central government level, which would partially trickle down to the local affiliations. But a quota plus 'actual requirement' principle with considerable flexibility was practised at the nominated provincial government levels.

This meant that, although the local governments might not receive the same quota as some of the central government agencies, or different local governments might receive unequal quotas among themselves, they could somewhat compensate for the deficiency by siphoning additional numbers from the locally controlled quota of normal immigrants to Hong Kong for the 'family reunion'. For example, certain provincial governments received a smaller quota from the central system as compared to Guangdong, but each year these governments jockeyed to use more of the locally controlled immigration quota to catch up with Guangdong, or at least tried hard not to fall too far behind.[4] Of course, proper justifications for such actions were expected to be lodged with the Central Organization Department. This meant a substantial reduction of actual quota for the genuine 'family reunion' applicants.

It is worth noting that the central government gave tacit consent to local adjustment as a way of balancing regional interests. In reality, however, the borders of the central and local quotas were often blurred, because instead of being in a neatly defined vertical relationship, a complex partnership network was formed horizontally as well as vertically to promote multiple interests and to radiate influence. This irregularity in practice complicated efforts to reach a firm headcount of the fifth columnists in Hong Kong.

It is believed that there was no uniform or rigid approach to recruit the fifth columnists from all ranks of ministries, departments, agencies and local bureaucracy, despite strict rules and regulations issued by the Central Organization Department requesting all its affiliates to comply with them. Interviews with dozens of CCP fifth column recruits[5] in Hong Kong at the end of 1996 revealed a very complicated situation that indicated the substantial erosion of the original guiding principles for the fifth column operation, the seduction of the fifth columnists themselves by the Hong Kong capitalist society, and the evaporation of the designed effectiveness of the mission.

One somewhat surprising selection practice observed is the absence of any institutional mechanism in the head-hunt. Instead, it seemed the process depended on a few people's assessment, opinions, power and networks. Contrary to the increasingly regularized and institutionalized Chinese bureaucracy in the reform era, the selection procedure virtually emulated the CCP's party member recruitment technique of the 1920s and 1930s – i.e. individuals in charge had the right to appoint or recommend candidates. Of course, the candidates' work units needed to give political clearance to the appointees, but they were not consulted beforehand and were left with little choice but to accept the *fait accompli.*

The interviewees reported that in the early years (early 1980s), the rules and regulations were more strictly observed than in later years (late 1980s and early 1990s). With the passage of time, this kind of practice was a sure guarantee of corruption. Some organizations and individuals with power turned the recruitment process into a lucrative market for themselves to cash in on, and the general loss of the central government's grip and subsequent laxity also allowed more room for corruption.

It is reported that the level of corruption worsened in those traditionally more 'protected' institutions, which had strong links with both central and local governments. The coastal provincial Department of State Security, for example, was a powerful unit, administered under the dual leadership of both the Ministry of State Security and the local provincial government. In the case of recruitment of fifth columnists, one particular provincial Department of State Security was given a quota directly by the MSS. At the same time it was also always successful in demanding an additional quota from local government. Although the Ministry of State Security was only established in 1983, it has since enjoyed a special status and treatment both at the central and local government levels because of its claimed importance in safeguarding the nation's security. Over the years, its need for deploying its own staff in Hong Kong was largely met, but with 'extra' quota at its disposal, it started to look for possible candidates from other departments and interested parties to trade-off the quota. The currency in this exchange could be money, favours, promotion, housing, jobs or other privileges. In reality, this strong bargaining position gave the local office of the MSS a powerful leverage over other agencies and individuals who were also eagerly trying to expand their sectoral and personal power base in Hong Kong. This practice was reported to be a great source for corruption, and caused considerable resentment among the fifth columnists.

There was a general understanding between the sponsoring bodies and the fifth columnists that, in guaranteeing them one-way exit permits, the government did not accept responsibility for giving their spouses and children the same treatment. In theory, their family members would need to join the long waiting queue for 'family reunion'. In reality, however, most of them brought their family members across the border in a relatively short span of time. This was again the pay-off for 'good connection plus good money'. For the mainland officials and authorities, this created yet another opportunity for them to seek personal gain.

Missions

Over the 13-year period, the original mission of the operation underwent a series of transformations and redefinitions in line with the fluid political developments in Hong Kong – from one of the instinctive and crude reaction of the early 1980s to the more sophisticated and targeted manipulation of today. The earlier approach was strongly influenced by the cold war's rigidity and the simplicity of Chinese foreign policy thinking, while the latter responded to the changing policy setting and work priorities.

While the CCP was strongly committed to a fifth column policy in Hong Kong from the outset, the policy objectives changed throughout these years, intentionally or otherwise, to serve perceived political needs. The irony is that, contrary to the official mission statement, which was mainly based on long-term political considerations, many individuals/groups involved in the process took a free ride and mainly aimed at obtaining immediate and quick personal gains.

Three stages can be perceived in the transformation of the fifth column's missions in Hong Kong. In the first stage (1982–1984), as mentioned above, the mission was initiated as a political insurance policy. It was a time when the cold war mentality still prevailed in China's foreign policy thinking, with strong distrust of British intentions for the future of Hong Kong. The second stage (1985–1989) witnessed smooth co-operation between the Chinese and British governments in resolving a series of transitional issues. It was during this period that the Chinese official establishments expanded rapidly and functioned well. It was against this backdrop that the original mission of the fifth column seemed out of context and faded into irrelevance. However, it was also during this period that the previous undercurrent of seeking personal profit through power and connections in the recruitment process of fifth columnists surfaced and spread widely across all levels of the bureaucracy. In fact, the practice became such a lucrative business that it generated a market and momentum of its own, which was somewhat independent of the original policy stimuli. In the third stage (1989–1997), a breakdown of the Sino-British consensus occurred on the scale and speed of political reform in Hong Kong following the 1989 Tiananmen incident, which to a large extent, saw the revival of the logic of the fifth column policy as stated in the first stage. Patten's 1992 political reform and two Legislative Council election results clearly implied, in the eyes of Beijing, that a future problem would lie in the need to woo votes and win 'numbers' under universal suffrage. It was this electoral imperative that added a new dimension to the mission of the fifth column – a new role as a voting bloc in the post-1997 period.

Loyalty control

The official selection process (i.e. expression of interest, clearance by the work unit and file with the organization department) stressed the primacy of political awareness and reliability as criteria for screening the candidates. Evidently, as part of the routine, the candidates were urged to contact XHNA in Hong Kong to 'keep each other informed', and to turn to XHNA for assistance when 'encountering difficulties'. This, in fact, referred to a reporting system as well as a surveillance mechanism. Candidates were also encouraged to keep in touch with the sponsoring bodies by submitting written 'progress reports' at regular intervals of 6 to 12 months. Other forms of contact included oral reports and facilitating visits by officials from the sponsoring bodies.

Most of the fifth columnists had irregular contact with Hong Kong XHNA in the early years of their arrival, but that quickly faded away as 'other work' took priority. The majority of them, however, kept regular contact with their mainland sponsoring bodies by establishing extended commercial networks or through business transactions. Informal oral reports were common when opportunities arose (e.g. two-way visits either to the mainland or to Hong Kong).

This meant that the fifth columnists' activities were largely outside the direct scrutiny of the party network in Hong Kong. Indeed, compared with those working within the official outlets and publicly identified CCP cadres, the fifth columnists enjoyed enormous privileges and freedom. Some of them had received a certain amount of financial assistance from sponsoring bodies in China to kick-start their new life in Hong Kong. When the businesses were rolling along, they usually tried to pay the 'loans' off quickly so that they could be 'debt-free' and have more autonomy in their business decisions. Others were just given the opportunity to 'swim' by themselves. Most of these people were doing well because of their close connections with the mainland and their sound knowledge of business norms in Hong Kong, due to the fact that most of them had previous working experience with Chinese official establishments in Hong Kong. These people usually were in their 30s or 40s, with good education, training and skills. Despite their relatively late entry into the game, generally they were survivors and faring well.

The presence of a large fifth column in Hong Kong with a loose loyalty control mechanism was, at least, suggestive of the CCP's poor management of, or an inability to handle effectively, the policy under the challenging circumstances of Hong Kong. It is hard to imagine that those mainland cadres who were used to party discipline and authoritarian supervision would not behave differently when a conflict of interests arose.

This state of inertia and lack of coordinated supervision were perhaps caused mainly by the CCP's inadequate command of resources in Hong Kong, which prevented it from putting in place a more efficient control regime. Some traditional mainland practices, such as political coercion and reward, would not be suited to Hong Kong's reality. Despite China's awareness of the potential danger of the lapse of loyalty – hence closer attention paid to the selection criteria and recruitment procedures – the apparent drifting of loyalty remained a sticking point for successful operation.

Loyalty control, however, took a different form, by linking up with commercial interests and opportunities. Maintaining loyalty to sponsoring bodies in the mainland was often rewarded handsomely with favourable trading conditions and business opportunities, which enabled the fifth columnists to succeed and prosper amid fierce competition in Hong Kong. This mutually beneficial arrangement was very important in the Chinese economic system, which was often marred by non-transparency and irregularity of the policy regime. As with many other aspects of Chinese politics, doing business with the mainland relied, to a large extent on the goodwill of party leaders and government agencies.

The political sources of Beijing's fifth column

As mentioned earlier, although China pursued the fifth column policy in Hong Kong from 1983, the perceived value of the policy to the PRC changed immensely over the years. For example, the need for the policy in 1983 arose from the fear that to fully rely on an institutionalized process would not serve China's best interest in Hong Kong. By the time of the handover, the perceived value of the policy seemed to be to shore up the pro-Beijing voting bloc in future HKSAR elections. In any case, the underlying rationale for the CCP to commit to the fifth column policy in

Hong Kong remains unchanged – namely, a political insurance policy for an uncertain future.

The atmosphere of suspicion and distrust between the Chinese and the British as a result of the dispute over sovereignty and political reform was mutual. For the British, the suspicion stemmed from distrust of communists, and from observing the post-1949 domestic record of the CCP, which featured drastic policy shifts and costly mistakes. For China, the roots of suspicion were buried deep in the history of nineteenth century imperialist expansion in China, the same history that created Hong Kong's colonial rule. The Chinese predisposition to distrust the British intensified after Margaret Thatcher's claim in 1982 to British sovereignty in Hong Kong, and her suggestion that the Chinese leadership should be careful to honour their international agreements (i.e. the three unequal treaties). Indeed, the atmosphere surrounding talks on the Territory's future was consistently poisoned by the sense among British officials that the Chinese could not be trusted to allow Hong Kong to prosper on its own, and the sense among Chinese officials that the British were seeking a means to continue their control of Hong Kong, or at least to enrich themselves with the colony's booty before they departed.

Up to this point, the operation of Beijing's fifth column in Hong Kong prior to China's resumption of sovereignty has been the focus of attention. The important question is this: why has China been pursuing such a policy given that its sovereign rights have already been recognized and guaranteed in the Joint Declaration and the Basic Law? In other words: why did China initiate, and continue to practise, the fifth column policy in a region that would soon be under its own jurisdiction?

The analysis that follows focuses on the political factors underpinning the CCP's decision to embark on the fifth column policy, in conjunction with its official effort, to expand the party's political power-base and to influence the future direction of Hong Kong. It demonstrates that, with a heavy historical burden and ideological tradition, the policy makers in Beijing actually had limited intellectual choice in their strategic thinking and policy approach to Hong Kong either in the early 1980s or in the mid-1990s. Domestic politics and international forces determined not only that China would take Hong Kong back, but also the way in which the restoration would be accomplished. Indigenous nationalist movements, the CCP's concept of sovereignty and its assessment of Hong Kong's political development throughout the transitional period are the keys to understanding China's fifth column policy toward Hong Kong.

Accordingly, this section will explore three issues. Firstly, Hong Kong in the Chinese revolutionary historiography is discussed to juxtapose the positions of nationalism and communism over the issue of Hong Kong. Secondly, China's attitude towards sovereignty on Hong Kong is highlighted to identify the CCP's intellectual basis for a fifth column policy in Hong Kong. Thirdly, the fluid Chinese domestic political situation and the changes in Hong Kong's political balance since the early 1980s are analysed to reveal the dynamic process of this policy.

Hong Kong in the Chinese revolutionary historiography

The Nationalist struggle to recover Hong Kong before 1949

Modern Chinese history has two major themes: the foreign occupation of Chinese territories through various treaties and conventions on the one hand, and strong anti-imperialist and anti-colonialist movements on the other. Dr Sun Yat-sen, the first President of the Republic of China after the Chinese Revolution of 1911, criticized the treaties concluded by the Qing Dynasty and the western powers as unequal. Sun argued that the western powers' political and economic oppression made China a 'hypo-colony',[6] and in his will, Sun urged his followers again that 'the abolition of unequal treaties should be carried into effect with the least possible delay'.[7]

At the 1931 National People's Convention, the Guomindang government proclaimed the 'Manifesto Concerning the Abrogation of Unequal Treaties' (Manifesto 1931, pp 461–465) and concluded:

> The Chinese people will not recognize all the past unequal treaties imposed by the Powers on China.
>
> The National Government shall, in conformity with Dr Sun Yat-sen's testamentary injunction, achieve with least possible delay China's equality and independence in the Family of Nations.

As a result of Chinese pressure and a stronger Chinese government, the western powers considered giving up part of their privileges in China, among them extraterritoriality. The UK was also pressured to renounce its concessions at Hankou and Jinjiang in 1928 and to return the leased territory of Weihaiwei in 1930, but the British did not return Hong Kong, including the New Territories. By the 1920s, Hong Kong was important to the British for Far Eastern trade and it remained in Britain's interest to continue to rule Hong Kong while relinquishing some extraterritorial privileges in China (Lane 1990, pp 44–45). The Guomindang government was not powerful enough to gain abrogation of all the treaties in one move. In 1931, Japan occupied Manchuria, and the next year attacked Shanghai. Japan's rapid encroachment upon large Chinese territories threatened China's survival, and responding to Japan was more urgent than abolition of the unequal treaties for the Guomindang government. In 1949, the Guomindang was overthrown by the Chinese Communists, ending its opportunity to settle the Hong Kong issue.

The CCP's position on the recovery of Hong Kong

The CCP was a strongly anti-imperialist and anti-colonialist party. The Manifesto of the Second Congress of the Party, published in 1922, pointed out that China was under 'the domination of international imperialism' and had been 'trampled underfoot by Britain, the United States, France and Japan'. The manifesto further stated that imperialist oppression of China and competition among imperialist powers for economic interests in China 'accounts for China's present special status in the field of international relations' (Hu 1955, pp 269–270).

In his 1939 Essay, *The Chinese Revolution and the Chinese Communist Party*, Mao argued that the Western powers 'forced China to conclude numerous unequal treaties', and that the primary task of the Chinese revolution was 'the national revolution for the overthrow of imperialism' (Mao 1954, pp 78–87). Mao, therefore, concluded that the Chinese revolution was to continue the national liberation movement of fighting colonialism and imperialism, dating from the Opium War of 1840 (North 1978, p 82).

In 1948, when the People's Liberation Army (PLA) was approaching the southern part of China, the total strength of forces available to the British to defend Hong Kong was at most 25 000 (Commonwealth Relations Office 1949). It was believed initially that the People's Republic of China was determined to take military steps to recover Hong Kong. Regarding itself as the leading power in the Chinese anti-imperialist and anti-colonialist movement, the Communist Party had no conflict of principles towards a takeover of the British colony, which would have wiped out the humiliation that the nineteenth century treaties represented. Moreover, a takeover could increase the new China's prestige among Third World countries.

However, the CCP decided not to take over Hong Kong immediately after it obtained power on the mainland. It is clear that the CCP's attitude towards the existence of Hong Kong as a British colony was significant for the island's survival. The emergence of the People's Republic as a military power after the Korean War had strongly reinforced this point. It is not clear how the Korean War affected British foreign policy towards Asia and in particular towards, Hong Kong, however, in 1952 Britain did change its position on Hong Kong and abandoned its plan to defend Hong Kong if it came under a large-scale Chinese military attack. A British Cabinet memorandum (which was not released at that time to the public) stated: 'We do not consider that our strategy in Hong Kong should be changed by a French withdrawal from Indo-China, although it may be necessary to maintain a larger garrison to ensure internal security and, if attacked, to cover an orderly evacuation' (Miners 1990, pp 223–246). This secret document revealed that in the early 1950s, Hong Kong's status became uncertain and that the British were prepared to withdraw from their colony if Beijing determined to recover Hong Kong militarily.

After the Korean War, the PRC was more confident of its military capability and demonstrated that it was willing to use force to take disputed border territories.[8] China's military capability may be one of the reasons that the Chinese were firm about sovereignty over Hong Kong in the 1980s.

The Qing Dynasty had lost Hong Kong 140 years earlier when the Chinese were defeated in the Opium Wars, but in the 1980s, although the UK was still one of the leading military powers, it had lost its dominant position in relation to China.

In conclusion, in the Chinese revolutionary historiography Hong Kong has been perceived as living evidence of the imperialist, in particular the British, carving of Chinese territory when China was weak, and as a symbol of national humiliation at the hands of western powers. Though the Communists and the Nationalists differed fundamentally in ideology, their strong nationalist sentiment on the Hong Kong issue was identical. It was unthinkable that during the Sino-British negotiations in the early 1980s, the policy makers in Beijing would agree to a continuation of British rule over Hong Kong because no Chinese leader wanted to be viewed by posterity as a traitor or to be condemned by the people. Deng Xiaoping may have summed up the real feelings of the policy makers in Beijing when he said that he would not be another Li Hongzhang. Strong Chinese nationalism was the real crux of Chinese efforts leading to the 1984 Hong Kong settlement, and the outcome of the settlement cannot be correctly explained without an understanding of that tradition.

Hong Kong and the issue of sovereignty

The concept of sovereignty is central to the CCP leadership's approach to the Hong Kong issue. The PRC also considers the principle of sovereignty to be one of the most important principles of international law and has always been sensitive towards the question of sovereignty.

The fundamental change in China's domestic politics and the shift of the CCP's focus from class struggle to economic development helped the emergence of a new pragmatism. This, in turn, enabled Chinese decision makers to be more flexible in dealing with sensitive issues, such as economic relations and foreign investment. China determined to accept the constraints of increased commercial and military links with the outside world, while at the same time making efforts to preserve its sovereignty and autonomy.

There were several reasons why the Chinese leadership chose to adopt this position on the question of sovereignty. Firstly, the top Chinese leaders were from the old revolutionary generation, which had long experience of fighting foreign powers and foreign influence. For them, the unification of China was particularly important and was a special task they were determined to complete.

Secondly, any concessions on the issue of sovereignty would bring about great political damage to those who made them. Prior to the Sino-British negotiations, Deng Xiaoping was on the point of consolidating his leading position in China. However, his power was far from being absolute. He had to balance different factions within the party, particularly the reformers and the orthodox leaders. To remain firm on China's position on recovering sovereignty would add to Deng's national prestige and further consolidate his authority.

Thirdly, the issue of sovereignty was a matter that applied not only to Hong Kong and Macao, but also had great relevance to the question of Taiwan and, potentially, to the position of Tibet and other national minority regions. Beijing considered that any concession on its position on sovereignty would lead to a domino effect.

In the final analysis, the Chinese leadership would not compromise over the issue of sovereignty. The proposal by the British government for 'divided sovereignty' only served as a reminder to Beijing that the British government was trying to extend its colonial rule in Hong Kong. This interpretation further alarmed the leadership in Beijing and impacted directly on the formation of the fifth column policy in Hong Kong. To Beijing, Chinese sovereignty in Hong Kong came close to meaning control over its affairs.

Dynamics of the policy process[9]

As observed previously, although the underlying rationale of the CCP's fifth column policy in Hong Kong was consistent, the objectives of the policy were nonetheless redefined several times to accommodate political volatility both in China and in Hong Kong. This dynamic nature of the policy itself has reflected the enormous complexity, subtlety and rapid changes in Chinese foreign policy during this period.

Chinese resumption of sovereignty over Hong Kong was an unprecedented event in world decolonization history. For Chinese leaders, the bottom line of the negotiation was the reversion of both sovereignty and administration to China. In accepting the burden of administration of Hong Kong, CCP leaders were clearly aware that in order to maintain Hong Kong's economic wealth, they had to allow it to practise different rules from those on the mainland. They were also prepared to bargain and to concede. On one hand, it is of great significance for China to live up to its international commitment to 'One Country – Two Systems', and to keep the present Hong Kong life style unchanged for 50 years. The highly experimental nature of this formulation would impact directly on the prospect of the future return of Taiwan. On the other hand, it is vitally important for Chinese leaders to consolidate and expand the CCP's real power in Hong Kong under such an arrangement. A strong and successful model in Hong Kong would not only serve to allay fears in Taiwan, but also would function inwardly to counter increasing separatist pressures from some remote areas.[10]

Once the date of handover was agreed, China's policy towards the Hong Kong transition was characterized as aiming at '13 years of great change and 50 years of no change' (*shisan nian da bian, wushi nian bu bian*) (Xu 1993, pp 131–162). This meant China was fully aware of the importance of the rule-laying 13 years leading up to 1997. Despite the unprecedented flexibility shown by Chinese leaders in conducting foreign relations, and despite a series of bilateral agreements guaranteed by international laws, some leaders in Beijing still found it hard to abandon totally the old revolutionary wisdom and practice in favour of a transparent and institutional process on their way to the handover. They were still worried by nagging doubts over where the CCP's power would lie after 1997, and whether the institutional framework was sufficient to guarantee the party's interests. For them, flexibility was acceptable only if the central government's political power was not placed in jeopardy.

During the transition period of 1984–1997, both the Chinese and British governments were actively engaged in a range of political manoeuvres to capture future political ground and maintain or expand economic influence. When the row occurred over Chris Patten's 1992 political reform package, Beijing's suspicion of the motives of the British colonial government in its sunset years was fuelled by 'hard' evidence. In the words of Zhou Nan, Director of XHNA Hong Kong Branch, as reported by *Ta Kung Pao*, the retreat of colonial power would never be a voluntary act, and a smooth transfer of power had to be fought for (BBC 1994).

Behind the furious open political disputes, something much more subtle had been quietly going on for some time. Drawing upon a rich repertoire of the CCP's underground struggle experience and Mao's base theory,[11] the fifth column policy was originally designed to be political insurance. As events unfolded, the policy was later intended to win support from the basic constituency in elections, and to maximize the CCP's influence among ordinary voters.

For the CCP, the painful revolutionary past fortified a deep-rooted suspicion of the western powers. Furthermore, the prevailing distrust of institutional and bureaucratic power among the ruling elite added complexity to the policy discourse. The united front, which contributed to the 1949 victory, found its contemporary application in the CCP's handling of transitional Hong Kong. Deng's 1983 definition of 'Hong Kong people' offered scope for Beijing to establish a broad 'united front' in Hong Kong.[12] This was implemented through the appointment of ever more prominent business figures to advisory and preparatory committees. Yet, the 'velvet glove' needed the backing of an iron fist, and this was the fifth column policy.

In the minds of Chinese leaders, the worst scenario would be that in Hong Kong, through democratic procedures, the extreme 'right' wing (personified by Martin Lee) would be elected to political prominence. Deng's views on political intervention by the central government in Hong Kong clearly indicated Beijing's deep concern that Hong Kong, left as it was, could become a base for subversion against the mainland.[13] The provision in the Basic Law on subversion[14] is clearly designed to institutionalize the illegality of political opposition to Beijing, and to minimize the political damage to China and Hong Kong. It is also for this reason that in the Basic Law, the formation of the HKSAR government and associated appointments were placed under the close supervision of the central government. Beijing thus ensured its share of power in the future Hong Kong, both at the nominal and actual levels.

Although in recent years the evolution of the CCP's influence in the upper levels of Hong Kong society roughly paralleled the increased official Chinese representation, Beijing had little leverage to manoeuvre the popular sentiment of the vast majority, given the CCP's vulnerability at the lower level of society, with many of the residents having fled the CCP's rule in China over previous decades.

This concern, too, was one of the original catalysts that caused Beijing to initiate its fifth column programme in Hong Kong in 1983. Chris Patten's reform package in 1992 confirmed to Beijing the wisdom of such a policy. Despite constant denials of its existence by both the Chinese and British governments, the fifth column in Hong Kong was an open secret and emerged to be a far from negligible political force.

The fifth column and Hong Kong's political future

The above analysis of Beijing's fifth column policy has touched on our understanding of the logic, sources and strategy of the fifth column policy in Hong Kong. This study has also shown a complicated and contradictory picture of the policy in practice. The recruitment procedures, goal setting, and loyalty control of the fifth columnists became increasingly problematic, raising genuine doubts about the necessity and effectiveness of continuing such a policy. There was no easy solution to these problems, however.

Beijing's rationale for the fifth column policy in Hong Kong can only be fully appreciated in the context of the interaction between international politics and domestic politics in China. Since Deng's reform era began in the late 1970s China's foreign policy has undergone a great change: 'a continuing process of learning and adjustment' (Chan 1989, p 154). The profound transformation in China's economic philosophy, structure and productivity have provided the conditions for the Beijing leadership to move gradually from rigidity toward flexibility in its foreign policy thinking. Furthermore, the dynamics of international power politics have significantly influenced China's foreign policy. Foreign policy can be rigid or flexible depending upon how Beijing calculates its own interests in the changing international environment, and the importance the policy may have for the regime's legitimacy. Such changes do not necessarily indicate a fundamental shift of principles in foreign policy thinking, however. China has remained consistent in its basic stand over a range of issues, despite the uncertain impact of power politics on the political discourse.

This study has identified the twin sets of factors that have been pro-pelling the fifth column policy, despite the problems of which the CCP was aware. First, there is the influence of domestic politics. When Beijing ini-tiated the fifth column programme, there was still strong influence on foreign policy calculation from Mao's era. As shown by the discussion in the previous section, the mission for the fifth columnists at that stage was both broad and vague. Later, the successful evolution of official Chinese political representation in Hong Kong in the mid- and late-1980s effec-tively advanced Chinese institutional power sufficiently to ensure the CCP's vested interests in the HKSAR.

One would assume that under such circumstances the original rationale of the CCP's fifth column programme in Hong Kong would become irrele-vant, therefore the policy might be terminated altogether. The evidence shows that the CCP continued this policy vigorously, however, even though the original rationale had gradually faded away.

The explanation for this highlights an interesting dimension of China's domestic politics. As noted earlier, within the Chinese bureaucracy there appeared a group of 'leeches' who preyed upon potential fifth columnists. These people possessed the practical power that enabled them to pursue an agenda that was not necessarily coincident with the party's objectives, and most of them seemed to concern themselves only with money grabbing or advancing their personal interests. This tendency reduced the party's 'strategic vision' and limited the effectiveness of the policy. The opportu-nity to become a fifth columnist was downgraded to a valuable commodity to be exchanged in the market place. In fact, the selection of fifth colum-nists represented such a lucrative business, and was so pervasive among officials at various levels, that many depended on it for continuing per-sonal prosperity. Strong resistance could therefore be expected from the bureaucracy should the operation be scrapped.

In addition, the fifth columnists, hand-picked by various party agencies, represented an elite group within the Chinese system. For the CCP, the operation of the fifth column policy served various interests: on one hand it strengthened Beijing's position in Hong Kong by grooming its new generation of proxies; on the other, it further cemented and expanded the patron/client relationship between the party and certain individuals/families/groups, thereby further consolidating the CCP's domestic political control and leverage.

In addition, as noted earlier, there was the influence of international events. Beijing's suspicions of British intentions regarding Hong Kong were renewed following the Major government's sanctions in late 1989, and Patten's 1992 political reform package. Both events impacted pro-foundly on Beijing's reading of Hong Kong's political situation. This was evidenced by the second peak of fifth columnists sent to Hong Kong in the early 1990s and the more conscious focus on electoral prospects.

There is no doubt that Beijing regards the HKSAR as highly experimental, and it remains jealous of any rules of the game set by others (e.g. Patten's democratic reform). By monopolizing political appointments and manipulating the ballot box, Beijing hopes to maintain sufficient numbers of pro-China people in the executive/legislative branches and in the business community and, importantly, to obtain a respectable vote in any future elections based on universal suffrage.

At a conservative estimate, around 20 per cent[15] of the total 'family reunion' immigrants to Hong Kong from China during the period 1983–97 were fifth columnists, a figure of more than 83 000, or over 1.4 per cent of the total Hong Kong population of 6 million. Taking as the parameter the 35 per cent of Hong Kong's 2.6 million registered voters (Stormont 1995) who cast their ballots in the 1995 Legislative Council election – the highest ever turnout in the Territory – the estimated 83 000 fifth columnists alone could have on that occasion accounted for more than 9.12 per cent of Hong Kong's active electoral voters. Of course, not all of them were then qualified to vote, as a seven-year residential status is required before the granting of voting rights. This number does indicate, however, that if Hong Kong is going to operate with a high degree of autonomy, and gradually evolve into a more democratic society as China has promised, then this voting bloc will become very significant, and will be well-positioned to play a strategically important role long after the handover. Viewed in this way, from the Chinese leaders' perspective, the fifth column policy, despite its many controversies, has indeed been a worthwhile effort after all.

Notes

1 Jonathan Mirsky, East Asia Editor of *The Times* (London) told the author that the information 'leaked' by a friend in Special Branch indicated that from 23 000 to 28 000 Communist Party members are currently active in Hong Kong. Willy Wo-Lap Lam, Associate Editor and China Editor of the *South China Morning Post* gave a more conservative figure of about 15 000. For a further discussion of the size and operations of the underground party cell, see 'Communists Mark Time Under Wraps', *Guardian* (London), 2 September 1995, and 'China's Magic Tool for Hong Kong', *The Economist*, 18 March 1995.

2 Although in the two basic documents – the Joint Declaration of 1984 and the Basic Law of 1990 – there is no mention of the roles of the CCP in the HKSAR, they do explicitly express the commitment of the Chinese government to maintaining a high degree of autonomy for the Hong Kong local government.

3 This section is based on notes of interviews with CCP officials in November and December 1996.

4 Interviews with senior Chinese officials, December 1996.

5 During fieldwork in November/December 1996, the author interviewed several dozen people who were recruited under the one-way exit permit scheme and currently work in Hong Kong. They are scattered all over the territory and engaged in a variety of businesses. One thing they have in common is that they all

assumed new names, changed identities and faked backgrounds when they registered with Hong Kong immigration authorities upon their first arrival in the territory. All the confidential material identifying these people has been documented and sighted by the Australian National University.

6   Sun Yat-sen wrote: The result is that China is everywhere becoming a colony of the Powers. The people of the nation still think we are only a 'semi-colony' and comfort themselves with this term, but in reality we are being crushed by the economic strength of the powers to a greater degree than if we were a full colony. China is not the colony of one nation but of all, and we are not the slaves of one country but of all. I think we ought to be called a 'hypo-colony.' See Sun's *San Min Chu I: The Three Principles of the People*, translator Frank W. Price, The Commission for the Compilation of the History of the Guomindang, Taipei: China Publishing, no date: I, 10.

7   *Ibid.* Sun's appeals represented the voice of the Chinese people. In 1895 Kang Youwei made a similar argument. He wrote, 'It is a well-known fact that in ancient times, countries were destroyed by the armed might of other countries. But today countries are ruined by foreign trade, a thing which is overlooked by everybody. When a country is conquered by the armed forces of another country, it perishes but its people remain; when a country is destroyed by trade, its people perish together with it. This is the danger now facing China.' *Nanhai Xiansheng Si Shangshu Ji* (Notes on Kang Youwei's Four Memorials to the Emperor), no date or publisher: 15, 21.

8   For example, in 1962 China defeated its neighbour, India, in a war over a disputed border, and in 1969 it fought with the Soviet Union for possession of Zhenbao Island, located on the Ussuri River border. In the 1970s and 1980s, the Chinese initiated several military attacks against the Vietnamese in the Spratly and Paracel Islands in the South China Sea, which both China and Vietnam claimed. Chinese military power could also be seen in its possession of an atomic bomb in 1964, its production of a hydrogen bomb in 1967 and in its launching of a satellite in 1970.

9   Hong Kong's transfer to China is more than just a symbolic act manipulated by emotion. This point was made clear when Deng rejected Margaret Thatcher's suggestion in the early stage of Sino-British negotiations in 1982 that China regain sovereignty while the British continue the mandate to exercise administrative power.

10   It is interesting to note parallel developments in other dimensions of Hong Kong life. In 1982 the PRC had already been debating the terms of reference for setting up Shenzhen and Xiamen Special Economic Zones, with a strong political consensus among the leadership to erect the second border to insulate Hong Kong from the rest of China. There existed a strong desire at the centre to exert bureaucratic and political control over the commercial southerners, particularly the Cantonese. Guangdong was, for centuries, a major trading centre of southern China. The Qing government wanted to keep all foreigners away from the centre and therefore decreed that all foreign trade was to be conducted through Guangdong. The Guangdong area had always posed difficult problems for the central government because it was far from the capital and also because of social differences. The Cantonese had been antagonistic towards the Manchus in the north.

After the establishment of the People's Republic, the leaders in Beijing were determined to guard against a flourishing of Cantonese localism. Through the campaign of land reform of 1950–1952, the centre achieved its aim of establishing a disciplined local administration with strong central control. As a result of land reform, 80 per cent of the local cadres of the rank of county-level leaders or above lost their position. However localism has continued and localist sentiment remains strong. The decentralization to provincial level of decision making in economic policy and the introduction of special economic policy in coastal areas have encouraged the regions to increase their strength. The coastal provinces, especially Guangdong, have become more confident in bargaining with Beijing and demanding more autonomy. In the 1980s, the leaders in Beijing became deeply concerned about a challenge from a powerful Guangdong or other coastal region. If local interests became linked with Hong Kong or Macao, such a challenge could have been even more critical. Localism, which had disrupted the nation during the previous century, continues to worry the CCP leaders in an era of reform and greater openness.

11 In the revolutionary era, the Chinese Communist Party built a large and strong contingent of cadres to spearhead and advance its cause from an inferior position. The party relied on Mao's 'base theory', that is to mobilize sufficient manpower and resources to form a solid base for the final victory. Later, Mao's personal prejudice encouraged a distrust of institutional arrangements and bureaucratic processes within the party. Although there are vast differences between today's Hong Kong capitalism and yesterday's guerrilla countryside in the hinterland of China, to the Chinese leadership these concepts remain strong and the basic principles apply. The main teaching of Mao's theory is that when encountered in an inferior position, the best survival tactic is to go underground to buy time to nurture and to build enough strength, to mobilize sufficient manpower and resources, and to form a solid base for the final uprising. The contemporary application of this strategic thinking to Hong Kong's reality shapes the uncompromising determination by the Chinese leadership to secure a high degree of political control, and also the means employed to do so.

12 On 22 June, 1983, Deng Xiaoping defined *Gangren* (Hong Kong people) to a group of Hong Kong industrialists: 'What are Hong Kong people? They are patriots in Hong Kong. The criterion for a patriot is that he agrees that sovereignty be ceded back to the mother country. Only this. Whether he agrees to capitalism or socialism or whatever passport he holds is not important here. Patriotism means agreeing to the recovery of sovereignty and agreeing that Hong Kong belongs to the People's Republic of China. If we have to add one more criterion, it would be love for the mother country and love for Hong Kong, as well as not doing anything detrimental to Hong Kong's prosperity and stability.' English text in H.K. Lame 1984, *A Date with Fate*, Hong Kong: Lincoln Green Publishing, p 201.

13 Deng Xiaoping once stated: 'If Beijing gives up all its rights, chaos might occur and this would be to the detriment of Hong Kong's interests. Therefore to leave some rights with the central authorities would do nothing but good.' 'Will some problems arise in Hong Kong some day which cannot be solved without the central authorities taking the matter up? When something happened in the past, Britain also took the matter up. There are certain things which can hardly be solved without the central authorities dealing with the matter. The central authorities will not infringe upon Hong Kong's interests with their policies. Therefore, I ask you to give consideration to these aspects in the Basic Law. After 1997, if there are people in Hong Kong who condemn the CPC and China,

we will allow them to do so. However, it will not be permitted for condemnations to be turned into actions, or for cloak of 'democracy' (to be used). In such a case, we would have to interfere. We would not necessarily have to call out the troops. Only if great turmoil occurred would troops be called out.' Hong Kong: *Ta Kung Pao*, 29 April 1987.

14 'The Hong Kong Special Administrative Region shall enact laws on its own to prohibit any act of treason, secession, sedition, or subversion against the Central People's government, or theft of state secrets, to prohibit political organizations or bodies of the region from establishing ties with foreign political organizations or bodies.' Article 23, the HKSAR Basic Law, 1990.

15 Interviews with high officials in China, December 1996. 20 per cent was a fairly conservative figure approximating Beijing's projection, but in reality the actual number far exceeded this percentage.

Bibliography

BBC 1994 *Summary of World Broadcasts*, part 3, Far East FE/1994 A2/3.

Chan, G. 1989 *China and International Organisations*. Hong Kong: Oxford University Press.

Commonwealth Relations Office 1949 *Approach to Our Commonwealth* Government *Asking Support of Hong Kong Policy*, FO371 75873. London: Public Record Office, 27 May.

Hong Kong Annual Report 1995, Hong Kong: Government Printing Service.

Hu Sheng 1955 *Imperialism and Chinese Politics*. Beijing: Foreign Language Press, (reprint 1973 Westport, Conn.: Hyperion Press).

Lane, K. P. 1990 *Sovereignty and the Status Quo*. Boulder: Westview Press.

Mao Zedong 1954 'On Chinese Revolution and the Chinese Communist Party', in *Selected Works of Mao Tse-tung*, Vol. 3. London: Lawrence & Wishart.

'Manifesto of the National People's Convention Concerning the Abrogation of Unequal Treaties' 1931. *Chinese Social and Political Science Review* 15 (supplement): 1931–1932, Beijing: National People's Congress.

Miners, N. 1990 *The Government and Politics of Hong Kong*. Hong Kong: Oxford University Press.

North, R. C. 1978 *The Foreign Relations of China*. Cambridge, Mass.: Duxbury Press.

Stormont, D. 1995 'Hong Kong: Polls Close in Historic Hong Kong Elections'. *Reuters News Service*, 17 September.

Xu Jiatun 1993 *Hong Kong Memoir*. Hong Kong: United Publishing House.

8
Power as Non-zero-sum? Central/Local Relations between the Hong Kong Special Administrative Region and Beijing: Opportunities and Closures

Linda Chelan Li

Hong Kong's reunion with China has posed unprecedented opportunities and challenges. What is at stake is not only the well being of the 6 million residents, but also the prospect of China developing a culture wherein open and institutionalized means are used to address conflicts and differences. Hong Kong has been a major source of capital and management know-how for China's modernization efforts; it is also intended, from the perspective of Beijing's leaders, that it should demonstrate how the 'historical problem' of Taiwan may possibly be resolved. Hong Kong's greatest challenge and most important contribution lies ahead, however, in the very fact that it has again become part of China and hence part of Chinese politics.[1] As a provincial-level special administrative region its interaction and relationship with Beijing will shed light on the eternally intriguing question: how can China possibly develop a sustainable and stable central-local relationship? This, in turn, will have tremendous implications for the conduct of politics in general in China.[2]

Against this background, this chapter argues that despite the immense magnitude of the differences between social and political practices in Hong Kong and on the mainland, the Hong Kong–Beijing relationship is not one of a simple zero-sum tug of war between local autonomy and central control. The definitive framework of the relationship is the pledge of 'One Country – Two Systems', which is the product of *both* central government initiative and local conditions and participation. Conflicts are, however, still 'normal' occurrences. This is not only because of the huge differences in circumstances and practices, but also because of the varying judgements by different actors, within and between the central government and Hong Kong, regarding the meaning of such differences, and regarding what is or is not tolerable within the framework of 'One Country – Two Systems'.

One Country – Two Systems

The constitutional pledge of 'One Country – Two Systems' was made by Beijing in the early 1980s to seize the initiative over the future of Hong

Kong. The context of the pledge is historical – that Hong Kong had been officially 'handed over' to Britain, and that a significant socio-economic-political gulf has subsequently developed between Hong Kong under British administration and the Chinese mainland. However, the pledge was made possible only by changes on the mainland (notably the end of Maoist radicalism), which opened up opportunities for a different assessment of national priorities and the perception of new possibilities.[3]

The definitive content of the pledge is, nevertheless, a product of interaction between Beijing, Hong Kong and the UK – through formal negotiations and bargaining by officials, as well as articulation and manoeuvring by societal groupings. The protracted process of the drafting of the Basic Law, the 'mini-constitution' for Hong Kong, which aims to fulfil China's promise, exemplifies how 'fluid' the working meaning of 'One Country – Two Systems' can be (Chan 1991). Interaction does not imply equal participation and influence by all parties. The room for participation for the more liberal groupings and the drafting of members from Hong Kong, for instance, were significantly diminished in the aftermath of the Tiananmen crackdown.[4] Asymmetry of influence notwithstanding, an interactive framework means that the manoeuvres of each party serve to constrain, and form the context of, the choices of the other parties. Moreover, the locus of asymmetry may change. As from 1 July 1997, Hong Kong has assumed a more important, though not exclusive, part in defining the practical meaning of the promise of 'One Country – Two Systems' through the conduct of daily routine in private and public life.[5]

More importantly, the situation is not one of zero-sum tug of war between the HKSAR government seeking autonomy and the central government in Beijing eager to impose control. In both Beijing and Hong Kong, political leaders and the people at large recognize the need for restraint. Beijing accepts that Hong Kong has to retain the high degree of autonomy it had under the British administration in order for Hong Kong to continue to prosper as a major international commercial centre. The people of Hong Kong, meanwhile, generally accept Chinese sovereignty over the territory, and independence has never been seriously considered by more than a few as an option.[6] With Beijing recognizing the need for Hong Kong to be relatively autonomous, and Hong Kong not contesting the claim of Chinese sovereignty and overall responsibility, there is, in fact, a good deal of common ground. Conflicts arise largely around issues of magnitude and circumstance: how far a high degree of local autonomy may extend; and how Chinese sovereignty and overall responsibility are translated into day-to-day administration of public life.

The opportunity for co-operation

The fluidity and ambiguity in the concept of 'One Country – Two Systems' provide ample room for conflict, as well as co-operation, between Beijing and Hong Kong. In contrast to the more common expectation among many observers for conflict, the short history of the HKSAR offers important instances of Beijing–Hong Kong co-operation. The announcement of the electoral system adopted for the 1998 Legislative Council election, for instance, illustrates how far the pre-existing delineation of Beijing–Hong Kong jurisdictions may be amicably redefined.

The point of contention lay in the delineation of jurisdiction of the Beijing-appointed Preparatory Committee[7] and the HKSAR government: whether the electoral system for the 1998 Legislative Council election, one year after the HKSAR was formed, should be decided by a body half of whose members were mainlanders, or by the local government itself. The Preparatory Committee was given the task of prescribing 'the specific method for forming the first Government and the first Legislative Council' by a decision of the Chinese National People's Congress (NPC) adopted on 4 April 1990. At the time, the plan was to have the 'through-train' between the last Legislative Council under the British administration and the first Legislative Council of the SAR. Article 6 of the NPC decision states that, 'if the composition of the last Hong Kong Legislative Council before the establishment of the Hong Kong Special Administrative Region is in conformity with the relevant provisions of this decision and the Basic Law of Hong Kong Special Administrative Region, … members … may, upon confirmation by the Preparatory Committee, become members of the first Legislative Council of the Region'. With the 'through-train' in place no new elections would be required, and thus the intended role of the Preparatory Committee in the formation of the first Legislative Council was largely symbolic and the legal prescription a matter of formality.

The situation changed with the 1992 constitutional reform proposal under the Patten governorship, which resulted in the Chinese government criticizing the British for contravening the Basic Law and subsequently declaring the 'through-train' arrangement dead. The Provisional Legislature was subsequently elected in early 1997 by a 400-member electorate, the formation of which was heavily influenced by Beijing. Without the 'through-train', and with the Provisional Legislature, intended as a transitory body to last for not more than one year,[8] and to be replaced by the first Legislative Council through a reconstituted election in 1998, the new situation saw the original 'symbolic' role of the Preparatory Committee in the formation of the first Legislative Council become one of substantive power.[9]

The dilemma was that with the formation of the HKSAR Government comprising entirely people from Hong Kong, the continuous active role of the Beijing-appointed Preparatory Committee after July 1997 became a strain on the smooth implementation of the central pledge of 'Hong Kong people running Hong Kong'. Electoral matters obviously lie within the domain of 'internal affairs' of the territory, wherein, according to both the Joint Declaration and the Basic Law, Hong Kong is to enjoy a high degree of autonomy.[10] The new Hong Kong leadership is also keen to avoid reinforcing the impression that Beijing is masterminding major decisions for Hong Kong, an impression gained previously due to the heavy involvement of Beijing in the election of the first SAR Chief Executive and the Provisional Legislature. The legitimacy of the new government lies in its ability to live up to the expectation of Hong Kong 'enjoying a high degree of autonomy'.

In the end, the Preparatory Committee (the First Legislative Council Election Sub-group) was approached by the new Executive Council, the 'quasi-cabinet' advising the Chief Executive, to 'exchange views' regarding the electoral arrangements. The Committee was tacitly asked to decide only on the major principles, leaving a lot of room for the SAR government to exercise its choice. In particular, it was mentioned that areas of controversy should be left to the SAR government for final decision, and this could be done by having the Preparatory Committee include a number of options in its 'decision'.[11] The Preparatory Committee had unambiguous legal authority over the election arrangements. Politically, however, a Beijing-appointed body exercising a high-profile role in a politically sensitive and well-reported 'internal' event of Hong Kong would almost certainly be counter-productive to the image of the SAR government in terms of its degree of autonomy. The mood among the new local leadership regarding the importance of conveying a 'proper' public image is indicated by the following observations from a member of the SAR Executive Council:

> Yes, the election system for the first Legislative Council may be under attack by liberal groups for being less democratic than the 1995 election. But this is a political responsibility the SAR government has to shoulder squarely. We cannot and should not seek to avoid becoming the target of attack by asking the Preparatory Committee to make the decision, which may be unpopular, for us. ... The crucial difference between the decision [on the election system] being taken by the Preparatory Committee or by the SAR government lies in that there are mainlanders within the Preparatory Committee, whilst the SAR government is constituted entirely by the people of Hong Kong. Having the SAR government take the decision will live up to the spirit of the central policy of 'Hong Kong people running Hong Kong, and Hong Kong enjoying a high degree of autonomy'.[12]

The request initially met a mixed response from the Preparatory Committee. There was displeasure among some members, including some Chinese officials, but the Hong Kong convenor of the Preparatory Committee sub-group, Lau Siu-kai, Director Lu Ping, and Vice-premier Qian Qichen were apparently receptive.[13] In the end, the Preparatory Committee passed a decision that left so much room for the HKSAR government that it may be better described as a 'suggestion', or at most a guideline. The decision of the Preparatory Committee was 'indecisive' with respect to the electoral system for the 20 directly elected seats, for which it offered two options for the choice of the HKSAR government. It listed 15 'candidates' for possible functional constituencies out of which the HKSAR government was to pick nine. Moreover, the decision basically left the allocation of the 20 per cent seat quota for which foreign-passport holders will be eligible to the discretion of the HKSAR government. The only definitive decision the Preparatory Committee made was regarding the electoral college: the 30 functional constituencies plus the six failing 'candidates' (which six fail depending on the decision of the HKSAR government) were to elect an 800 member electoral college, in accordance with the divisions in categories as prescribed in the Basic Law (Oriental Daily, 24 May 1997, A15).

Upon announcement Chinese officials hastened to add that the decision of the Preparatory Committee would be binding on the HKSAR government, and that the latter may only make decisions from within the boundaries as prescribed by the Preparatory Committee (Oriental Daily, 24 May 1997, A15). The purpose of such a statement was to reiterate the legal position, but, given the width of the boundaries, the discretion for 'implementation' was imaginatively huge. This is further evidenced by the fact that when the HKSAR government made its choice, after nearly one-and-a-half months and not before a brief public consultation was conducted, the original preferences within the Preparatory Committee for the various options were not always followed.[14]

Moreover, upon the delivery of its 'decision' on the first Legislative Council, the Preparatory Committee was instantly declared to have 'basically completed all its duties'.[15] It was officially wound up on 11 July, less than two weeks after the HKSAR was formed. This contrasts markedly with the earlier expectation among some members of the Committee that their work would stretch to the second half of 1998 when the first Legislative Council election would be held.[16]

Thus, apparently, the agenda of the Chinese leadership for Hong Kong had changed in anticipation of the formation of the HKSAR. With the departure of the British and with the HKSAR government in place, the pledge of 'One Country – Two Systems' has arrived at a real test – and passing here requires Beijing to do less, not more. Qian Qichen was thus found, on the eve of the passage of the Preparatory Committee decision on the first Legislative Council election, to have argued for a 'facilitating' decision, laying down only the general principles and leaving a lot of discretion for the HKSAR government. The guiding principle behind the decision should be, Qian was reported to have advised the committee members, what needed to be done in the interest of fulfilling the overriding policy of 'One Country – Two Systems' (Ming Pao, 23 May 1997). The members who originally were less prepared to see their power watered-down were urged to toe the new central line.[17]

The change in context has, therefore, demanded corresponding changes in strategy and choice of action. There is common interest between Beijing and Hong Kong in seeing the pledge of 'One Country – Two Systems' fulfilled, or at least perceived by observers to be fulfilled, especially during the early period of the change in government, when Hong Kong is in the international limelight. Too much is at stake. For the central government there is China's reputation for honouring an international agreement, the desired demonstration effect aimed at Taiwan, and national pride in not being outdone by the British in its administration of Hong Kong. For the new local leaders the worst scenario would be to be perceived as merely the agents of Beijing. Like the future of Hong Kong as an international city, their own political future depends on the realization of the vision of 'One Country – Two Systems'. There is a confluence of interests in making the pledge work. As a result we witnessed this readiness of Beijing leaders to silence the 'dissenters' within their own house,[18] and to co-operate with the HKSAR government, acceding to its demand for control over its 'internal affairs'.[19]

Conflict as normality: varying tolerance of difference

Notwithstanding goodwill on both sides, the potential for conflict and difficulties abounds. The concept of 'One Country – Two Systems' implies a tolerance of differences between the two systems. Difficulties arise when opinions as to what is tolerable differ. Differences in levels of tolerance may arise in many ways: between significant segments of the population within Hong Kong; within the mainland; and between Hong Kong as a whole and the mainland as a whole. Moreover, social systems are under constant change, which exacerbates the possibility of different expectations, as different segments of the society may have divergent judgements regarding what constitutes the essence of the social systems in question.

The following discussion focuses on two cases of conflict, each illustrating a different example of the gap in expected tolerance in the area of freedom of expression and civil liberties. The first case focuses on the gap between central leaders and the people of Hong Kong, a 'typical' scenario for the Beijing–Hong Kong relationship. The situation becomes more complicated, however, when the 'Hong Kong' party is put under closer scrutiny. The second case addresses the tension between the new local leadership and a considerable segment of the local community regarding proposed amendments to public order laws. It reveals the gap in expectations within Hong Kong regarding what constitutes an appropriate response to central government initiatives. The fact that Hong Kong is not a monolithic whole makes the Beijing–Hong Kong relationship a multi-faceted, complex set of interactions between multiple parties.

Beijing vs. Hong Kong: freedom or restraint?

In the eyes of many observers as well as people of Hong Kong, freedom of expression has long been one of the two major sources of tension in the imaginative scheme of 'One Country – Two Systems'. In a sense, it is the natural complement of the other major source of tension: the differing economic systems and huge gaps in the affluence level of the average person in the two systems. Differences in the political sphere reflect, if only partly, differences in the socio-economic sphere. The Basic Law prescribes a government structure for Hong Kong largely in line with its previous existence. The local population is also promised, in the Joint Declaration as well as in the Basic Law, a continuation of its usual 'way of life'. The difficulty is that what constitutes the 'Hong Kong way of life' is not amenable to any definitive description in a document. However authoritative the document may be, and however strictly it is adhered to, the fulfilment of the promise depends on the subjective realm – whether the 'Hong Kong way of life' in daily practice, as perceived by the central leadership of the day, falls within their range of tolerance of differences between the two systems.

Conflict occurs when expectations about what is tolerable differ between the parties, and there are bound to be differences in expectations when the general pledge of 'One Country – Two Systems', made at a vague systemic level, enters the stage of meticulous day-to-day implementation. One major clash over expectations occurred when the Director of the Hong Kong and Macau Office, Lu Ping, in an interview with CNN of the USA in May 1996, assured the Hong Kong press that it would continue to enjoy freedom of expression after 1997, but added that such freedom would not cover reports which 'promote or incite the division of the country'. Moreover, whilst government policies could be criticized, turning words into acts would not be allowed (Hong Kong Economic Daily, 1 June 1996, A7; Apple Daily, 1 June 1996, A1). In October 1996, Vice Premier and Foreign Minister Qian Qichen, in an interview with the *Asian Wall Street Journal*, added that whilst the Hong Kong press could continue to criticize Chinese leaders, personal attacks would not be allowed. There should also be no more political activities in Hong Kong aimed at directly influencing developments within the mainland, such as the Tiananmen vigils and related mass rallies (Apple Daily, 17 October 1996, A1).

Ironically, the original intention of the Chinese leaders was apparently to give assurance to the Hong Kong community that no major changes were envisaged regarding the freedom of expression it used to enjoy. However, the qualifications they added to the general principle of 'no change' when prompted during the interviews suggested there would be important tightening up of civil liberties. There was grave concern about the ambiguous distinction drawn between expression of words and 'action'. Questions were asked, for instance, regarding the circumstances when a certain expression of words criticizing the central government would be classified as forming part of a 'programme of action' aiming at inciting hatred towards the government, thus becoming illegal. Critics drew attention to the practice within the mainland that oral or written criticisms of the government were often regarded by the government as sufficient evidence of 'actions' directed at overthrowing the government.[20] The attempt to categorize some forms of verbal or written expression as 'action', it was pointed out, would significantly constrain freedom of expression, and effectively ban all harsher criticisms against the government.

In response to critics, Lu Ping and other Chinese officials made clear that the Hong Kong press would be allowed to report news related to controversial themes in an 'objective' manner, and it was only advocacy in support of such developments (the 'two Chinas', for example) in the press that would not be tolerated. The demarcation between 'objective' reporting and 'advocacy', the critical point of contention, was to be defined by law to be enacted by the HKSAR government. This fell short of providing effective assurances, however, as the local press, and the community at large, was concerned that secessionist advocacy would be used as a pretext for curtailing criticism of the government. Fear over the allegation of advocacy, it was felt, would significantly reduce the room for 'objective' reporting.

The conflict comes down to the very different assumptions, on the part of Chinese leaders and the Hong Kong community respectively, as to the range of political opinions to be regarded as tolerable, and desirable, within an international city. Chinese leaders believe they are already very open-minded in conceding to the people of Hong Kong the 'privilege' of openly criticizing, or even opposing, the central government and its policies. Still, central leaders are hesitant to accept criticism on a personal level, as Qian Qichen's warning has shown. They are even more disinclined to tolerate open reporting of political opinions related to sensitive issues, especially those on secession. The Chinese leadership is clearly trapped between its instinctive dislike of political criticism, and the implications of its own pledges of 'One Country – Two Systems', and 'Hong Kong maintaining its own way of life unchanged for 50 years'. These promises require the Chinese government to agree to Hong Kong continuing to engage openly in criticism against it, as the people there have previously done under British administration. Its natural instinct, however, causes it to attempt to impose a restraint on such freedom.

On the other hand, the Hong Kong press and the community at large has been used to enjoying a relatively high degree of freedom, especially since the 1980s, to criticize the authorities. This is not to say that there have been no problems with press freedom under the British administration. There have been draconian laws on the books, and until recently the British administration did not hesitate to use the law to crush social movements and to silence 'trouble-makers'.[21] The important difference, nevertheless, is that while in the 1990s British governors and Hong Kong civil servants may have lacked the will to correct historical wrongs, or to provide positive protection for freedom of expression through progressive law reforms, the threat from China is more immediate. Reports abound of crude interference in the dissemination of news, and intimidation of reporters and publishers, ranging from outright trial and imprisonment, through deportation and bribery, to economic pressure (Sciutto 1996). Aware of the possibility of further tightening of political control after 1997, the community has been very sensitive to moves suggesting new areas of taboo, lest they turn out to be only the tip of an emerging iceberg. For many, the difference between 'objective' and 'inciting' reporting is inherently subjective and murky, and in any event is a question of taste rather than legality. These reactions, if they surprised central leaders, address more than the immediate substantive issues *per se*. They reflect deep-seated worries among the local community about the prospects for civil liberties and the perceived gaps in understanding and expectations between Hong Kong and the mainland.

Internal contradiction? Anticipation and choice

The formation of the HKSAR government on 1 July 1997 symbolized the beginning of the implementation of the constitutional pledge of local autonomy. Whilst 'One Country – Two Systems' has long been a subject of debate, and debates will always affect popular expectation about the prospective fulfilment of the pledge, since July 1997 action (or inaction) by the HKSAR government and Beijing has constituted part and parcel of the pledge itself. In other words, the policies of the HKSAR government and its responses to Beijing by themselves define and redefine, in a continuous process, the practical meaning of 'One Country – Two Systems'.

In this circumstance the choices and perceptions of the local leadership about what is tolerable, and thus legitimate, are critical. Equally important is the context whereby a perception becomes dominant, and a choice of action made. Given the ambiguities inherent in the constitutional pledge, and the evident gap in expected tolerance between Beijing and Hong Kong, how do the local leadership arrive at their judgements regarding legitimate differences?

In this section we shall examine a case whereby the incoming HKSAR government acted in response to a central government initiative, but its choice of action attracted widespread criticism from a sizeable segment of the local community. The purpose is not to go into the motives of the choice, but to locate the choice of action within the context of central government actions and local opinion, and to highlight the coexistence, and thus the relativity, of freedom of choice and contextual constraints in a central–local relationship.

The background is that the National People's Congress Standing Committee (NPCSC), acting on the advice of the Beijing-appointed Preparatory Committee for the formation of the HKSAR, passed a resolution in February 1997 that, among other things, major amendments to public order legislation during the British administration would not be adopted as the laws of the SAR.[22] Under Article 160 of the Basic Law, the NPCSC is empowered to declare, upon the establishment of the HKSAR, any pre-existing laws in Hong Kong that in its opinion contravene the Basic Law not to be adopted as laws of the Region. The incoming HKSAR government was then left with the task of filling the legal gaps by proposing new legislation.

The legislation in question comprises the amendments made in 1992 and 1995 respectively to the Societies Ordinance and the Public Order Ordinance. The amendments at the time were intended to bring the law in line with the Hong Kong Bill of Rights Ordinance. The Chinese government was highly displeased, and the amendments were pushed through by the British Governor with the support of local liberals. The backdrop was a period of Sino-British strain and mistrust in the aftermath of the Tiananmen crackdown. The Chinese had been skeptical of the plans by the British to grant the right of abode to 50 000 Hong Kong families, the legal and political implications of the Bill of Rights Ordinance (enacted in 1991), and the possible financial strain of the plan to build a new and larger airport in Hong Kong.[23] The strain reached its peak when the new Governor, Christopher Patten, announced in 1992 his political reform package, designed to liberalize radically the election system without prior consultation with, or the endorsement of, the Chinese government. The Chinese felt that the British had betrayed their earlier co-operation, so that negotiations after the unilateral announcement were doomed from the beginning. Eventually, having gained the support of the more liberal legislators, Patten's political reform package was adopted for the last round of pre-1997 elections despite continued Chinese opposition, and China responded by declaring dead the 'through-train' arrangement for the first HKSAR Legislature.

The opposition of the Chinese government to the amendments to the public order legislation, which reduced restrictions on the formation of organizations and the launching of public processions, thus extended beyond their specific content. While they did not welcome liberalization of the laws themselves, the situation was further aggravated by unfriendly Sino-British relations during the period when the amendments were passed. One question that the Preparatory Committee was often asked was in what ways the amendments contravened the Basic Law, since the latter also contains provisions on protecting the civil liberties and human rights of Hong Kong residents. Tung Chee-hwa, then Chief Executive-designate and Vice-Director of the Committee, once replied that the amendments contravened Article 3 of the Joint Declaration and Article 8 of the Basic Law, both of which stipulate that the laws 'previously' in force in Hong Kong will remain basically unchanged (Ming Pao, 5 February 1997). The relevant time-frame is ambiguous, however. The Chinese understanding was always that, in accordance with the spirit of the Joint Declaration, there should be no major changes to the laws during the post-agreement transition period, and if changes needed to be made as required by circumstances, China had a right to be consulted (Ching 1994, p 176).

The displeasure of not being consulted thus extended from the political reform package to all associated initiatives by the Patten governorship. In fact, Chinese officials emphasized time and again that whilst the amendments were about civil liberties and human rights, the opposition to the amendments had nothing to do with the debate on human rights.[24] The decision not to adopt the amendments as laws of Hong Kong after 1 July was *not* directly based on the preferences of the Chinese government regarding freedom of association – the substantive matter in question. The amendments were opposed, the argument goes, because they were enacted unilaterally without the participation of the Chinese, and thus in the eyes of Chinese leaders exemplified a breach of the spirit of the Joint Declaration by the British. A reply to this argument was that if the Chinese government had participated in the amendment process for these laws, the amendments would never have taken place.

Distinguishing the subject matter from the overall critical spirit which gives rise to opposition regardless, enables us to locate an action within its context, and identify possible areas of opportunity and closure. One possibility is that, since the opposition of the Chinese government to the amendments was primarily directed at the procedure of their being enacted, according to the official Chinese position, and not at the content of the amendments, the incoming HKSAR government should enjoy full autonomy in determining the content of the new laws. The HKSAR government, and the Provisional Legislature, could then theoretically decide on whatever public order laws they saw as appropriate, to the point that they could go further than the previous amendments in terms of human rights protection.[25]

This argument is firmly based on the constitutional principle of 'One Country – Two Systems'. The spirit of this principle calls for minimal intervention in Hong Kong affairs by the central government, so that the local government, constituted wholly of, and accountable to, the people of Hong Kong, will take charge and make its choice of policies in accordance with local conditions. The formation of organizations and societies, and the organization of public processions, issues in question in the amendments, have nothing to do with the few areas for which the central government is responsible in Hong Kong, in accordance with the Basic Law. Legislation in these areas, the logic goes, should therefore be entirely the responsibility of the HKSAR government, which should then make its decisions on the basis of thorough understanding of local opinion.

There is an indication that the HKSAR government did regard the legislative exercise as a matter of local autonomy, and that despite Chinese opposition to the original amendments, felt that how the laws should be revamped was entirely within its discretion. The consultative document on the legislative proposal, for instance, was reportedly issued by the Office of the Chief Executive-designate in April 1997 without prior consultation with the central government.[26] Chinese leaders apparently also adopted a 'hands-off' attitude, stressing that how the legal gaps should be filled was entirely a matter for the HKSAR, and refrained from being drawn into local debates on the subject.

On the other hand, other indications signaled significant qualification to the exercise of local autonomy. As early as in February 1997, the newly appointed Secretary of Justice-designate, Elsie Leung Oi-sie, doubted the possibility of following the results of public consultation, if the dominant opinion was against tightening up the relevant legislation. The Secretary was reported to say:

> If the results of the public consultation really call for not 'diluting' the laws … it would be left to the provisional legislature to decide whether to accept it or not. The chances of not diluting the laws will be very low because that would mean overruling the suggestions of the Preparatory Committee.
>
> (South China Morning Post, 23 February 1997)

Thus the Secretary of Justice-designate presumably believed that although the original amendments were scrapped because of problematic procedures, somehow their content, though not directly criticized by the Chinese government, was also unacceptable. The message seemed to be that, politically some dilution of the original laws was mandatory, though theoretically the HKSAR government should enjoy unrestrained autonomy in the exercise. Here it should be noted that Leung's remarks were made before the consultative document was drafted. Upon her appointment she became the principal person in charge of the drafting of the document, which was released in early April 1997.

The proposal that was put forward in April claimed to strike a 'middle ground' between returning the laws to their pre-amendment version and the 1992 and 1995 amendments. In other words, there would be some increase in regulation and social control but not to the point that civil liberties would return to the pre-amendment days.[27] The proposal, released through a consultative document, immediately met a huge wave of criticism. There was widespread discontent over the tightening up of the right to form societies without *a priori* registration, and the right to organize public processions without *a priori* application for approval. Critics were also adamant about the irrelevance of the concept of 'national security' in public order legislation, which the proposed bills included for the first time. The concept of 'national security', critics pointed out, was intended to protect the integrity of sovereignty from external threat, not to restrain the exercise of basic rights of association by local residents.[28] The proposal also included a provision (Section 4.7) banning the establishment of ties between local political organizations or bodies and a whole catalogue of foreign political organizations, foreign organizations, or simply aliens. Specifically, financial assistance could not be solicited from these sources, and the policies and management of local bodies should not be influenced by foreign organizations. The ban was considered too harsh and wide-ranging, and likely to suffocate the valuable international linkages of a whole range of local bodies. Hong Kong as an international city needed to foster a multifaceted network of international links in various arenas, it was contended. Terms, such as 'foreign' and 'international political organizations', were criticized as ill-defined and ambiguous.[29] The inclusion of individual foreigners in the banned list exemplified the broad control envisaged, and was against the Basic Law, which allows the right of political participation to foreigners residing in Hong Kong.[30]

The crux of the criticism was that the proposal conflated the issue of national security and concern over espionage with the exercise of rights of association. Article 23 of the Basic Law requires the HKSAR government to enact laws on its own to prohibit any act of treason, secession, sedition, subversion against the Central People's Government, or theft of state secrets. Critics argued that national security was a separate matter to be dealt with on its own, and should not be 'smuggled' into other legislation in a piece-meal manner.[31] The rightful concern of public order legislation was, it was maintained, only to ensure that the basic rights of association of local residents were appropriately exercised. It was asked, given the good past record of public processions in terms of public order, whether it was legitimate to impose further control on the exercise of such rights.[32]

The spate of criticism presented a major challenge to the new government-in-waiting, which found itself obliged to make concessions. Eventually, the requirement for public processions to obtain a notice of 'no objection' was relaxed, and the reference to 'aliens' (individual foreigners) in the prohibition of foreign links for local political bodies was deleted. The concept of 'national security', however, has remained as one of the reasons for the government to ban an organization or a public procession, though attempts were made to clarify the concept with reference to 'the protection of the territorial integrity and independence of the People's Republic of China' (Hong Kong Economic Journal, 16 May 1997). Despite the concessions, the final version has, however, remained by and large intact, thus preserving the major tightening in the original proposal.

Interestingly, despite the declaration of 'no intervention' by central leaders, and empirical evidence suggesting that the central leadership did not play an active role in the exercise, the new local leadership still chose to ignore the local demand for more liberal laws. Apparently, they reached a judgement that despite the *carte blanche* the HKSAR government appeared to enjoy in filling the gap, it was politically advisable to be prudent.[33] This is suggested by the comments of Leung Oi-sie, the Secretary of Justice-designate in February 1997, to the effect that the decision of the Preparatory Committee, and the NPCSC, to scrap the amendments made it politically difficult, if not impossible, to leave the legislation undiluted in the subsequent enactment exercise. Moreover, there were indications that the Chief Executive-designate, Tung Chee-hwa, was very concerned about the need to ward off 'controversial' political activities during the early days of the HKSAR. Tung and his officials explicitly warned on several occasions that public processions in support of the independence of Tibet or Taiwan would not be allowed under the new administration.[34] It appeared that Tung had felt it necessary to have national security included in the legislation so that the HKSAR government would be legally empowered to act on these controversial political activities. The feeling within the central government on these activities was strong and the possibility of seeing these activities occur in the HKSAR could not be excluded. The new HKSAR government needed to be seen by the central government as capable of controlling controversy, especially during its early days.[35]

Actors make their choice of action within the constraints and context in which they operate. The new HKSAR government has its operating environment defined by the constitutional principle of 'One Country – Two Systems', which allows it much greater autonomy than any provincial-level government in China. At the same time, its choice of action is also 'constrained' by this principle. It needs to display a high degree of autonomy and responsibility in order to live up to the expectation of the local population as well as the international community, which has been keeping a close watch on Hong Kong, and whose views will have an impact on Hong Kong's continuing reputation as a major international city. The central government shares its interest in seeing Hong Kong thrive, but it also has other concerns. One major dilemma for Beijing is that while Hong Kong needs to be highly autonomous, it cannot be too autonomous lest it becomes a 'base of subversion' used by Taiwan and other 'enemies' of the Chinese state. Thus, Beijing seeks to balance both components in the 'One Country – Two Systems' schema. 'Two Systems' is the special design and focus of action, but the goal of having 'Two Systems' is to attain 'One Country'. This is why Qian Qichen and Lu Ping kept on saying that advocacy for Taiwanese or Tibetan independence was not tolerable in Hong Kong, while at the same time stressing continuing freedom of expression in Hong Kong.

This sense of insecurity among the central leadership over the 'One Country' side of the schema is not, however, shared by the entirety of the local community. Indicative of dissenting opinion within Hong Kong is the view articulated by the law profession, which holds that while treason is certainly a crime in any country, the rules of evidence should be much stricter than those adopted on the mainland. Specifically, the existence of the use of physical force should be a definitive element in what constitutes a genuine threat to national security. All other expressions of opinion belong to the realm of civil liberties and should be protected, not restrained, by law.[36]

In the end, the 'middle ground' posture adopted by the new HKSAR leadership regarding the public order amendments suggests that in the leadership's judgement they found it necessary to accede more to the concerns for the 'One Country'. They might have thought it politically prudent to lean more towards the concerns of the central government, especially in the early days after the handover, when they had yet to win the trust of the new sovereign.[37] Alternatively, they might genuinely think that the change in government offered Hong Kong a novel chance to review its previous policies, and the proposed legislation reflected their judgement of what constituted a better balance between civil liberties and public order.[38] Whatever their underlying motives, which may be both or neither of the above, the difficulty of the new government was to convince *both* the central leadership and the local community (and to an extent the international community) that the constitutional schema of 'One Country – Two Systems' was alive and well. The local community tends to be more concerned about the 'Two Systems' component, and takes 'One Country' as non-problematic. The concerns of the central leadership are more complicated. It definitely wants the 'Two Systems' to succeed, but is not as relaxed as the local population about the 'One Country' component.

As Tung Chee-hwa has often said since his election as Chief Executive 'if Hong Kong fares well, China as a whole will benefit; … thus the non-zero-sum nature of the Beijing-Hong Kong relationship'.[39] By emphasizing the interdependence and common interests of Hong Kong and the mainland, Tung seeks to enlarge the room in which his new government can fruitfully manoeuvre. Given the immense gaps in expected tolerance the task of bridging the gaps and striking common ground will not be easy. The HKSAR government needs to be able, for instance, to convince Beijing that free expression of a whole range of political opinions will not necessarily harm the integrity of the Chinese state, whilst at the same time explaining to the local population the concerns and worries of the central government. The legislative exercise regarding the public order legislation is a classic case in which the local government has sought to strike a balance. The question is whether they have succeeded to the satisfaction of both parties, the central government as well as the local community.

The ambiguity and inherent conflicts within the 'One Country – Two Systems' schema therefore point to the importance of good political judgement on the part of political leaders, both in Hong Kong and Beijing. The greater burden falls on the former, however, as Beijing can fulfil its part by mere inaction. The HKSAR government has to carry on the daily routine of administration of Hong Kong, and bears the onus of initiative in requesting intervention or assistance by the central government. As local political leaders they need to understand fully, as well as to articulate and represent, the expectations of various segments of the local population regarding the bounds of tolerance. To get things done they need also to understand the expectations of the mainland and the central government. The challenge for the fruitful implementation of the pledge, for the mutual benefit of Hong Kong and China as a whole, is to strike the right balance to meet these varying expectations, and since the views of Beijing are more often in the limelight, not to lose sight of expectations within Hong Kong.

Notes

1   This is notwithstanding the famous saying of President Jiang Zemin, 'the well water does not interfere with the river water', prescribing that Hong Kong should stay away from politics on the mainland. This remark was made when Jiang received visitors from Hong Kong in Beijing in the aftermath of the Tiananmen crackdown when there were massive rallies in Hong Kong protesting against the crackdown. See *People's Daily*, 12 July 1989, and quoted in Ching 1994, p 179.
2   The notion that changes in central–local politics, and in particular at the central–provincial interface, will have significant impact on the conduct of politics in general in China is put in Li 1998, in the context of the experience of two important provincial units, Guangdong and Shanghai.
3   The linkage between the 'One Country – Two Systems' initiative and changes in the wider context and the definition by the Chinese leadership of its environment and possible options is elaborated in Chen 1992, pp 1–11.
4   This was largely a result of the active participation of the Hong Kong community in the Tiananmen developments, especially after martial law was declared on 19 May 1989 in Beijing. Hong Kong was branded as 'a base of subversive activities' in the aftermath of the crackdown by some Chinese officials. Two Hong Kong members resigned from the Basic Law Drafting Committee, and another two boycotted the meetings after the crackdown. See Chan 1991, p 24.
5   The more likely active role of Hong Kong in fulfilling the pledge of 'One Country – Two Systems' post-1997 was also noted by the former director of New China News Agency, Hong Kong, Xu Jiatun, who had fled to the USA in the aftermath of 4 June 1989. According to Xu, the major role of Beijing lies in non-interference. See interview with Xu, reported in the *Hong Kong Economic Journal*, 1 July 1997, p 14.
6   A majority of the local population favoured the continuation of British administration over reversion to China, according to a widely reported and cited opinion poll commissioned by the Hong Kong Observers, a group of liberal-minded local elites. See Tang and Ching 1994, p 157.
7   The Preparatory Committee for the HKSAR is established under the decision of the National People's Congress on the method for the formation of the first government and the first legislative council of the HKSAR, adopted by the Seventh

NPC on 4 April 1990, when the Basic Law was also promulgated. No fewer than half of its members were to be from Hong Kong, and all members were to be appointed by the NPC standing committee.

8   According to a decision by the Preparatory Committee in March 1997 on the jurisdiction of the Provisional Legislature, the latter was to last for not more than a year, starting from 1 July 1997, and would only undertake tasks strictly necessary to the smooth functioning of the HKSAR government. See *Hong Kong Economic Journal*, 1 July 1997.

9   The importance of this 'newly found' role was suggested by the sheer number of Preparatory Committee members volunteering to join the sub-group on the first Legislative Council election. Altogether 64 members volunteered to join, of whom about 20 per cent were Chinese officials. The Hong Kong member convenor, Professor Lau Siu-kai, in an interview anticipated that much importance would be attached to this sub-group, especially after the selection of the Chief Executive (*Sing Tao Jih Pao*, 5 January 1996, A15).

10   The relevant article in the Joint Declaration reads, 'The Hong Kong Special Administrative Region will enjoy a high degree of autonomy, except in foreign and defence affairs which are the responsibilities of the Central People's Government' (Article 3(2)). This semi-language of 'residual power' is not adopted in the Basic Law, which states explicitly the delegated nature of the autonomy to be enjoyed by the HKSAR.

11   The approach took place in the form of an invitation issued by the convenor of the HKSAR Executive Council, Chung Sze-yuen, to the Hong Kong convenor of the first Legislative Council election sub-group of the Preparatory Committee, Lau Siu-kai, for lunch on 7 April together with other ExCo members. The areas of controversy were largely areas where the 1992 Patten reform package made major changes, which the Chinese found unacceptable. The most important were: (1) the electoral system for the 20 directly elected seats, whether by way of first-past-the-post single seat constituency (the pre-existing system), proportional representation, or single-vote-multiple-seat constituency; (2) the reconstitution of the new 9 functional constituencies that Patten introduced as 'quasi-direct election' in the 1995 election; (3) the reconstitution of the electoral college returning 10 seats; (4) the allocation of the quota of seats (no more than 20 per cent that may go to holders of foreign passports, according to the Basic Law. *Ming Pao* (Hong Kong), 8 April 1997, A7.

12   Henry Tang, Executive Councillor and provisional legislator, in answer to queries from the press in response to earlier comments from Lau Siu-kai, said that a definitive decision (on the first Legislative Council election) by the Preparatory Committee would save the HKSAR government from political criticism regarding the controversial changes. *Apple Daily* (Hong Kong), 10 May 1997, A9.

13   According to one Hong Kong member of the sub-group, the participation of the HKSAR government in designing the election system had been discussed in a previous meeting, prior to the approach of the ExCo, and many were against the dilution of the authority of the Committee, see *Apple Daily*, 9 April 1997: A9. The New China News Agency (Hong Kong) was reportedly behind this opposition, whilst the Hong Kong and Macau Affairs Office supported the position of the HKSAR government, see *Sing Tao Jih Pao*, 15 April 1997.

14   The 'mainstream' preference within the Preparatory Committee sub-group regarding the electoral system for direct election was for the single-vote-multiple-seat

constituencies. The HKSAR government chose the other option, proportional representation. The functional constituency of 'mainland enterprises' ranked eight among the 15 functional constituency candidates in the Preparatory Committee decision, but was replaced by the insurance constituency (ranking tenth) in the HKSAR government announcement. See *Apple Daily*, 9 July 1997, A4. However, it should be emphasized that these preferences were always intended to have no binding effect on the HKSAR government (*Ming Pao*, 23 May 1997).

15   Qian Qichen, Vice-Premier and Director of the Preparatory Committee, made this announcement in his closing remarks to the Ninth session of the Preparatory Committee on 23 May 1997, right after the Committee passed its decision on the election (*Ming Pao*, 24 May 1997).

16   Some committee members argued that the Preparatory Committee had to endorse the election results and could thus be disbanded only after the first Legislative Council election in 1998. See *Sing Tao Jih Pao*, 15 April 1997. This view was, however, apparently not shared widely. Lu Ping, director of the Hong Kong and Macau Affairs Office, State Council, stated explicitly on 19 May 1997 that the Preparatory Committee needed only to arrive at the election methods, and leave the implementation of the election entirely to the HKSAR government. The Committee could thus be dissolved even before 1 July 1997. *Ming Pao*, 20 May 1997.

17   The new central policy of 'no intervention' was precipitated by the public pledge of President Jiang Zemin, to Tung Chee-hwa after Tung's election, that the central government 'will definitely not intervene in affairs in the HKSAR which fall within the realm of local autonomy' (*Apple Daily*, 19 December 1997, A1).

18   As with many other issues there have been different shades of opinion within the Preparatory Committee and among different groups of Chinese officials. For instance, it was reported that New China News Agency had been behind some members of the Preparatory Committee insisting on a longer tenure of the Committee, so that it would oversee the first Legislative Council election. The Hong Kong and Macau Affairs Office, as noted previously, was against this idea, and Qian Qichen finally supported the latter view. See *Sing Tao Jih Pao*, 15 April 1997.

19   There has been speculation regarding whether Tung Chee-hwa had requested an early end to the work of the Preparatory Committee during his meeting with Chinese leaders. Tung, also a vice-director of the Preparatory Committee, refused to confirm or deny such speculation (*Ming Pao*, 24 May 1997).

20   Notable examples are the cases of Wei Jingsheng and Wang Dan.

21   The Hong Kong Journalists Association (HKJA) has been adamant in criticizing the reluctance of the British administration to reform the law. See its annual reports, starting in 1994. In the 1995 report (HKJA, 1995: 2), it was asserted that 'the Hong Kong government ... has singularly failed to amend those laws which most threaten this fundamental freedom (of expression)'. For recent recitals of some major cases in which the government employed public order laws to silence social opposition, see *Apple Daily*, 21 January 1997: A1; 22 January 1997: A2.

22   See *Gazette of the NPCSC*, No. 1, 1997; *Ta Kung Pao* (Hong Kong), 24 February 1997.

23   These plans were announced in the policy address of the then governor, David Wilson, to the Legislative Council in October 1989, four months after the

Tiananmen crackdown. For a personal account of the background of these moves see Wilson 1996, p 182.

24 In response to widespread criticisms by the Western media of the implications for human rights in Hong Kong, Vice-Premier and Foreign Minister Qian Qichen stated that the move to scrap the laws had been part of a continuous process initiated by the establishment of the Preliminary Working Committee, a new organization set up in 1993 by China to prepare alternative plans for the 1997 take-over subsequent to the announcement of the Patten political reform package and the souring of Sino-British relations. See *Ming Pao*, 1 February 1997. New China News Agency (Hong Kong) official Zhang Zin-sheng stressed that the proposed scrapping of the laws had nothing to do with the human rights issue. The Chinese government had been very concerned about the human rights of Hong Kong residents and had made adequate provision in the Basic Law for that purpose, he said (*Ta Kung Pao*, 5 February 1997).

25 This possibility is pointed out in Li 1997.

26 This was reported by *Apple Daily*, 9 April 1997, A9. Sources at the Office of the Chief Executive-designate reportedly told the press that neither the Hong Kong and Macau Affairs Office of the State Council nor New China News Agency (Hong Kong) participated in the drafting of the consultative document on civil liberties and social order. The Chief Executive-designate reportedly saw the exercise as an entirely 'internal' affair of the HKSAR, in which the principle of 'Hong Kong people running Hong Kong' should apply.

27 The 1992 amendment to the Societies Ordinance, amongst other changes, replaces the previous requirement of seeking *a priori* approval for registration (or exemption from registration) before a society may be legally formed with a notification system. The 1995 amendment to the Public Order Ordinance relaxes the issuance of licenses for public processions. The new proposal seeks to reinstate the registration requirement for the formation of societies, and tighten up control on public processions. See Annex B of the Consultative Document.

28 Proposals in the Consultative Document allowed the government to refuse the registration of societies or ban the organization of public processions on grounds of public order, national security, public safety, the protection of public health or morals or the protection of the rights and freedoms of others. Members of the legal profession, including barristers, solicitors and law professors, were almost unanimous in maintaining that the inclusion of the reference to 'national security' in public order legislation was highly inappropriate, and might be used against people exercising their basic rights. *Apple Daily*, 26 April 1997; *Ming Pao*, 1 and 17 May 1997. A major local newspaper in its editorial called for the delinking of the concern for national security and freedom of association, the latter being the subject of the legislation concerned (*Hong Kong Economic Journal*, 19 April 1997).

29 The ban on 'foreign links' attracted a wave of criticism when the consultative document was first released on 9 April 1997. See *Apple Daily*, 10 April 1997. A prominent law professor criticized the concept of 'international political organization' as very ambiguous and 'non-existent' in international law (*Sing Tao Jih Pao*, 17 April 1997).

30 Article 26 of the Basic Law stipulates that 'permanent residents of the Hong Kong Special Administrative Region shall have the right to vote and the right to stand for election ...', and 'permanent residents' of the HKSAR include persons not of Chinese nationality, i.e. foreigners who have ordinarily resided in

Hong Kong continuously for not less than 7 years and have taken Hong Kong as their place of permanent residence (Article 24 (4)). Article 67 of the Basic Law makes it explicit that 'permanent residents of the Region who are not of Chinese nationality or who have the right of abode in foreign countries may also be elected members of the Legislative Council of the Region, provided that the proportion of such members does not exceed 20 per cent of the total membership of the Council'. Foreigners are thus allowed explicitly to participate in local politics and to be elected to the legislature, provided that they are permanent residents.

31 This is a major argument in the editorial of the *Hong Kong Economic Journal*, 19 April 1997, and in the position paper of the Hong Kong Bar Association. See *Apple Daily*, 26 April 1997.

32 Such objections were voiced by the more liberal provisional legislators as well as members of the outgoing legislature (*Express News* (Hong Kong), 27 April 1997).

33 Tung was once reported to have privately admitted to the press that the proposals contained in the consultative document reflected his personal opinions, and in his view had been very prudent in terms of their impact on existing practice (*Apple Daily*, 12 April 1997, A1).

34 Tung confirmed during an interview with the foreign press that his administration would not allow inciting writings or public processions in support of the independence of Taiwan or Tibet. See *Sing Tao Jih Pao*, 7 May 1997. When asked for one single major difference in civil liberties as a result of the new legislation, a senior official in Tung's office responded that 'before 1 July public processions in support of the independence of Taiwan are legal. They will not be after 1 July' (*Ming Pao*, 16 May 1997).

35 This suggestion was made by *Ming Pao*, 16 May 1997, quoting a source from within the Office of the Chief Executive-designate, but was immediately denied the next day by Michael Ming-yeung Suen, Director of Policy Co-ordination for the Office (*Ming Pao*, 17 May 1997).

36 This argument was fully articulated by the law profession in their submission to the consultative document on civil liberties and public order (*Ming Pao*, 1 May 1997).

37 Senior Minister and former premier of Singapore, Lee Kuan Yew, had explicitly advised Tung Chee-hwa to do only what would be seen as appropriate by Beijing, rather than what would be seen as appropriate by local people, in order to obtain the trust of Beijing and gain the autonomy to manage Hong Kong's affairs (*Ming Pao*, 3 July 1997, A8).

38 Tung Chee-hwa emphasized the opportunity during the new era to chart new plans and improve on past achievements time and again during his campaign, and since being elected, to the office of Chief Executive. For an example of an explicit reference to the need to reprioritize potentially competing values, see his speech to an American audience in Hong Kong, in which he addressed the differences in values between western and Asian societies, and remarked that 'now it is time to put more emphasis on the traditional values (of the Asian societies), including order and stability (*vis-à-vis* the Western values of freedom and rule of law)' (*Ming Pao*, 16 May 1997). Leung Oi-sie, the new Secretary of Justice, in defending the consultative document, once remarked that the proposal reflected an attempt to reappraise existing values and reorder priorities (*Express News*, 27 April 1997).

39 For example, see Tung's speech on the scrapping of public order legislation, given on 23 January 1997, in which he said, '... the future success of Hong Kong

is closely linked up with the success of China. If Hong Kong is successful, China will benefit. Alternatively, if China is successful, Hong Kong will benefit even more.' (*Ming Pao*, 24 January 1997, B11).

Bibliography

Apple Daily, various.

Chan, M. K. 1991 'Democracy Derailed: Realpolitik in the Making of the Hong Kong Basic Law, 1985–1990', in Chan, M. K., Clark, D. J. (eds) *The Hong Kong Basic Law: Blueprint for 'Stability and Prosperity' Under Chinese Sovereignty*. Armonk, New York: M E Sharpe.

Chen, L. 1992 *Study of Deng Xiaoping's Thought on 'One Nation, Two Systems'* (*in Chinese*). Shenyang: Liaoning renmin chubanshe.

Chief Executive's Office, Hong Kong Special Administrative Office, PRC. 1997 *Civil Liberties and Public Order: Consultative Document*. Hong Kong: Chief Executive office.

Ching, F. 1994 'Toward Colonial Sunset: The Wilson Regime, 1987–92', in Chan, M. (ed.) *Precarious Balance: Hong Kong between China and Britain, 1842–1992*. Armonk, New York: M E Sharpe.

Express News, 27 April 1997.

Hong Kong Economic Daily, 1 June 1996.

Hong Kong Economic Journal, various.

Hong Kong Journalists Association. 1995 *Broken Promises: Freedom of Expression in Hong Kong*, Joint report with Article 19.

Johnson, C. 1984 'The Mousetrapping of Hong Kong'. *Asian Survey* XXIV(9) (September): 887–909.

Li, L. C. 1997 'A Less-than-beautiful Misunderstanding: Comments on the "Civil Liberties and Social Order Consulation Document"' (*in Chinese*), *Hong Kong Economic Journal*, 14 April: 6.

Li, L. C. 1998 *Centre and Provinces: China, 1978–93. Power as non-zero-sum*. Oxford: Clarendon Press.

Ming Pao, various.

National People's Congress Standing Committee, *Gazette*, No. 1, 1997, Beijing: NPC.

Oriental Daily, 24 May 1997.

People's Daily, 12 July 1989.

Sciutto, J. E. 1996 'China's Muffling of the Hong Kong Media', in Skidmore, M. J. (ed) *The Future of Hong Kong*. London: Sage Publications.

Sing Tao Jih Pao, various.

South China Morning Post, 23 February 1997.

Ta Kung Pao, various.

Tang, J. T. H., Ching, F. 1994 'The MacLehose-Youde Years: Balancing the"Three-Legged Stool", 1971–86', in Chan, M. K. (ed.) *Precarious Balance: Hong Kong between China and Britain, 1942–1992*. Armonk, New York: M E Sharpe.

Wilson, D. 1996 'Learning to Live with China', in Blyth, S., Wotherspoon, I. (eds) *Hong Kong Remembers*. Hong Kong: Oxford University Press.

Yahuda, M. 1993 'Hong Kong's Future: Sino-British Negotiations, Perceptions, Organization and Political Culture'. *International Affairs* 69(2): 245–266.

Xu Jiatun 1997 Interview reported in the *Hong Kong Economic Journal*, 1 July 1997.

9

The Public Service in Transition: Sustaining Administrative Capacity and Political Neutrality

Ian Scott

Definitions of administrative capacity commonly focus on the management skills required for successful policy formulation and the effective delivery of services (Umeh 1992, p 58; see also Turner and Hulme 1997, pp 88–91). In this technical, managerial sense, most under-developed countries do not possess, and may never have had, sufficient administrative capacity to achieve their policy objectives. In apparent contrast to this view, however, there is a substantial literature documenting the actual loss of administrative capacity in post-colonial bureaucracies. World Bank structural adjustment studies, for example, suggest that a range of factors may lead to a decline in bureaucratic capacity under conditions of environmental turbulence (Langseth 1995). These include: structural reorganization disrupting established routines; corruption; political interference in administration; difficulties in retaining personnel; and an absence of the 'governance' values of accountability, openness and transparency (Barratt Brown 1995, Baker 1992, Grindle and Thomas 1991, Tordoff 1980, Cohen and Wheeler 1997). Any bureaucracy, in this wider, political sense of the term, could potentially be faced with a loss of administrative capacity.

At first sight, the Hong Kong public service would seem to be about as far removed from such concerns as it would be possible to be. It is a very efficient organization with excellent managerial skills, an impressive record of policy implementation under budget and within time, and a revenue base that is the envy of many developed countries. Its capacity is, if anything, enhanced by the small size of the territory, limited involvement in some social policy areas, autonomy from political interference and a high degree of societal compliance with its directives and regulations. Nonetheless, administrative capacity is critically important in the post-handover polity because the ability of the public service to continue to deliver goods and services efficiently and effectively is arguably the key element in maintaining a level of support for the regime. The Chinese government, in common with its colonial predecessor, has seen performance legitimacy as a necessary, if not sufficient, condition in winning the tacit consent of the governed. In 1995, for example, a committee set up by the Chinese government to advise on the transition attributed the territory's success to the civil service system, noted that the Chinese government believed that stability was related to the ability of the public service to function effectively and indicated that it would monitor its operations closely (Preliminary Working Committee 1995). With what were in effect appointments to the Chief Executive's position and the Provisional Legislature, a judiciary that was unwilling to pass judgement on the legality of the legislature and the blatant gerrymandering of the future electoral system, the public service became even more important as the last repository of institutional integrity (Scott 1998).

This chapter examines the prospects for sustaining administrative capacity in both the narrow managerial sense and in the wider political context in which the public service operates. It is divided into three parts. In the first part, the underlying values and culture on which capacity is currently based are assessed against their potential for erosion under the present regime. In the second part, the ability of the public service to sustain its managerial capabilities in the face of personnel changes and concern over retention rates in key civil service positions is examined. Finally, two factors that might lead to a loss of capacity – corruption and the possibility of increased political control and the consequential difficulty of maintaining political neutrality – are considered.

Values and culture

Administrative capacity is a product of history, values and culture as much as it is a result of existing technical, professional and managerial skills. If the values and culture are destroyed, it is very difficult to replace them; what is lost is institutional memory or, in more concrete terms, routine ways of dealing with problems. The Hong Kong public service has not been significantly affected by the wave of managerialist reforms affecting other parts of the world. Nor has the handover provoked explicit challenges to its structure, operations or authority; the Chinese government, at least formally, supports the status quo. Nonetheless, inherent in the nature of the transition, are potential threats to the way in which the public service functions. To examine these threats further, we need to consider the central characteristics of Hong Kong's bureaucracy and to identify the values and culture that have underpinned its high level of performance.

A syndrome of characteristics, which might help explain the success of the public service, is presented below. The significant features relating to administrative capacity, it is argued, are:

- fiscal frugality
- clear lines of authority

- a career civil service and qualified personnel selected on merit
- a focus on effective and efficient delivery of goods and services
- political neutrality.

These characteristics might be thought of as the embodiment of the ideal virtues to which traditional public administration aspired. But they are also a result of the territory's unique history and the changing accommodation of the bureaucracy to the demands of the wider polity. The following sections deal with the central characteristics of the public service, the ways in which they have been modified and adapted over time, and their standing under the new regime.

Fiscal frugality

The Hong Kong government learned early to value fiscal frugality. The British government was insistent that colonies should as far as possible meet their own expenses and concern with balancing the budget, eventually to be written into the Basic Law, was to become the dominating principle of colonial financial administration. By the 1890s, when Hong Kong had begun to prosper, businessmen were able to secure a majority of the unofficial positions on both the Legislative and the Executive Councils. A consistent theme of their advice ever since has been that, if taxation were increased, the money would only be spent on unnecessary social and welfare programmes. This argument has occasionally also been stretched to embrace an opposition to moves towards democracy. Democrats, so the syllogism runs, are elected. Elections require votes. Votes require expensive social and welfare policy promises. Ergo, democracy is a threat to the public purse. Since the Provisional Legislature and the Executive Council are largely composed of those with pro-business interests and since the electoral system has been fudged to ensure their continuing dominance, there is no reason to suppose that these attitudes will not persist.

In 1993, the then Financial Secretary, Sir Hamish MacLeod, described government policies as ensuring that 'merit can find its way to the top, that talents can be fully developed through subsidized education; to provide incentive for hard work through a low taxation system; [and] to provide a safety net for those who need help, through social spending on housing, on welfare, on health and on hospitals' (Hong Kong Hansard 1992/93, Session: 3996–3997). In his 1997–1998 budget, which received prior approval from the Chinese government, the new Financial Secretary, Donald Tsang Yam-kuen, essentially endorsed these principles. Noting that the formulation of the budget was constrained under the Basic Law by the requirement that it should be balanced, that it should be based on low tax policies and that public expenditure should not outstrip economic growth, he described his budget as one of 'continuity in a time of change' (Hong Kong Government 1997: 6; Basic Law 1990: Articles 107, 108). Public expenditure continues to range between about 15 and 18 per cent of Gross Domestic Product projected forward to 2001 (Hong Kong Government 1997: Appendix A, p 12; see also Ho 1996, p 26). Provision for social policy expenditure, although far short of the aspirations of the democrats, remains in line with previous policies. Salaries tax has been reduced for those on lower incomes. Whether these policies will continue in possibly less favourable economic times remains to be seen. There is strong pressure from some members of the post-handover Executive Council to reduce profits tax, and negative attitudes towards workers' rights, including collective bargaining and unfair dismissal, carry with them implications for possibly reduced public expenditure on labour. For the moment, however, the public service holds the ring. Fiscal frugality seems well entrenched and even reinforced under the present regime.

Clear lines of authority

In many underdeveloped countries, lines of authority within public bureaucracies become confused, resulting in a loss of administrative capacity, as post-independence governments attempt to adjust to the demands of new development goals. Colonial bureaucracies are typically characterized by centralized, hierarchical structures with power usually concentrated in the Treasury. As new social policy objectives, requiring more co-ordinated and more decentralized policy implementation come into play, the disjunction between hierarchical and collegial decision-making agencies becomes more pronounced. Hong Kong is fortunate that this disjunction did not occur at the point of the handover but rather has been a feature of public policy-making since 1972. In this respect, the crisis that many independent countries face has already been experienced and, while the adaptation of a colonial structure to post-colonial social policy-making has not been easy, and even now has not been fully accomplished, it is a problem with which Hong Kong civil servants are long familiar (Scott and Cheek-Milby 1986, Scott 1987).

For much of its history, the Hong Kong public service functioned along classical colonial lines. Following the riots of 1966–1967, a series of reforms to labour legislation, complaint-handling procedures and control of corruption were introduced. In 1972, a new Governor, Sir Murray (later Lord) MacLehose committed the Hong Kong government to considerably increased expenditure on housing, social welfare, health and education (Scott 1989, pp 127–170). In the following year, McKinsey consultants were employed to devise a structure that would better facilitate the delivery of these services. Their major recommendation was the separation of branches, which were to be concerned with policy-making, from departments which were to be responsible for implementation (McKinsey 1973). The reforms did not subvert the public service's strongly hierarchical structure or detract from the powers of the Finance Department, but it did spread policy-making across the civil service to accommodate the new emphasis on social policy-making.

Subsequent reforms have been equally cautious. Sensitivity to the Chinese government's suspicions during the transition and some resistance to managerialist reforms have meant that the basic structure of the public service has not changed. Independent statutory bodies have been created for housing and hospitals; financial decentralization, including trading funds, public corporations and the establishment of non-department public bodies, has been approved in principle but implemented in only a few instances; and some measures have been taken to decentralize human resource management (Burns 1994, Cheung 1995, Cheung and Lee 1995, Law 1994, Hong Kong Government 1989). But the structure essentially remains that of a modernized colonial bureaucracy. This carries with it the advantages that lines of authority are clear and that implementation is swift, efficient and effective. These benefits are counterbalanced, however, by three significant costs. First, inadequate attention is paid to policy formulation at the top of the pyramid because resources are concentrated instead on implementation. Second, co-ordination of social policy-making, which requires flatter structures and lateral cooperation between departments, is often impeded by the hierarchical, autonomous structure of those departments (Scott 1987). Third, the bureaucracy still shows at times a lack of responsiveness to public concerns.

It is unlikely that these problems will be resolved in the short term. There has, of necessity, been some concern with bureaucratic responsiveness as the Chinese government threatened, and subsequently introduced, a Legislative Council which was unrepresentative (Hong Kong Government 1995). There have also been mild moves in the direction of introducing more private sector practices in the civil service. In Tung Chee-hwa's first address as Chief Executive, he revealed that he had set up a special group to develop and implement a target-based management process which would focus its early efforts on housing and care for the elderly (Tung 1997, p 51). There are also serious questions about the power relationships between the policy secretaries and Executive Councillors. But the structure of the rest of the public service, its lines of authority, and hence its continuing high levels of achievement of a particular kind of administrative capacity, are not likely to be significantly affected.

A career civil service and qualified personnel selected on merit

Since 1862, when a cadet system, the forerunner of the present administrative grade, was established, a career public service has been an essential component of the Hong Kong government (Lethbridge 1978, pp 31–51; Miners 1990, pp 85–111). Administrative and executive grade officers may be transferred within the service but the majority of officers spend their entire careers within a single department. While there may be tensions between these departmental officers and administrative grade officers, who may be brought in as their superiors, the system has generally tended to promote stability and to reinforce a hierarchical structure (Scott and Burns 1988). When promotion works on seniority rather than merit, professionals are employed on contract when needed, salaries are generous and there are sufficient financial resources available for the public sector to avoid the need for radical change, there are likely to be considerable forces in place in favour of maintaining the status quo.

In terms of administrative capacity, a career public service has several important advantages over a managerialist system. It is, first, easier to replace those who leave without a loss of institutional memory and decision-making precedents. By contrast, managerialist systems, which rely on the development of individuals with generic skills, who may serve on short-term contracts, tend to be more fragmented. Second, a career system is more likely to sustain and promote a public service ethos. The question of what this ethos might be, how it relates to the loyalties of public servants and what consequences it may have for the wider polity are significant issues that are discussed later in this paper. Third, and this is particularly important in the case of Hong Kong, a career public service provides a bulwark of stability in times of volatile political change. In the Sino-British agreement of 1984, the two governments emphasized their commitment to continuity in the practices and procedures of the civil service (Joint Declaration 1984: Annex 1, Sections I, III, IV, V and XII). It was stressed that appointments, promotions, recruitment, discipline, pay and conditions of service would be dealt with in accordance with existing principles (Letter from the current Chief Secretary, 27 September, 1984). The only changes envisaged were that British nationals would not be entitled to special benefits and that they could no longer hold the highest positions in the public service. The Chinese government has subsequently reiterated its support for these provisions (Preliminary Working Committee 1995). There is little reason to suppose that it, or its surrogate government in HongKong, would countenance a major restructuring of the public service, although there are justifiable concerns about the possibility of political appointments.

A focus on effective and efficient delivery of goods and services

All governments are concerned, to a greater or lesser degree, with the efficient and effective delivery of goods and services. For the Hong Kong government, however, efficiency has become something of an obsession. Lui has explained this fixation as a consequence of the colonial government's inability to develop legitimating political institutions (Lui 1994). If policy is being made and implemented without more than the cursory involvement of a weak legislature and a compliant Executive Council, accountability by results to a distant public becomes the justification for the regime's existence. Because of fiscal frugality, clear lines of authority and a well-qualified career public service, the Hong Kong government has the administrative capacity to deliver some goods and services at a high level of efficiency. It is generally able to do what it says it will do, particularly in the implementation of infrastructural projects. Successful projects and policies are unlikely to be seriously challenged by the Legislative Council, a factor that reinforces public service views on the importance of efficiency and effectiveness.

What is seemingly less subject to formal accountability processes is the efficiency and effectiveness of the Hong Kong government in the social policy arenas. Housing, education, health and social welfare standards all fall well below what might be expected from a government with the budgetary surpluses that the Hong Kong government generates. Part of the reason for this is structural: the public service is still not well adapted to providing these services. Part of it is ideological: there is resistance in influential circles inside and outside the government to the provision of some of these services. The end result is that social policy demands, often poorly articulated in the present climate, meet with an inadequate response. The government, given its ideological mindset, is unlikely to see social policy areas as priority issues in the future and there is a possibility of an increasing, and fractious, distance between civil society, whose autonomous groups often relate to social policy questions, and the public service.f

Political neutrality

Political neutrality is a short-hand way of describing a series of inter-related concepts which include *inter alia* loyalty to the government within the limits of the law and prescribed policy; anonymity and the secrecy of the bureaucratic decision-making process; responsibility to implement government policy regardless of the political affiliation of the civil servant; limited political rights for senior civil servants; impartiality of policy advice; and impartiality in the administration of rules and regulations (Scott 1996). In the Hong Kong context, it also implies, in the muted language of post-handover debate, non-interference from political and business interests and, especially, the Chinese government, in the affairs of the public service.

Hong Kong's senior leaders appear to have seen the threat to the political neutrality of the civil service principally in terms of political appointments. Patten's first benchmark for the continued success of Hong Kong, for example, contained the question:

> Are … key positions filled by individuals who command the confidence of their colleagues and the community and owe their appointments only to their ability?
>
> (Patten 1996, p 29)

One of his aides apparently believed that if senior civil servants 'were unable to sustain the pressure from China, Hong Kong... would soon be left with a "flabby Third World bureaucracy" which would rapidly succumb to the predators from the mainland' (Dimbleby 1997, p 353). And Anson Chan Fang On-sang, the Chief Secretary and head of the civil service, when asked what worried her most about the future, said:

> I think its very important for the civil service to remain politically neutral, for our system of recruitment and appointment to be based on the merits of the individual and not on political considerations.
>
> (Newsweek, 9 June 1997)

Political appointments would certainly shake the Hong Kong civil service to its foundations, but violations of any of the various dimensions of political neutrality could have serious implications for administrative capacity. In practice, political neutrality, as the term is used by Hong Kong's senior civil servants, simply describes the central features of the public service over the past two decades: its power and its autonomy.

For many years, the Hong Kong public service has been under the virtually exclusive political direction of senior civil servants, the policy secretaries. The last three Governors, Youde, Wilson and Patten, have been so pre-occupied with relations with China that the public service has almost run itself. It cannot be said in this sense to be politically neutral; the civil service has a view on how Hong Kong should be administered and what policies are appropriate for the territory and, in recent times, its views have almost always prevailed. Any challenge to its political power in the past – for example, from the democrats – has been resisted. It is possible that future challenges from the Chinese government or from the Chief Executive will also be resisted, or at least that the thrust of proposed changes will be modified. Closely related to the question of political power is the autonomy of the public service from business interests. Although business interests had an influential voice in government in colonial times, they did not dominate the government's agenda and they were not always happy with its policies. Hong Kong's present government is a government of business. If it seeks to impose policies designed to make short-term profits, it is likely to come into conflict with public servants who believe that they have longer-term responsibilities to the economy of the territory and who will seek to protect the notion of the 'level playing field' from those who seek to make expedient gains.

In sum, the syndrome of characteristics that made the Hong Kong public service strong and effective is likely to be only partially sustained in the post-handover era. Fiscal frugality, clear lines of authority and a public service recruited, for the most part, on the basis of merit are likely to be retained. But there are serious questions about whether turnover, possible rising levels of corruption and the threats to political neutrality in all its various manifestations might not lead to reduced administrative capacity. In the following sections, we consider, first, retention and wastage rates; second, the issue of bureaucratic corruption, which some see as a major problem for morale and eventually for declining efficiency; and, finally, the range of questions relating to administrative capacity that are incorporated in the term 'political neutrality' and which include important issues relating to the loyalty of civil servants.

Retention and turnover rates

Limited professional expertise and the inability to retain qualified and experienced personnel are often seen as major reasons for declining administrative capacity (Cohen and Wheeler 1997). In the Hong Kong context, a well-educated population, competitive civil service salaries, a defined career structure and the ability to recruit successfully outside the territory have all reduced the impact of political change on retention and wastage. At various times, however, concern has been expressed that rapid turnover in some groups, grades and occupations – for example, the directorate level, younger public servants taking early retirement, senior policy officers, nurses, social workers and local legal counsel – would have an effect on administrative capacity. While it is difficult to measure precisely what this effect would be, indicators could be lower levels of efficiency in the provision of goods and services and perceptions, both within the civil service and outside, that public servants were over-worked and that morale was low. To date, there is little evidence of lower levels of efficiency. Turnover has, however, created strains in some areas with increasing workloads and a significant number of officers acting above their substantive positions.

The Chinese government has been concerned about turnover at the directorate level, the thousand or so public servants who hold the most senior positions in the service. Under the Basic Law, the most senior public servants of all, the policy secretaries and heads of major bureaus, are appointed by the Chinese government (Basic Law: Act 48). Below this level, however, the Chinese government was concerned that it knew too little about potential turnover. In 1995, it demanded, through the Preliminary Working Committee, that the British government should inform it of 'any case of resignation, early retirement or normal retirement of the directorate officers' (Preliminary Working Committee 1995: 3). On a *prima facie* level, there was perhaps some reason for the Chinese government's concern. As Table 9.1 shows, the wastage rate of the directorate grade is significantly higher than the remainder of the public service and rose substantially in three of the five years prior to the handover. However, this can be explained by the decision not to renew a significant number of contracts over this period, by localization policies and by the fact that a higher proportion of the directorate than the civil service as a whole is nearing

Table 9.1   Turnover and localization at the directorate level

Year	Directorate level strength	Directorate turnover (i)	Civil service turnover (ii)	Local directorate (iii)
1985	900	7.67	3.74	49.11
1986	939	9.16	3.17	50.69
1987	997	5.42	2.82	52.26
1988	1057	5.58	4.04	55.63
1989	883	8.15	5.80	62.74
1990	972	7.61	5.73	66.36
1991	1032	6.49	5.16	68.60
1992	1006	16.40	8.00	66.70
1993	997	11.03	6.03	67.50
1994	1008	7.34	5.35	68.85
1995	1005	10.45	5.09	71.94
1996	1052	7.60	4.37	74.52

Source: *Civil Service Personnel Statistics* (1985–1996) Hong Kong, Civil Service Branch.
Notes: (i) Turnover as a percentage of directorate strength; (ii) Turnover as a percentage of civil service strength; (iii) Local directorate as a percentage of total directorate.

retirement age. The turnover rates in themselves do not seem sufficiently large to affect administrative capacity. However, if it were perceived that the motivation for directorate-level personnel leaving was because they were not politically acceptable, this would have serious repercussions for morale in the rest of the service.

As Table 9.2 shows, a growing number of public servants are opting to retire between 45, the earliest possible age, and 55, the normal retirement age. This can partly be explained by the changing age profile of the public service. In a workforce that has grown by only a small amount over the past 12 years, the number of public servants in the eligible age category has also increased. Between 1985 and 1996, civil servants between 20 and 29 dropped from 39.9 per cent of the establishment to 18 per cent, while the number between 40 and 49 rose from 16.3 per cent to 28.3 per cent (calculated from *Civil Service Personnel Statistics* (1985–1996)). While this explains part of the rise in early retirements, it is not the only cause. The Tiananmen Square massacre had a significant effect on the morale of the civil service. Resignation rates increased considerably in the aftermath of the massacre (see Table 9.2). There was probably also a delayed effect on the number of early retirements because some civil servants may have postponed their departure until they reached the age of 45 when they would be entitled to a pension. Turnover of staff has been at historically high rates in the transition period and, while it has been possible to fill vacancies with qualified replacements, there has also been a substantial number of new recruits to the service. In 1995 alone, for example, some 15 000 new appointments were made (Civil Service Personnel Statistics 1996). Many of

Table 9.2 Strength, retirements and resignations in the Hong Kong civil service, 1985–1996

Year	Total workforce strength	All retirements (%)	Voluntary early retirements (%)	Resignations (%)
1985	172 641	0.68	0.19	1.95
1986	175 481	0.64	0.20	1.54
1987	179 053	0.50	0.16	1.39
1988	182 843	0.59	0.19	2.22
1989	186 054	0.68	0.19	3.84
1990	188 393	0.68	0.17	4.20
1991	190 448	1.01	0.22	3.52
1992	185 685	1.22	0.29	3.09
1993	182 099	1.50	0.32	2.54
1994	180 695	1.93	0.32	2.12
1995	179 972	1.95	0.49	1.94
1996	182 675	2.18	0.50	1.55

Source: *Civil Service Personnel Statistics* (1985–1996) Hong Kong, Civil Service Branch.
Notes: 1. All percentages are in relation to 'Total Workforce Strength'; 2. 'Voluntary early retirement' covers those taking early retirement (below 55 years) and excludes those taking re-employment without a break in service.

the new recruits have experience in the private sector or public services elsewhere, but the ability of the public service to continue to employ able new recruits is by no means certain. Much will depend on its perceived attractiveness as an employer, on the stability of the service itself, and the political considerations that impinge upon its work.

Some grades in the civil service have experienced shortfalls in strength and recruitment as a result of factors largely beyond their control. The Legal Department, for example, has relied heavily on expatriate lawyers in the past, principally because it has had difficulty in recruiting local lawyers. The police force has also employed a disproportionately large number of expatriates in senior positions. Many of these will leave or will be replaced in the immediate post-handover period and there has been some concern among legislators that the numbers departing would put 'the law at risk' (South China Morning Post, 29 October 1996). If this is critical to the way in which services, such as policing, are delivered, then there could be serious, although probably temporary, repercussions. In general, however, it does not seem that turnover rates whether at the directorate level, among middle-ranking, middle-aged civil servants or among specific grades will affect administrative capacity in the short term.

Bureaucratic corruption

Bureaucratic corruption need not in itself lead to a loss of administrative capacity but it is generally assumed that it will act on the environment, eroding morale within the service and reducing public confidence in its integrity and in the equity of its decisions. There is a widespread belief in Hong Kong that corruption is on the increase; an Independent Commission Against Corruption (ICAC) survey in 1996 found that 70 per cent of those surveyed expected to see corruption rise (ICAC 1997a). There is some support for this belief found in the number of non-election corruption reports to the ICAC in 1996 (see Table 9.3 and ICAC 1997b). However, the increase is small and it is too early to judge whether these trends will continue. At present, the majority of public sector corruption complaints relate to the police (44 per cent of all complaints), housing (10 per cent), urban services (9 per cent) and buildings and land (6 per cent). There has been little change in this pattern over the years 1992 to 1996. If there is an increase in corruption, it seems probable that it will occur disproportionately in these departments and in the private sector.

Public perceptions about corruption in the civil service are probably more important than the reports or complaints received by the ICAC. A major blow to the clean image of government were the events surrounding what was in effect the dismissal of the Director of Immigration, Lawrence Leung Ming-yin. As it eventually transpired, Leung was given an ultimatum in July 1996 to either retire or be dismissed. He chose to retire, citing work pressure and health problems linked to the murder of his daughter in Canada three years previously (South China Morning Post, 11, 13 January 1997; Hong Kong Standard, 11 January 1997). Following his retirement, rumours, based on the assumption that he had been forced out, began to circulate (Gilley 1996). One rumour was that he had unexplained assets beyond his income, an offence under Hong Kong's corruption laws. Another was that he had assisted illegal immigration into the territory and that he had compromised the British Nationality Scheme by leaking

Table 9.3 Corruption reports, 1995–1996

	1995	1996	Percentage change
Corruption reports (non-election)	2987	3086	+3
Police	561 (19%)	576 (19%)	+3
Other government departments	687 (23%)	738 (24%)	+6
Private sector (non-election)	1630 (54%)	1651 (53%)	+1
Public bodies	109 (4%)	131 (4%)	+20

Source: Independent Commission Against Corruption, *Key Statistics for Briefing/Media Interviews* Hong Kong, Mimeo, May, 1997.

information to the Chinese government about which senior civil servants had British passports (Gilley 1996; Dimbleby 1997, p 391–393). The Chinese government, which had always been opposed to the nationality scheme, would almost certainly have regarded Hong Kong civil servants with British passports as disloyal. Morale in the service would have been adversely affected and resignations and retirements of senior officials would have increased.

In October 1996, the Legislative Council decided to launch an enquiry into the incident. When Leung gave evidence before the Select Committee appointed to deal with the case, he was able to dispel some of the rumours. He revealed that the ICAC had indeed investigated his financial affairs but had concluded that there was insufficient evidence to warrant a prosecution, a fact that was confirmed by the ICAC itself (Hong Kong Standard, 11 January 1997). Although Leung did live a lifestyle far in excess of his income, his wealth was inherited or attributed to the commercial activities of his wife. In response to Legislative Councillors' questions about the reasons for his retirement, Leung said that the Secretary for the Civil Service had told him that the government no longer trusted him but that he did not know why this was so (South China Morning Post, 11 January 1997). His relationships with the Chinese government also came under scrutiny. A caller to a radio station revealed that he had seen Leung in conversation in a coffee shop with a Chinese official, Chen Zuo'er, shortly after his meeting with the Secretary for the Civil Service. Leung admitted that he had met with Chen but said that the meeting had been pre-arranged and lasted only ten minutes. Chinese officials had previously called for a full enquiry into Leung's case and the communist press in Hong Kong described him as a victim of 'political persecution' (see Yeung 1997).

The Hong Kong government was understandably reluctant to see the dispute widened into a Sino-British confrontation or into one that might pit loyal civil servants against those supported by, or close to, the Chinese government. The Secretary for the Civil Service, Lam Woon-kwang, emphasized that the case was '…an employment matter between the Hong Kong Government and Mr Leung himself. I want to state that the UK Government was not involved in the matter in any way' (South China Morning Post, 11 January 1997).

The Governor, Chris Patten, was apparently also keen to scotch the rumour that the names of civil servants with British passports could have been leaked to the Chinese government; Leung did not have access to the list, which was to be returned to Britain at the time of the handover (Dimbleby 1997). When the Secretary for the Civil Service gave evidence to the Select Committee, he gave further details of the reasons for the decision to force Leung to retire. First, he had failed to repay a HK$1.76 million government housing loan immediately after a Canadian flat he bought with the money was sold. Second, he had failed to make full disclosure of his investments in a company owned by the legislator and landowner, Lau Wong-fat. Third, he failed to report an investment of HK$100 000 in a business that intended to develop advertising in China, a company that was found to have links with the Chinese leadership (South China Morning Post, 16 January 1997). Legislators pressed for the release of the ICAC report and a police integrity report on Leung. The Chief Secretary and the Secretary for the Civil Service did present the reports to the Select Committee in camera, the Select Committee chair reportedly describing the contents as 'shocking' (South China Morning Post, 23 January 1997). There the matter rested.

The Leung case brought together two key public concerns about the state of the civil service. First, it involved suspicions of corruption at the highest level. ICAC investigations of a senior official were bound to confirm public perceptions that bureaucratic corruption was on the increase even though the official concerned was cleared of wrong-doing. Second, the Leung case raised the vexed question of the loyalties of civil servants. Leung's loyalty was not in itself an issue, for the government did not believe that he was guilty of leaking critical information to the Chinese side. However, evidence that he had close relationships with senior Chinese officials touched sensitive nerves in a charged situation. Was it appropriate that senior civil servants should develop such relationships? Could this be squared with commitments to the traditions and culture of the Hong Kong civil service, the Special Administrative Region government and the people of Hong Kong?

Loyalty and political neutrality

The greatest potential threat to administrative capacity in Hong Kong is the erosion of what is vaguely referred to as political neutrality. Senior civil servants tend to define neutrality as the diametrical opposite of a politically appointed service. But there are other implications of impending changes to the relationship between the executive of the HKSAR government and the Chinese government and the public service. These may be divided into three categories: questions about the loyalties and attitudes of civil servants; increasing political authority of the HKSAR Executive Council and policy branches in the civil service; and the possibility of direct interference in Hong Kong affairs by the Chinese government.

Loyalties and attitudes

Maintaining the loyalties of public servants has always been a problem for Hong Kong governments. Under British colonialism, some public servants, such as police officers, may have sworn allegiance to the Crown, but the majority probably felt that their primary loyalties were to the people of the territory or to the culture and traditions of the service itself (Lui 1988). Possible contradictions between these, and other, values intensified as the transitional period drew to a close. Chinese government claims on the loyalty of public servants, the rise of the democrats and the response of Hong Kong citizens to the Tiananmen Square massacre all made for potentially volatile changes in attitudes within the service.

The Chinese government was suspicious of the relationship between senior public servants and the British government, suspicions that were exacerbated by the conflict over the 1995 electoral system and its belief that the British government was attempting to impede the transfer of sovereignty. The concept of political neutrality and the notion that governments of whatever complexion could be impartially and objectively served by top officials was completely contrary to the experience of the Chinese leaders. Yet the assumption that senior civil servants had pledged their allegiance to London was not valid: 'They accept orders from above out of respect for authority and to avoid conflict. There is not any need for Beijing and the SAR chief to be highly suspicious about the senior civil service' (Wong 1997, p 98).

Towards the end of the transitional period, a number of retired senior public servants openly identified themselves with the Chinese government and there were rumours that they might be brought back to ensure the loyalty of the service. Although the Preliminary Working Committee had promised that there would be no settling of scores or major reshuffles in the senior civil service, the issue of the abolition of the elected 1995 Legislative Council and its replacement with one that was essentially appointed made the position of senior civil servants extremely difficult (Preliminary Working Committee 1995, pp 2, 4). A committee set up by the Chinese government voted in March 1996 to proscribe the legislature. The British government and most of the territory's citizens were understandably opposed to the cavalier way in which their electoral rights had been treated. The Chief Secretary and head of the Civil Service, Anson Chan Fang On-sang, made it clear that she regretted the decision, echoing the views of the Governor, Chris Patten (Eastern Express, 25 March 1996). In response, the Chinese government demanded that policy secretaries support the proscription of the legislature or face demotion after the handover (Hong Kong Standard, 25 March 1996; Financial Times, 27 March 1996). In the event, the threat was not acted upon and the new Chief Executive, with the approval of the Chinese government, endorsed the incumbent policy secretaries.

Both the Chinese and the HKSAR governments know that the 'right of abode' provision in the Basic Law will be sufficient to maintain compliance with political directives, if not to ensure positive support. Article 101 states that 'only Chinese citizens among Permanent Residents of the Region with no right of abode in any foreign country' may hold the 27 most senior positions in the civil service (Basic Law, Article 101). The Law makes senior civil servants vulnerable to political manipulation simply because they have no right to leave Hong Kong. Beyond this negative sanction, the Chinese government, and probably most of the HKSAR Executive Council, want to see a civil service that responds positively to developments in China. In an interview with the *South China Morning Post*, Leung Chun-Ying, an Executive Councillor who has been given a brief for producing improvements in housing policy, argued that civil servants knew little about China. Using an analogy, he said that a civil servant's office, prior to the handover, always had two things: a portrait of the Queen and a large map of Hong Kong. Beyond the map, however, there was a blank space where China ought to have figured prominently. Leung saw this as reflecting the attitudes and mind-set of civil servants and he did not expect them to change for many years, although he felt that it was imperative that they should (South China Morning Post, 10 May 1997).

Leung may well be correct. Surveys conducted by Lui and Cooper in the last two decades, which focus on the attitudes of senior public servants, suggest that they hold values that might well be antithetical to those held by the Chinese and HKSAR governments. Lui and Cooper found that a majority of senior civil servants tend to favour liberal and democratic values (Cooper and Lui 1990); that the Hong Kong official is 'not the archetype of a bureaucrat who would carry out the dictates of his superiors without any moral reflection' (Lui and Cooper 1996, p 193); and that they had a strong commitment to their community and the values of their organization (Lui and Cooper 1997). These findings do not sit easily with the view that the Hong Kong civil service can be moulded to new tasks beyond the parameters of its present value framework. If the political objectives envisaged by Leung, his colleagues on the Executive Council and their counsellors in Beijing, are imposed on the Hong Kong public service, it will be at the expense of some tacit resistance and some loss of administrative capacity. There may be no reason to question the loyalty of senior public servants to the regime in power, but to suggest that they might be persuaded to share its values and attitudes is stretching the point.

The Executive Council and the civil service

Hong Kong's constitutional development was very different from that of other British colonies. Although there was a belated attempt to introduce more democratic electoral practices in the 1990s, nothing was done to create a more responsible executive. Executive Councillors were simply advisers to the Governor and, although they were occasionally drawn from among Legislative Councillors, there was no requirement that they should be representative of any particular section of the population. Patten went further and separated the Executive and Legislative Council membership. Had he conceded the demand of democrats that their electoral victories warranted seats on the Executive Council, he would have immediately been condemned by the Chinese government. The separation of Executive and Legislative Council membership made his task easier (Dimbleby 1997, p 123) and it left policy secretaries in effect as ministers, but it did nothing to resolve questions of accountability and of the relationship between the political executive and the civil service.

When Tung Chee-hwa acceded to power, he did so in the context of a series of Chinese-appointed committees that had been preparing for the handover, principally by identifying those laws that the Chinese government wanted repealed. The team that Tung Chee-hwa set up to advise him soon came into conflict with the policy secretaries. Neither side was accountable to the Legislative Council, nor in any direct sense to the population, but the senior civil servants did enjoy considerable respect in the community. Anson Chan Fang On-sang, the Chief Secretary, for example, had more support among the population for the Chief Executive's position than Tung Chee-hwa himself (DeGolyer 1998). The senior civil servants clearly resented intrusions from the new team and, particularly, from Executive Councillors who were given portfolios with responsibility for such areas as housing and social welfare. From the civil service standpoint, this represented an unjustified erosion of their previously autonomous position.

Anson Chan had indicated her own reservations about the changing role of the civil service when she declined to stand for the office of Chief Executive. In an interview in June 1997, she said that she might resign on matters of principle and implicitly criticized the Chief Executive claiming, '... he has *some* understanding of the way the government works [but] he doesn't have a real deep understanding of how the government machinery works' (Newsweek, 9 June 1997).

The interview was taken in Hong Kong to signal two developments. First, that the Chief Secretary was being side-lined by the new regime (Dimbleby 1997, p 421). And, second, that, by speaking out in the interview in defence of civil liberties, she had staked out a position rather different from that of the more evasive future Chief Executive (South China Morning Post, 11 June 1997).

Subsequent developments after the handover suggest that the new executive is attempting to impose its will on the civil service. Less than a month after assuming office, it was announced – first by the New China News Agency and then by the HKSAR government – that the policy secretaries were to be re-shuffled (South China Morning Post, 28 July 1997). Among the appointments was a new Secretary for Electoral Affairs who was to prove instrumental in introducing a system for the May 1998 elections designed to discriminate against the democrats. The announcement that some Executive Councillors would be given what were in effect portfolios and calls by one of them, Leung Chun-Ying, for the civil service to be given more direction were portents of impending changes in political control.

The basic problem for the new executive is that it does not have popular support, owing its presence almost entirely to the preferences of the Chinese government. For the executive to attempt to assert control over the civil service, it will require the services of compliant senior officials who do not have misgivings about its political agenda. While there may be sufficient numbers of these officials, there are likely to be others, like Anson Chan, who might wish to resign or who, in the time-honoured tradition of the Hong Kong civil service, frustrate some of the aims of their political masters. In either event, the administrative capacity of the service is diminished; coherence and continuity in the formulation and implementation of policy will almost certainly be affected.

The Chinese government and the civil service

There seems little doubt that the Chinese government is monitoring developments in the civil service actively and that it has full dossiers on senior officials. It will seek assurances of the loyalty of these officials either directly, or more likely through an executive that has already articulated its belief that the civil service should be more responsive to Chinese demands. If this loyalty is achieved through expeditious promotions and the demotion of those who cannot be trusted, the morale of the service will be prejudiced. If it is achieved through threats, damage may spread to the community as the integrity of the service itself is called into question. Whether political control is achieved through gradual changes by the executive, as seems likely, or through more overt intervention by the Chinese government, political neutrality will be eroded. When that happens, a range of other values – impartiality, the rule of law and the integrity of the service – will also be threatened. This will reduce administrative capacity simply because the conflict of values that will ensue will adversely affect the culture of the service, challenging its raison d'etre and eroding its authority.

Conclusion

Provided that the Hong Kong civil service remains insulated from political interference, there is no reason to suppose that it cannot continue to deliver goods and services efficiently and effectively. Its key structural features – fiscal frugality, clear lines of authority and recruitment on merit – remain in place. Its present establishment is well qualified and the territory continues to produce able graduates from whom new recruits can be drawn. Increasing bureaucratic corruption may be a problem, but it is not likely to have an immediate effect. Even if the strength of its key structural features are gradually eroded, the loss of administrative capacity in the civil service will not be felt in the community for some years to come.

The political issues are of a different order. Neutrality of the civil service essentially means recognition of the impartiality and objectivity of its senior officials. Once the loyalty of civil servants is in question, their actions are in effect subject to political criteria. If this, in turn, is linked to issues relating to control, if the Executive Council begins to act as a set of unelected ministers without mandates, the response of the service and the community it serves is not likely to be positive. In a worst case scenario, evidence of direct intervention from the Chinese government in the form of political appointments and of directions to the service to take a particular line, will have wider ramifications for the political future of the territory and the strength of the 'One Country – Two Systems' concept. Administrative capacity is sustained and reinforced by a reiteration of the importance of the values and culture of the service; political interference cuts across these values by undermining established decision-making routines and practices. The cost of such expediency is a rapid loss of administrative capacity.

Bibliography

Baker, R. (ed.) 1992 *Public Administration in Small and Island States*. Connecticut: Kumarian.

Barratt Brown, M. 1995 *Africa's Choices*. Harmondsworth: Penguin.

Burns, J. P. 1994 'Administrative Reform in a Changing Political Environment'. *Public Administration and Development* 14.

Chan, Fang On-Sang Anson (Chief Secretary) 1984 Letter to the author, 27 September.

Chan, K. M. 1997 'Combating Corruption and the ICAC', in Cheng, J. Y. S. (ed.) *The Other Hong Kong Report 1997*. Hong Kong: Chinese University Press.

Cheung, A. B. L. 1995 *The Politics of Administrative Reform in Hong Kong: Corporatization of Public Services During the 1980s*. Unpublished PhD thesis, University of London.

Cheung, A. B. L., Lee, J. C. Y. 1995 (eds) *Public Sector Reform in Hong Kong*. Hong Kong: Chinese University Press.

Citizens Party 1997 *Hong Kong: A Model for Economic and Social Enterprise: A Five-Year Plan*. Address by Citizens Party, Hong Kong, 28 September 1997.

Civil Service Branch, Government Secretariat 1985–1996, *Civil Service Personnel Statistics*, mimeo, Hong Kong.

Cohen, J. M., Wheeler, J. R. 1997 'Building Sustainable Professional Capacity in African Public Sectors: Retention Constraints in Kenya'. *Public Administration and Development*, 17(3) (August).

Consultative Committee for the Basic law of the Hong Kong Special Administrative Region of the People's Republic of China 1990, *Basic Law of the Hong Kong Special Administrative Region of the People's Republic of China 1990*, Hong Kong, April 1990.

Cooper, T. L., Lui, T. T. 1990 'Democracy and the Administrative State: The Case of Hong Kong'. *Public Administration Review* 50(3).

DeGolyer, M. 1998 'Public Opinion on Hong Kong's Transition', in Scott, I. (ed.) *Institutional Change and the Political Transition in Hong Kong*. Basingstoke: Macmillan.

Dimbleby, J. 1997 *The Last Governor: Chris Patten and the Handover of Hong Kong*. London: Little Brown.

Eastern Express, 25 March 1996.

Financial Times, 27 March 1996.

Gilley, B. 1996 'Loud Silence'. *Far Eastern Economic Review*, 7 November.

Grindle, M. S., Thomas, J. W. 1991 *Public Choices and Policy Changes*. Baltimore: John Hopkins University Press.

Ho, H. C. Y. 1996 'The structure of public finances', in Ho, H. C. Y, Chau, L. C. (eds) *The Hong Kong Economy in Transition*. Hong Kong: Asia Research Service.

Hong Kong Government 1989 *Public Sector Reform*. Hong Kong: Finance Branch, February.

Hong Kong Government 1995 *Serving the Community*. Hong Kong: Government Printer.

Hong Kong Government 1997 *Hong Kong: The 1997–98 Budget*. Hong Kong: Government Printer.

Hong Kong Hansard 1992/3, Government Printer: Hong Kong.

Hong Kong Standard, various.

Hope, K. R. 1995 'Managing the Public Sector in Botswana: Some Emerging Constraints and the Administrative Reform Responses'. *Public Administration and Development*, 15.

Independent Commission against Corruption 1997a *Key Statistics for Briefing/Media Interviews*. Hong Kong: Government Printer.

Independent Commission Against Corruption 1997b *Annual Report 1996*. Hong Kong: Government Printer.

Langseth, P. 1995 'Civil Service Reform in Uganda: Lessons Learned'. *Public Administration and Development*, 15.

Law, F. 1994 'Hong Kong: The Challenge of Managing the Government's Human Resources', in Scott, I., Thynne, I. (eds) *Public Sector Reform: Critical Issues and Perspectives*. Hong Kong: AJPA.

Lethbridge, H. J. 1978 *Hong Kong: Stability and Change*. Hong Kong: Oxford University Press.

Lui, T. T. 1988 'Changing Civil Servants' Values', in Scott, I., Burns, J. P. (eds) *The Hong Kong Civil Service and its Future*. Hong Kong: Oxford University Press.

Lui, T. T. 1994 'Efficiency as a Political Concept in the Hong Kong Government: Issues and Problems', in Burns, J. P. (ed.) *Asian Civil Service Systems: Improving Efficiency and Productivity,* Singapore: Times Academic Press.

Lui T. T., Cooper, T. L. 1996 'Bureaucracy, Democracy and Administrative Ethics: a Study of Public Service Values in Hong Kong'. *International Review of Administrative Sciences*, 62(2).

Lui, T. T., Cooper, T. L. 1997 'Administrative Ethics and the Hong Kong Public Servant'. *Administration and Society* 29(3).

McKinsey and Company 1973 *The Machinery of Government: A New Framework for Expanding Services*. Hong Kong: Government Printer.

Miners, N. 1990 *The Government and Politics of Hong Kong*, 5th edn. Hong Kong: Oxford University Press.

Newsweek 1997, 9 June.

Patten, C. 1996 *Hong Kong: Transition*. Address by the Governor at the opening of the 1996/1997 session of the Legislative Council, Hong Kong: Government Printer, 2 October.

Preliminary Working Committee 1995 *Some Views of the Preliminary Working Committee of the HKSAR Preparatory Committee on Maintaining the Stability of the Hong Kong Civil Service and its System.* mimeo, Hong Kong, 8 December.

Scott, I. 1987 'Policy Implementation in Hong Kong'. *South East Asian Journal of Social Science,* 15(2).

Scott, I. 1989 *Political Change and the Crisis of Legitimacy in Hong Kong*. London: Hurst.

Scott, I. 1996 'Civil Service Neutrality in Hong Kong', in Asmeron, H. K., Reis, E. P. (eds) *Democratization and Bureaucratic Neutrality*. Basingstoke: Macmillan.

Scott, I. 1998 (ed.) *Institutional Change and the Political Transition in Hong Kong*. Basingstoke: Macmillan.

Scott, I., Burns, J. P. 1988 *The Hong Kong Civil Service and its Future*. Hong Kong: Oxford University Press.

Scott, I., Cheek-Milby, K. 1986 'An Overview of Hong Kong's Social Policy-making Process'. *Asian Journal of Public Administration* 8(2).

South China Morning Post, various.

Tordoff, W. (ed.) 1980 *Administration in Zambia*. Manchester: Manchester University Press.

Tung Chee-hwa 1997 *Building Hong Kong for a New Era*. Address to the Provisional Legislative Council, Hong Kong: Government Printer, 8 October.

Turner, M., Hulme, D. 1997 *Governance, Administration and Development: Making the State Work*. Basingstoke: Macmillan.

Umeh, O. J. 1992 'Capacity Building and Development Administration in Southern African Countries'. *International Review of Administrative Sciences* 58(1): 57–70.

Wong, F. 1997 'The Civil Service', in Cheng, J. Y. S. (ed.) *The Other Hong Kong Report 1997*. Hong Kong: Chinese University Press.

Yeung, C. 1997 'Everyone Loses in the Leung Debacle', *South China Morning Post*, 15 January.

10
Constitutional Dilemmas in the Hong Kong Special Administrative Region

Peter Wesley-Smith

The courts of the Hong Kong Special Administrative Region (HKSAR) have operated only since 3 July 1997, and in that time only a handful of cases of much constitutional significance have been decided. The first, and arguably the most significant so far, was *HKSAR v. David Ma Wai-kwan* [1997] HKLRD 761. In that case the Court of Appeal (sitting to determine questions of law reserved by the Court of First Instance) discussed the continuity of the British Hong Kong legal system into the HKSAR period and the constitutional validity of the provisional legislature. It is proposed in this paper to consider these primary questions. (On other aspects of the case, see Chan 1997b and Watson-Brown 1998.)

It should be noted at the outset that, although the Court of Appeal in the *David Ma* case confidently asserted the legality of the provisional legislature, the question cannot be regarded as finally settled. This is because the Court of Final Appeal has not so far had to express an opinion. However, given that complete constitutional paralysis could well be the result of a contrary decision, it seems unlikely that the Court of Final Appeal would disagree with the lower court. In any event, this is a question that would probably require, or at least provoke, the interpretive intervention of the Standing Committee of the National People's Congress (NPC) (see Article 158 of the Basic Law, BL158), and it is unimaginable that the Standing Committee would support the destruction of the provisional legislature. The Court of Appeal gave two reasons for its decision, and it was thought by some, including this author, that the second reason, relating to the provisional legislature, was technically *obiter* and thus not binding on the Court of Appeal itself or on lower courts. However, the court had another opportunity to consider the legality of the provisional legislature in *Cheung Lai-wah v. Director of Immigration* (1998) CA, Civ App Nos 203 & 216 of 1997, and all three judges held that both reasons were part of the *ratio decidendi* of the earlier decision and thus binding on the court. They therefore declined to reconsider the matter.

Background

The Basic Law, adopted by the NPC on 4 April 1990 and put into effect on 1 July 1997, is the HKSAR's codified (or written) constitution (Wesley-Smith 1994, pp 2–3, pp 68–69): it establishes the institutions of HKSAR government and defines their functions, it specifies the law that is to apply in the HKSAR, it provides for the fundamental rights and duties of residents, and it prescribes the relationship between the HKSAR and the PRC. Article 66 of that Law states that the Legislative Council (Legco) shall be the legislature of the HKSAR. The method for forming Legco 'shall be specified in the light of the actual situation in the Hong Kong SAR' (BL68). Annex II provides for the formation of the first Legco in accordance with an NPC decision made when the Basic Law was adopted: an NPC-appointed Preparatory Committee was to be 'responsible for preparing the establishment of the Region and shall prescribe the specific method for forming the first Government and the first Legislative Council in accordance with this Decision'. The first Legco's composition is prescribed by the decision, which goes on:

> If the composition of the last Hong Kong Legislative Council before the establishment of the HKSAR is in conformity with the relevant provisions of this Decision and the Basic Law of the Hong Kong SAR, those of its members who uphold the Basic Law of the Region may, upon confirmation by the Preparatory Committee, become members of the first Legislative Council of the Region.

That is, in the terminology widely used in Hong Kong during the transition, the Legislative Council to be elected in 1995 was to be on the 'through train' and its members were to hold office in the first Legco until 1999.

As is well known, however, this through train was derailed by the PRC's reaction to Governor Chris Patten's package of proposals for election of the 1995 Legco. Governor Patten sought to exploit what he saw as an opportunity in the Basic Law to extend the degree of democracy to be afforded the territory's citizens. Whether his programme did, in fact, conflict with the Basic Law, as well as the Sino-British Joint Declaration on the Question of Hong Kong 1984 and less formal agreements or understandings between Britain and China, as the Chinese authorities alleged, could be endlessly debated. China may have objected more to the manner of the announcement than to the actual content of the proposals, but in any event Chinese opposition was implacable.

The Hong Kong government nevertheless persevered with electoral reform and, in consequence, on 31 August 1994 the Standing Committee of the NPC decided that the last Hong Kong British Legco would terminate on 30 June 1997. The Preparatory Committee, invoking its mandate regarding 'matters relating to the preparation for the establishment of the Hong Kong SAR', then resolved to form the 'Provisional Legislative Council of the Hong Kong SAR', which was to begin work after appointment of the first Chief Executive (see Chen 1997a and, for a chronology and reproduction of all essential documents in English, Chen 1997b). The PC's work report was approved (perhaps ratified) by the NPC on 14 March 1997. The Provisional Legislative Council (PLC) was duly established well before the HKSAR came into being and, sitting in Shenzhen, began passing bills. An application for judicial review to challenge its constitutionality was thrown out, on technical grounds, in June 1997 (*Ng King-luen v. Rita Fan* [1997] HKLRD 757). On 1 July the PLC passed the Hong Kong Reunification Ordinance, which purported to validate certain matters and, lest there be doubt about transitional arrangements, provide for the continuity of laws and institutions. The ordinance could be effective, of course, only if the PLC had been validly created.

The legal issues in the *David Ma* Case

David Ma and two others were charged in August 1995 with conspiracy under the common law and were committed to stand trial before the High Court. The trial began in June 1997 and was adjourned on the last working day of the month. Three days later British sovereignty and jurisdiction over Hong Kong ceased and the HKSAR was born. On 3 July, the case was resumed before the same judge, now appointed by the Chief Executive as a deputy judge of the Court of First Instance; the defendants challenged his jurisdiction and the matter was reserved for determination by the Court of Appeal. The principal question formally posed was whether the offence of conspiracy at common law was part of the laws of the HKSAR. Other matters were also raised: whether the termination of British sovereignty put an end to the proceedings and whether the Court of First Instance could properly assume jurisdiction over a case begun in the pre-HKSAR High Court. The defendants' main contentions, however, were that BL160 ('Upon the establishment of the Hong Kong SAR, the laws previously in force in Hong Kong shall be adopted as laws of the Region except for those which the Standing Committee of the NPC declares to be in contravention of this Law' (first paragraph)) required a positive, express, formal act of adoption of the laws. This included the common law, previously in force (see BL8), that no such act of adoption had been performed by the NPC or its Standing Committee, and that, insofar as the Hong Kong Reunification Ordinance purported to adopt the laws previously in force, it was futile because the ordinance was passed by the PLC and the PLC, being unlawfully established, was incompetent at law to make valid legislation. Thus was raised the crucial question of the constitutional propriety of the PLC and with it the authority of the NPC *vis-à-vis* Hong Kong.

The political issue

The people of Hong Kong have been constantly reassured that the Basic Law, being a controlled (rigid) constitution in the care of an independent judiciary, and implementing a treaty registered with the United Nations, would provide a solid legal buffer between Hong Kong and the PRC. This entails that the Basic Law be as binding on the PRC authorities as on the HKSAR people and government, and in particular that it constrain the NPC in its dealings with the HKSAR. However, if the NPC could ignore the Basic Law, for example, by authorizing the establishment of a provisional legislature that seems to be inconsistent with that Law, or at least could make decisions that the HKSAR courts could not review, the constitution would fail, in legal terms, to implement the promises made. This was raised early in 1997 by Professor Albert Chen. Referring to the NPC's (then anticipated) resolution approving the PC's work report, Chen wrote:

> As the resolution will, under the constitution and legal system of the PRC, be legally binding on the courts of the HKSAR, it will suffice for the purpose of forestalling any legal challenge to the PLC mounted before the courts of the HKSAR.
>
> (Chen 1997a, p 8)

This seemed to blend the HKSAR and PRC legal systems, contrary to the notion of 'One Country – Two Systems', and to ensure the subordinacy of the HKSAR courts to the political institutions on the mainland (Wesley-Smith 1997, p 126).

Thus, there seemed to be much at stake in the *David Ma* case, and there was great interest in how the judges, whose professional concern it is to uphold the rule of law, would handle issues of such grave import.

The principal legal decision

All three justices of appeal agreed that the Basic Law itself had sufficiently arranged the transition such that legal proceedings against Ma and his co-defendants could continue beyond the end of June. No express act of adoption was necessary to maintain the common law previously in force, since BL8 had already provided for the previous law to continue. 'Shall be adopted' was imperative and declaratory, with no connotation of some future act. BL81 (courts *shall be* established and the judicial system previously practised *shall be* maintained) and BL87 (principles previously applied in criminal or civil proceedings *shall be* maintained) were similarly declaratory, reflecting the continuity and 'seamless transition' that the Basic Law was at pains to ensure. These provisions, as well as the second paragraph of BL160 ('Documents, certificates, and rights and obligations valid under the laws previously in force in Hong Kong *shall* continue to be valid ...') and BL19 (the courts *shall* have jurisdiction over all cases in the Region), maintained the indictment, the rights and obligations of prosecution and accused, and the courts themselves, their jurisdiction, and the principles by which they exercised it.

On this basis, the case for Ma was lost. Whether a specific act of adoption had occurred, and whether the Hong Kong Reunification Ordinance was valid, were quite immaterial. It was thus unnecessary to consider the further arguments. Nevertheless, all three judges proceeded to analyse and debunk any suggestion that the courts were empowered to examine the legality of NPC decisions or that the PLC was of dubious validity.

The reviewability of NPC decisions

The PLC was validly established because: (1) it had been created by the PC in the proper exercise of that body's powers; (2) in any event the NPC had ratified its creation; and (3) the NPC's decisions are beyond judicial review in the HKSAR. It is this last proposition that is of the greatest importance.

The reasoning seems to be based on the provision in BL19 that the restrictions on the HKSAR courts' jurisdiction 'imposed by the legal system and principles previously in force in Hong Kong shall be maintained'. Mr Justice Patrick Chan CJHC thought it difficult to imagine that the British Hong Kong courts could challenge the validity of a UK Act of Parliament or an Order in Council passed by the Queen for Hong Kong; the PRC now being sovereign over Hong Kong, its highest organ of state power, the NPC, can act for Hong Kong without restraint enforced by HKSAR courts (pp 780I–781F). Nazareth VP accepted that, under inter alia the doctrine of parliamentary sovereignty, the British Hong Kong courts were incompetent to review imperial legislation (pp 793H–794B). Mortimer VP simply regarded it as self-evident that the legality or validity of laws made by the NPC and its Standing Committee was not open to challenge in the HKSAR courts (p 807G). Further, establishment of the PLC was not in any event contrary to the Basic Law: the PLC was not the first Legco and therefore did not need to comply with the Basic Law's stipulations for that body: 'The establishment of the PLC was outside the Basic Law and collateral with it. It was part of the arrangements and method for establishing the first Legislative Council' (Mortimer VP, p 809B).

Consequences

Immediately after the decision was handed down, the Solicitor General, Mr Daniel Fung SC, who had argued the case before the court, stated his view that an amendment to the Basic Law which did not observe the prescribed requirements would not be valid (Fung 1997) Albert Chen, a Hong Kong member of the Beijing-appointed Committee for the Basic Law, believes that the decision does not mean 'that any act, decision, or resolution of the NPC that is relevant to or touches upon Hong Kong has the force of law in Hong Kong': once the Basic Law came into operation the NPC could not act inconsistently with it, and its normative acts could only have legal force in the HKSAR if made applicable to it under BL18 (Chen 1997c, p 390). There is a distinction, therefore, between what was necessary to establish the SAR and implement the Basic Law prior to 1 July 1997, and what can be done after the Basic Law has entered into force.

Can such a distinction be maintained? This author does not believe there is authority for it in the judgements handed down by the Court of Appeal. This is because each judge relied on the notion of sovereignty as precluding any inquiry by HKSAR courts as to the constitutional propriety of whatever the sovereign does. 'There is simply no legal basis' for regional courts 'to query the validity of any legislation or acts passed by the sovereign', ruled Chan CJHC (p 780J). Nazareth VP's logic ran thus: if the PC is a working committee under the NPC, which it is, the Court of Appeal could not review its constitutionality or the legality of its actions, and it must follow that the constitutionality of the PLC was equally beyond judicial scrutiny (p 794A–B). What counted was sovereignty. If the acts of the British sovereign in its colonies could not be questioned – merely confirmed and implemented – the acts of the NPC in its SAR could equally not be questioned.

The court did not of course consider NPC decisions taken after 30 June, but the reasoning is equally applicable to such decisions. The only question, ultimately, was whether the PC had acted within the authority conferred on it by the NPC (e.g. p 796I); once that was answered affirmatively there was nothing more to be said. 'The NPC being the sovereign of the HKSAR, the validity of the acts of establishing this interim body cannot be challenged in the HKSAR courts' (p 786D). Nor did the court have to consider an apparent breach of the Basic Law, since it held that the PLC was not a creation of the Basic Law, was not the first Legislative Council nor was it ever intended to be (p 786A), and if its creation produced any inconsistency with the Basic Law the NPC decisions had to prevail (p 796H). 'Far from breaching the Basic Law', said Mortimer VP, '...the formation of the PLC was consistent with efforts to comply with the law...' (p 809B). Again, however, the clear ground relied on by all three judges was that sovereign acts were immune from challenge in the courts. 'No legal basis' existed for such a challenge.

Evaluation

The great flaw in the Court of Appeal's reasons for decision lies in the notion of unimpeachable sovereignty. It smacks too much of Hobbes and Austin, as though legal theory has progressed no further and presents no alternative paths of analysis; it is too redolent of strident legislative supremacy for it to apply comfortably in a territory newly lost to the British empire. There is no *a priori* reason why sovereignty – which, after all, is just 'an organizing idea' and a 'notoriously elusive' one at that (Harris 1997, p 325) – cannot be divided between different institutions in the state. When Patrick Chan, Gerry Nazareth and Barry Mortimer went to school the sovereignty of Parliament was thoroughly orthodox, though not unquestioned, and it was accepted largely because no standard of positive law existed by which to measure the validity of its legislation (standards of the common law or morality or natural justice had been abandoned long before). Almost as soon, however, as an alternative and competing statement of law was created – through British entry into the European Community – the sovereignty of Parliament collapsed (the *Factortame* litigation: see Wesley-Smith 1994, pp 183–184). And had the question of conformity of an Act of Parliament with the European legal order arisen in the British Hong Kong courts, those courts would have been duty bound to resolve it, if necessary by 'disapplying' the Act. There cannot be any doubt about this. In the event of prerogative legislation such as an Order in Council or the Hong Kong Letters Patent being found to be inconsistent with an Act of Parliament applying in the colony, the Hong Kong courts – supplied thereby with a standard by which to measure the validity of the prerogative legislation – would have been obliged to 'disapply' the inferior breed of law (see also Chan 1997a, pp 378–382.) Whatever the restrictions on the courts' jurisdiction, which, in the words of BL19, were 'imposed by the legal system and principles previously in force in Hong Kong', they did not include the inability to decide which of two conflicting rules to apply.

In the HKSAR a normative order that is at least capable of competing with NPC decisions and resolutions does of course exist: the Basic Law, promulgated by the NPC, but requiring applicable national laws to be listed through a specified procedure (BL18) and a prescribed method of amendment (BL159). If NPC law is alleged to conflict with the Basic Law, this issue – of determining which law is to prevail – must be squarely faced, and it is surely an abdication of the judicial function merely to assert fusty old notions of sovereignty. There is a choice: between supremacy of the PRC over the HKSAR and the promises made in the Joint Declaration and the Basic Law – between 'One Country' and 'Two Systems'. And keeping faith with the Hong Kong community requires that choice to be made in favour of the Basic Law.

It would seem that the Court of Appeal has already made its choice, and it has in the process denied the Basic Law and the high degree of autonomy of the HKSAR. Its reasoning allows no other conclusion. It is as though the judges, being British-trained, were quite insensible to the different parameters of a legal system containing a codified constitution (compare Jordan 1997, p 356.) But this does not, or should not, prevent the court from reconsidering the matter should the occasion arise: its decision on the validity of the PLC is distinguishable in that no conflict was recognized in the *David Ma* case between NPC decisions and the Basic Law. Should such conflict be recognized in a future case, the opportunity will exist for the Hong Kong courts to renounce subservience to some supposed sovereign and to proclaim the principles of the HKSAR's separate legal system. Chan CJHC, indeed, has resiled from the full force of his reasoning, stating in the *Cheung Lai-wah* appeal:

> It would seem that my analogy with the colonial courts in the *David Ma* case might not have been entirely appropriate. It may be that in appropriate cases...the HKSAR courts do have jurisdiction to examine the laws and acts of the NPC which affect the HKSAR for the purpose of, say, determining whether such laws or acts are contrary to or inconsistent with the Basic Law which is after all not only the Constitution of the HKSAR, but also a national law of the PRC. But as counsel has pointed out, my views on the courts' jurisdiction in the *David Ma* case were expressed in the context of the case and cannot be understood to mean that NPC laws and acts would prevail over the Basic Law. Nevertheless, whether this point may have any effect on the final conclusion on the legality issue is for the Court of Final Appeal to decide...

The other judges made no such recantation. It may be that no litigant in Hong Kong will consider it a prudent use of resources to take the issue to the Court of Final Appeal. The PLC, of course, is now dead, though its works live on.

It has been claimed by Richard Kay that alternative positions that might have been taken by the court are not right or wrong on legal grounds: 'They are assumptions *about what the law is*. Ultimately the quality of legality cannot be defined in legal terms' (Kay 1998, p 192). In his view we cannot know whether the method of decision making in *David Ma* – the application of clear principles of law – 'arose from a genuine inability to see the deeper issues that were at stake or a conscious determination to avoid and obscure those questions' (Kay 1998, p 193). Trevor Allan, however, would reject Kay's premise: when ultimate questions of sovereignty arise we cannot merely accept what politicians decide: the courts must rely on a systematic theory of the constitution. 'Judicial decisions which settle doubts about the scope of parliamentary sovereignty must inevitably draw on such a theory, if they are rational and legitimate, even if they are generally presented, implausibly, as the ineluctable result of contemporary politics' (Allan 1997, p 451). It may be suggested, that in seeking a solution in legal terms, the court in *David Ma* relied on a theory of sovereignty that was too unsophisticated, too impoverished to provide a rational and legitimate decision likely to compel consent. But it did the job in political and pragmatic terms.

Other matters

A number of other questions arose, all of which may arise again, and may be briefly noted.

1. At least in disputes involving constitutional aspects of the Basic Law, a purposive approach to its interpretation is appropriate. In this case the principal purpose of the Basic Law was identified as continuity of the laws and legal system through the transition.
2. It was correctly pointed by Chan CJHC (p 776F-J) and Mortimer VP (pp 803J–804A) that the non-adoption by the Standing Committee of the Application of English Law Ordinance, which declared the extent to which English law applied in Hong Kong, did not affect the existence and effect of the common law in the HKSAR. The ordinance was redundant, since BL8 already provides for maintenance of the laws previously in force, including the common law, and insofar as s 4 provided for the reception of imperial Acts of Parliament and Orders in Council in Hong Kong it was in conflict with the Basic Law. However, both judges referred to the ordinance as declaratory. Chan said the ordinance neither imported nor re-applied English law but merely continued its application.

This is curious, however, for two reasons. In the first place, there being no common law rule that the common law necessarily exists in a ceded colony, a specific act, preferably legislative, was required in order to supplant the previous laws. English law applied to Hong Kong because and only because an ordinance of the Hong Kong legislature so provided. When, in 1966, the Application of English Law Ordinance repealed s 5 of the Supreme Court Ordinance 1873, which had previously been the authority for the reception of English law, it replaced the earlier provision and thus itself directly caused English law to apply. Although the ordinance in one sense merely continued the application of English law, it did not maintain the previous regime, and in providing anew it changed the rules significantly.

The second curiosity is the irrelevance of the supposed declaratory nature of the ordinance to the circumstances of the case. Counsel had argued that the common law was not maintained by the Basic Law, there being no act of adoption by the NPC, and the Hong Kong Reunification Ordinance was ineffective to do so because it was not passed by a valid legislature. The declaratory effect of the ordinance could have been important only if some other pre-1966 basis existed for the reception of English law; none was suggested, but if one had been discovered it would not in any event have survived the cessation of British sovereignty. Labelling the ordinance declaratory served no purpose.

It should be noted that the Application of English Law Ordinance is not now consigned to the legislative dustbin. Any inquiry as to the content of the common law in the HKSAR must relate back to 30 June 1997, and thus to the common law as received under s 3 of the ordinance (and as affected by Acts of Parliament, which had impinged upon it under the previous formula). Although not adopted – or rather 'non-adopted', since the purpose of BL160 is to provide for non-adoption – and thus not in force, it remains to be considered and applied in the future. It survives in the same limbo as repealed legislation that abolished part of the common law and whose repeal did not bring back to life that which it had destroyed.

3. There cannot be any doubt that the common law previously in force must be, as each judge decided (pp 777B–C, 790G, 801E–H), 30 June 1997. What is obscure is how this matter arose. It seems to have been argued that the indictment was valid when proceedings commenced because of a saving provision in the Crimes (Amendment) Ordinance 1996 that abolished the common law offence of conspiracy, but that no such provision would have existed if the cut-off date was in 1984 or 1990. Since the common law in 1984 and 1990 included conspiracy (the 1996 abolition not yet occurring), selection of either year as a cut-off date could not possibly have jeopardized the indictment. Selection of 30 June 1997 was therefore, not necessary for the decision and was *obiter*, though indubitably correct.

4. Two judges referred to the desirability of expert evidence on Chinese law (pp 798E, 807I), not available in the present case. It is plainly unsatisfactory for Hong Kong judges to venture opinions on the meaning in Chinese law of certain acts by legal institutions in the PRC: they are not equipped to do so.

5. The Joint Declaration may be used as an aid in interpreting the Basic Law (pp 775D, 803D).

6. The case was decided on the English text of the Basic Law, even though the Chinese version of BL160 was recognized as unambiguous. Since the Chinese text prevails it would seem odd that it was not resorted to from the beginning (see Gunter 1997, p 44).

7. There are many other provisions in the Basic Law that employ the words 'shall be': whether they too are to be regarded as imperative and declaratory will depend on their particular context, no doubt, but the *David Ma* decision may well be relevant to their interpretation. Thus, for example, certain matters 'shall be prohibited', such as arbitrary restriction of personal freedom (BL28) or arbitrary search of a resident's home (BL29); others 'shall be implemented' (BL39) or 'shall be protected by law', such as welfare benefits (BL36), freedom of communication (BL30), and the lawful traditional rights and interests of New Territories indigenes (BL40). If HKSAR legislation does *not* prohibit, implement, or protect, etc, can residents argue that the Basic Law has already declared the law and that local legislation is not strictly necessary for the preservation of rights and interests?

8. For all the supposed clarity that the Court of Appeal found in the Basic Law to justify the maintenance of judicial proceedings, it is evident that the matter was dealt with inadvertently by the drafting committee, if at all. The provision in BL19 that HKSAR courts 'shall have jurisdiction over all cases in the Region' was clearly never intended to cover previous proceedings, and its use begs the question whether prosecutions begun in the name of the Queen are in fact 'cases in the Region'. 'The judicial system previously practised in Hong Kong shall be maintained' (BL81), the courts 'shall adjudicate cases in accordance with the laws applicable in the Region' (BL84), and maintenance of the 'principles previously applied ... and the rights previously enjoyed by parties' in civil and criminal proceedings (BL87): none of these supplies obvious authority for the continuation of prosecutions not completed by 30 June. 'Documents' and 'rights and obligations', which shall continue to be 'recognized and protected' by the HKSAR (BL160, second para.), can perhaps more plausibly be conscripted to justify survival of the indictment, the rights of the prosecution, and the obligations of the accused.

The assertion that the Court of First Instance has jurisdiction to hear an indictment filed before it existed is much more difficult to accept. The High Court under the British regime ceased to exist. The Basic Law *established* the Court of First Instance. It made no express transitional provision to maintain previous proceedings. The Hong Kong Reunification Ordinance did so (and shows that the Hong Kong authorities recognized, rather late in the day, the lack of attention paid to the issue in the Basic Law), but the judges ruled that the Basic Law provided for transition without the help of the ordinance. Nazareth VP held (p 791F) that the courts referred to in BL81 needed no additional act of establishment but 'stand established by the imperative words of the Basic Law upon the coming into force of that Law'. This cannot assist the argument, since it does not address the question of the Court of First Instance's jurisdiction to hear cases begun in another court. The Court of Appeal seems on this question to have treated the Basic Law in so broad and generous a spirit as to appear almost cavalier, or desperate to ensure continuity come what may.

Concluding remarks

The Hong Kong legal profession (including academics and judges) were woefully unprepared for the transition to Chinese sovereignty, despite having had over seven years to study the Basic Law before it came into operation. *David Ma* exemplifies this. The judges did not seem at ease with public law reasoning and have not adjusted their legal thinking to accommodate the new style of legal order. Sovereignty to them appears to mean simply locating a body that has supreme power within the state and paying obeisance to it, with the consequences that the transition was simply a matter of replacing British imperial authority with another, and the Basic Law was merely the device by which this transformation was achieved. In time, however, such attitudes may be discarded and full recognition given to the dominant purposes of the Basic Law: to preserve in the HKSAR a high degree of autonomy, the maintenance of the HKSAR's separate systems and way of life, and the erection of a legal barrier to assist in keeping out unwanted interference from the PRC.

Bibliography

Allan, T. 1997 'Parliamentary Sovereignty: Law, Politics, and Revolution'. *Law Quarterly Review* 113: 443.

Chan, J. 1997a 'The Jurisdiction and Legality of the Provisional Legislative Council'. *Hong Kong Law Journal* 27(3): 374–387.

Chan, J. 1997b 'Amicus Curiae and Non-Party Intervention'. *Hong Kong Law Journal* 27(3): 391–404.

Chen, A. 1997a 'The Provisional Legislative Council of the SAR'. *Hong Kong Law Journal* 27(1): 1–11.

Chen, A. 1997b 'Legal Preparation for the Establishment of the Hong Kong SAR: Chronology and Selected Documents'. *Hong Kong Law Journal* 27(3): 405–431.

Chen, A. 1997c 'The Concept of Justiciability and the Jurisdiction of the Hong Kong Courts', *Hong Kong Law Journal* 27(3): 387–390 (an abridged version appeared in the *South China Morning Post*, 5 August).

Fung, D. 1997 'A Win for the Rule of Law'. *South China Morning Post*, 1 August.

Gunter, J. 1997 'HKSAR v. Ma: The Basic Law "Shall Be" Given a Purposive Interpretation'. *The Loophole* (newsletter of the Commonwealth Legislative Council Association) December 1997: 38.

Harris, J. 1997 'China, Hong Kong and Divided Sovereignty after 1997', in Krawietz, W., Pattaro, E. and Erh-Soon Tay, A. (eds) *Rule of Law: Political and Legal Systems in Transition*. Berlin: Duncker and Humblot.

Jordan, A. 1997 'Lost in the Translation: Two Legal Cultures, the Common Law Judiciary and the Basic Law of the Hong Kong SAR'. *Cornell International Law Journal* 30: 335.

Kay, R. 1998 'Sovereignty in the New Hong Kong'. *Law Quarterly Review* 114: 189.

Watson-Brown, A. 1998 'Do We Still Need "Shall"?' *Hong Kong Law Journal* 28(1): 29–44.

Wesley-Smith, P. 1994 *Constitutional and Administrative Law in Hong Kong*, 2nd edn. Hong Kong: Longman Asia.

Wesley-Smith, P. 1997 'The SAR Constitution: Law or Politics?', *Hong Kong Law Journal* 27(2): 125–129.

11

Towards a Democratic Audit in Hong Kong: Some Issues and Problems

Robin Porter

Recent attention given to democracy in Hong Kong has tended to follow the development of democratic institutions, and in particular the elections to the Legislative Council and the evolution of the political parties. Yet a case can be made to say that democracy in Hong Kong is far more complex than this, with roots that go much deeper than the institutional changes back and forth over the past few years.

This chapter will begin by offering an outline of recent approaches to the study of democracy in Hong Kong. It will then review briefly trends in the use of systems of democratic audit that have been most commonly applied to other countries, and especially to societies in the throes of rapid socio-economic and political transition, notably in Eastern Europe and in parts of the former Soviet Union. In Pacific Asia a different path to development has been followed.[1] The unique position of Hong Kong, as a Pacific Asian society undergoing a transition *to* communist rule will be underlined, posing as it does very distinctive requirements for the measurement of the features of its democracy, especially as they may evolve over time. Several commonly heard arguments against the need to preserve democracy in Hong Kong will be addressed.

How the key principles and indices devised by the political analyst David Beetham for an audit of democracy in the UK might be used as a possible model for assessing democracy in Hong Kong will then be considered.

The questions at the heart of the audit will be presented in four groups, and the apparent characteristics of political, legal and social life in the territory will be profiled in the light of these questions. A brief contrasting profile, corresponding to these points, will be given for mainland China. An indication will be given for each group of questions of where the main pressure points lie for democratic practice following the transfer of sovereignty, based on responses given in semi-structured interviews by figures active in public life, and on comment by locally based academic observers.

Despite some drawbacks, it will be maintained that the Beetham approach provides a convenient and relatively comprehensive framework for understanding the central features of Hong Kong's democratic culture.

Recent work on democracy in Hong Kong

The issue of democracy in Hong Kong has always been highly problematic. The notion that the territory was a 'borrowed place, on borrowed time' – shared in large measure by both 'sides', those who advocated greater democracy, and those who for various reasons opposed it – has conditioned the debate over political institutions and values over several decades.[2]

Up until the Joint Declaration of 1984 relatively little academic work of *any* kind specifically on Hong Kong was published in the UK, the territory being widely disregarded as a legitimate focus of study in its own right. In Hong Kong itself, the 'East Asian' series of monographs from Oxford University Press Hong Kong included work that shed light on the functioning of government and aspects of the law in Hong Kong (Hopkins 1971, England and Rear 1975), but inevitably, such studies as existed of political life reflected, quite accurately, a picture in which the citizens of Hong Kong were seen as the objects, rather than the subjects, of policy (Miners 1975). In the United States and elsewhere at this time, Hong Kong featured only rarely in academic work.

It was the Joint Declaration of 1984, and Britain's commitment to hand the territory back to China by 1997, which above all focused minds on Hong Kong's political arrangements. It may also be supposed that the growing prosperity of Hong Kong's economy, the rising standard of education, the increasing domination of the professions by local people, and the absorption of 'international' middle-class values through the spread of telecommunications technology all played their part in inducing a sense of relative political deprivation among a significant part of the population.

Political change was clearly on the agenda for many of Hong Kong's educated middle class, though it would still take the Tiananmen incident in 1989, and the appointment of the reforming Governor Chris Patten in 1992, to bring about long overdue changes in the responsibilities of, and arrangements for election to, the Legislative Council. Meanwhile, the hybrid nature of Hong Kong's growing democratic culture came increasingly under analysis.

Academic study of legal matters began to extend to a discussion of civil rights, and the whole future framework of law in Hong Kong (Wacks 1988, 1989, 1992). Political institutions too began to merit serious academic concern, especially as the territory approached its first full elections to the Legislative Council in 1995, to be held under the new voting arrangements (Davies and Roberts 1990). At several of Hong Kong's now more numerous universities, projects were established to evaluate the rapid changes taking place – notably the ongoing research at the University of Hong Kong into the implications of legal change for Hong Kong, and the Hong Kong Transition Project at Hong Kong Baptist University. In 1989, the Chinese University of Hong Kong Press began to publish its annual *'Other Hong Kong Report'*, doing much to refocus political analysis away from policy making to the impact of policy on ordinary people.[3]

In the atmosphere of rapid change taking place against a fixed deadline, Hong Kong's news media also inevitably took a prominent role in debate, probing the boundaries both in reporting and analysis, and itself becoming the object of much speculation about its future independence. The media, in turn, fed and encouraged a wider public debate about life after the transfer of sovereignty, in which almost everyone became engaged or at least had a view. This has influenced everything from individual decisions about whether to emigrate, or what line to take in personal or business relations, to overseas perceptions of the climate for investment in Hong Kong, and the performance of the economy as a whole.

Thus, it is that academic work on democracy in Hong Kong, taken in its broader sense, has flourished only recently in the context of a thorough-going discussion in the community at large of political possibilities following the resumption of Chinese sovereignty, and conditioned by the timetable leading up to that event. The stakes are such that, even given the inevitable constraints, some attempt to measure and assess the extent of the democratic culture in Hong Kong at the point of the transfer and beyond would seem to be worthwhile.

Systems of democratic audit

There has for some time been discussion among students of politics of ways and means of 'measuring' democracy (Dahl 1971; Inkeles 1991; Huntington 1991; Beetham 1993). Much of the early discussion was predicated on the cold-war assumption that the forms of democracy to be found in North American, western European and certain other developed western societies were normative, and a model to which other 'developing' countries could approximate in time. Democracy was often defined in the narrow sense of the electoral system, the degree of responsible government, and the institutions and patterns of political behaviour that reinforced them. Some work on the measurement of democracy attempted, through surveys and sampling, to project a quantifiable assessment of the degree of conformity in any particular country to western, often American, norms. In this way, a country could be assigned a figure, supposedly enabling it to be compared objectively in the extent of its democracy to other countries (Vanhannen 1990).

More recently, account has been taken of the possibility of more diverse forms of democratic expression, with allowance made for distinct cultural influences on the form democracy might take (Parekh 1993), and for the effect of the level of economic development on democratic institutions and practice (Hadenius 1992).[4] The transition underway in the former states of the communist world has, in some degree, forced this broader view. Simultaneously, there has more recently been some disenchantment with the quantitative approach to the measurement of democracy, and greater experimentation with qualitative and experiential approaches to assessment (Beetham 1993, 1995).

The aspiration to democracy among the peoples of the former Soviet 'bloc' has, in particular, prompted a move to emphasize the dynamic aspect of democracy, and to relate it to the pace and scale of economic change (Przeworski 1991). Culture and previous political history have also been more explicitly brought in to explain the differing rates of democratic change in former Soviet bloc countries. In Pacific Asia, meanwhile, analysts have become fascinated by the interrelationship between strong economic growth in many states and the relative absence of democratic institutions and behaviour as these would be understood in the west; most recently, provisional conclusions about this relationship have been challenged by the Asian financial crisis, with its suggested causes rooted in part in a lack of transparency and democratic accountability. Yet, there has so far been remarkably little attention given to the specific possibility of auditing democracy in Pacific Asia.[5] Once again, culture is advanced as the explanation for local variations, both in the degree of growth achieved, and in the apparent extent and local nature of democracy. It is widely perceived that democracy does not necessarily follow development, nor even that there is any observable relationship between the two.[6]

It may be asserted that the need to confront more closely widely differing political experience has hastened the movement among analysts to experiment with more qualitative assessments of democracy. These have included attempts to embrace many of the more diverse and perhaps elusive aspects of 'democratic culture' not addressed when the concern was primarily with voting systems. Thus, democratic culture has come to comprise a whole range of questions to do with the responsiveness of institutions, access to people in authority, accountability, equality of opportunity, civil and political rights, the role of non-government organizations in preserving those rights, and indeed the whole character of civil society. In some cases, analysis may encompass the extent to which specific economic and social rights are enjoyed by the population.

Such a wide-ranging discussion must inevitably rely on research techniques the results of which are less quantifiable. It may, therefore, be that using these techniques one country's democracy cannot in consequence be 'measured' against that of another, while at the same time it may have been described more usefully and in greater depth. Another consequence of this more eclectic approach has been to produce a greater acceptance of alternative forms of democracy. Gordon White has argued, for example, that in Asia, democracy is 'corporatist'.[7]

In the context of this discussion, the particular circumstances of Hong Kong stand out as unique. For so many years until very recently denied all but token institutions of electoral democracy, Hong Kong has steadily, and especially over the past 30 years or so, acquired a strong democratic culture in many other respects. Whatever may be the experience elsewhere in Pacific Asia, it may be argued that this is both a consequence and a cause of its spectacular economic success. Culturally, Hong Kong has long been a place where Chinese and western ideas could exist in synthesis, or at least in harmony. In stark contrast to what is happening in many other parts of the world, Hong Kong is in some measure facing a transition *to* communism, a process of change that will undoubtedly place extraordinary pressure on many aspects of its democratic culture. These points will all be the subject of further elaboration below.

For all these reasons, a broader, more qualitative approach to the study of democracy in Hong Kong would seem to be the most appropriate.

Some reservations addressed

In any discussion of the possible application of a democratic audit to Hong Kong, the issue should first be addressed as to whether it is appropriate even to look for democracy in Hong Kong, or to hold it up as a desirable objective.

One argument might take the form of asserting that on democracy, as on human rights, there is an Asian, or even an ethnic Chinese perspective, which places a posited need for harmony in society above any conformity to what may be regarded as imposed western values. The case for Asian values is familiar, and has been made periodically since the late 1980s, most notably in the form of the Bangkok Declaration of 1993[8], when a number of Asian states dissented from western notions of universal human rights. This matter is also addressed elsewhere in this book (see chapter 12).

Several points may be made here. On the issue of democracy, just as in the case of human rights, the dissenting argument is often put forward by those who stand to benefit from democracy's absence. It can also be argued that as a way of mediating differences in society, democracy can be seen as an instrumentality that is value-free. Moreover, in this particular case, critical to the nature of Hong Kong is that it has had 150 years of development separate from China, a period sufficiently lengthy to see much of the map of the world re-arranged. In this time, and especially since the Second World War, western ideas have flourished in Hong Kong, so much so that Hong Kong has often been a springboard for these ideas into China. As education has become much more widespread and sophisticated in Hong Kong, western political concepts have taken firm root. In the light of these considerations, it would seem entirely appropriate to monitor the condition of democracy in Hong Kong.

There is a related argument sometimes put forward by those who are prepared to sacrifice democracy because they do not see it as essential to Hong Kong's continued prosperity, and indeed see pressure for its continuation as likely to destabilize the HKSAR.[9] Those who advocate this point of view argue that for most people in Hong Kong what matters is their livelihood, which can best be guaranteed by an HKSAR government primarily of corporate interests working closely with the authorities in Beijing.

Yet a strong contrary argument can be made that, in Hong Kong's synthesis of Chinese and Western ideas, beliefs about freedom of thought and of action have had much to do with the territory's commercial success. It is not only the electoral and representative institutions of democracy that matter, important as they are symbolically, but the intellectual and political climate that they guarantee.

Few who have worked for or with the institutions of a one-party state would deny that tactical and strategic decision making in such states is carried on all too often in a climate of inhibition and fear. In such a context, to use initiative is often dangerous. The system is seen as all powerful, determining the distribution of benefits within society and conditioning life chances for every one of its members. Citizens respond by covertly manipulating the opportunities that come their way, a process that may rapidly cross the line into corrupt activity, hidden from view by the habitual secretiveness of the state.[10] The root cause of this self-censorship of initiative is political, and in no small degree the solution may lie in democratic institutions and the possibility of healthy and stable political change from time to time. Only in this way may the legitimate activity of the institutions and organizations of society remain paramount, and the hidden personal agendas of the individual recede in importance.

A further argument is sometimes heard that suggests that, in consequence of its increasing level of economic activity (a trend that may now be in some jeopardy), China itself will in the course of time become more democratic, and that Hong Kong has only to wait for it to catch up. To press for the retention of the existing level of democratic practice in Hong Kong, it is suggested, will only aggravate a delicate situation, and may even retard progress to democracy in China.

This argument ignores the fixed conceptual approach to the analysis of political forces associated with Marxism–Leninism and Mao Zedong's thought, which holds that there can be only one correct view of any political situation, only one correct policy. This approach asserts that there is a dialectical relationship between theory and practice, and through continual engagement in political practice, and frequent modification of theory in the light of practice, a higher level of truth will emerge.[11] A consequence of this, however, must be that there is only one truth. Thus, individuals who hold a contrary view must either have not yet reached this level of truth, in which case they must be helped through political education to achieve it, or if they persist in asserting their point of view they must be enemies of the state, or, in an extreme case, counter-revolutionaries.

While this fixity of purpose may be what is required to win a civil war and create revolution, it would naturally tend to reinforce the continuation of authoritarian institutions and practices in more settled times. For those who think in this way, democratic institutions are to be opposed because they might result in 'the wrong people, holding the wrong views', taking power. Moreover, there is no concept of loyal or constructive opposition. Those who are not with the party in power, are against them.

This has clear consequences for the prospects for the natural evolution of democratic government in China. So long as the Communist Party retains power there, it may be naive to assume that democracy will emerge in any significant form or to any significant degree. The implication for Hong Kong must surely be that it is better to try to defend what it has than to wait to benefit residually from any change in China.

The scope and range of the Beetham audit: its application to Hong Kong

The systematic audit contrived by the political scientist David Beetham and his team for application to the United Kingdom may be a useful model on which to build a democratic audit for Hong Kong.[12] The model is broad, qualitative, and by and large avoids judgements about what is 'normative' in political institutions. Moreover, Hong Kong under colonial rule derived much of its democratic culture and practice, if not the detail of its electoral system, from the UK.

According to Beetham, 'democracy' rests on the two related key principles of popular control (over political decision making) and political equality (in voting, standing for office, in treatment by legislators, in simply making one's voice heard). The practice of these principles in any given society may be tested by the application of a series of 30 indices, expressed in the form of questions, in four groups.

In this section, the groups of questions are first set out, as indicated in a recent formulation by Beetham. A brief profile is then given after each group of questions to outline, in summary form, the situation in Hong Kong in June 1997 in respect to these points. At this stage this profile should be regarded as no more than a common perception, which would need to be thoroughly documented in any proper audit. This is then followed by a brief profile of the corresponding situation in mainland China, which should be regarded in the same light. An indication will then be given of the kind of developments that should deserve particular attention if the state of democracy is to be monitored now that sovereignty has passed to China, and of the kind of evidence that might be gathered in establishing a trend.

It should be pointed out that the information presented here is not new. Rather, the object is to look at the evidence in a particular way that will be helpful to our understanding of democracy in Hong Kong on the eve of the transfer, and any trends which may have been established in the period since, and to suggest an analytical framework for observers who may wish to follow developments there. The particular points for monitoring are based on views expressed in interviews by people active in the political process in Hong Kong, and by academic and other commentators.

So what are Beetham's indices of democracy, and how could they be applied in the case of Hong Kong?

The *first* group of indices concerns popular control over the legislature: the 'reach' of the electoral process, its inclusiveness, its fairness, its independence. Following Beetham's approach in his 1997 paper (see endnote 12), in Hong Kong this would mean asking the following six questions or sets of questions:

1. How far is appointment to legislative and governmental office determined by popular election, on the basis of open competition, universal suffrage and secret ballot?
2. How independent of government and party control are the election and procedures of voter registration, how accessible are they to voters, and how free are they from all kinds of abuse?
3. How effective a range of choice and information does the electoral and party system allow the voters, and how far is there fair and equal access for all parties and candidates to the media and other means of communication with them?
4. To what extent do the votes of all electors carry equal weight, and how closely does the composition of parliament and the programme of government reflect the choices actually made by the electorate?
5. How far is there equal effective opportunity to stand for public office, regardless of which social group a person belongs to?
6. What proportion of the electorate actually votes, and how far are the election results accepted by the main political forces in the country?

Broadly speaking, as of June 1997 in Hong Kong, appointment to the Legislative Council was principally based on popular election through a dual system of geographical and functional constituencies, on the basis of open competition, and secret ballot.[13] Universal suffrage was the rule for geographical constituencies, and universal suffrage of the working population for the functional constituencies, many people having two votes. The Executive Council was appointed by the Governor at his discretion.

The consensus is that voter registration and elections were largely free from abuse. The media were accessible to candidates, and openly discussed the issues; a full range of information was available to voters.

Where the elective principle was followed, votes carried equal weight, but the disjunction between the elected representatives of the Legislative Council and the wholly appointed Executive Council meant that government programmes did not necessarily reflect choices made by the majority of the electorate.[14]

Opportunity to stand for public office was, as in many democracies, conditioned in part by the financial resources of the candidate, though there was no ban on candidates from any particular social group. In the 1995 elections to Legco, 36 per cent of electors actually voted.[15] The results were accepted as valid by all the main political parties in Hong Kong, but not by the Chinese government, which opposed the holding of elections.

In China, appointment to legislative and government office is determined in secret procedures of nomination and selection orchestrated by the Communist Party, of which most government leaders are members. Only at the village level is there some measure of popular election to positions of leadership, and here too the Communist Party may intervene if it disapproves of successful candidates.[16]

As there are no elections to high legislative and governmental office, there is no information disseminated about selection processes. The media are controlled by the Communist Party, and represent its views alone. The composition of the National People's Congress and the programme of government do not in any discernible way reflect the popular will, as there is no way of telling what the popular will might be.

The way to public office lies through membership of the Communist Party, and for many years after 1949 former landlords, capitalists, and many members of the bourgeoisie were excluded from membership on the basis of their social origin.[17]

As there are no national popular elections, so the issue of acceptance of election results does not arise.

Indicators that could establish trends for this first set of indices on electoral processes could include the following.

- changes to electoral law and practice (already begun by the Provisional Legislature in respect of Legco and the May 1998 elections) affecting:
  — the proportion of legislative and government office holders elected
  — the extension of functional at the expense of geographical constituencies
  — the secrecy of the ballot, and the possible introduction of electronic voting
  — the frequency of elections, and term of office of government

- changes in procedures for voter registration
- any possible developments in the role of the Chinese Communist Party, Xinhua News Agency, and other mainland organizations in influencing the outcome of elections
- changes in the degree of access of some parties to the media, either through legislation, influence brought to bear, or self-censorship in the media; any possible reduction in the opportunities of candidates to publicize their platforms
- any possible expansion or reduction in the degree of responsibility of the executive to the legislature
- any possible exclusion of certain candidates or parties by virtue of their views
- any reduction in the franchise; any trend to rejection of legitimate election results.

It will be clear that the proroguing of the sitting Legco in July 1997, and its replacement with one elected in May 1998 with substantially reduced popular input into the choice of 40 out of 60 candidates, falls into this general category.

The *second* group of indices addresses the degree of openness and accountability of government: political accountability of the government to the elected legislature, legal accountability to the courts, financial accountability to the legislature and the courts, as well as the monitoring of government by independent bodies. This would lead to a further 12 themes for questions:

7. How accessible to the public is information about what the government does, and about the effects of its policies, and how independent is it of the government's own information machine?
8. How effective and open to scrutiny is the control exercised by elected politicians over non-elected executive personnel, both military and civilian?
9. How extensive are the powers of parliament to oversee legislation and public expenditure, and to scrutinize the executive; and how effectively are they exercised in practice?
10. How publicly accountable are elected representatives for their private interests and sources of income that may affect the performance of their public office, and the process of election to it?
11. How far are the courts able to ensure that the executive obeys the rule of law; and how effective are their procedures for ensuring that all public institutions and officials are subject to the rule of law in the performance of their functions?
12. How independent is the judiciary from the executive, and from all forms of interference; and how far is the administration of law subject to effective public scrutiny?

13. How readily can a citizen gain access to the courts, ombudsman or tribunals for redress in the event of maladministration or the failure of government or bodies to meet their legal responsibilities; and how effective are the means of redress available?
14. How far are appointments and promotions within public institutions subject to equal opportunities procedures, and how far do conditions of service protect employees' civil rights?
15. How systematic and open to public scrutiny are the procedures for government consultation of public opinion and of relevant interests in the formation and implementation of policy and legislation?
16. How accessible are elected politicians to approach by their electors, and how effectively do they represent constituents' interests?
17. How far do the arrangements for government below the level of the central state meet the above criteria of openness, accountability and responsiveness?
18. To what extent does sub-central government have the powers to carry out its responsibilities in accordance with the wishes of its own electorate, and without interference from the centre?

As of June 1997, there was a substantial degree of openness in the work of government, with the regular publication of the proceedings of the Executive and Legislative Councils, the publication of reports and proceedings of most committees, the publication of draft and final versions of legislation, as well as the reports of individual government departments, and the proceedings of some of their committees.[18] Special reports on the workings of policy in practice were also published from time to time. In addition to these government sources there was active reporting by the media on the implementation of policy, and an ongoing debate on the pros and cons of different aspects of policy.[19]

The security forces and the public service were accountable to the Executive, though less obviously to elected members of Legco. Legco was able to oversee legislation and public expenditure, and scrutinized, but did not control the Executive.[20]

Elected representatives were generally accountable for their private interests, and it was unacceptable for these to be confused with the public interest. More widely, the Independent Commission Against Corruption, over the previous two decades, sought to enforce probity throughout the public service.[21]

The courts by and large ensured that the Executive, and other public officials and institutions obeyed the rule of law. The judiciary was very largely independent of the Executive, and its workings were open to public scrutiny.[22] Citizens enjoyed access to the courts, though in practice this was constrained by the financial means of the citizen or the degree of commitment of the government-administered legal aid programme.

Appointments and promotions in public institutions were subject to equal opportunities procedures in recent years, though employees' civil rights were not always paramount.

In the few years immediately prior to 1997, government was more attentive to public opinion, as well as to employers, professional and other interest groups, in the formulation of policy. Submissions and comment by the public were frequently invited on draft legislation, and by commissions of enquiry into the effects of legislation that had been implemented. Elected politicians were generally accessible to their constituents.

Government below the 'centre', at the Urban and District Council levels, varied in the degree of its accountability and openness, though the elective principle in Hong Kong in fact began with the Urban Council.

In China, the plenary meetings of the National People's Congress, which occur once a year, are public but stage-managed, while the Standing Committee and smaller steering groups meet in secrecy. More importantly, the plenary sessions of the Congress of the Communist Party, though widely reported, are also stage-managed. The real debates over issues and policy are carried on in secret by the Party Central Committee, its Politburo and Standing Committee. All domestic reporting on proceedings of state and Party organs is undertaken by New China News Agency, which is charged with the dual function of reporting news and disseminating propaganda.[23]

As delegates to both state and Party Congresses are not popularly elected, there is no control by elected representatives over civilian and military personnel.

While the National People's Congress technically has the power to oversee legislation and expenditure, it very seldom challenges the agenda set by the Party.[24] There is no monitoring of any possible clash between public and private interests, apart from occasional campaigns against corruption in the government and Party.

The judiciary in China is not independent of the Executive, and indeed may be seen more accurately as an arm of the Executive. The courts effectively rehearse the evidence and pass sentence on citizens deemed by the police to have committed a crime.[25] The judiciary does not monitor public officials, institutions, or the Executive to ensure that they obey the rule of law.

By and large, there is no means of redress available through the courts to citizens who believe they have been mistreated by government or by public officials or institutions. Appointments in public institutions are not subject to equal opportunities procedures; employees do not have civil rights.

There are no procedures for government consultation of public opinion in the formulation of policy, and no elected politicians to represent electors' interests. Below the level of central government, administration is similarly secretive, unaccountable, and unresponsive, although most recently elections at the village level to administrative councils hold out a small glimmer of hope for the future.

There is a range of practices here that could be monitored to establish the trend in Hong Kong following the transfer of sovereignty in June 1997:

- a possible reduction in the number and variety of sources of published information about the workings of government
- a possible reduction in extent or thoroughness of debate of policy issues in the media
- legislated or voluntary change in the scope of elected representatives to oversee legislation, expenditure, and to critically monitor the activity of the Executive
- the progressive overlap of private and public interests
- a loss of independence by the judiciary, manifest in the erosion in practice of their power to ensure that the Executive, public officials and institutions obey the rule of law, in the political appointment of judges, in the allocation of cases to certain judges known to be sympathetic to a certain outcome, and in other ways
- the growth of political favouritism in appointments and promotions within public institutions
- the diminution in practice of public consultation in the formulation of policy and legislation.

It can be argued that there has been a perception of growing secrecy in the functioning of particularly the Executive branch of government since July 1997, and a weakening of the judiciary evident, for example, in the extension of immunity to Xinhua News Agency, and the failure to prosecute in the Sally Aw corruption case.

In the *third* group of questions, guarantees of civil and political rights and liberties which are crucial to effective popular democratic control over government, are examined. A further five questions explore this aspect of democracy:

19. How clearly does the law define the civil and political rights and liberties of the citizen, and how effectively are they defended?
20. How equal are citizens in the enjoyment of their civil and political rights and liberties, regardless of social, economic or other status?
21. How well developed are voluntary associations for the advancement and monitoring of citizens' rights, and how free from harassment are they?
22. How effective are procedures for informing citizens of their rights, and for educating future citizens in the exercise of them?
23. How free from arbitrary discrimination are the criteria for admission of refugees or immigrants to live within the country (territory), and how readily can those so admitted obtain equal rights of citizenship?

Since 1991, and up to June 1997, Hong Kong had a Bill of Rights to set out clearly the principles governing the political rights and liberties of the territory's residents. The Bill of Rights frequently took precedence over other legislation, and defence of rights in court under the legislation was vigorous, with precedents cited from Canada, India, and other countries with similar legislation.[26]

Voluntary organizations, including Amnesty International, Asia Watch, Hong Kong Monitor and others with an interest in rights matters, took a strong hold in Hong Kong and were able to function effectively. Citizens were made aware of rights through both government campaigns and a lively discussion of them in the media.[27]

Hong Kong's planned retrocession to China, its size and density of population, conditioned its policy on refugees, which was primarily to seek resettlement for them elsewhere.

In China, while the constitution guarantees economic and some political rights, in practice decades of civil war before 1949, the revolution, and the Cultural Revolution have perpetuated a political culture of precipitate measures to resolve differences in which western notions of the rights of the individual have little place. This is as much true of China now as it was before the economic reforms began in 1979.

The law, therefore, does not effectively define or defend civil or political rights for the individual. Not all citizens are equal. In recent decades members of former landlord, capitalist or bourgeois families have been denied equal treatment, and even today in some instances and in some areas they remain objects of suspicion. Persons considered hostile to the Communist Party's objectives are frequently denied justice.[28]

There are, as yet, very few voluntary organizations within China to monitor citizens' rights. Apart from the most general statements in the Constitution, there is no official effort to inform citizens of any rights they may have, nor any education in their use.

Refugees or immigrants, relatively few in number, and usually ethnic Chinese, have generally been obliged to integrate rapidly into the broader community, enjoying no more rights than anyone else.

The trend since June 1997 with respect to civil and political liberties in Hong Kong may be monitored in several ways. Points to watch for may include:

- most obviously, the fate of the Bill of Rights in the period immediately following the transfer of sovereignty
- the use of arguments to do with national security to repeal existing provision and tolerance for demonstrations and other means of protest
- the denial of rights to specific individuals known to be opposed to the policies of the government

- the categorization of voluntary human rights associations as 'political', and in this way the severance of their financial and other ties to similar organizations overseas; or the use of other legal or practical means to proscribe the activities of these organizations
- the progressive substitution of mainland Chinese ideas of patriotism and obedience to authority in place of dissemination of information about rights in education and among the citizenry at large
- a tightening up of provision for even temporary acceptance of refugees.

Of particular concern here since July 1997 are the fate of the Bill of Rights, the court rulings that acts of the National People's Congress of China will take precedence over Hong Kong's constitution, as well as subsequent court rulings that assert the opposite but are rejected by Beijing, and the proposed introduction of laws to counter 'subversion'.

The *final* group of indices is concerned with the nature of 'civil society' – those associations through which people independently manage their own affairs. Seven sets of questions are proposed to address this dimension of the democratic culture:

24. How far is there agreement on nationhood within the established state boundaries, and to what extent does support for political parties cross regional, linguistic, religious or ethnic lines?
25. How tolerant are people of divergent beliefs, cultures, ethnicities, life-styles, etc., and how free are the latter from discrimination or disadvantage?
26. How strong and independent of government control are the associations of civil liberty, and how accountable are they to their own members?
27. How publicly accountable are economic institutions for their activities, and how effective is their legal regulation in the public interest?
28. How pluralistic are the media of communication in terms of ownership and accessibility to different opinions and sections of society; and how effectively do they operate as a balanced forum for political debate?
29. How extensive are literacy and education for citizenship, and how equal are the chances for future citizens to participate in economic, social and political life?
30. To what extent do people have confidence in the ability of the political system to solve the main problems confronting society, and in their own ability to influence it?

In Hong Kong in the decades leading up to 1997, there was apparent, especially among the young, a growing sense of identity as Hong Kong people, very largely ethnically Chinese, but with a way of life and outlook distinctly different from those of people in mainland China.[29] It is notable that in June 1997, even most of those political parties in the territory that supported re-unification with China recognized and wished to sustain this difference. In other respects, the political parties differed widely on ways and means, though there are no clear cleavages on regional, linguistic, religious or ethnic lines.

There was widespread tolerance of differing beliefs and cultures in Hong Kong, and in particular an openness to westerners and western influences, which contrasted sharply with periodic outbursts of anti-foreignism in China.

Almost all the associations of civil society in Hong Kong were independent of government control, and many were accountable to their own members. Economic institutions were accountable, and strictly regulated by law. The media were, by and large, free and open in their treatment of the news, though there was a tendency to self-censorship on sensitive issues as 1st July approached.[30]

The population had a high rate of literacy, and in recent years education prepared people for citizenship with increasing effect. Opinion polls generally showed that, crisis periods apart, the population had confidence in the political system, and a growing feeling that they could have some influence over it.[31]

In China, there has historically been a strong consensus on nationhood based largely on Chinese ethnicity and civilization.[32] This has been projected onto other territories with ethnic and historic ties to China, such as Taiwan, Hong Kong and Macao, and to areas historically acknowledging Chinese suzerainty, such as Tibet.

The only fully functioning political party in China, the Communist Party, is a Leninist party with restricted access and functioning largely in secret.

In the period since 1949, there have been extended periods of extreme intolerance of divergent beliefs and cultures, and especially of foreign influence.

All significant associations in civil society in mainland China have been controlled by and accountable only to the Communist Party. Economic institutions, though they report to the appropriate Ministry, are not publicly accountable; the degree of legal regulation varies, and may or may not be geared to the public interest.

Xinhua News Agency for many years originated *all* news, for distribution to other organs of the media. Though this is no longer the case, Xinhua remains the main front of all important news reports, especially about policy matters. Journalists in China operate under guidance from the Communist Party to both report the news *and* disseminate Party propaganda.[33] Access to the media is therefore restricted, and only limited debate of the issues is tolerated.

Citizens are under constant pressure through education and propaganda campaigns to show patriotism and support for the policies of the

Communist Party. Those who do not, find their opportunities to participate fully in the country's economic, social and political life severely
proscribed.

It is impossible to assess the degree of genuine support for and confidence in the political system, as research of this kind is effectively impossible to conduct in China. Anecdotal evidence suggests that, following
Tiananmen especially, citizens feel they have very little ability to influence
political outcomes.

Possible developments which, if monitored, might indicate a trend on
these issues in Hong Kong following the transfer of sovereignty may include:

- the progressive introduction of a concept of citizenship based on race
  and ethnicity
- a growing insistence on the diminution of the Hong Kong identity in
  favour of clearly stated allegiance to the People's Republic of China
- a growing intolerance of beliefs, cultural influences, ethnicities and life-
  styles that would not be tolerated in mainland China, with pressure to
  support periodic campaigns in China which have some degree of anti-
  foreign tone to them
- evidence of pressure brought to bear on civil associations that may in
  some way be considered to be hostile to China
- a diminution in law or in practice of Hong Kong's strict regulation of
  the activities of economic institutions, and a gradual reduction in their
  effective accountability
- the possible intervention by the SAR government in the editorial freedom of the media, possibly preceded by the growth of self-censorship
  on critical issues by journalists and the owners of media organizations
- evidence of any reduction in the opportunities for citizens to participate
  fully in economic, social and political life; evidence of changed attitudes
  towards citizenship consequent on the promulgation in schools of the
  new Civic Education Curriculum
- any indication of a loss of confidence in the political system, evidenced
  by incidents of protest, whether effective or abortive, a growth in apathy
  and political fatalism, possibly with a corresponding decline in the territory's economic success, and the incidence of emigration overseas, especially by ethnic Chinese Hong Kong residents with foreign passports.

As of late, Hong Kong remains cosmopolitan and outward-looking, with
the dispute over the editorial content at RTHK (Radio Television Hong
Kong) being resolved in favour of freedom of speech. The 53 per cent
turnout in the May Legco election, and the moral standing of the
Democratic Party and its allies, having achieved 63 per cent of the popular
vote (despite this translating into only 31 per cent of the seats), should help

the institutions of Hong Kong's civil society to resist pressure for unwanted change.

Applying the audit in practice

At the time of writing, a year and a half after the transfer of sovereignty to China, the prospects for carrying out a survey of the democratic culture in Hong Kong using the Beetham audit still appear to be quite good. Although, as noted above, there has been some pressure on certain aspects of this culture, the critical test of the authorities' reaction to the first Tiananmen commemorative demonstration since the handover has been passed without major incident. It is therefore possible to contemplate ways and means.

First, in view of the importance for Hong Kong of maintaining a strong international profile as a guarantee of its present degree of autonomy, it would seem appropriate for the study to be carried out by mixed teams of researchers from institutions both inside Hong Kong and overseas.

It is proposed that a team should be formed to address each of the four groups of issues delineated by Beetham, those concerning: (a) the 'reach' of the electoral process, its inclusiveness, its fairness, its independence; (b) political, legal and financial accountability; (c) guarantees of civil and political rights and liberties; and (d) the nature of 'civil society' in Hong Kong.

Ideally, among the researchers should be political scientists, experts in civil rights, constitutional, criminal and commercial law, sociologists, sinologists and perhaps one or two with a knowledge of business and of the functioning of non-governmental organizations.

Information would be gathered through a combination of techniques appropriate to the particular issue. These would include interviews with prominent participants in the political and legal processes of Hong Kong, questionnaires submitted to a representative sample of targeted constituent groups within society, scrutiny of significant political events such as elections or instances of constitutional change, analysis of the handling of legal cases through judicial records and accounts, the monitoring of the functioning of significant bulwarks of good government, such as the Independent Commission Against Corruption, and the non-governmental organizations, through their records and through personal interviews, and the day-by-day monitoring of media coverage of political events, and assessment of the degree of continued independence of that coverage.

It should be possible to build up in this way an image of the pattern of political practice in Hong Kong following the handover, in consequence of which trends in the behaviour of government and other political and legal institutions will emerge. Changes in the democratic culture of Hong Kong will clearly have significance, not only in the possibility that democratic freedom may be about to contract somewhat in Hong Kong, but also in the reverse possibility that the extent of survival of democratic practice in Hong Kong, tolerated indirectly by the Chinese Communist Party, may in due course embolden those in China who wish to see democratic practice expand there. This remarkable daily tug of war over ideology and the bounds of individual freedom under two distinct jurisdictions within the same country must surely be without precedent, and for that reason alone should be of interest to all students of politics. That this should be taking place against a background of an Asian crisis of which it is said a major cause has been a lack of transparency and democratic accountability makes the subject of all the more pressing interest.

Conclusion

Taken as a whole, the Beetham audit, although originally contrived for the UK, may offer a useful tool with which to assess the ongoing impact on democracy in Hong Kong of the transfer to Chinese sovereignty. To the extent that the electoral arrangements and political institutions of democracy up to 1 July 1997 had evolved partially based on British practice, the model would clearly have relevance. More than this, however, in its provision for analysis of the broader 'democratic culture', and its concern with the general principles of democracy rather than solely with mechanisms, it may be particularly suitable.

Where drawbacks exist, these may have more to do with the model's ability to effect a comparison with China, and with the way in which the economic level of a society such as China may bear on its capacity to develop or sustain democracy. The Beetham model cannot, and indeed does not set out to, tell us much about this. The challenge of developing a model that would simultaneously embrace two societies with some common cultural roots, but markedly different recent political experience and differing levels of development must be a subject for future enquiry.

Acknowledgement

The author wishes to acknowledge the generous advice and assistance of David Beetham in the preparation of this chapter.

Notes

1   The path of export-led development followed by many of the states of Pacific Asia – the former British colonies Hong Kong, Singapore, Malaysia and the former Japanese colonies Taiwan, South Korea, and others – is now widely known. Less understood is the relationship between political institutions and the success of development strategy, or the influence on either of cultural values. Hong Kong's own success is *widely acknowledged* to have been due in part to the haven it provided from precisely that system which has now taken it over.

2 Although Hong Kong Island and Kowloon were ceded in perpetuity to Britain, it had long been accepted that Hong Kong could not exist without the New Territories, on which the lease ran out in 1997.

3 *The Other Hong Kong Report* has become a focus for informed and scholarly criticism of Government policy.

4 Parekh (1993) asserts the incongruity of applying what he regards as western culture-bound ideas about democracy out of context. Hadenius (1992) offers recent insights into the complex relationship of democracy and development. See also Huntington (1991) on this.

5 To some extent, this must reflect the fact that studies of democracy have tended to focus on societies regarded as being 'in jeopardy', either because (in cold war terms) they might join the 'communist camp', or because their lack of political stability in other ways threatened international peace and order. In the case of most Pacific Asian countries, economic prosperity was seen as the best bulwark to the spread of communism, and indeed most received investment in part as a consequence of the project to 'contain' China.

6 Examples might include South Korea, Singapore, Malaysia and Indonesia.

7 Gordon White, Institute of Development Studies, University of Sussex, on BBC Radio 4, 1996.

8 The Bangkok Declaration, in which the Chinese Government played an active part, sought to stem the flow of criticism, especially from the United States, of Asian governments with poor human rights records. No evidence was adduced, however, to suggest that popular opinion in the countries concerned would repudiate rights if they were offered. In some measure, the debate about rights has obscured concerns about democracy in Pacific Asia.

9 See especially Sir Percy Cradock, former British Ambassador to China, in his testimony to the Foreign Affairs Committee of the House of Commons, in *Relations between the UK and China in the Period Up To and Beyond 1997*, Volume 2, House of Commons, 1994.

10 Porter develops the argument that politics and culture combine in mainland China to create hidden agendas that impinge upon decision making in all areas of life. See Robin Porter, *Politics, culture and decision making in China*, in Brown and Porter (1996).

11 See the *Selected Works of Mao Tse-tung*, especially 'On Practice' (1937), 'On Contradiction' (1937), and 'On the Correct Handling of Contradictions Among the People' (1957), part 1.

12 David Beetham's ideas for a democratic audit have developed over a period of years, and are elaborated most recently in: Beetham 1993, Beetham 1994, Beetham 1995, and Beetham & Boyle 1994. The precise questions used here are from the recently revised document *Conducting a Democratic Audit*, Beetham, unpublished paper (1997). Permission to use this paper and David Beetham's generous assistance is gratefully acknowledged.

13 Under the Patten reforms, the 60-seat Legislative Council would comprise 20 geographical seats chosen by universal suffrage, 30 functional seats chosen by the whole working population (some 2.7 million), and 10 seats filled by an electoral college of the 300 District Board members, who were themselves directly elected.

14 Martin Lee, leader of the Democrats, the party that achieved some 65 per cent of the popular vote in the 1995 elections, had unsuccessfully urged the Governor to open up 'at least 50 per cent' of Legco seats to popular election through the

geographic constituencies with universal franchise. (Interview with the author, May 1997). Lee had put the same demand to the previous Governor, David Wilson. See Wang, 1995, p 176.

15 *Far Eastern Economic Review*, Sept. 28, 1995, p. 16. Given the lack of previous experience of elections to Legco on this scale, this figure was regarded as significant.

16 For a discussion of the constraints on political autonomy at the village level see John Dearlove, *Village Politics* in Benewick and Wingrove 1995, especially pp 124–127.

17 Although there is much increased scope in China for entrepreneurial activity that can bring personal wealth, it is contended that upward mobility and the consolidation of gains is still very much dependent on political connections.

18 The requirement for publication of reports and proceedings on the work of government has in recent years been broadly similar to that in the UK.

19 Hong Kong has some 60 daily newspapers, mostly in Chinese, with a few in English, and many television channels and radio stations in Cantonese, Mandarin and English.

20 In practice, the Executive Council and Governor have in recent years had to justify themselves and their policies to the Legislative Council. Legco has been free to debate these policies, and often to influence their implementation in Committee, but the majority party in Legco has not formed a 'government', and has not as a body been able to initiate policy.

21 The Independent Commission Against Corruption (ICAC) was established in 1974 following a particularly difficult period for corruption in the police and in government. See Hong Kong Government (1981, p 11).

22 The courts in Hong Kong function largely in English. One reason for this, it is suggested, is the difficulty of expressing concepts from English Common Law in Chinese (Raymond Wacks, Faculty of Law, University of Hong Kong, interview with the author, May 1997).

23 For the structure and function of Xinhua, see Robin Porter, *Shaping China's News*, in Porter (1992).

24 There can occasionally be exceptions to this general rule. Recent research by the author showed up an encouraging example of the National People's Congress sending back the draft Energy Conservation Law (1995) to the State Council for amendment because it considered the level of detail in the law to be inadequate. Although this was not a direct challenge to the Party, it was some departure at least from the NPC's normal role as a rubber stamp.

25 The author has directly observed Chinese criminal court procedures. See also, for example, Donald C. Clarke, *Justice and the Legal System in China*, in Benewick and Wingrove (1995, pp 83–93).

26 Raymond Wacks, interview with the author, May 1997. On the various precedents, and the process of introduction of the Bill of Rights in Hong Kong, see especially Peter Wesley-Smith 'Protecting Human Rights in Hong Kong', and Nihal Jayawickrama 'The Bill of Rights', both in Wacks ed 1992.

27 Wacks, in his introduction to Wacks (1992), notes that the Bill of Rights bound 'only government, public authorities, public officers, and employees of public authorities' and was not applicable to 'inter-citizen relations'.

28 See especially Carlos Wing-hung Lo (1997, pp 90–107). Perhaps one of the best-known cases is that of Wei Jingsheng, in prison from 1979 to 1992 for advocating democracy as the 'fifth modernization', and again from 1995 for a further

14 years for continuing to speak out against the Chinese government. Wei was finally released in 1998 and took refuge in the United States.

29 Janet Salaff addresses the complex matter of Hong Kong identity in Chapter 13 of this volume, suggesting that Hong Kong people stress different identities for different purposes.

30 Controversy in this respect has surrounded not only the Chinese-language newspapers, but also the English-language *South China Morning Post*. The disappearance from the Post of the much-admired but, in mainland Chinese terms unacceptably irreverent, cartoonist Larry Feign was regarded by many local journalists as a warning sign.

31 Hong Kong has become well versed in recent years in the use of opinion poll techniques. Among the many organizations involved in testing political opinion, the Social Science Research Centre of the University of Hong Kong and the Hong Kong Transition Project at Hong Kong Baptist University, stand out. See, for example, Chang and Chuang (1998, pp 149, 153).

32 The survival of the Chinese state over more than 2000 years, despite occasional occupations and temporary break-ups, is often attributed to the strength and unifying force of Chinese civilization and culture. One consequence of this is that even in the modern day, all ethnic Chinese are regarded as potential citizens of China, no matter where they may have been born.

33 See *Xinwenxiezuo* (Newswriting), an official guide to the journalist's art in China published by Yunnan University, translated by Jennifer Grant, Australian National University, unpublished paper, 1979.

Bibliography

Apter, D. E. 1987 *Re-thinking Development: Modernization, Dependency, and Post-modern Politics*. Newbury Park, CA.: Sage.

Baker, H. 1983 'Life in the Cities: the Emergence of Hong Kong Man'. *China Quarterly* 95 (September): 469–479.

Baker, H. 1993 'Social Change in Hong Kong: Hong Kong Man in Search of Majority'. *China Quarterly* 136 (December): 864–877.

Barme, G. 1995 'To Screw Foreigners is Patriotic: China's Avant-garde Nationalists'. *China Journal* 34 (July): 209–234.

Beetham, D. 1993 *Auditing Democracy in Britain*, Democratic Audit Paper no.1, University of Essex: Human Rights Centre.

Beetham, D. 1993 'Liberal Democracy and the Limits of Democratization', in Held, D. (ed.) *Prospects for Democracy*. Cambridge: Polity Press.

Beetham, D. (ed.) 1994 *Defining and Measuring Democracy*. London: Sage.

Beetham, D. 1995 *The Democratic Audit of the UK*. London: Routledge.

Beetham, D., Boyle, K. 1995 *Introducing Democracy: 80 Questions and Answers*. London and Lanham, MD.: Polity Press and UNESCO.

Beetham, D. 1997 'Conducting a Democratic Audit', unpublished paper.

Bell, J. D., et al. 1990 *An Orderly Rebellion: Bulgaria's Transition from Dictatorship to Democracy*. Washington D.C.: IFES.

Benewick, R., Wingrove, P. (eds) 1995 *China in the 1990s*. London: Macmillan.

Bollen, K. A. 1980 'Issues in the Comparative Measurement of Political Democracy'. *American Sociological Review* 45: 370–390.

Brown, D., Porter, R. (eds) 1996 *Management Issues in China: Volume One, Domestic Enterprises*. London: Routledge.

Burns, J. P., Falkenheim, V. C., Lampton, D. M. (eds) 1994 *Hong Kong and China in Transition*. Canada and Hong Kong Papers, no. 3. Toronto: Joint Centre for Asia and Pacific Studies.

Chan, Ming K., Clark, D. J. (eds) 1991 *The Hong Kong Basic Law: Blueprint for Stability and Prosperity under Chinese Sovereignty?*, Hong Kong: Hong Kong University Press.

Chang, D. W., Chuang, R. Y. 1998 *The Politics of Hong Kong's Reversion to China*. Basingstoke and New York: Macmillan/St.Martin's Press.

Cheng, J. Y. S., Kwong, P. C. K. (eds) 1992 *The Other Hong Kong Report, 1992*. Hong Kong: Chinese University Press.

Clark, D. J. 1992 'The Basic Law: one document, two systems', in Cheng, J. Y. S. Kwong, P. C. K., *The Other Hong Kong Report, 1992*. Hong Kong: Chinese University Press.

Cottrell, R. 1993 *The End of Hong Kong: the Secret Diplomacy of Imperial Retreat*. London: John Murray Publishers.

Cradock, P. 1994 *Experiences of China*. London: John Murray Publishers.

Cradock, P. 1997 *Relations between the UK and China in the Period up to and beyond 1997*, vol. 2, 118–128.

Dahl, R. 1971 *Polyarchy: Participation and Opposition*. New Haven: Yale University Press.

Dahl, R. 1989 *Democracy and its Critics*. New Haven: Yale University Press.

Davies, S., Roberts, E. V. 1990 *Dictionary of Politics for Hong Kong*, Basingstoke: Macmillan.

Deng, Xiaoping 1993 *On the Question of Hong Kong*. Beijing: Foreign Languages Press.

Domes, J., Shaw, Y. (eds) *1988 Hong Kong: a Chinese and International Concern*. Boulder, CO: Westview Press.

England, J., Rear, J. 1975 *Chinese Labour under British Rule*, Hong Kong: Oxford University Press.

Gastil, R. D. 1991 'The Comparative Survey of Freedom: Experiences and Suggestions', in Inkeles A. (ed.) *On Measuring Democracy: Its Consequences and Concomitants*. New Brunswick, NJ and London: Transaction Publishers.

Goodman, D. S. G., Feng, Chongyi 1994 'Guangdong: Greater Hong Kong and the New Regionalist Future', in Goodman, D., Segal, G. (eds) *China Deconstructs*. London: Routledge.

Hadenius, A. 1992 *Democracy and Development*. Cambridge: Cambridge University Press.

Held. D., Pollitt, C. 1986 *New Forms of Democracy*. London: Sage.

Held, D. (ed.) 1993 *Prospects for Democracy*. Cambridge: Polity Press.

Holden, B. 1988 *Understanding Liberal Democracy*, London: Phillip Allan.

Hong Kong Government 1981 *Hong Kong 1981*. Hong Kong: Government Printer.

Hong Kong Government 1995 *Hong Kong 1995*. Hong Kong: Government Printer.

Hook, B. 1991 'The External Relations of Hong Kong', in Sung Yun-wing and Lee Ming-kwan (eds) *The Other Hong Kong Report, 1991*. Hong Kong: Chinese University Press.

Hopkins, K. (ed.) 1971 *Hong Kong: Industrial colony*, Hong Kong: Oxford University Press.

Huntington, S. P. 1991 *The Third Wave: Democratization in the Late Twentieth Century*. Norman, Oklahoma: University of Oklahoma Press.

Inkeles, A. (ed.) 1991 *On Measuring Democracy: Its Consequences and Concomitants*. New Brunswick, NJ and London: Transaction Publishers.

Lau, E. 1989 'A "subversive" alliance: China attacks territory's democrats'. *Far Eastern Economic Review*, August 3.

Lau Siu-kai Kuan Hsin-chi 1988 *The Ethos of the Hong Kong Chinese*. Hong Kong: Chinese University Press.

Lipset, S. M. 1959 'Some Social Requisites of Democracy: Economic Development and Political Legitimacy'. *American Political Science Review* 53: 69–105.

Lo, Wing-hung Carlos 1997 'Criminal Justice Reform in Post-Crisis China: a Human Rights Perspective'. *Hong Kong Law Journal* 27 (part 1): 90–107.

McMillen, D., Man Si-wai (eds) *The Other Hong Kong Report*. Hong Kong: Chinese University Press.

Mao, Zedong 1975 *Selected Works of Mao Tse-tung*, Beijing: Foreign Languages Press.

Miners, N. 1994 *The Government and Politics of Hong Kong*, 5th edn. Hong Kong: Oxford University Press.

Moran, M., Wright, M. (eds) 1991 *The Market and the State: Studies in Interdependence*. Basingstoke: Macmillan.

Mueller, R. 1995 Speech to the Foreign Correspondents' Club, 1995, in the *South China Morning Post*, weekly edition, May 6.

National People's Congress 1990 *The Basic Law of the Hong Kong Special Administrative Region of the People's Republic of China*. Beijing: National People's Congress.

Parekh, B. 1993 'The Cultural Particularity of Liberal Democracy', in Held, D. (ed.) *Prospects for Democracy*. Cambridge: Polity Press.

Patten, C. 1994 'Hong Kong: A Thousand Days and Beyond'. Address by the Governor, the Right Hon. Christopher Patten at the Opening of the 1994/95 Session of the Legislative Council, Hong Kong Government Press, 1994.

Porter, R. (ed.) 1992 *Reporting the News from China*. London: Chatham House.

Przeworski, A. 1991 *Democracy and the Market: Political and Economic Reforms in Eastern Europe and Latin America*. Cambridge: Cambridge University Press.

Pye, L. W. 1995 'Chinese Politics in the Late Deng Era'. *China Quarterly* 142 (June): 573–583.

Rafferty, K. 1991 *City on the Rocks: Hong Kong's Uncertain Future*. London: Penguin.

Schell, O. 1994 *Mandate of Heaven: A New Generation of Entrepreneurs, Dissidents, Bohemians and Technocrats Lays Claim to China's Future*, New York: Simon and Schuster.

Segal, G. 1983 *The Fate of Hong Kong*. London: Simon and Schuster.

Sorensen, G. 1993 *Democracy and Democratization: Processes and Prospects in a Changing World*. Boulder CO.: Westview Press.

Sullivan, J. C., Sutter, R. 1995 'Hong Kong's Political Transition: Implications for US Interests'. *Congress Research Service Issue Brief*. Washington DC: CRS, April 11.

Tsang, S. 1988 *Democracy Shelved*. Hong Kong: Oxford University Press.

Tucker, N. Bernkopf 1994 *Taiwan, Hong Kong and the United States, 1945–1992 Uncertain Friendships*. New York: Twayne Publishers.

Vanhannen, T. 1990 *The Process of Democratization: A Comparative Study of 147 States, 1980–1988*. New York: Taylor and Francis.

Verba, S., Nie, N., Kim, J. O. 1971 *The Modes of Democratic Participation: a Cross National Comparison*. Beverly Hills, CA: Sage.

Wacks, R. (ed.) 1988 *Civil Liberties in Hong Kong*. Hong Kong: Oxford University Press.

Wacks, R. 1989 *The Future of the Law in Hong Kong*. Hong Kong: Oxford University Press.

Wacks, R. 1992 *Human Rights in Hong Kong*. Hong Kong: Oxford University Press.

Wang, Enbao 1995 *Hong Kong 1997: the Politics of Transition*. Boulder, CO. and London: Lynne Rienner Publishers.

Welsh, F. 1994 *A History of Hong Kong*. London: Harper Collins.

Wilson, D. 1990 *Hong Kong! Hong Kong!* London: Unwin Hyman.

Yahuda, M. 1990 *Hong Kong: China's Challenge*. London: Routledge.

Yahuda, M. 1996 'Hong Kong's Future: Sino-British Negotiations, Perceptions, Organization and Political Culture'. *International Affairs*, 69(2) (April).

Part III
Social Discourse

12
Reflections on the Hong Kong Discourse on Human Rights

Susanne Weigelin-Schwiedrzik

The question of human rights in Hong Kong has been a focus of attention since 4 June 1989. Following the mass demonstrations in Hong Kong in support of the Beijing students' movement and in protest against its bloody suppression by the Chinese government, people inside and outside Hong Kong were to become more aware of the human rights issue and to regard it as one of the main problems to be solved during the transition process.

It is not only because of the obvious political implication of the human rights issue that we need to address this question in our research, however. Analysing the discourse on human rights in Hong Kong also means addressing the question of the Hong Kong identity, and even more than that turns out to be a question of universal concern. Hong Kong used to be a Chinese city under colonial rule and is now an international city under Chinese rule. Thus, Hong Kong is also a place where European values should be more commonly accepted than in most other cities in Asia, and at the same time is a westernized place with strong connections to the larger Chinese community across the boundary, and hence to a great variety of currents in Chinese culture and thought. It is this special situation that makes Hong Kong an ideal place to explore the acceptability of ideas about human rights in the context of Asian cultures, the compatibility of human rights and Asian values, and the question of whether or not the notion of human rights, as it has been generated in the west, can be rooted into an Asian context.

The development of the human rights issue

When the Joint Declaration was signed by the British and Chinese governments in 1984, the human rights issue was not yet of major concern. With the Soviet Union still in existence, the world-wide discussion on the implementation of human rights was focused on what was happening in the Soviet Union. And with China embarking on a reform course, there was no interest in criticizing it for deficiencies in the field of human rights. Moreover, most people involved in the process of negotiation as well as a sound majority of Hong Kong people shared the view that the Beijing government would, in its own interest in modernizing China, never dare to do any harm to Hong Kong. Under these circumstances, the British government did not feel any pressure to stress the implementation of human rights after 1997, and seemed to have been satisfied to have the Joint Declaration guarantee the applicability of the International Covenant on Civil and Political Rights as well as of the International Covenant on Economic, Social and Cultural Rights as passed by the United Nations in 1966 (Jayawickrama 1992, pp 162–165). The British side, as well as the majority of Hong Kong residents, were optimistic about the territory's future and confident that reforms in China would eventually lead to a convergence of the two political systems.

This situation changed dramatically when the student movement in Tiananmen Square was bloodily suppressed on 4 June 1989. People in Hong Kong who were widely regarded as politically indifferent, suddenly joined mass demonstrations against the Beijing government to express their grief about the massacred students, their anguish about the removal of then party leader Zhao Ziyang from power and their fears about the future of Hong Kong. Suddenly, the main presupposition on which the optimism about Hong Kong's future had been based turned out to be invalid. With the 'reformers' in the CCP leadership repelled and Zhao Ziyang removed from power, confidence in the future convergence of the two political systems was shaken. The newly established leadership in Beijing was widely viewed as a group of old-fashioned politicians making irrational decisions no matter what the Chinese people, the people of Hong Kong and the world at large would think about them.

It was under these circumstances that concerns spread about the 'autonomy' guaranteed in the Joint Declaration being subject to interpretation, with the views of the original undersigners diverging more and more obviously. That is why 'checks and balances' were needed to ensure that the people of Hong Kong would not be arbitrarily deprived of their freedoms after 1997. It was at this juncture that the human rights issue moved into the centre of the political discourse in Hong Kong and about Hong Kong (Wacks 1988; and the foreword for the second edition of 1989).

The Hong Kong Bill of Rights

On 8 June 1989, a full-page advertisement appeared in Hong Kong newspapers saying:

> Power does not come
> out of the muzzle of a gun.
> It comes from the will of the people.

The people of Hong Kong need their
Bill of Rights now!

(Jayawickrama 1992, p 70)

The Foreign Affairs Committee responded to this demand by a suggestions that 'a Bill of Rights should be introduced as soon as possible so that
it becomes entrenched in the Hong Kong system, and a substantial body of
case law on it can be built up. Hong Kong should not arrive at 1997 with its
rights and freedoms new minted and untested' (Jayawickrama 1992, p 71).

Confronted with the changed situation in both Beijing and Hong Kong,
and with pressure from both Hong Kong and the international media, the
British government departed from its former policies. The then Foreign
Minister Sir Geoffrey Howe announced that a Bill of Rights '... will be introduced as soon as possible. It will form part of the existing law and be able to
continue after the transfer of sovereignty' (Jayawickrama 1992, p 71).

Even though this reaction to the situation might have been understandable under the circumstances, it was quite astonishing given the human
rights policy the British government had previously displayed in Hong
Kong. After the ratification of the European Convention on Human Rights
in 1951, it was applied to 42 overseas dependent territories, but not to Hong
Kong. After Nigeria had become the first British colony to be provided with a
constitutional Bill of Rights in 1959, other colonies followed, but not Hong
Kong. The above-mentioned UN covenants passed in 1966 and ratified by
Great Britain in 1976 were translated into the Common Law system all over
the Commonwealth, except in Hong Kong. That is why, as late as 1988, the
UN Committee on Human Rights criticized the British government for vio-
lating human rights in Hong Kong and urged immediate changes regarding
political freedoms in the city (Jayawickrama 1992, pp 41–44).

It is still quite unclear why the British government acted in this way.
As the related documents are still classified, there are no archival sources
to help explain the attitude the British government had taken in the context of the Hong Kong human rights issue before 1989. Why should the
British government regard the Hong Kong people either as unable or
unwilling to cherish human rights, if it believed other people in Asia and
Africa to be ready for the implementation of human rights? Was it fear of
communist subversion, or disregard for the so-called politically indifferent
population of Hong Kong? One possible explanation comes from the PRC.
There, this author was told, in 1949 when Communist troops had reached
Shenzhen and were ready to march into Hong Kong, a secret agreement
was reached between the then Governor of Hong Kong and the Communist Party of China to the effect that Hong Kong would be left untouched
if it helped in supplying China with necessary commodities that were otherwise unobtainable, and as long as Hong Kong did not serve as an initia-
tor or transmitter of subversive acts against the new Communist regime.[1]

With civil war continuing after the People's Republic had been established, it seems reasonable to believe that the Governor of Hong Kong would have tried to inhibit Communists as well as Nationalists from engaging in a continuous battle over China from Hong Kong, at least during the first few years after the founding of the PRC. Furthermore, Hong Kong was, in fact, in a difficult situation after the end of the war with the city devastated and masses of refugees pouring in (Blyth and Wotherspoon 1996, pp 1–54). In later years, the constraints on political rights for the people of Hong Kong could be explained by fears that the PRC government and the CCP might destabilize the situation in Hong Kong with the help of their supporters in the colony. When, finally, the crisis had reached Hong Kong in the context of the Cultural Revolution, these fears proved to be justified.

This interpretation is at least partly backed by the publication of two letters from the British Foreign and Commonwealth Office to Professor Harro von Senger, professor of Sinology at Freiburg University (Senger 1997, pp 101–116). In one of these letters, an official of the Hong Kong Department of the Foreign Office explains why the European Convention on Human Rights had never been extended to Hong Kong, saying:

> Hong Kong was not included, because in June 1952 we had concluded that in many respects Hong Kong would not have been able to comply with the Convention. This was primarily because of the emergency measures then in force in the Colony.
>
> (Senger 1997, pp 111–113)

No explanation if offered for the period between 1952 and 1976 when the UN Covenants were extended to Hong Kong, or June 1991 when the Hong Kong Bill of Rights was enforced. Only for the period immediately after the Communist take-over of the mainland does this official refer to the fact that this question was not openly discussed for fear of communist propaganda seizing upon the obvious conflict with the European Covenant on Human Rights (Senger 1997, p 112). In a second letter from the same office, it is pointed out that 'the political situation in China remained unstable until the late 1970s' and therefore threatened the stability of public order in Hong Kong well beyond the early 1950s (Senger 1997, pp 115–116). The then Governor of Hong Kong, Sir Alexander Grantham, was quite aware of the 'abnormality' of the situation, noting that: 'to deal with the day-to-day administration of [the refugees] in dangerously congested conditions calls for rapid and sometimes arbitrary action such as could not, rightly, be tolerated under normal conditions' (Senger 1997, p 111). Thus, the implementation of human rights in Hong Kong has always been subject to the evaluation of the concrete political situation. And in this respect, the British Government's agreement to demands asking for a Bill of Rights in 1989 was consistent with its earlier policies.

After the masses had demonstrated in the streets, experts from the legal profession took over, drafted a first version of the Bill of Rights, organized committees and participated in the public consultation following the publication of the so called White Bill on 16 March 1990 (Jayawickrama 1992, pp 71–75). In these discussions, they were confronted with resistance both from Beijing and Hong Kong. The Beijing government insisted that the Bill of Rights violated the essence of the Joint Declaration, as it was not part of the status quo agreed upon in 1984, and as it was supposed to claim a superior status to other laws in Hong Kong. Hong Kong voices criticizing the draft expressed their fears that they would not be able to enforce law and order in the territory (Jayawickrama 1992, pp 73–75).

The Bill of Rights published for consultation in March 1990 differed from the original in not endowing the bill with a special and superior status. These and other changes that had been undertaken in the course of consultation led Nihal Jayawickrama, who had actively taken part in the drafting of the original version of the Bill of Rights, to conclude that, 'With incredible alacrity, the demands of the Chinese authorities had once more been accommodated' (Jayawickrama 1992, p 75). This harsh criticism of the Bill of Rights is quite understandable if the Hong Kong situation is measured against the human rights situation in other parts of the western world. But it may in some respects be too severe as it ignores the situation under which the enforcement of the Bill of Rights was to be undertaken.

Had Britain decided to revise its policy of limiting the enforcement of human rights in Hong Kong immediately after the end of the Cultural Revolution (1966–1976), the discussion in Hong Kong could possibly have developed without the Beijing government interfering as strongly as it did later when the Hong Kong take-over had already been agreed upon. The 'lifestyle' of Hong Kong referred to in the Joint Declaration would have included the implementation of human rights, and a 'substantial body of case law' would have been built up long before the Hong Kong handover. In 1989–1990 the discussions were not only impeded by a Beijing government that was by itself under severe international and national pressure, but also by rapidly deteriorating relations between the UK and the PRC, which made finding a solution acceptable to both sides extremely difficult. As a consequence, the Bill of Rights seems to have been appreciated by none of the parties concerned. The Beijing government could not be persuaded to accept it, just as the pro-China business elite was unhappy about it, the Hong Kong democrats could not agree to it, and the Hong Kong population did not show any direct signs of support, relief or gratitude. The only positive long-term effect of the Bill of Rights may have been that a discussion on the human rights issue had for the first time in the history of Hong Kong openly taken place.

The Hong Kong discourse on human rights

The general discourse on the human rights issue outside the political and business elites of the territory presents us with a picture contrary to expectation. Discussions on the Bill of Rights issue, as well as on the human rights issue in general, have up to now been largely limited to the daily press, especially the English-speaking daily press, while, with the exception of the *Apple Daily* (Lai 1996, pp 251–258), the Chinese-language press seems to pay less attention to this question. Even in highly politicized magazines such as *Jiushi niandai* (The Nineties) or *Dongxiang* (The East) we find that the question of human rights in Hong Kong is not a question of major concern (Weigelin-Schwiedrzik 1999). These magazines publish articles on human rights quite frequently, but their focus is on the human rights situation in China (He 1991, pp 33–35; Yan 1995, pp 11–13; Ai 1991, pp 48–49; Liu 1991, pp 48–50; Yu 1991, pp 44–47). Their main argument is that even though the Chinese people are still afraid to demand the implementation of human rights, people outside the PRC should continue to press for the improvement of the human rights situation as this is the best way to destabilize the Beijing government (Nan 1989, pp 36–38; Li 1989, pp 16–19 on the democracy movement; Qi 1989, pp 29–31; Ming 1990, pp 53–54 on human rights foreign policy). A destabilized Beijing government would be unable to interfere with Hong Kong's affairs and would eventually retreat in order to make way for people whose views are more compatible with Hong Kong's hope for a convergence of the two systems. Thus, only a change of policies and politicians in Beijing could help Hong Kong (He 1991; Guo 1995, p 10; Wu 1991, pp 40–41).

This reasoning is interesting in several respects. First of all, it starts out by instrumentalizing the human rights question while refraining from discussing its juridical or philosophical implications. The question of universality versus particularity of human rights is not discussed and the universality taken for granted in the premise of 'exporting' human rights to the PRC (for an exception, see Ming 1993, pp 44–46).

Secondly, the reasoning reflects the close interdependency between the situation in Hong Kong and the PRC. Authors belonging to this segment of the discourse do not stress the special status of Hong Kong and the fact that it is and should be different from the PRC, but treat the HKSAR as any other city or region belonging to the PRC. This, of course, can be explained by the fact that the majority of them have been exiled from the PRC since 1989, and that some of them publish in Hong Kong magazines although they do not live in Hong Kong.

Quite in contrast to this segment of the discourse, the Hong Kong democrats conceive of the human rights issue as a major concern in the context of developing a Hong Kong identity (Wacks 1989, Wacks 1992, Davis 1995).[2] The entrenchment of the human rights issue into the process of democratization in Hong Kong is what makes Hong Kong different from the PRC, and the question of whether or not democracy and human rights in Hong Kong will have any effect on what is going on in China is only of minor importance. Just as the Hong Kong government reacted to demand by formulating a Bill of Rights for Hong Kong in order to regain legitimacy and restore confidence, Hong Kong democrats use the public discourse on human rights to define the so-called missing identity of the people of Hong Kong. They want Hong Kong to be a modern, cosmopolitan city with a democratic system based on the implementation of human rights; and they want this not only to be the collective identity of the newly evolving political elite in contrast to that of the pro-China business elite, they also want this to be the identity of the people of Hong Kong as a whole (McNeil 1992, pp 86–119). They do not explicitly dwell on the issue of universality versus particularity. They take for granted the universality of human rights in their political form. And this also means that they regard external support for their demands as just as valid and legitimate as popular support from inside Hong Kong.

Indeed, the 'outside' factor has increasingly become important for their cause, as public support for human rights activities has declined since its high tide in 1989. Although many non-government organizations are active in this field, their main area of operation seems to be the Internet and, with the exception of the 4 June rallies every year,[3] not the streets of Hong Kong. Constituting an identity for Hong Kong through discussion of human rights as well as the democracy issue forms part of the political elite's struggle for supremacy in the political debate in Hong Kong, as well as a tactic in its contest for power with the business elite, strongly backed by the Chinese government.

The third segment of the discourse is formed by a small group of authors who also start out from the special situation of Hong Kong, but conclude, in contrast to the Hong Kong democrats, that the Hong Kong situation does not yet allow for a full implementation of human rights. In their eyes, the special situation of Hong Kong is its colonial legacy, which itself makes the implementation of human rights impossible (Mingbao 1992, p 50). With the handover, the special situation of Hong Kong consists in it being part of a country with a political system so different that it will be as far away from Hong Kong – though in a different sense – as the former colonial motherland (Zha 1992a, pp 4–9; Zha 1992b, pp 51–53). In other words, they see the situation of dependency in Hong Kong quite unchanged.

In following this reasoning, this group of authors seem to back the opinion of the enlightened part of the business elite searching for a *modus vivendi* under the given circumstances. The magazine *Mingbao* sometimes lends its pages to these authors. For them, the identity of the people of Hong Kong is not to be defined by the special status of the territory but by the Hong Kong people being Chinese and partaking of Chinese culture

(Jin 1992, pp 50–56). By avoiding active involvement in the human rights discussion, they avoid having to back the standpoint of either the incompatibility of Asian cultures with the universality of human rights, or the standpoint of the PRC government, which by now acknowledges the universality of human rights as laid down by the UN, but focuses solely on social and economic rights (Guowuyuan 1991). Implicitly, they stress the 'eastern' orientation of Hong Kong more than the 'western', and in doing so, they write the countertext to the democrats' attempt at defining a Hong Kong identity on the basis of human rights and democracy.

Public consultation on the Public Order and Societies Ordinances

During the last 100 days before the change of sovereignty in July 1997, the human rights issue had again been moved into the centre of the political debate about Hong Kong's future. The administration under Chief Executive Designate, Tung Chee-hwa, came out with the proposal for the Public Order and Societies Ordinances in April 1997, which heated up the above-mentioned contest between the business and the political elites, involving all political and media forces in the territory. What Tung Chee-hwa had intended as a 'rational, reasonable and intellectual debate on how to strike best the balance between civil liberties and social order' (Tung, 1997a) was met with a variety of different responses on the part of the Hong Kong as well as the international press, and 4575 submissions from individuals, 932 submissions from groups and organizations, and 293 Internet communications, which expressed opinions about the ordinances to the Chief Executive's office (see Chief Executive's Office 1997a).

While political forces backing the Chief Executive Designate stressed that in the period of transition Hong Kong should not forget the necessity of public order and stability and should avoid any risks,[4] the democratic forces in the city criticized the proposals as 'a step back' in the process of democratization (Lau 1997). As a result of approximately one month of consultation, the original version of the ordinances was slightly changed and the outcome of the contest tested by an opinion poll. According to the *South China Morning Post*, 'the survey found 50.3 per cent [of the respondents] were uncertain or concerned that the amendments would restrict the freedom of assembly' which compared to '49.7 per cent who said the amended law would not affect civil liberties' (Cheung 1997).

The discussion was focused on two questions: the degree to which the Hong Kong political forces would be able to retain their international connections; and reaching a common understanding of the balance between individual freedom and the need for social order and stability (Tung 1997a). Tung Chee-hwa embedded the discussion in what he called the uniqueness of Hong Kong. By combining the best from the east and from the west, he pointed out, Hong Kong could avoid the problems of modernization in the form of the 'permissiveness' that western cities confronted (Tung 1997a). That meant limiting individual freedom in favour of public order as well as adhering to 'traditional' Chinese values such as 'humbleness, patience, persistence and hard work' (Tung 1997b), combining them with the western orientation of democracy and freedom:

> Hong Kong will not become like Beijing or Shanghai. Nor will we want to become like Washington, New York, or London. I am confident that we will find our own way forward in part based on our own culture, history and values which we hold dearly.... We want to live in the type of society in which we ourselves and our future generation will feel proud of. We know we will succeed in our efforts.
>
> (Tung 1997b)

On the basis of this definition of the uniqueness of Hong Kong, the Tung Chee-hwa administration feels that it is legitimate to limit the possibility of foreign intervention in Hong Kong's 'internal' affairs. Tung Chee-hwa's proposals are, of course, not primarily aimed at political forces active in the PRC, but quite clearly at political forces in Taiwan as well as in the United States. He justified the limitations by observing, that:

> Most of the countries in the world are sensitive about influences of foreign political parties on their domestic political scene. Indeed, the federal election laws of the United States are much tougher than the proposed provisions of our Societies Ordinance.
>
> (Tung 1997b)

The limitation on international funding for political parties will not only pose a major problem to political parties that are not funded by the Hong Kong business elite. It will obviously weaken the political elite, which has up to now been strongly supported by outside forces. And it might also touch the cosmopolitan character of the Hong Kong lifestyle, which is closely linked to unlimited international contact in the economic sphere. Quite obviously, Singapore is the model Tung Chee-hwa wants to follow, but, contrary to his expectations, the way in which globalization in the economic sphere is combined with Chinese values in Singapore might be regarded as a step back in Hong Kong. In Hong Kong, western influence has been able to freely compete with traditional Chinese values just as easily as commodities freely flow in and out of the territory.

The special status of Hong Kong, which has been the focus of the human rights debate as put forward by the democratic forces in Hong Kong, is no longer a domain of discourse solely occupied by the democrats. The appointed political leadership in Hong Kong has stepped into this domain and, in contrast to its earlier stance, seeks to provide the population of Hong Kong with some kind of value orientation. That is why in this new round of discussion on human rights, the conflict between them and the evolving political elite comes out more clearly than before, when the business elite and its intellectual adherents tried to avoid the discussion.

The main argument the democrats in Hong Kong raised against the Public Order and Societies Ordinances can be summarized with the words 'a step back'. Members of democratic organizations do not see Hong Kong threatened by social disorder. On the contrary, in their minds, stressing the political and organizational freedom of the people totally accords with Hong Kong being a modern and international city dependent in its further development on the creativity of its population, as well as on the free flow of goods and information. As Christine Loh put it in one interview: 'We are more modern!'[5]

On the other hand, the limitation on individual freedoms and financial support from foreign political organizations is regarded as a sign of mistrust of the political active forces in Hong Kong. To quote Gladys Li, member of the Hong Kong JUSTICE group:

> I think that there is absolutely no doubt that the proposals are a regression from what we currently have. And what we have to look at is: have we had civil disorder as a result of the laws as they currently are? And I think the answer is quite clear – that we have had no civil disorder as a result of relaxing constraints that used to exist in the past. Now the proposals seem to restore the restraints that existed in the past. And to me that is a very sad thing. Because what it says to people in Hong Kong is: we can't trust you. We can't trust you to behave responsibly. And that I think is a very sad message to begin with.[6]

On 15 May 1997 the HKSAR Chief Executive's Office finally presented a revised version of the two ordinances to the public. While the changes undertaken obviously did not reflect the kind of fundamental criticism voiced by the Hong Kong democrats, they did respond to criticisms regarding the inexact wording of the original draft. The meanings of words like 'national security', 'political' and 'international political organizations' were redefined and other wording made more comprehensible. Wording like 'safeguard public health and public morals' that did not easily accord with the nature of an ordinance were removed. Spontaneous rallies, which under the first version would have been impossible, became possible because the requirement for a minimum of 48 hours for advance notice was removed (Chief Executive's Office 1997).

These changes are more or less in line with the meticulous criticism the office of Governor Patten had published directly after the ordinances had been presented to the public. And they are also in line with the criticisms voiced by the English-language, as well as some of the Chinese-language press in Hong Kong: 'We have listened carefully to public opinions on the consultation document and have taken positive steps to address the concerns expressed' (Chief Executive's Office 1997a), said Michael Suen Ming-yeung, Secretary for Policy Co-ordination for Chief Executive Tung Chee-hwa. And as a result of this, the future administration of Hong Kong found a middle-of-the-road solution when confronted with sharp criticisms by the democratic forces in Hong Kong, as well as with highly tuned expectations voiced in Beijing. As we have seen above, nearly 50 per cent of the respondents in the *South China Morning Post* poll did not find their personal freedom intruded upon, and the 'level of satisfaction with Mr. Tung's performance increased two points over the April reading to 57 per cent', with those not satisfied increasing from 17 to 24 per cent (Cheung 1997). In their contest for the supremacy over the political discourse in Hong Kong, the business elite, as represented by the Chief Executive Tung Chee-hwa and backed by the Beijing government, reached the point where it could offer value orientations to the public, to which approximately 50 per cent of the people responded positively. On the other hand, the democrats, with their criticisms of the Tung Chee-hwa propositions, still in May 1997 influenced more than the 25.1 per cent of voters who would have elected their candidates if given the possibility to vote at that time (Cheung 1997). This means that even though, in the course of the second round of discussions on the human rights issue, the Tung Chee-hwa administration had gained more support than expected, the position of the democrats also had sound backing among the population. This kind of backing is not evidenced by rallies in the streets of Hong Kong, nor by people participating in human rights activities. With the sole, but important, exception of rallies on 4 June, the activists in human rights organizations are quite isolated, and because of their isolation they complain about the lack of political culture, of identity, and of a feeling of self-consciousness. In short, they complain about the political indifference the majority of people in Hong Kong display when it comes to questions of human rights.[7]

Universality versus particularity of human rights

The Hong Kong discourse on human rights, starting off as a discourse on the general political orientation of Hong Kong, has developed to become a discourse on the post-colonial identity of Hong Kong. It first gained momentum when nearly one million people gathered in the streets of Hong Kong to protest against the Beijing government's solution to the student movement on Tiananmen Square in 1989, and when the British government as well as the administration of Hong Kong responded to demands asking for the immediate drafting of a Bill of Rights. In the course of the discussion, basically two chains of argument were put forward with the

political elite demanding what they called the full implementation of political human rights for Hong Kong, and the business elite stressing the necessity to find the correct balance between civil liberties and social order. Both
chains of argument were developed in relationship to 'outside' forces interfering with the political discussion in Hong Kong. The arguments developed
by the political elite are obviously linked to international discussions on
the question of human rights as promoted by the UN, the USA and certain
European countries. On the other side, the initial avoidance of the topic by
the business elite as well as its later attempt to step into the debate were
influenced by the fact that the government of the PRC was the main target
of criticisms voiced in the international debates. But, as both sides aimed at
defining the special status or uniqueness of Hong Kong, they were eager to
distance themselves from those 'outside' forces. The political elite, although
clearly backed in its demands by the reform strategies of Governor Patten,
openly criticized the British government as well as the administration of
Hong Kong for their attitude towards the human rights issue (Ng 1995).[8]
The business elite, although eager to co-operate closely with the Beijing
government, does not follow the official line in Beijing of giving supremacy
to economic and social rights as compared to political rights.

Outside the range of this inner elite contest, only one group of discus-
sants has offered a third variety of arguments, which is mainly addressed to
the situation in the PRC and the necessity to change the overall political
situation in mainland China. Their arguments direct attention to a second
underlying topic in the human rights discourse, a topic that neither the
political nor the business elite directly address: the future relationship
between the situation in Hong Kong and the situation in the PRC. The reason the democratic movement started in the first place was the changing
political situation in China, which prompted people to go out into the
streets and ask for human rights in Hong Kong also. And it is not fear of
despotism on the part of the HKSAR government, but distrust in the Beijing
government that accounts for concern over the future of freedom in Hong
Kong. No matter how much autonomy is guaranteed to Hong Kong, people
there conceive of the situation in the city as being to a high degree determined by Sino–Hong Kong relations.

This interpretation is backed by polls, the findings of which show a
strong correlation in two respects: between the degree of satisfaction with
the Hong Kong administration on the one hand and their policies towards
Beijing on the other; and between the degree of satisfaction with the
Beijing government on the one hand and its policies towards Hong Kong
on the other.[9] Whoever is regarded as being able to adequately relate to
the Beijing government is to be trusted, just as the Beijing government
can only overcome the lack of confidence on the part of the Hong Kong
population if it shows itself to be able to adequately cope with the difficult
relationship between Beijing and Hong Kong.

Thus, for the above-mentioned discussion on the identity of Hong Kong, only those solutions that include a resolution of the human rights issue as part of both the identity problem and Sino–Hong Kong relations can hope for wide support among the population of Hong Kong. While the Hong Kong democrats seem to refrain from direct interference with the political situation in the PRC, they do see the possibility of Hong Kong exerting an indirect influence through its emerging modern political culture. Fundamentally, however, they regard Hong Kong as totally autonomous and view the Beijing government as a counterpart rather than a partner in the discussion. This means that their definition of the identity of Hong Kong implies separateness, and stresses difference, rather than pointing to the necessity of friendly relations with the PRC. And while the business elite stresses the necessity of guaranteeing stability, at the same time they feel compelled to conform with the UN covenants and to reply to demands for civil liberties in Hong Kong.[10] With their definition of the identity of Hong Kong, they try to respond to the twin character of Hong Kong as a Chinese as well as an international city. And this means under the new circumstances that it can only be international as far as the latter does not conflict with it being Chinese. The fact that in a recent poll, 70 per cent of the respondents said they trusted Mr Tung and his legislation to be supportive of the Hong Kong people, while only 23.5 per cent said they were not confident, shows that the project of defining a Hong Kong identity complying with both the international and the Chinese character of the city is gaining more and more support (Cheung 1997).

The human rights discourse in Hong Kong is not a discourse on fundamental philosophical or juridical questions such as typically form the focus of the human rights discourse in Europe. In this respect it quite obviously differs from what a western observer would normally expect a human rights discourse to be. In stressing political rather than economic and social rights, it is part of the international human rights discourse as promoted by most western, highly industrialized and wealthy nations. But by making the human rights issue the focus of a debate on the future identity of Hong Kong and its people, it responds to local political needs and therefore develops its own style. The Hong Kong example provides us with arguments both for universality as well as particularity, universality here meaning that the Hong Kong human rights discourse is part of a world-wide discourse on the subject, and particularity meaning that this discourse is a Hong Kong discourse, which differs from discussions in other parts of the world. However, universality in this sense does not have the same meaning everywhere. It refers only to the ubiquity of the discourse. Similarly, particularity does not mean human rights may be valid only in some parts of the world, despite the particular value systems of some other parts. It simply means that the discourse can develop only in particular political and cultural contexts, which finally determine the (particular) form it will take.

Notes

1 This information emerged from a discussion with Professor Dou Hui, Shanghai, when he delivered a paper at the Center of Chinese Studies, University of Heidelberg, on 13 May 1997. When asked for written proof, Dou stated that he himself was referring to oral information. Dou has given permission for this reference.

2 These comments on the democrats' position in the human rights discourse are also based upon the author's personal interviews with Emily Lau, Christine Loh and Gladys Li, which took place in March and April 1997.

3 Even though these magazines, such as *Jiushi niandai* and *Zhengming* have increasingly become critical of the so-called democratic movement of 1989, people in Hong Kong still seem to be very interested in what was going on in 1989. Interest in the film by Carma Hinton about the spring of 1989 in Beijing has been continuously high, and the numbers participating in the 1997 rally in remembrance of the 4 June incident, before the transfer of sovereignty, was around 50 000. Even after the transfer, in June 1998 approximately 3000 people participated in the rally to commemorate the 4 June incident.

4 This comment is based on the author's personal interview with Donald Yap, President of the Law Association of Asia and the Pacific, in April 1997.

5 When asked about future Sino–Hong Kong relations, Christine Loh stressed in a personal interview with the author that she not only sees the PRC exerting an influence on Hong Kong, but also the other way around – Hong Kong by its lifestyle and political culture influencing the PRC. Interview with Christine Loh, 24 March 1997.

6 Quoted from the author's personal interview with Gladys Li, 7 April 1997.

7 In this context, Emily Lau seems to be especially outspoken. In several interviews with the international press, she repeatedly pointed to the fact that the Hong Kong people did not fight enough for their rights. She further repeated this criticism during a personal interview with the author in April 1997. Christine Loh however, expressed the view to the author that people in Hong Kong can be mobilized for political ends, depending on what they are asked to support. Loh herself had collected a quarter of a million signatures against land reclamation from Hong Kong Harbour.

8 Personal interviews with Emily Lau and Christine Loh.

9 These were the findings of the Hong Kong Transition Project 1996, directed by Dr Michael E. DeGolyer, Hong Kong Baptist University. The project is publishing the results of opinion polls conducted since 1994, which includes questions on the degree of satisfaction with the Hong Kong government as compared to satisfaction with the Hong Kong government's policy towards Beijing (and the same for the Beijing government). For the latest updates see: http://www.hkbu edu.hk: 80.

10 Here it is interesting to note that the press release on the changes applied to the Public Order and Societies Ordinances includes three principles, one of which reads: '...we must uphold the Basic Law and the International Convention on Civil and Political Rights as they are applied to Hong Kong'. Earlier statements only referred to the problems of foreign influence and the balance between individual freedom and social order. See Chief Executive's Office 1997a.

Bibliography

Ai Kesi 1991 'Lun renquan baipishu de weida' (On the glory of the white book on human rights), *Dongxiang*, 12: 48–49.

Blyth, S. Wotherspoon, I. (eds) 1996 *Hong Kong Remembers*. Hong Kong, Oxford, New York: Oxford University Press.

Cheung, S. 1997a 'Trust in Tung Dips, Says Poll', *South China Morning Post*, 19 May, http://www.scmp.com/news/template.

Cheung, S. 1997b 'Democrats Favorite with Voters, says Poll', *South China Morning Post* 19 May, http://www.scmp.com/news/template.

Chief Executive's Office 1997 'Consultation Yields Changes', Press releases, 15 April and 15 May 1997, http://www.ceoffice.org.hk.

Davis, M. C. (ed.) 1995 *Human Rights and Chinese Values, Legal, Philosophical and Political Perspectives*. Hong Kong, Oxford, New York: Oxford University Press.

Gregor, P., Robertson Wensauer, C. Y. (eds) 1997 *Traditionelle chinesische Kultur und Menschenrechtsfrage*. Baden-Baden: Nomos.

Guo Qiming 1995 'Dalu de jintian shi Xiang'ao de mingtian' (Mainland China's today is the future of Hong Kong and Macao), *Zhengming* 12: 10.

Guowuyuan 1991 *Zhongguo renquan zhuangkuang* (On the human rights situation in China). Beijing: Zhongyang wenjian chubanshe.

He Li 1991 'Renquan faan: Zhizhi da men?' (Is the Bill of Rights nothing but a piece of paper?). *Jiushi niandai*, 7: 33–35.

Jayawickrama, N. 1992 'Hong Kong and the International Protection of Human Rights', in Wacks, R. (ed.) *Human Rights in Hong Kong*, Hong Kong, Oxford, New York: Oxford University Press.

Jin Yaoji 1992 'Zhongguo zhengzhi chuantong yu minzhu zhuanhua' (Chinese political tradition and democratic transformation). *Mingbao*, 4: 50–56.

Lai, J. 1996 'Freedom and Information', in Blyth, S., Wotherspoon, I. (eds) *Hong Kong Remembers*. Hong Kong, Oxford, New York: Oxford University Press.

Lau, E. 1997 'Peking Abandons Pretence of Respect for Freedoms and Rule of Law', 22 April, http://www.emilylau.org.hk

Li Moren 1989 'Renquan minyun xin yi zhang' (A new chapter in the history of the movement for democracy and human rights). *Jiushi niandai*, 4: 16–19.

Liu Gong 1991 'Zhonggong renquan baipishu de lailong qumai' (On the genesis of the CCP white book on human rights). *Dongxiang*, 12: 49–50.

McNeil, W. 1992 'Righting and Difference', in Wacks R. (ed.) *Human Rights in Hong Kong*. Hong Kong, Oxford, New York: Oxford University Press.

Ming Lei 1990 'Xifang zhidai yu dalu renquan' (Western boycott and human rights in mainland China). *Zhengming*, 12: 53–54.

Ming Lei 1993 'Zhonggong yi fazhanquan ya renquan' (The CCP suppresses human rights with the right for development), *Zhengming*, 8: 44–46.

Mingbao 1992 'Zhimindi shang jue fei minzhu, ru you minzhu, fei zhimindi' (There is absolutely no democracy in a colony, and if there is democracy, its not a colony), Mingbao 12: 50.

Nan Fangshuo 1989 'Fang Beijing, kan dalu minzhu yundong' (Throwing an eye on the democratic movement in mainland China during a visit to Beijing), *Jiushi niandai*, 4: 36–38.

Ng M. 'Are Rights Culture-Bound?', in Davis, M. (ed.) *Human Rights and Chinese Values. Legal Philosophical and Political Perspectives*. Hong Kong, Oxford, New York: Oxford University Press.

Qi Xin 1989 'Fang Lizhi shijian yu zhongmei guanxi' (The Fang Lizhi incident and Sino-US relations). *Jiushi niandai*, 4: 29–31.

Schubert Gunter (ed.) 1999 *Menschenrechte in Ostasien*, Tübingen:Mohr-Siebeck.

Senger H. von 1997 'Die Ausgrenzung Hongkongs aus dem europäischen Menschenrechtsschutz', in Gregor, P. Robertson Wensauer, C. Y. (eds) *Traditionelle chinesische Kultur und Menschensrechtsfrage*. Baden-Baden: Nomos.

Tung Chee-hwa 1997a 'Mr Tung Chee-hwa at the 8th Annual Governors' Dinner of the Canadian Chamber of Commerce', speech, 16 April, http://www.ceoffice.org.hk/press/p970413.htm.

Tung Chee-hwa 1997b 'Address by Tung Chee-hwa, Chief Executive of HKSAR at CNN World Report Conference', speech, 1 May, http://www.ceoffice.org.hk/press/p970501.htm.

Wacks, R. (ed.) 1988 *Civil Liberties in Hong Kong*, Hong Kong, Oxford, New York: Oxford University Press.

Wacks, R. 1992 (ed.) *Human Rights in Hong Kong*, Hong Kong, Oxford, New York: Oxford University Press.

Weigelin-Schwiedrzik S. 1999 'Menschenrechte und Demokratie – Eine Diskussion unter chinesisch-sprachigen Intellektuellen in Hongkong', in Schubert, G. (ed.) *Menschenrechte in Ostasien*. Tubingen: Mohr-Siebeck.

Wu Jingguan 1991 'Fanhuazhe, zhongguo Gongchandang' (The CCP is anti-Chinese!). *Zhengming*, 7: 40–41.

Yan Jiaqi 1995 'Xianggan renquanfa he "lingjia" wenti' (The Hong Kong Bill of Rights and the question of supremacy) *Zhengming*, 12: 11–13.

Yu Guanghua 1991 'Renquan baipishu shi qishi zhi zuo' (The white book on human rights is deceiving the public). *Zhengming*, 12: 44–47.

Zha Lianyong (Louis Cha) 1992a 'Xianggang he zhongguo – 1997 ji qihou wunian' (Hong Kong and China – 1997 and the first five years). *Mingbao*, 4: 4–9.

Zha Lianyong (Louis Cha) 1992b 'Baochi xianzhuang chongfen liyong' (Stick to the status quo and use it as well as possible). *Mingbao*, 11: 51–53.

13
Church–State Relations in the Transition: A Historical Perspective

Beatrice Leung

Introduction

In the modern world, Christian ideology has, at various times had a significant impact on the socio-economic and political development of societies. The relationship between church and state can positively or negatively affect political stability in a society (Weigel 1987, 1992). There are several models of church–state relations. In many colonies, there was a partnership or contractual relationship between church and state to share the workload in areas such as education, social services and medicine. Often the government would grant land and financial aid for recurrent expenditure to church schools, as well as helping medical and social service institutes (Igwe 1967). This was a mechanism for channelling resources to the Church, when its members became involved in progressive social movements (Chan 1995, McCarthy, Britt and Wolfson 1991). Depending on the path of development of the church–state relationships, the channelling mechanism had various socio-political implications (McCarthy 1991).

In the British colonies, most officials did not want to be criticized for using public money to support the evangelical work of churches (McClell 1988). Catholic and Protestant missionaries in Hong Kong, however, were assisted by the government to run their prestigious schools and refugee services in the 1950s. Later, evangelistic motives were obvious in many of Hong Kong's social services.

Partly because of financial aid and partly because of their high standard of education, Christian schools were considered 'reputable' and attracted Hong Kong's elite (Hong Kong Public Records Office, HKRS 147 2[1]). On the government Education Board, three church leaders (two Catholics and one Protestant) were among the 17 appointed members who advised the government on the education policy of the colony after the Second World War (Hong Kong Public Records Office, HKRS 147 2[2]). Under the Sino–British agreement, when Hong Kong reverted to Chinese rule, the church–state relationship in Hong Kong was expected to change from the British 'partnership' or 'contractor' model to the 'politics absorbs religion' model that is practised in China (Chan 1995).

This chapter aims to explore how the 'contractor' model developed between the Hong Kong government and the Catholic Church, through church services such as education, social services and socio-political involvement. Then, how the Church in Hong Kong prepared for the handover will be studied. This will be followed by a discussion of the role of the Hong Kong Catholic Church as a 'bridge' between China and the Vatican, and the dynamics and complexity of the triangular relationship between China, the Vatican and Hong Kong. Finally, church–state encounters during the first year of the HKSAR will be analysed to illustrate the strengths and weaknesses of the Church as it tries to survive under a socialist regime.

The Catholic Church and the Hong Kong government since the Second World War

Before and after the establishment of the PRC in 1949, many of the refugees from the mainland were accompanied by missionaries who were expelled by the PRC for political reasons (Ryan 1959; Motte 1971; Leung 1992a, pp 73–103). The inflow of personnel and other resources enabled Hong Kong Christian churches to offer relief services such as food provision, education and housing. Thus began large-scale church relief and education services even before the Hong Kong government started offering aid to refugees in 1954 (Luo 1967, pp 45–75 and Maryknoll Archives, MPBA Hong Kong 9/8). During the cold war period, the Hong Kong government saw the church as an ideal partner in this work.

The Cold War and British policy towards the communist bloc

Being a traditional partner of the USA in international politics, the UK undertook an embargo against the PRC that caused the Hong Kong economy to suffer in the 1950s. Britain was very careful not to allow Hong Kong, with 90 per cent of its population being Chinese, to be the recipient of communist revolution when the Chinese Communist Party (CCP) exported its revolutionary ideology. Thus, with a clear policy of keeping communism at bay, Hong Kong, under instructions from London, adopted a strategic plan to prevent the spread of communism at the grassroots level.[1] The (Catholic) church–state co-operation in Hong Kong after the Second world war was based on the common political orientation of anti-communism. The development of that co-operation has gone through various stages since then. In co-operating with the government's education policy, the Christian churches, including the Catholic Church, who share similar anti-communist fears, united and formulated a contract with the government.

Education

At the end of 1948, the Hong Kong Governor, Sir Alexander Grantham, openly echoed the London view, saying that he would not tolerate communist propaganda in Hong Kong schools (South China Morning Post, 16 December 1948, p 7). In 1948–1994, Hong Kong received an influx of refugees unparalleled in its history. Hundreds of thousands of people entered the territory during 1949 and the spring of 1950. By mid-1959, the population had swelled to an estimated 2.2 million, of whom 30 per cent (677 000) were political refugees.[2]

In response to the rapid increase in population from 600 000 to 2.2 million in six years, Bishop R. O. Hall, the Anglican bishop of Hong Kong (a member of the Education Board), suggested to the government that Christian church schools alone should be allowed to provide urgently needed primary and secondary education to prevent communist infiltration into education (Hong Kong Public Records Office, HKRS 147 2/2 [17, 119]). Suggestions made by church leaders were accepted by the Hong Kong government, because the ideology of church education was in line with the British policy towards communism in Hong Kong. With education in the hands of the Christian churches, whose teaching is directly opposed to atheism, infiltration by communism was made much less likely. This explains why, from the 1950s onwards, many subsidized primary and secondary schools were assigned to Protestant and Catholic churches; until in the 1970s there were not enough church personnel to meet the growing demand for staff in new schools.

Christian schools, but not schools run by traditional Chinese associations like the Tung Wah Hospital Group or pro-communist organizations, were assisted in developing education to cope with the influx of refugee children in the 1950s and 1960s. There are at least two possible interpretations of the Anglican Bishop's view on assisting the Hong Kong government in education. First, with additional manpower from the mainland, Christian leaders, both Protestant and Catholic, found a way for the Church to provide education as a means of evangelism. Second, the strategy of having Christian schools exclusively funded by the government suited the government's anti-communist policy. In education, a two-front strategy was devised. Firstly, the Hong Kong government was determined to prevent schools from being used to disseminate political propaganda. The government intervened in the operation of pro-communist schools by deporting the principal of Heung Tao Middle School in January 1950, de-registering several teachers at the Portland Street Motor Car Workers' Children's School in late 1950 and early 1951, and closing Nanfang College in March 1951. In each of these cases, the Hong Kong Teachers' Welfare Association and the leftist press protested strongly against the government action (Sweeting 1993, pp 192–220).

The Catholic Church put tremendous effort into building Catholic schools. In 1953, the number of new Catholic schools was 22 (14 in the New Territories, 8 in Hong Kong and Kowloon). However, ten years later 33 new Catholic schools had been added (16 in the New Territories, 17 in Hong Kong and Kowloon). The number of students added to Catholic schools from 1953–1963 increased from 3909 to 28 029 (Hong Kong Catholic Diocesan Archive Office, HK-DA S.6–01, F/03).

The rapid construction of Catholic schools was necessary to meet the needs of a growing number of school-age children. In practice, the government first built schools and invited churches to run them with large government subsidies. At first, the government allowed school halls and playgrounds to be converted for Sunday worship, then later allowed land adjacent to the school to be used for church building for two-thirds of the lease price. However, the full lease price of land for the living quarters of clergy had to be paid. Both Catholic and other Christian churches were eager to use these subsidized schools according to this government plan because it allowed the Catholic authority either to have church buildings erected on the land bought at a cheap price, or to use school buildings for worship.[3]

Social services

As early as 1869, Governor Sir Richard MacDonnell justified the policy of contracting with the church and the channelling mechanism, saying that the church could offer a better quality of service at a quarter of what it would cost the government (Luo 1967, pp 45–74, and Maryknoll Archives, MPBA Hong Kong 9/8). Orders of nuns, such as the French Sisters, the Italian Sisters and the Chinese Sisters of the Precious Blood, were the main sponsors of Catholic social services before the Second World War. Later, lay groups like the St Vincent de Paul Association joined in, but on a much more limited scale.

After the Second World War, the inflow of refugees from mainland China put great pressure on the territory, whose economy was already weakened by the embargo against China imposed by the West. Foreign missionaries from the mainland brought much money for refugee projects in Hong Kong, especially through the American Catholic Relief Service of New York, and donations from the American Prelate Cardinal Spellman. In the 1950s, the American Foreign Missionary Society (Maryknoll Fathers) turned their attention from China to Hong Kong's refugees (Luo 1967, pp 45–74 and Maryknoll Archive, MPBA Hong Kong 9/8). New districts, such as Diamond Hill and King's Park, were developed as centres of relief and medical aid. As years went by, the number of these centres grew (Ryan 1959, pp 243–58). In due course the government established resettlement areas and started large-scale housing projects. The Catholic social centres – usually a Catholic school with an adjoining mass centre – were the result of the government's policy of assistance to Christian education and social services. Later, these became big parishes by extending their religious programme and by erecting big church buildings to accommodate the growing population of converts. Parish churches in Shamshuipo, Wongtaisin, Cheungshawan, Diamond Hill and King's Park in Kowloon, and Chaiwan and North Point on Hong Kong Island are parishes of this model. Rennis Hill was exclusively for refugees – served by Christian missionaries exiled from the mainland.

Caritas-Hong Kong was established in 1953.[4] It was the creation of the Hong Kong Catholic Authority, which wanted to co-ordinate services within the church at a time of influx of refugees and rapid change in Hong Kong society. The role of Caritas evolved over time. In 1968, it functioned as the service arm of the Catholic Church, dependent upon the support of the community to render welfare aid to the less fortunate.[5] It sought to function as a pioneer in the field of social welfare by initiating new services as needs emerged. It aimed at co-operating with the government and other agencies in developing services as funds and facilities became available, and 'promoting the growth of the individual through love and kindness' (Caritas Hong Kong Annual Report, 1968–1969).

As the years went by, Hong Kong became increasingly affluent and living standards improved. Accordingly, in the early 1990s, services provided by Caritas-Hong Kong were redesigned to include social services for the family, the elderly, childcare and rehabilitation services. Exchange and training programmes with mainland China and services for Vietnamese refugees/boat people, including counselling and educational programmes, hospital visitation and social assistance schemes formed an important focus of Caritas-Hong Kong's work (Caritas-Hong Kong Annual Report, 1968–1969).

Changing society and a changing church: 1970s to 1990s

Hundreds of thousands of mainland Chinese fleeing the Chinese communist revolution of 1949 were attracted to the political stability of Hong Kong and its free market economy (Yang 1984, pp ix–xxv). By the 1990s the once quiet colonial outpost had become an international financial centre and metropolis of 6 000 000 people. Hong Kong rapidly transformed itself into one of the industrial world's great urban centres and forced the government to ensure a stable socio-political order by developing a disciplined labour force, educated in technical skills, and by providing financial stability. Thus, the government's social services and education policies evolved to meet the changing needs.

The Catholic Church responded positively to these new developments and changing government policies because, internally, it was also going through a process of renewal. In the 1960s, the Catholic Church underwent great changes as a result of the Second Vatican Council (1963–1965). Vatican II encouraged the Church to have a more outward-looking relationship with the modern world for the good of humanity (see Lumen

Gentium [Dogmatic Constitution of the Church] and Gaudium et Spes [Pastoral Constitution of the Church in the Modern World]). Thus, the Catholic Church in Hong Kong became more flexible *vis-à-vis* education and social services and began to be more concerned with socio-political issues. This explains why the partnership between the Church and government became even firmer after the 1960s.

The Catholic Church gave its full co-operation and support by sponsoring more schools.[6] At the same time, many of the religious institutes of missionaries found that they could not take responsibility for more schools because they did not have the religious personnel to cope with the rapid increase in demand for schools (Lam 1995, pp 439–472). In 1997, there were 327 Catholic schools, half of them run by religious institutes and the rest by the Hong Kong Diocese and Caritas-Hong Kong (Hong Kong Catholic Church Directory 1998, p 553). Approximately one-quarter of school children in Hong Kong attend Catholic schools. Catholic schools not only serve the Catholic community but the community of Hong Kong as a whole. In the last decade 91.6 per cent of students attending Catholic schools have been non-Catholics (Ha 1992).

In 1978, at the invitation of the government, Bishop Francis Hsu, the first Chinese Catholic Bishop of Hong Kong, mediated between the government and teachers in a salary dispute. He was able to prevent a teachers' strike in the public examination period and to peacefully resolve the labour dispute.[7]

At the request of the government, the Catholic Church also began to offer various types of schools, such as evening and pre-vocational schools, special education courses for the disabled and handicapped, along with classes for adults. Its own plan of promoting tertiary education never materialized, despite the fact that the Irish Jesuits were invited to come to Hong Kong in 1920 to offer Catholic tertiary education. The Jesuits ran Ricci Hall at the University of Hong Kong from 1929 and Adam Schall Hall at the Chinese University from 1960. In 1926, the Irish Jesuits were asked to run two secondary schools, the Wah Yan Colleges on Hong Kong and in Kowloon. Both were soon considered elite schools in Hong Kong. Many Catholic primary and secondary schools became the cradle of the elite of Hong Kong society, producing leaders in the Democratic Party and many top civil servants, such as the first Chief Secretary of the HKSAR.

According to Xu Jiatun, later head of the Xinhua branch in Hong Kong, in 1967, during the Cultural Revolution, the Hong Kong government was not only able to control the situation but also successfully cracked down on the underground network of the CCP in Hong Kong. With sinophobia greatly diminished, the value of Christian education in serving the government's political ends was reduced. Special privileges formerly given to the Catholic churches were withdrawn.[8] Now, schools run by Chinese associations such as the Tung Wah Hospital Group and Po Leung Kuk were invited to receive government aid in education.

The Catholic Church did not abandon the idea of running Catholic tertiary education. In 1961, its leader again proposed the plan of building a tertiary education institute. It was proposed as a post-secondary college that would offer studies in Social Sciences and Languages. The government turned down this proposal (Fang 1997, p 37).[9] In the late 1960s and 1970s, plans for setting up Catholic tertiary education were again rejected by the government, which had been asked to assist the plan by providing aid and leasing free land on which to build institutes (Hong Kong Catholic Diocesan Archive Office, HK-DA S.6–02 F/01). The Catholic policy of higher education, which aims at full personal development, did not fit the government's policy of tertiary education, which aimed at training the elite to assist in Hong Kong's administration.

In the field of social services, as Hong Kong progressed economically in the 1970s, the focus switched from supplying immediate relief to improving quality of life. The government, seeing the need for change, tried to streamline social services, and encouraged charitable organizations to provide a larger share. The Director of Social Services in his Annual Department Report of 1963–1964 reflected this attitude. He remarked that the public provision of social services was not a gratuitous act of charity, but a concomitant privilege of citizenship. Thus in the 1970s, the welfare service of the Catholic Church began to concentrate on family and community needs, largely through Caritas-Hong Kong. The work was divided into three categories: childcare services, children and youth centres, and services for the elderly. However, the Catholic Marriage Advisory Council, the Birthright Society for unwed mothers, social projects for Filipino domestic help and China services had to be funded by the Church alone, because these projects were not considered a priority of the government.

Non-traditional church activities and planning for Chinese rule

The Second Vatican Council of the Catholic Church (1963–1965) suggested more integration of the Catholic faith with the secular world (Abbott 1966). The setting up of the Pontifical Commission of Justice and Peace as an office in the Vatican, with its branches in Catholic dioceses across the world, showed that the Church wished to promote justice and peace within the context of gospel values (Gaudium et Spes). The Diocesan Commission of Justice and Peace (DCJP) was an indication of the Church's concern for social issues, such as demanding justice for workers, better welfare for the poor, opposing the repatriation of Vietnamese refugees (boat people) by force, the protection of human rights and the promotion of democracy (Ha 1992).

Although the 1984 Sino-British Joint Declaration promised 'One Country – Two Systems', and the Basic Law of the HKSAR guarantees that religious freedom will continue unchanged following the handover to

Chinese rule, Hong Kong Catholics are concerned that the definition of religious freedom under Chinese rule will be different from that under British rule.[10] China, so far, has not replaced Hong Kong's capitalist system with the Chinese socialist system. However, in political and ideological matters, Chinese interference has been increasingly felt. China denounced the semi-democratic 1995 Legislative Council elections, and after the handover, did not allow the elected councillors to retain their seats. Contrary to the provisions of the Basic Law, Beijing decided to set up a temporary legislative body right after the transfer of sovereignty. Religious freedom is an important indicator of social freedom, and is closely linked with ideological and political freedom. When political freedom is curbed and freedom of the press is under threat, Hong Kong Catholics, aware of the history of the Catholic Church on the mainland, fear that following the handover, church–state relations in Hong Kong will change from the 'contractor' model to the 'political absorption of religion' model that is practised in China (Chan 1995).[11]

Due to the ideological incompatibility of religion and atheistic communism, and the track record of church–state disputes between Chinese Catholics and the communist Chinese regime, Hong Kong Catholics sought political participation as a means to keep the autonomy promised by 'One Country – Two Systems'. By doing this, they intended to protect themselves from being persecuted like their Chinese counterparts (Chan and Leung 1996).

Catholic participation in politics during the transitional period (1984–1997)

The transitional period (1984–1997) provided a good opportunity for adjustment in church–state relations, and afforded time for each side to initiate appropriate policies in dealing with the other. On the Catholic side, the exhortation of Cardinal Wu, titled 'March in the bright future', was the blueprint for Catholic policy after 1997 (Wu 1989). This two-pronged strategy aimed firstly at encouraging the Church, guided by Christian principles, to become more involved in Hong Kong's socio-political affairs, and secondly at strengthening the Christian community through deepening of religious belief. It was intended that through sermons, preaching and catechizing on the parish level, the social teaching of the Church would spread to grassroots Catholics. The role of being a 'bridge' between the Church in China and the universal church was outlined in the document (Wu 1989, p 8).

Legislative Council elections

The Catholic Church's political participation in Hong Kong affairs was first seen in its support for the 1988 Legco elections. Instruction was issued by the Chancellor's office of the Diocese to support the elections (Leung 1992b). In fact, during the entire transitional period, Catholic social concern groups have been pushing for a faster pace of political development and for a more accountable governmental structure before and after 1997. Catholic social concern groups have formed coalitions and mobilized the laity to express their opinions, for these are the basic rights of political participation. Since Hong Kong entered the transitional period, Hong Kong citizens have been urging the government to introduce a more democratic political structure. In 1987, Catholic groups joined the heated debate on the first direct elections to the Legco planned for 1988. Surveys were carried out in parishes to solicit opinions from Catholics on direct elections, and large-scale gatherings were convened to show the solidarity of Catholics in striving for a democratic political system. Fr. J. B. Tsang, Vicar General of the Diocese, spoke at one of these gatherings in the Ko San Auditorium.

In 1991, the Catholic Church in Hong Kong celebrated the 150th anniversary of its inauguration. Catholic laity organized a large part of the celebration, and its members, who were mostly middle-class professionals, chose the theme 'hand in hand towards the future', which meant that the Church would work in solidarity with the Hong Kong people. Catholic lay leaders wished the Church to be more closely involved in democratic activities to shape Hong Kong's future (So and Kwitko 1990). Thus, the Catholic Laity Council assisted many parishes in setting up campaigns for the registration of voters. Banners were flown within church grounds to remind Catholics of their duty as citizens to vote. Volunteer workers were stationed at churches on Sundays to help parishioners go through the voting registration process. Sermons from pulpits were delivered to remind churchgoers to take part in voting. Booklets and pamphlets were distributed by the Diocesan Commission of Justice and Peace to advise readers how to select their own candidates. With such intensive involvement, the Hong Kong Catholics' political participation in terms of voting in the Legco in 1991 and 1995 was much higher than that of the public in general (86.5 per cent versus 39.5 per cent in 1991, 81.5 per cent versus 35.8 per cent in 1995) (Chan and Leung 1996). Research suggested that both the social-economic status of Catholics (middle class) and the 'China factor' were the major reasons for their high turnout rate and their party preference for Democrats. In other words, most Catholics are middle class and they opted for Democratic Party candidates. This implies that Catholic concern about the consequences for Catholics during and beyond 1997 had influenced them to vote Democratic (Chan and Leung 1996). However, in the 1995 Legco election, when active promotion among Catholics was less, the Catholic voting rate dropped slightly from 86.5 per cent in 1991 to 81.5 per cent.

After the 1991 Legco election, pro-democratic associations within the Catholic Church, such as the Hong Kong Catholic Social Communication Office, the Hong Kong Central Council of Catholic Laity and the Diocesan Commission of Justice and Peace, jointly formed the Catholic Monitors of Legislative Councillors (CMLC). According to Mary Yuen, executive secretary of the Diocesan Commission of Justice and Peace, the main tasks of the CMLC were to promote social justice through monitoring the performance of Legislative Councillors, and to promote social awareness in the Church, as well as to actualise the social mission of Christians. However, the CMLC indirectly also achieved its aim of making the councillors more accountable to the public in the democratic manner.

Supporting the pro-democracy movement in China

Catholic groups have also been involved in local democratic movements in China. The union of Hong Kong Catholic Organizations in Support of the Patriotic and Democratic Movement in China was set up by the joint efforts of progressive Catholic associations led by the Diocesan Commission of Justice and Peace. The Diocesan centre was made available for workshops and meetings of the Union for the pro-democracy movement. Hundreds of volunteers worked around the clock preparing for four major rallies in Hong Kong before and after the military crackdown in Tiananmen Square on 4 June 1989. Priests and nuns in full religious habit marched under Catholic banners chanting religious songs, as a distinctly Catholic part of the huge crowd. Fr Louis Ha, a diocesan priest, was deeply involved in the Alliance of Hong Kong Citizens in Support of the Democratic Movement in China, headed by leading democrats such as Szeto Wah and Martin Lee.[12] Ha was the key figure in bringing together the Catholic Union and the Alliance during the Tiananmen Square incident. At the annual general meeting of the Alliance in 1989, he received the highest vote in the election to the steering committee.

However, the Catholic authorities suddenly instructed the Catholic Social Communication Centre headed by Ha, to withdraw from its membership in the Alliance.[13] Ha requested the Catholic Church to let him remain on the Steering Committee as an individual, but the Church would not allow him to do so. He was asked to leave the directorship of the Catholic Social Communication Centre. He went on to do research on church history as a sign of detachment from sensitive political involvement that might antagonize Beijing and jeopardize the future relationship of the Church with the HKSAR government. The Church never admitted that this action followed pressure by Beijing. Ha, however, believed that conservative clergy close to the Cardinal, were concerned that his intensive involvement in the Alliance and in promoting the democratic movement in Hong Kong and in China would antagonize Beijing, and cause negative results. Thus, self-regulating action was taken in removing Ha.[14]

The triangular relations of the PRC, Hong Kong and the Catholic Church

Ideological conflict between the PRC and the Catholic Church led to the expulsion by Mao Zedong of the Papal Nuncio in 1951. The Sino–Vatican dispute could not be resolved even in Deng's era of 'open door policy'. It is the policy of the Vatican to build a bridge to link the Catholic Church in China to the Catholic Church in the world, to prevent the Catholic Church in China from being separated from the leadership of the Holy See.

The China policy of Caritas-Hong Kong and other Hong Kong-based Catholic institutes is part of the Church's endeavour to establish a warmer relationship with China in order to facilitate rapprochement between the Vatican and China. The Hong Kong Catholic Church responded to the call of Pope John Paul II in 1981 to establish communication and offer services to China (Leung 1992a, pp 189–256). Caritas has been offering social services as a non-governmental organization for the needy, especially in rural China, first in 1983 in Guangdong province and then spreading to many other remote areas. In 1997, both in terms of quality and quantity, the services of Caritas-Hong Kong have increased handsomely. It now acts as an agency for other European Catholic social welfare organizations such as Caritas International, German Caritas and Swiss Caritas, which entrust Caritas-Hong Kong with funds for China projects. Social services in terms of vocational training, medical and social work are well received in China, as Caritas makes clear that it will not use its services to promote Catholic teaching.

Despite the fact that Catholicism is not promoted directly on the mainland, the impact of aid to China from overseas Catholics via Hong Kong has been a major factor behind the revival of religion in general and Catholicism in particular. The revival has been so significant that is has caused concern among top leaders, such as Chen Yun and Jiang Zemin (Documentation Centre 1995, p 177). This development is taking place at a time when the CCP is suffering from its own crisis, and communism, as an ideology, is gradually being undermined. The revival of the Catholic Church, especially through the assistance of foreign religious groups, does not sit easily with the interests of the CCP. Its policy on freedom of religion, as revealed by Ye Xiaowen, Head of the Religious Affairs Bureau, is to eliminate the influence of religion in a socialist society (Ye 1996). Ye indirectly warned the Hong Kong Catholics that as the mainland was not going to force Hong Kong to conform to mainland rules, according to the 'One Country – Two Systems' principle, Hong Kong should not attempt to interfere in the mainland's internal affairs. Ye also quoted HKSAR Basic Law, Article 148, which states that 'non-subordination, mutual respect and non-interference' are the three main guidelines of interaction between Hong Kong and mainland Catholics. He remarked that these guidelines should be observed 'with great care' (Sunday Examiner, 5 July 1996).

Church–state relations since the transfer of sovereignty

After the handover of Hong Kong to Chinese rule, the dilemma of the Catholic Church in Hong Kong was exposed during an Asian Bishops Synod held in Rome from 19 April to 14 May 1998. Bishop Joseph Zen, the

Coadjutor Bishop of Hong Kong, and Bishop John Tung, the Auxiliary Bishop of Hong Kong, were invited to speak at the Synod. Bishops Zen and Tung's presentations were not on Hong Kong (Sunday Examiner, 3 May 1998: Kung Kao Po, 3 May 1998). While some problems have been experienced by the Church in Hong Kong since the territory came under mainland rule, the two Hong Kong bishops concentrated their attention on the Catholic Church in China. From Beijing's point of view, Bishops Zen and Tung could be accused of interfering in the internal affairs of the Chinese Catholic Church. However, at this juncture, when Hong Kong is troubled by the economic crisis, Beijing is also anxious to preserve the HKSAR's positive image. Thus, the issue was kept low key. This reveals the dilemma the Catholic Church in Hong Kong faces as it attempts to act as a bridge in aiding the Church in China. This role could jeopardize its relations both with the HKSAR government and with China.

In his policy address on 8 October 1997, the HKSAR's new Chief Executive, Tung Chee-hwa, addressed issues of education, care for the aged, as well as housing (Tung 1997b, pp 29–35). He outlined his vision for the future of Hong Kong as

> a society proud of its national identity and cultural heritage; a stable, equitable, free democratic society with a clear sense of direction; an affluent society with improved quality of life for all, a decent society with a level playing field and fair competition under the rule of law; a window for exchange between China and the rest of the world; a renowned international financial, trading, transportation and communication centre; a world class cultural education and scientific research centre.
>
> (Tung 1997a, pp 6–7)

Tung believes that the foremost task for the HKSAR government is 'to enhance Hong Kong's economic vitality and sustain economic growth', and that 'education is the key to the future of Hong Kong' (Tung 1997a, p 3). Catholic education also had a vision of 'promoting Christian transformation of the world by which natural values, viewed in the full perspective of humanity as redeemed by Christ, may contribute to the good of society as a whole' (Abbott 1996, pp 637–651). The issue of the language of instruction has rapidly come to the fore. Tung Chee-hwa emphasised that 'mother-tongue teaching' will be given priority (Tung 1997b, pp 29–35). The Education Department announced, in December 1997, the guidelines on mother-tongue teaching. Schools were asked to assess their standard of English before being allowed to continue in the medium. 114 schools successfully appealed to continue teaching in English while the rest had to switch to mother-tongue.

The Education Department was criticized for its hasty ruling, which many argued would have a major impact on the quality of education in

Hong Kong, and reduce Hong Kong's strategic position in the greater China region and in the global context. The government's policy was not based on extensive research into whether the study of English presented a real learning barrier, or into its relationship to learning and entertainment habits, changing cultural values, peer influence, school-family co-operation and so on. Rather, it was finding the easy way out by forcing most students to learn only through Chinese simply because they did not receive proper training in English in their primary school days. This policy will cost Hong Kong dearly because effective usage of English by Hong Kong people would help to make them more competitive through their ability to communicate with foreigners in English. As their counterparts in Asia, particularly in China and Taiwan, are becoming proficient in the use of English in dealing with their nation's speedy economic development, Hong Kong may soon lose its place as the bridge between China and the rest of the world. This is due to the government's 'instruction medium policy', which contradicts Tung's own stated principle that the education system 'must cater for Hong Kong's needs' (Tung 1997a, p 5). While Catholic schools foresaw these problems, they, unfortunately, made no study of ways to counteract them.

In the 1970s, long before Tung's 'mother-tongue teaching' policy was launched, a number of Chinese priests advocated 'mother-tongue teaching' within the Church. However, this suggestion received little attention. In Cardinal Wu's exhortation 'The March Towards the Bright Decades', mother-tongue teaching was one of the suggestions made regarding Catholic education (Wu 1989, p 7). The Catholic Board of Education of the Diocese supported mother-tongue teaching in principle, but their support was not based on careful study of whether it could 'contribute to the good of society as a whole' (Declaration on Catholic Education 1996, pp 637–635).

Catholic schools in Hong Kong can be divided into two categories: Catholic diocesan schools, and mission schools run by religious congregations. Mission schools have a much longer history than diocesan schools and are of superior quality. These mission schools have contributed most to local education. Catholic schools were divided over the mother-tongue policy, although the Cardinal's guidelines coincided with government policy in promoting the mother tongue. Most mission schools were classified as English-speaking schools and these same religious orders teach throughout the world. They have good reason to stand firm on the policy of English as the medium of instruction, rather than supporting the mediocrity of the Catholic Diocesan schools. Most diocesan schools that already used Chinese as the teaching medium supported Cardinal Wu and the Chief Executive, while the Catholic Board of Education did not listen to the view of mission schools, and also supported the government policy without any in-depth study of the issue. In the first year of Chinese rule, therefore, the Catholic Church in Hong Kong, despite the dissenting voice of the old mission schools, supported the HKSAR government's language policy. Internally, it revealed the division of opinion within Catholic education circles and the failure of the church authorities to resolve it.

Following Hong Kong's reversion to Chinese rule, it is of paramount importance to change the image of Catholic schools as bastions of anti-communism, while keeping the Catholic identity intact. The recent project on 'nationalism in civil education', undertaken by the Catholic Institute for Religion and Society, is one endeavour seeking this goal (Kung Kao Po, 14 June 1998).

Points of conflict

In recent years, the Catholic Justice and Peace Commission has openly expressed its views on social, economic and political issues. It has indirectly criticized Hong Kong government policy on issues such as the repatriation of Vietnamese boat people, the treatment of children, illegal immigrants from the mainland, labour policy and social insurance. Often, Christian groups have formed ad hoc committees to press for change. At times, these pressure groups have been able to influence government policy. However, their campaigns are often cries in the wilderness. Christian pressure groups were among a number of protesters who met the Secretary of Justice designate, Elsie Leung Oi-sie, on 21 April 1997 to demand that the government not re-introduce the draconian Civil Liberties and Social Order Ordinances. These Ordinances bar local Hong Kong political organizations from soliciting or accepting cash or loans from foreign organizations, or affiliating with foreign political organizations. A document of the laws, issued before the handover by the office of the Chief Executive designate Tung Chee-hwa on 9 April, allowed a three-week consultation with the public (Asia Focus, 9 May 1997).

The non-comformist views of Catholic groups have become clear to the Hong Kong government. Although the Church has not been involved in government decision making, the government was aware of the Catholic Church's position through grassroots groups and, at times, the government has made some adjustments in policy. In the last three decades of British rule, the Hong Kong government has tried not to suppress minor criticism generated by pressure groups and religious institutes. Mass media gave coverage to these non-conformist views on socio-political issues. The British in Hong Kong were generally not afraid of criticism because the Hong Kong bureaucracy is remarkable for its stability, efficiency in delivering services, and freedom from corruption (Lau 1984, p 25). The recent economic performance of Hong Kong proves that the outspokenness of non-conformist groups has never threatened Hong Kong's well-being. Demand for political participation by Hong Kong citizens did not drive away foreign investors in the 1980s and 1990s. On the contrary, it served Hong Kong's interest in an open society, which is a conducive atmosphere for international business.

The lack of contact between the Hong Kong Catholic Church and Beijing signifies a lack of confidence in each other. Co-operation between the Catholic Church and the HKSAR government may become difficult, given that China does not entrust education to religious groups. Now, Hong Kong Catholic leaders have questions about the future of Catholic education. Will Catholic schools be nationalized? They know that the PRC in its Constitution states that religion cannot interfere with education, but what is the implication for the HKSAR's education policy? These are basic concerns of Hong Kong Catholic leaders. Also, the political support of Catholics for democratic parties reflects the fact that Catholics in Hong Kong tend to be anti-communist (Chan and Leung 1996). With these basic but negative elements, it will not be easy for Hong Kong Catholics to develop a positive and smooth relationship with the HKSAR in the years to come.

Conclusion

The Roman Catholic Church with its sovereign head, the Pope, has been defined by political scientists as an international actor. The Catholic Church's influence in politics has been subtle but continuous. The social involvement of the Catholic Church and its socio-political stance on many issues does not always coincide with government policy. This has been the main difficulty in church-state relations in many western democracies. In the 1960s, the US Catholic Bishops Conference issued a statement against the national policy of armament. Catholics in Singapore in the 1970s did not support the state's population policy. Since the establishment of Hong Kong as a colony, the Catholic Church's role in humanitarian work, education and social service is an indication of its influence. Its services helped to expand the colonial government's capacity to cope with the various socio-economic and political crises that arose as Hong Kong developed. As a result, the church and state enjoyed a harmonious relationship because they pursued common goals. Sharing a common ideology with the British, the Catholic Church in Hong Kong began to co-operate so closely with the government that it eventually lost its bearings.

Now the Catholic Church is charting a new relationship with the HKSAR. While it may be too early to see how things will turn out, indications are that the relationship is not going to be as easy as before because of ideological differences between China and the Catholic Church. Religious freedom is an important indicator of social freedom, which, in turn, is an important indicator for foreign investors who are carefully scrutinizing the territory's socio-political environment. Their decision to invest in Hong Kong will depend on whether they will be able to reap high profits, and they will only invest if the environment is stable. In short, good church–state relations in Hong Kong after the handover will serve China's purpose in the long term.

Notes

1 Discussions between the Governor, Sir Alexander Grantham, and the Secretary of State in 1949 led to legislation to prevent the spread of communism and to facilitate control over subversive elements in education and labour, reflecting British policy.
   Malcolm MacDonald, the British Commissioner-General for South-East Asia, further recommended that Christian churches should be a partner to implement this plan. He remarked that for its own security, Hong Kong could not afford not to seal off the communist infiltration. Given the need to combat the Chinese, the Hong Kong government would trust Christian churches more than traditional Chinese associations when it sought partners or contractors to launch the much-needed projects of providing education and social services to the inflow of refugees in the 1950s. It was felt that foreign church leaders with their anti-communist ideology could be trusted, while local Chinese leaders of charity organizations could be sympathetic to communism out of patriotism and nationalism. See: Hong Kong Public Record Office Grantham to Secretary of State, 311 secret, 1 April 1949, in C0537/4824 and Grantham to Secretary of State, 384 secret, 30 April 1949, in F037/5839.

2 After the Japanese occupation of Hong Kong, Chinese civilians, many of whom had moved into China during the war, returned at the rate of almost 100 000 a month. The population, which by August 1945 had been reduced to about 600 000, rose by the end of 1947 to 1.8 million. See Information Service Department 1997.

3 Information given by Father Mencarini, Vicar General in the 1950s and 1960s, with responsibility for the building of churches and schools to cope with the expansion of the Catholic population at the time, when interviewed in March 1997.

4 This organization was instituted originally as the Catholic Social Welfare Conference in July 1953, and was affiliated to Caritas International in March 1955. In December 1957, it became the official social welfare bureau of the Roman Catholic Church in Hong Kong. In 1961 it was renamed Caritas-Hong Kong, and in 1969 it was accepted as a member of the Community Chest of Hong Kong. See *Caritas-Hong Kong Annual Report, 1984–1985*, pp 6–7.

5 In the early years, the services were concerned with the immediate needs of refugees such as sheltering orphans, abandoned children, the deaf, the blind and the aged. Later support for the sick and suffering began to be offered when Hong Kong was flooded with refugees needing food (milk powder, vitamin tablets and flour), housing, medical care, education immigration and professional training. However, as the economy of Hong Kong steadily progressed, more professional services were required.

6 In the field of education, the government in 1971 launched a six-year free education campaign and nine-year free education in 1978.

7 This issue was fondly remembered in the mass commemorating the 25th anniversary of Bishop Francis Hsu's death. See *Kung Kao Po* (Catholic Weekly News) 31 May 1998 and also Louis Ha 1992.

8 The special price for leasing land to Christian churches was cancelled and Christian school halls and playgrounds could not be used for Sunday worship.

9 This was recalled by Father Mencarini when interviewed in March 1997. See note above.

10 In every version of the Chinese constitutions religious freedom is included. Yet, even now religious believers continue to be arrested for non-religious reasons. Chinese leaders have their own interpretation of 'religious freedom' and religious activities are circumscribed by regulations issued by the CCP. See document 19, 1982 in Documentation Centre, Policy Section of Religious Affairs Bureau, *Xinshiji Zongjiao Gongzuo Wenjian Xuanbian* (Selected Documents on Religious Work of New Age), Beijing: Zongjiao Wenhua Press, 1995: pp 53–73.

11 Sociologists take the present model of interaction between the state and religion in China as the 'politics absorbs religion' model. See Chan 1995.

12 Later on Martin Lee left the Alliance and gave focus to the democratic movement in Hong Kong by establishing the Democratic Party.

13 At that time the joining of the Alliance was by organization. Anyone from the organization could be elected as a member of the Steering Committee and then this member could put himself/herself forward as an individual.

14 Father Ha spoke of this when interviewed by this author on 2 October 1998.

Bibliography

Abbott, W. (ed.) 1996 *The Documents of Vatican II*. New York: Guild Press.

Asia Focus, Hong Kong, 9 May 1997.

Caritas-Hong Kong Annual Report, various.

Chan Che-po, Leung, B. 1996 'The Voting Behaviour of Hong Kong Catholics in the 1995 Legislative Council Election', in Kuan Hsin-chi *et al.* (eds) *The 1995 Legislative Council Election in Hong Kong*. Hong Kong: Hong Kong Institute of Asia-Pacific Studies (Chinese University).

Chan Shun Hing 1995 'The Future Development of Hong Kong's Church-State Relations', in Wong, A. (ed.) *Christian Faith and Hong Kong Society*. Hong Kong: Hong Kong Christian Institute, (in Chinese).

Chen Yin, Guo Qiguan (eds) 1997 *Xianggang Jilu* (The Total Record of Hong Kong), vol. 1. Hong Kong: Zhonghua.

'Declaration of Catholic Education' 1966, in Abbott, W. (ed.) *The Documents of Vatican II*. New York: Guild Press.

Documentation Centre, Policy Section of Religious Affairs Bureau, *Xinshiji Zongjiao Gongzuo Wejbian Xuanbian* (Selected Documents on Religious Work of New Age) 1995, Beijing: Zongxiao Wenhua Press.

'Dogmatic Constitution of the Church' 1996, in Abbott, W. (ed.) *The Documents of Vatican II*. New York: Guild Press.

Fang Hao (ed.) 1997 *The Late Bishop Francis Hsu's Letters: An Incomplete Collection*. Taiwan: Window Press.

Ha Louis 1992 'Catholicism in Hong Kong', in Sung Yun-wing, Lee Ming-kwan (eds) *The Other Hong Kong Report*. Hong Kong: Chinese University of Hong Kong Press.

Holmes, B. (ed.) 1967 *Educational Policy and the Mission Schools: Case Studies from the British Empire*. London: Routledge and Kegan Paul.

Hong Kong Catholic Church Directory 1998. Hong Kong: Catholic Truth Society.

Hong Kong Catholic Diocesan Archive Office, various.

Hong Kong Record Series, Hong Kong Public Record Office, various.

Igwe, S. O. 1967 *Education in Eastern Nigeria 1847–1975, Development and Management: Church, State and Community*. London: Evens Brothers.

Information Service Department 1997 *Hong Kong 1997*, Hong Kong: Hong Kong Government.

Kung Kao Po (Catholic Weekly News), various.

Lam, A. 1995 'Christianity and Buddhism', in Cheung, S. Y. L., Sze S. M. H. (eds) *The Other Hong Kong Report 1995*. Hong Kong: Chinese University Press.

Lau Siu-kai 1984 *Society and Politics in Hong Kong*. Hong Kong: Chinese University Press.

Leung, B. 1992a *Sino–Vatican Relations: Problems in Conflicting Authority, 1976–1986*. Cambridge: Cambridge University Press.

Leung, B. 1992b 'The Catholic Voters', in Kwok, R. *et al.* (eds) *Votes without Power: The Hong Kong Legislative Council Election 1991*. Hong Kong: Hong Kong University Press.

Leung, B. 1998 'Church, State and Education during the Colonial Period: Hong Kong and Macau', in Bray, M. (ed.) *Hong Kong and Macau Education: A Comparison*. Hong Kong: Comparative Education Research Centre (HKU).

Luo Kuong (ed.) 1967 *Tianzhujiao Jihua Chanjiao Lishi* (The History of Catholic Missions in China). Taiwan: Guangchi Press, Hong Kong Catholic Truth Society.

McCarthy, J., Britt, D., Wolfson, M. 1991 'The Institutional Channelling of Social Movements by the State in the United States'. *Research in Social Movements' Conflict and Change* 13: 45–76.

McClell V. A. 1998 'Census Fidelium: the Developing Concept of Roman Catholic Voluntary Effort in Education in England and Wales', in Broack, C., Tulasiewicz, W. (eds) *Christianity and Education Provision in International Perspective*. London: Routledge.

Maryknoll Archives, various.

Motte, J. 1971 *History of the Catholic Church in China* (translation Joseph Tarc. Hou). Taichung: Kwongchi Press.

'Pastoral Constitution of the Church in the Modern World' 1966, in Abbott, W. (ed.) *The Documents of Vatican II*. New York: Guild Press.

Ryan, T. 1959 *The Story of a Hundred Years: The Pontifical Institute of Foreign Mission (PIME) in Hong Kong, 1858–1958*. Hong Kong: Catholic Truth Society.

So Alvin, Kwitko, L. 1990 'The New Middle Class and the Democratic Movement in Hong Kong'. *Journal of Contemporary Asia* 20(3).

South China Morning Post, 16 December 1948.

Sunday Examiner, Hong Kong, various.

Sweeting, A. 1993 *The Phoenix Transformed: the Reconstruction of Education in Post War Hong Kong*. Hong Kong: Oxford University Press.

Tung Chee-Hwa 1997a 'A Future of Excellence and Prosperity for All', speech at the ceremony to celebrate the establishment of the Hong Kong Special Administrative Region (HKSAR), 1 July.

Tung Chee-hwa 1997b 'Building Hong Kong for a New Era', address by the Chief Executive at the Provisional Legislative Council Meeting, 8 October.

Weigel, G. 1987 *Tranquillitas Ordinis: The Present Failure and Future Promise of American Catholic Thought on War and Peace*. New York: Oxford University Press.

Weigel, G. 1992 *The Final Revolution: The Resistance Church and the Collapse of Communism*. New York: Oxford University Press.

Wu, B. J. 1989 The March into the Bright Decade, pastoral exhortation of Cardinal John B. Wu on the Pastoral Commitment of the Catholic Diocese of Hong Kong (unpublished).

Wu, B. J. 1995 *Proclaim the Gospel of the Lord, Spread the Kingdom of God*, interim report, 4 June (unpublished).

Yang, C. K. 1984 'Introduction', in King, A., Rance Lee (eds) *Social Life and Development in Hong Kong*. Hong Kong: Hong Kong Chinese University Press.

Ye Xiaowen 1996 'Dongqian Woguo de Zongjiao Wenti' (Contemporary Religious Questions of the Motherland), in *Zhonggong Zhongyang Dangxiao Baogao Xuan* (Selected Reports of the Party Central School) vol. 101, no. 5, internally circulated document. Beijing: Central Party University.

14
Migration and Identities in Hong Kong's Transition*

Janet W. Salaff[1]

Introduction: migration and identity

Hong Kong's reversion to China on 1 July, 1997 was unusual. Not only did an underdeveloped Communist country incorporate a world-class city, but scheduled far in advance, the community had time to reflect on the meaning of the transition in their daily lives. There has thus been much interest in how the Hong Kong people defined reversion, and made strategies to meet the challenges.

For six years leading up to the 1997 event, this author studied how 30 Hong Kong Chinese families planned to cope with the uncertainties of the transition. The families were chosen from a random survey list of 1552 households from different backgrounds living in Hong Kong in 1991. Prompted by the massive move of the middle class to the western democracies in the late 1980s and early 1990s, emigration was, at first, identified as their strategy to confront Hong Kong's uncertain future. Talks with the study families led the researchers to question this assumption that migration is a uniform response to an external shock. These families held a range of views on the transition. At the same time, a number of circumstances contributed to the decision to move abroad. The talks with these people over time evolved into multifaceted discussions of many themes. Here, we seek to disentangle identities from migration behaviour to look more deeply at how migration and identity intersect, drawing on their life stories, locating structures that shape views. The unfolding of some of these views in the period just before reversion and six months later is also described. The reversion was followed by a sharp dislocation of the economy, and we look for the stability of views. Were they shaken by these events or not?

Identities

Salaff and Wong (1994) found that people's social class backgrounds underlay distinct views of the reversion. However, our subject families raised more themes about reversion than about family economy and status. We explore some of these here, including three major issues.

Nationalist sentiment is often voiced in anti-colonial movements. Central to a nationalistic evaluation of the transition is identification of the return to China as a feature of the families' *Chinese roots*. To understand the diversity of their views, we look into their family history. We posit that their construction of being Chinese was linked to the family's concrete relationship to China as a nation state. Since 1997 signalled a return to a place where they or their kin had come from, the recall of the family's past dealings with China figures in their stance towards reversion (Bertaux-Wiame 1981). Most crucial in their sense of continuity or discontinuity in the return of their territory to a place they once lived is whether they or their parents fled China's politics or poverty.

Their evaluation of their economic future featured in their views of reversion. Many had enjoyed an unprecedented rise in living standards (Shen and Lai 1997). Not only did they have full employment, but they also invested heavily in the Hong Kong system. Many working-class families bought homes (albeit with kin help, and some were non-home buyers) and invested in stocks. Some were already affected by the structural changes of the past few years, and might have misgivings about future downturns under Chinese rule.

Their assessment of democratic politics also influenced the families' views towards reversion. It has been argued that the region's economic stability is grounded in authoritarian political systems, and that an 'Asian' value system that subordinates individuals to the group interest provides the political stability needed for development (Deyo 1990). Many maintain that the Hong Kong populace cares little about the franchise (Lau and Kuan 1988). Others dispute this, arguing that a modern economy demands democratic institutions, and further record local popular movements (So, 1997; Scott, 1989). To learn whether the families we met were likely to trade political rights for economic growth and thereby favour reversion, we sought their assessment of the balance between the two – *economy versus polity*.

People perceive cultural artifacts as meaningful group symbols, which draw them to act towards common goals (Baumeister 1986, Coleman 1995). We might expect that their common *cultural identity* would rally Hong Kong people to resist reversion (Choi 1990, Thomas 1997, Anderson 1983, Chan 1997). As a basis of a distinct identity, we looked into the ways these people expressed a different lifestyle from that of their Chinese brethren on the mainland.

International migration itself is more than a simple response to an external shock. A study of Hong Kong professional immigrants to Scotland detected that their early childhood values and circumstances underlie the desire to migrate. The history of family migration and location of kin abroad, which eases the costs of a long-distance move, increase its likelihood (Basch *et al.* 1994, Bertaux 1997, Bertaux-Wieme 1981, Boyd 1989, Massey 1990, Ng and Cheng 1994). To understand structural conditions associated with a desire to emigrate, we turned to the families' *social networks*. Social network theorists remind us that the circles in which people move shape their identities. Densely concentrated social networks of family and friends reinforce a core identity (Bott 1957). We found that the locations of their kin shape these people's desire to move (Salaff *et al.* 1998). In this chapter, we link the formation of identities to the factors shaping emigration.

After a discussion of sources, the remainder of the paper describes a broad range of views towards reversion to China. We describe how migration careers are associated with these identities. While there is no one response to the reversion of Hong Kong to China, views are grounded in early life experiences and are reinforced by the structural conditions encountered as adults.

Sources

We gained our understanding of types of views Hong Kong people hold towards reversion to China from a panel of 30 people interviewed yearly from 1991 to 1997. These people were chosen based on two background features: social class and the intent to emigrate. We expected that class experience would shape views towards reversion.[2] Although the working and lower-middle classes are most numerous in Hong Kong, we sub-sampled equal numbers of workers, lower-middle and middle-class families to have enough of each group to study. Our larger random 1991 sample survey found that 12 per cent intended to emigrate and 7 per cent had applied for papers.[3] We wished to explore the reasons underlying the intent to emigrate and for the in-depth study, chose equal numbers of those who had applied to emigrate and those who had not. We interviewed people in each social class group; those who had applied to emigrate and those who had not. Such an in-depth study of 30 families is called a 'theoretical sample' because it draws on those groups that can best answer our queries.

We spoke to the families in detail on their views toward reversion and intentions to emigrate. We gathered life history, demographic and ethnographic contextual materials. We placed them in their social contexts. Visiting them at home, we noted details about their environment. We spoke with husband and wife and children and often had the opportunity to include friends and other kin in our chats. We also sought information from each on the emigration experiences of their children, brothers and sisters, and parents. We call these 'kin units' and in the tables below describe how the location of kin units is associated with views towards reversion to China.

Our regular discussions over the years revealed a number of sea changes. We began when Hong Kong was still reeling from the 1989 Tiananmen incident. By the mid-1990s, economic prosperity had created enough wealth for the working class to be investing in stocks. Our final discussions with a quarter of these families took place six months after the Asian economic crisis began, and gave us insights into the more pessimistic views of the local conditions families now held.

Although the families studied are not unrepresentative, having been chosen from the original random sample survey, we cannot learn from this sub-sample the proportion of Hong Kong people who hold each type of attitude. We can, however, describe a range of attitudes and also link these to their social bases. Our study over time helped us to explore the stability of their attitudes in the period leading up to reversion, and included the early months of the downward economic spiral in the region following reversion. Where possible, we will assess how the economic climate modifies the families' evaluations of the transition.

Four broad types of identification with Hong Kong in transition

Those we met hold four distinct sets of views of reversion. We have called them the 'Loyalists', the 'Hong Kong Locals', the 'Waverers', and China's 'Class Enemies'.[4] Each group exhibits a somewhat different constellation of responses to the themes of nationalism and Chinese roots, politics versus economics, and Hong Kong lifestyle. However, they are not mutually exclusive, and there is some overlap. Nevertheless, by characterizing the study families in this way, and then looking for common past histories, we can begin to understand the social roots of identity formation.

While each attitude type can be considered in relation to any family experiences, in practice some crucial forms of identification are associated with particular family experiences. Most Loyalists and Locals take continuity with the past in their lives for granted and stress their Chinese roots. Few had suffered politically in China. In contrast, Waverers and Class Enemies fear discontinuity and had been politically disenfranchised in China.

There are associated family networks as well. The more kin people have on the Chinese mainland, the more they build a local identity on their Chinese roots, whereas the more kin they have in Hong Kong, the more they view themselves as locals. In contrast, those whose networks are in diverse places have more cosmopolitan identities. Whereas the Loyalist perspective is characteristic of families with kin in China, the close kin of those with Waverer and Class Enemy views have applied to emigrate or live abroad.

Similarly, some types of identification are much more typical of particular social groups. Those from working-class backgrounds, proud of their

Table 14.1 Attitude types and typical social class location

	Working	Lower middle	Affluent
Loyalist	X	X	
Locals	X	X	
Waverers	X	X	X
Class enemies			X

improved family economies, see reversion in pragmatic terms as more of the same. In contrast, those who have had property confiscated, many of whom have regained their standing in Hong Kong and are middle class, question the Basic Law assurances around the reversion. They are most likely to be Waverers or Class Enemies.

In using the word 'family' we do not suggest unity in either strategies or attitudes towards the transition among all members. It is true that spouses share backgrounds, develop and exchange views. Parents pass attitudes to the younger generation. Nevertheless, there is disagreement within families. For instance, there are different proclivities by gender (Salaff 1998). These various dimensions result in a complex of possibilities that we cannot discuss here. Rather, we group views by couple, and give them a single perspective. While views of individual partners about reversion at times differed, most couples arrived at a working consensus well before 1 July 1997 about the actions they would take. This agreement was clearest on the decision about whether to emigrate, remain or re-migrate as 'astronauts'.[5]

Our purpose is to offer a preliminary framework within which we can link attitudes to family experiences and strategies. In the discussion that follows, we sketch out this relationship between family experiences and views towards the transition, and suggest some of the principal variations in terms of social groups. We discuss the four characteristic attitudes in turn.

Pattern 1 – Loyalists: 'your roots will always "come back to China"'

Six of the 30 respondent couples are Loyalists: half working class and half lower/middle class. Our sample contains no upper/middle class Loyalists. Loyalists accept the idea of returning to China, which they identify as their birthplace and a place they visit often. They voice attachment to China and feel Hong Kong is historically part of China. Some go so far as to see reversion as good for their family. Others would prefer a separate Hong Kong. All believed a separate Hong Kong was historically impossible.

Most are middle-aged to elderly, were born in China, and spent their formative years there.[6] Two men were caught on the Hong Kong side when the border closed after 1950. The lower/middle class couples came legally to Hong Kong to join family members, and left others behind. They could not reproduce their mainland cultural capital in Hong Kong and lost the position they had enjoyed in China. The youngest had fled China by boat, and had only to 'touch base' in Hong Kong to remain. Since his experiences were formed in village China, his identity differs little from that of his older counterparts.

Economic concerns dominate Loyalists' views. Their political experiences in China were not particularly negative. Most had fled China's poverty. The family of only one Loyalist spouse had had its property confiscated, but his wife had not, and her views dominate their assessment of reversion. Three couples lived in China during the Cultural Revolution, but had not suffered its most demoralizing features.

Although we term them Loyalists, these families do not seek to return to the past, which is associated with hard times. They are grateful that the turn towards privatization in China has improved the position of those in their family left behind, whom they no longer have to support.

They professed confidence in the HKSAR economy. Most credited Hong Kong's success to local Chinese merchant families, others to Hong Kong's standing as an 'international city'. On the eve of the transition, they expected that as China continued its progress to economic modernity, Hong Kong would also prosper. The Loyalists further saw no reason for China to upset the Hong Kong rice bowl.

We interviewed two of the six Loyalists six months after the Hong Kong economy began a downturn. At that time, they still maintained optimism towards the reversion. They did not attribute much to the colonial state; rather they criticized the British for monopolizing profitable opportunities and distorting the economy. Transportation was often mentioned. The litany of complaints started with the double-decker buses imported from England ('just their castoffs'), to automatic toll machines (not suitable for Hong Kong), going on to the new airport (British firms get the contracts).

Their way of life in Hong Kong and that of the mainland is for them intertwined. Because they emigrated late in their lifetimes, their ongoing and dense ties to Chinese kin are important to them. They cross the border to see these Chinese kin often, and hope they can have closer contact after reunification. They may give kin money, and their economic fates are intertwined with those of kin. Four of the six have shared occupations with kin. Some of them work in a traditional ethnic enclave with links to China.

Loyalists are not politically involved. In the pre-transition power vacuum, it does not make sense to them to throw their weight behind the retreating colonial regime. They do feel that they participate in the Hong Kong lifestyle that has emerged. They optimistically believe the 'One Country – Two Systems' formula will protect their way of life in Hong Kong.

Table 14.2 describes the whereabouts of 73 'kin units' of Loyalist couples. Although most are in Hong Kong, a substantial proportion lives in

Table 14.2   Location of Loyalists kin units*

	China	H.K.	The west	Asia (other)	Total
No.	16	40	8	9	73
%	22	55	11	12	100

*Six couples, or 12 respondents, their parents, siblings and children.

China. Western nations claim few. As many live in other Asian communities (Taiwan, Indonesia, the Philippines) as live in the west. That most have kin in Hong Kong or China helps explain the basis of their turning towards China. With few kin living abroad at the time of our study, these people have no plans to go west. They turn their attention to China. Indeed, three of the six couples have recently bought new homes in China for their elders or themselves.

The Laus, an elderly Loyalist couple, live in the traditional Hong Kong western district. Mr Lau uses the abacus to render accounts in a firm trading in dried imported fungi and other foodstuffs from China and Japan. The wife is a homemaker, who dotes on her new grandson, and earns pin money by cleaning birds nests for a neighborhood importer.

The Chinese Communist Revolution divided his family, and for years the husband could only travel to visit his wife and two children a few times a year. After decades of effort, his wife and youngest daughter legally joined him in Hong Kong. Another married daughter and her family remain in China. They keep close contact, and the Hong Kong branch used to send money to those in China. Yet Mr Lau remarks that they no longer need the kind of help he used to give them because China's economy has improved so much. Their daughter's family does not wish to move to Hong Kong now that they can get solid, working-class jobs, such as a driver or factory worker, suited to their skills in China. Comparing family improvements like theirs increases pride in China's accomplishments. Mr Lau greatly enjoys the Hong Kong lifestyle. Like other Loyalists, Lau sees Hong Kong as a Chinese subculture akin to that of Guangzhou province.

Although some might see this Hong Kong Loyalist, concerned mainly with family matters, as apolitical (Lau and Kuan 1988), his apathy is more a result of political conflict. This keen follower of local history saw positive contributions from the local political system, but since his allegiances were firmly on the side of China, he held back from voting.

Lau reads Chinese history and is familiar with the seaman's strike and other major Anglo-Chinese confrontations. He is qualified to vote, but has never used the ballot, which he saw as a compromise. He did not support the British colonial electoral system of 'so-called democracy'. He anticipates he can survive the narrowing of political expression in the press. When asked about former Governor Patten's moves to expand voting, he replied that the new policies were 'just too theoretical'. He viewed the British colonial establishment cynically. He admitted being in conflict over whether to be loyal to the political groups supporting reversion or to the new democratic figures who did so much for people like him in his neighborhood. This conflict led him to abstain from voting.

Lau believes that the two territories are economically interdependent. In his case, the Pacific rim trade in dried seafood and bird's nests serve as an example, and he concludes that the Hong Kong people need Chinese trade: 'Hong Kong has to exist with China.' Six months after reversion we revisited this family who credited the Chinese government with helping Hong Kong survive the Asian meltdown. 'All of Asia has this problem,' said the husband.

How did he evaluate British colonial rule? 'They fulfilled their historical mission, but they weren't good for Hong Kong.' He feels that Hong Kong belongs to China. Proud of his roots in China, he sees reversion as historically inevitable. The husband does not worry that much will change in his family's circumstances in Hong Kong or China after 1997, and would never emigrate. 'In each place, there will always be a time of adjustment. But you get used to it. The difference is roots. Even if you have a good life abroad, your roots will always "come back to China".'

Improving his family's economic situation by crossing the border was central to our youngest Loyalist family's plans.

A young construction worker fled his impoverished Paoan village in a 'snake boat' a decade ago. He then joined his older brother and sister who already lived in the colony. His parents and five other siblings remained on the mainland. Now, the two brothers live with their families in an apartment they bought together. They work in interior decoration and construction with their elder sister, her husband, and their uncle.

Although the two brothers visit their China kin only on major Chinese holidays, they are familiar with conditions 'back home'. They know that China's economic reforms have raised the living standard of his village. They expect reunification to bring the two parts of the family closer in many ways. But they strongly feel that life in Hong Kong is much better, and are not willing to return to China. 'Go back to live? What an idea!' the youth retorted rhetorically.

While the lad may not welcome the return of Hong Kong to China, ('The best would be not to take back Hong Kong!'), he had great confidence in Hong Kong's future. 'I don't believe that China will ruin Hong Kong because there's no point in doing so.' Asked whether his parents told him about the Cultural Revolution, he responded forcefully, 'It was China's policy! How could we dare to talk about it?' Nevertheless, he thought that what the Communists had done on 4 June, and during the Cultural Revolution, would not happen in Hong Kong. 'According to my friends' opinions, there should be no great change after 1997.'

The brothers were critical of the Hong Kong government's economic policy, which they felt was directed to improving the position of the rich. Elder Brother complained that the elevation of the English language harmed people of their class.

Did they vote? Their nonparticipation again spoke of fear of committing an error by not knowing enough. Younger Brother replied, 'Voting doesn't make a difference to me. I told my wife to throw the form away. I don't know the candidates, how can I vote?' The use of English in documents affronted Elder Brother, 'I did vote, but just blindly chose among the candidates'.

Indifferent to politics, they treated 1 July as a holiday. 'It has nothing to do with us. We work as usual.' Even construction workers got the day off however, which they spent dining out and playing cards. Six months after reversion their view of the situation was that 'Everywhere is pretty much the same.' The economic downtown had already affected them. They had just bought their first stocks, and lost money because these construction stocks had invested heavily in Thailand. They flippantly equated it with their losses in horse racing. They did not attribute this downturn to politics, but to the wider economy.

The wife added, 'It's not just Hong Kong, but it's the whole global problem. Like Thailand. This time it's HK. Then it's Korea. It's all related. It has even gone to the States. The whole world is linked together.'

Family economies shape the terms through which Loyalists voice acceptance of reversion. Their view of economics, based on their own and their China kin's improved livelihood, dominates their politics. Six months into the region's economic downturn, they maintained a sense of continuity. Ties with China contributed to their construction of an identity that stressed their Chinese 'roots'. Reunification is inevitable, natural, and acceptable.

Pattern 2 – Hong Kong locals: 'but I also feel a struggle within me'

Nine couples, whom we call 'Locals', are firmly Hong Kong-based. Locals expected China to continue to progress economically and politically, but have scant personal contact with China. Nor do they express an affinity to the British. They are glad that the British pulled out and left Hong Kong for local people. Firmly attached to Hong Kong, they accepted reversion without fanfare, because they expect little change.

Their view towards the transition is rooted in these social and demographic characteristics. Born of working and lower/middle-class families that were not subject to political movements on the mainland – most are young. Most were raised in Hong Kong, where they built their cultural capital, struggling hard to finish school and secure a career. They own their apartments and bought domestic goods from their own earnings and family loans. They plan their future. To them, their advance mirrors Hong Kong's development.

They see Hong Kong as an economic colony, transferred from the UK to China, and at the time we met them they expected continued prosperity. Reversion to China symbolized the inevitable integration of the two economies. However, they recognized that China and Hong Kong cannot be unified overnight, and there would be switchbacks. Three applied to emigrate, 'as insurance' against economic chaos. But they do not expect chaos, and do not plan to leave. Wait and see is a common view. We interviewed two of the nine Local couples six months into the HKSAR regime. 'Give the Chinese time, they have to learn how Hong Kong works' was their attitude.

Most feel politically naive and characterize themselves as non-involved. They, too, worry about the outcome of an uninformed vote. However, they are more likely to have voted than not.

Table 14.3 Location of Hong Kong locals' kin units*

	China	H.K.	The west	Asia (other)	Total
No.	4	93	8	4	109
%	45	85	8	4	100

*Nine respondent couples, or 17 respondents, their parents, siblings and children.

Their view of themselves as Hong Kong 'locals' flows more from attachment to the local cultural lifestyle and access to economic opportunities, than to politics. Within lifestyle, they include personal expression. They give voice to identity, nationalism, a search for roots, and anti-colonialism. Their uneasiness about reversion turns on concern to maintain this life style.

Hong Kong locals no longer recognize close bonds to kin who are in China, and most of their important kin are in Hong Kong (Table 14.3).[7] No husband and wife in this group have close kin abroad; only 22 per cent of their kin units applied to emigrate. They are not torn in different geographical directions. Their focus is Hong Kong.

The Gwans are a young lower/middle-class couple who work in large Hong Kong bureaucracies, one a lower level member of the administrative civil service, and the other an engineer with a diploma, employed by an airline. They have been promoted rapidly in the years since we met. Although both have worked for the British, they do not identify with the colonial order. They are proud to be Hong Kong Chinese and at the same time looked forward to China's regaining sovereignty.

In a tentative emigration step, the wife applied for the United Kingdom Right of Abode. She later dropped the application as it appeared more trouble than it was worth, and sensed she might be turned down. After her elder sister graduated from a marketing course in England and married a Hong Kong Chinese naturalized UK citizen, our couple saw even less reason to apply to emigrate. They reasoned if life in Hong Kong became too chaotic, Younger Sister would return to England and would sponsor them to England. The couple did not expect this, however. They had faith in the Sino-British Joint Declaration. Family orientiated, they are loath to separate from local kin, whom they visit weekly.

Neither was overly concerned about the economy. They anticipated a drop after the reversion but thought locals with relatively better skills would come out on top:

> I think the living standard will drop in the years to come. There won't be enough space for all the people who will flood into Hong Kong from China. So, if you're interested in changing your life, you should do it now, or it will be too late. That's why we've already bought our own apartment. On the other hand, the effect of '97 will be minimal on the overall financial situation of the colony.

A cautious couple with no major investments, they remained optimistic despite sharp downturns in the stock market in the fall of 1997. They anticipated leaving the stock they had bought for their daughter's education as 'it might rebound in value'.

Furthermore, the linking of the Hong Kong economy to that of China promised ongoing projects for the husband. When the airport has been completed, 'That is not a problem for there is a North-West Railway to be constructed. We hope that the job opportunity will not end before he retires. Hopefully, projects will go on, one by one'.

They did worry about law and order after 1997:

> The most important thing is to make the society a safe place. Politics, laws and public order are most important. If the SAR does not change the laws, our society won't be in trouble. In China, it's common that 'there's no law except for the officials'. If they say you have made a mistake, even if you have proven yourself innocent, as long as the accuser is a high ranking official you'll be charged and found guilty. There's a lot of red tape, and black can even turn into white. It's different in Hong Kong where they have to go to court to prove that you are guilty. So, I worry about this part. I don't worry much about the economy. Maybe because I don't expect too much for myself, that's why the economy aspect doesn't seem a big problem. I think basic necessities like food and housing will not be affected at all.

Regarding the political transition and former Governor Patten, Mrs Gwan said,

> I don't have much of an opinion about him because I don't like politics. But I feel he's in a bit of a rush, and that can't benefit the Hong Kong people. He doesn't work for us, just thinks of himself. We all know who asked him to come here!

She commented rhetorically referring to the British. 'But we can't blame him. Because a lot of Hong Kong people, including me, don't know whether democracy is good or bad.' Asked whether legal reforms have been done in haste, she said, 'Yes, so fast that I feel it's a bit unsafe.' Further, she felt insecure that her fate depended on just the few lower-class voters who turned out.

> Actually, few people voted. Take night watchmen. The Governor just goes and talks to these people, then they will vote for him. But what do they represent? Nothing compared to the rest who don't vote and who're the most influential in Hong Kong.
>
> I don't have any interest in politics, I wasn't the type who joined activities even when I was in school. So, nothing has really changed. My activity is just my family, and other things are minor. In Hong Kong, a lot of people are like me. They only care about their own business.
>
> At the time of 4 June, I felt the Chinese government made a mistake. But looking back at it now, they must have had their own reasons for doing it. There's no perfect government. A government can't please everybody!

This family expressed alienation from local politics because of lack of expertise.

Mr. Gwan thought voting was so important that only experts should vote. He did not feel knowledgeable enough.

I won't waste my time knowing in detail the election dates and the people involved, because I don't believe in what they say. That's why I decided not to concentrate on this election thing. Actually, the candidates have their good points. I think they are good people. But it is very difficult to tell who works hard and who doesn't. You can't do research on them. As with salesmen, there are good and bad things about a product, and it all depends on what the customer wants. Hong Kong is just starting to hold elections. That's why not everybody wants to spend time on it. Most of us don't have the time to play this 'game'. But even if I was to spend enough time, I don't think it would make a difference. You don't really know the candidate. Like, for instance, in a certain district, if you feel that the candidate is not good, you can't even complain. The only thing you can do is not to vote for him, but instead vote for the other candidate. There's nothing you can really do about elections. So sometimes you can feel that it's just a waste of time. Suppose I didn't vote for him, and he won! So for me, elections don't mean anything. As long as it doesn't affect me, then it is okay. But I won't waste my time. Whoever wins, I won't feel bad for the other party who lost.

It's just like horse racing. Some just bet for fun, while some really read and study it carefully before placing their bet. Elections also depend on the seriousness of the person voting. If I am going to spend a lot of time knowing the candidate, I might as well spend it on horses.

As long as it doesn't affect the lifestyle of the people, who can continue to work and live, then who owns the place is not important.'

This Local family's acceptance of the new order is drawn from their modest upbringing, tinged with their strategy of survival. Their expectation that China will let Hong Kong be on its own flows from their limited interaction with mainland life. Although they were affected like others by the recession in the colony, they did not blame the mainland for this setback.

Pattern 3 – Waverers

The eight respondent couples in this group are mixed in class and motivations, but all prefer British rule to what they see in China. They presume China will act in Hong Kong as it does in China. Thus, they worried about the reversion. Most felt political disappointment and were even outraged by the 4 June Tiananmen events. They were cynical and negative about China when we first met. Several are Christians. The youngest is active in an evangelical church, and fears Chinese control over his sect. Religious links compound their anticipation that China will change Hong Kong. Waverers' networks reach abroad and increase their ambivalence to reversion.[8] Forty per cent of their siblings applied to emigrate to a western nation, or already live there. They recognize few mainland kin (Table 14.4).

Nearly all in this group had applied to emigrate, but only one has left. In the years since we have known them, they have adjusted to remaining in Hong Kong – hence the title for their category. Those who were working class among them were unsuccessful applicants because of lack of resources. Those with brighter economic futures at home than abroad,

Table 14.4   Location of waverers' kin units*

	China	H.K.	The west	Asia (other)	Total
No.	1	84	24	6	115
%	1	73	21	5	100

*Nine respondent couples, or 15 respondents, their parents, siblings and children.

chose to carry forward their careers in Hong Kong. All have reframed their views since the reversion, and now expect no immediate change in Hong Kong. While they still mistrust the Chinese system, they do not expect their children to suffer. Let us turn to a family that sought to leave and failed. Their bitter choice was sweetened by Hong Kong's prosperity for people of their class. They reasoned that while they could not leave, at least they would be economically better off in Hong Kong.

A van driver has emigrant kin with restaurant and construction businesses in a Toronto suburb and this prompted him to apply to emigrate. He hoped to work with them abroad. His eldest brother had gone to high school in Canada, and become a citizen. When his parents retired and sold the store, Eldest Brother sponsored them. They invested the proceeds of the store in two small Canadian enterprises, and the van driver applied to join them.

He was eager for better economic opportunities abroad. He also liked the quiet Canadian way of life. Finally, the possible civil disorder after reversion concerned him. He spoke of the small daily freedoms, not democratic representation.

> Without a lot of money, we can still live. The most important thing is 'freedom'. We Hong Kong people are used to speaking freely. If you don't like the boss, you can attack him directly. It's not sinful. But in China, you may commit a sin without knowing you're doing it.

A frank person, he wanted to speak his mind. As a working-class man, he valued the importance of public facilities. 'I visited China as a tourist, and found it disorderly; people don't follow traffic and other rules.'

In contrast, his wife did not wish to leave her Hong Kong kin. Several times a week she visits her maternal kin, who helped care for her youngsters when small. Although her brother, of whom she was fond, joined his wife's family in Toronto, she was reluctant to leave her female kin. She appeared to have had no say in the emigration project of her husband's kin. Knowing no English, afraid to leave her kin in Hong Kong, his wife was not keen on depending on her husband's family for their livelihood, or on serving them. 'If you have a day's life, just live it. It's not bad in Hong Kong. If you can work and can eat, let it be.'

She attributes her fatalism towards politics to her low education and lack of experience. 'To engage in politics is not my business. I am not qualified.' Speaking of the students in the 4 June Tiananmen massacre, she said politics was for the well educated.

Maybe for those students with a lot of education, there is something to do. But still they died. Sometimes I think, why should we be afraid to live here? There are still so many people, millions. How could each of us be afraid? It is ridiculous to worry that the Chinese can punish us and send us to the countryside to farm; there is no farm here! Sometimes I think there's no point fighting the mainland Chinese. You can't win. Maybe this is the personality of us Chinese.

When family feuds and a recession in the Canadian economy reduced the emigration opportunities, their plans changed. They had intended to emigrate to align their own family economy with that of the husband's family. Yet, the husband speaks of the rejection in positive terms. In the winter of 1997, the downturn of the economy and decline in demand for dining out affected the wife's job in the food service industry. Nevertheless, as they were not investors, so long as they could keep their jobs they felt they had made the right choice in staying in Hong Kong.

Pattern 4 – Class enemies of China: 'just like mixing lemon tea with water' (the worst of both worlds)

Class Enemies harbour deep misgivings about the Chinese political system, which they fear will be imposed on an unwary Hong Kong. Most opposed reunification with China, they prefered life as it was. There are seven couples in this group. Most Class Enemies have upper-class backgrounds. Five of the seven families are now in Hong Kong's upper middle class. The remaining two never regained their position after their family property was confiscated.

Political justice is important to those three couples whose close family members suffered deeply in China. The collective memory of having lost family property fuels their anxiety about the transition. While the others have not personally experienced problems, they have become aware of the difficulties upper-middle-class people like themselves have living under Chinese communist rule. Their experience as businessmen or professionals in China means that they do not trust in China's ability to handle the delicately balanced Hong Kong economy. They attribute Hong Kong's economic development to the presence of the British colonial government and the absence of China's 'rule of people not of law'.

They spoke about reversion to China in detached terms. As 'Chinese', they wanted to 'help' China; and criticized the authorities, which did not use their professional talents properly. They did not consider themselves to be members of China's body politic.

They are alienated from the Chinese political system, but not from politics entirely. Of those about whom we have information, as many voted as declined to vote. Even more joined the demonstrations surrounding the events of 4 June, 1989.

Most applied to emigrate. They organized for emigration well in advance of reversion. Their response is not to panic and exit. Instead, they planned their escape for years.

Table 14.5 Location of kin units of class enemy couples*

	China	H.K.	The west	Asia (other)	Total
No.	5	67	28	3	103
%	5	65	27	3	100

*Seven respondent couples, or 14 respondents, their parents, siblings and children.

They do not maintain on-going ties with China, reinforcing negative attitudes towards China.[9] They either lack mainland kin or do not take kin located in China into account in their daily actions. The decision to leave China for Hong Kong was not shaped by the need to help kin, nor do they contribute to a common family economy with mainland kin. Those who were born in China left siblings behind when they fled with their parents whose property was taken away. Their flight ruptured contact with these kin. Several remain alienated from the kin left behind. Others, however, have since met their siblings, and increased contact moderates their negative views of China. Two locally born couples come from a long line of Hong Kong kin (Table 14.5).

In contrast, they are part of a stratum that spans the seas. They have many close friends and classmates, as well as kin, abroad in the major western receiving nations. Three of the four upper-middle-class couples who have exited Hong Kong already have siblings or children abroad. These kin most shape their opinions. Their kin describe life overseas, they provide information, and tend to reinforce negative views about Chinese anti-democratic processes.

Most Class Enemies applied to emigrate. Some have left, expressing their lack of faith in the institutional protections in the Joint Declaration. The greatest misgivings are over corruption. Those that have not left stress China's inability, not lack of integrity, to improve its economic system. These relatively weak negative views do not propel them outward.

Not all Class Enemies had their family property confiscated. This family man, one of a long line of middle-class kin, and an employee of a large Hong Kong bureaucracy, has reason to feel disaffected from China.

An administrator, keen to leave Hong Kong, increased contacts with his wife's kin in Canada. The family had no kin in China, nor did they lose property there. Rather, the husband's desire to emigrate was grounded in his British-orientated cultural capital. From his position as a senior manager in the real estate department of a major British firm, he saw the orderliness of British rule. He contrasted this with his experience of 'lawlessness' in China. He thought there would be no hope for his family in Hong Kong. He also thought his challenged son could find a better life abroad. The family 'landed' in Canada at considerable cost, and the husband has returned to Hong Kong to a new job to secure his family finances.

Having struggled through adult evening school for an MA, he felt that the Chinese Government put too little effort into education. He thought that the education standard of the Chinese can be raised only after 'the age-old rulers go'. He had hoped to contribute what he learned to educate the Chinese people. 'I have Chinese blood. I wish to help China modernize.' He tried to give his expertise to China, but the experience of teaching in China disappointed him. 'Several hundred [of us in Hong Kong] to educate several billions are just like a drop of water in the ocean! I love China but China doesn't love us [Hong Kong people].' Having had dealings with China, he found Chinese bureaucrats hard to work with. He feared the corruption he saw in China was already coming to Hong Kong.

> We have increased our vigilance here, but we Hong Kong people have a double standard. When we go there, we pay. We give people gifts. Maybe we hire Chinese police officers to protect our buildings. If you build in Hong Kong, it's simple, you can get gas, water, light. Here, we have guards, or our own people. In China, it's hard. You have to visit the offices of gas, water, light one by one, go to the higher ups, give them gifts and only then can you get service.

The raging debate on political reforms before reversion further confirmed the 'One Country – Two Systems' proposal to be insincere. He was disappointed by the comments of the Chinese officials who had undermined Sino-British relations. He exclaimed, 'Seven million people are under the control of these kind of people!'

'The future of Hong Kong and China is just like mixing lemon tea with water. Hong Kong will be worse off by sharing her benefits with China. China will be better off because she gets the benefits of Hong Kong' He thought that there was too much uncertainty in Hong Kong's future. 'No one wants to leave Hong Kong, but the environment forces us to.'

The family waited until 1996 to sell their apartment. Until then they lived as other Hong Kong people. The only difference was that their passports enabled them to leave whenever necessary. The husband told us in 1995, 'I'm not afraid. I have a British passport. I can leave at any time.' He also said, 'Emigration is the last resort. Holding a passport is like buying an insurance policy. When you have bought the insurance policy, you put it aside. When you need it, you take it out again.' The family finally landed in Canada in early 1996.

The husband maintained that he emigrated for his son's sake. In 1993 he told us, 'I am now 45 years old. In 1997, I'll be an old man. It doesn't mean much to me whether I stay in Hong Kong or not, but it's for the next generation.' Although he believes that he 'cannot become rich in a foreign country', he hopes that his son can 'live in a liberal land'.

His search for a job abroad was fruitless and he returned to Hong Kong. Hong Kong's financial downturn limits his local prospects, which are tied to the property sector. He remained uncertain whether to risk his fate in the Hong Kong transition or in Canada. He was more resigned to than approving of the transition. He gave China credit for buffering the impact of the recession and protecting Hong Kong from its worst effects (see Ash and Kueh 1995).

Those who already saw the reversion to China in black terms were most critical of the transition government. They were sensitive to the corruption in the Chinese businesses in Hong Kong. They were critical of the administration's style during the transition, citing the malfunctioning of the new airport and the authoritarian Chinese management system as exacerbating the problems encountered.

Conclusion: linkages between elements of the patterns

Our thematic analysis of in-depth interviews with 30 families in Hong Kong indicates the broad range of identities. We grouped these into four sets of views, based on their attitudes towards their Chinese roots, the political and economic system, and cultural identification with the Hong Kong way. Loyalists and Locals were most likely to believe that China would respect Hong Kong's distinct institutions. Waverers and Class Enemies maintained China would impose its own political system.

Seeking the roots of these identities, our analysis suggests how family experiences contribute to political values and identity formation. First, experiences in the hands of the mainland Chinese were crucial. Those who fled China's politics were the most likely to have had upper/middle-class backgrounds, and were the least eager to live under Communist rule. Those who fled China's poor economy most likely had working and lower/middle-class backgrounds, with only labour to sell, and were most likely to accept reversion.

Next, the place where husband and wife grew up, and the age at which the respondents came to Hong Kong, were also significant. The longer our respondents lived in Hong Kong, the more they were used to local life styles and felt they would not be able to adjust to life under mainland rule.

Networks shape attitudes also, and the location and interaction of their kin figured in their identities. This ranged from those for whom China was the home of kin whom they often visited, to those without personal links to the mainland, and on to those cosmopolitans whose kin lived mainly in the west.

Just as responses to reversion to China are complex, the desire to migrate abroad is more than a simple response to an external shock. We found the locations of their kin shaped these people's desire to migrate abroad. Having a history of family migration, and having close kin abroad, are associated with making a greater effort to move. Thus, both the formation of identities and factors shaping emigration are rooted in family histories and experiences. It is therefore not surprising that we found remarkable persistence over time. The passing of nearly a decade and many sea changes did not greatly reshape popular views. We traced them through early pessimism to optimism and on to the early stages of economic downturn of Hong Kong and the wider region. Those we revisited in the short period after reversion have maintained their views although they are more pessimistic about the economy than before. We concluded that identities are dynamic and changeable, but are deeply grounded in lived experiences, in structured socio-economies, and in networks.

Notes

* This chapter is based on research undertaken for the 'Emigration from Hong Kong Project' by a research team at the Centre for Asian Studies of the University of Hong Kong, Principal Investigator Professor Wong Siu-lun.

1 An earlier version of this paper was published in Ming Chan (ed.) 1997 *Hong Kong's Reintegration with China: Transformation and Challenge*, Armonk, NY: Sharpe. We acknowledge the funding of the Hong Kong Universities Grants Association, administered by the Centre for Asian Studies, University of Hong Kong. We are grateful for the assistance of Fung Mei-ling and comments by Lisa Fischler, Ed Friedman, Michael DeGolyer and Nick Thomas on the earlier draft.

2 Details of our sample are as follows: we chose ten blue-collar labourers, composed of unskilled and semi-skilled manual workers. The lower middle class were mainly white-collar workers. The upper-middle-class group includes managers and professionals. One limitation should be mentioned: although interviews in the large-scale survey were conducted with several wealthy upper-class families, none responded to us when we recontacted them to participate in our follow up in-depth study.

   We classified married respondents' occupational class by the highest occupation of either spouse. For our in-depth study, we increased this proportion to the half who had taken steps to get papers, including those who have foreign papers and those who applied but had been rejected. Our respondents were different ages. They ranged from two unmarried men aged 30 when we met, to an elderly retired ivory carver, since deceased. For further details of the survey from which we drew the sample see Wong 1995.

3 This number is matched by the data from the Hong Kong Transition Project surveys, which found that 9 per cent had a right of abode overseas and 3 per cent were seeking it (DeGolyer 1997, p 10).

4 Two people working independently arrived at these classifications from the clustering of the data. We classified the families based on their attitudes and actions on the political themes discussed above. The few times we disagreed, we discussed and reclassified them.

5 While most held the same views towards the reversion to China, in four cases, or 13.7 per cent, the husband and wife disagreed over their assessment of Chinese rule. We classified them by the pattern that dominated the couples' actions. Despite their disagreements, the four couples fell into adjacent categories. Similarly, surveys by the Hong Kong Transition Project found 12 per cent of couples held divergent views towards the transition (Michael E. DeGolyer, personal communication, 15 December 1997).

6 Nine of the 12 husbands and wives in this group were born in China.

7 There were 17 individuals in this group, six born in China, ten born in Hong Kong, one elsewhere.

8 Of the 16 in this pattern, only one was China born, 12 were born in Hong Kong, one elsewhere. We lack information on two.

9 Ten of the 14 husbands and wives in this group were born in Hong Kong, three were born in China, one elsewhere.

Bibliography

Anderson, B. 1983 *Imagined Communities: Reflections on the Spread of Nationalism*. London: Verso.

Ash, R., Kueh, Y. Y. 1995 'Economic Integration within Greater China: Trade and Investment Flows Between China, Hong Kong, and Taiwan', in Shambaugh, D. (ed.) *Greater China: The Next Superpower?* Oxford: Oxford University Press.

Basch, L., Glick Schiller, N., Szanton Blanc, C. 1994 *Nations Unbound: Transnational Projects, Post-Colonial Predicaments and Deterritorialized Nation-States*. Newark, NJ: Gordon and Breach.

Baumeister, R. F. 1986 *Identity: Cultural Change and the Struggle for Self*. Oxford: Oxford University Press.

Bell, D. 1975 'Ethnicity and Social Change', in Glazer, N., Moynihan, D. P. (eds) *Ethnicity and Experience*. Cambridge Mass: Harvard University Press.

Berger, M. T., Borer, D. A. (eds) 1997 *The Rise of East Asia: Critical Visions of the Pacific Century*. London: Routledge.

Bertaux, D. (ed.) 1981 *Biography and Society*. Thousand Oaks: Sage.

Bertaux, D. 1997 'Transmission in Extreme Situations: Russian Families Expropriated by the October Revolution', in D. Bertaux and P. Thompson (eds) *Pathways to Social Class*, Oxford: Oxford University Press.

Bertaux-Wiame, I. 1981. 'The Life-History Approach to the Study of Internal Migration', in Bertaux, D. (ed.) *Biography and Society*, Thousand Oales: Sage.

Boyd, M. 1989 'Family and Personal Networks in International Migration: Recent Developments and New Agendas'. *International Migration Review* xxiii(3): 638–663.

Bott, E. 1957 *Family and Social Networks: Roles, Norms and External Relationships in Ordinary Urban Families*. London: Tavistock Publications.

Chan, Hoiman 1997 'Labyrinth of Hybridization: The Cultural Internationalization of Hong Kong', in Postiglione, G. A., Tang, J. T. H. (eds) *Hong Kong's Reunion with China: The Global Dimensions*. Armonk, NY: ME Sharpe.

Cheng, S. L. 1995 *Hong Kong on a Plate*, Hong Kong: Department of Sociology, University of Hong Kong, M.Phil.

Choi, Po-king 1990 'Popular Culture', in Wong, R. Y. C., Cheng, J. Y .S. (eds) *The Other Hong Kong Report 1990*. Hong Kong: The Chinese University Press.

Cohen, A. 1969 *Customs and Politics in Urban Africa*. London: Routledge and Kegan Paul.

Coleman, J. 1995 'Rights, Rationality, and Nationality', in Breton, A. *et al.* (eds) *Nationalism and Rationality*. New York: Cambridge University Press.

DeGolyer, M. E. 1997 'Squaring the Circle: Civil Society in Hong Kong and China', conference paper, typescript, *American-Asian Review* forthcoming.

Deyo, F. C. 1990 *Beneath the Miracle: Labor Subordination in the New Asia Periphery*. Berkeley: University of California Press.

Guldin, G. E. 1980 'Multilineal Modernity: Ideologies of Modernization in Hong Kong', in *Proceedings of the 2nd International Symposium on Asian Studies*, Vol. I: 69–86.

Harding, H. 1995 'The Concept of 'Greater China': Themes, Variations and Reservations' in Shambaugh, D. (ed.) *Greater China: The Next Superpower?* Oxford: Oxford University Press.

Johnson, G. 1994 'From Colony to Territory: Social Implications of Globalization', in Leung, B., Wong T. (eds) *25 Years of Social and Economic Development in Hong Kong*.

Hong Kong: Centre of Asian Studies Occasional Papers and Monographs, University of Hong Kong.

Kwok, R., Yin-wang, So, A. Y. (eds) *1995 Hong Kong-Guangdong Link: Partnership in Flux*. Hong Kong: Hong Kong University Press.

Lau Siu-kai, Kuan Hsin-chi, 1988 *The Ethos of the Hong Kong Chinese*. Hong Kong: The Chinese University Press.

Lee Ming-kwan 1995 'Community and Identity in Transition in Hong Kong', in Kwok R. Yin-wang, So, A. Y. (eds) *Hong Kong-Guangdong Link: Partnership in Flux*, Hong Kong: Hong Kong University Press.

Li, F. L. N., Jowett, A. J., Findlay, A. M., Skeldon, R. (no date) *Discourse on Migration and Ethnic Identity: Interviews with Professionals in Hong Kong*. Dundee, Scotland: Department of Geography, Centre for Applied Population Research, University of Dundee.

Li, F. L. N., Jowett, A. J., Findlay, A. M., Skeldon, R. 1994 *Talking Migration: An Interpretation of the Migration Intentions of Hong Kong Engineers and Doctors*. Dundee, Scotland: Centre for Applied Population Research, University of Dundee.

Lodge, G., Vogel, E. (eds) *1987 Ideology and National Competitiveness: An Analysis of Nine Countries*. Boston: Harvard Business School Press.

Massey, D. S. 1990 'Social Structure, Household Strategies and the Cumulative Causation of Migration'. *Population Index* 56(1): 3–26.

Ng Sek-hong, Cheng Soo-may 1994 'The Affluent Migrants as a Class Phenomenon: The Hong Kong Case', in Lau Siu-kai, Lee Ming-kwan, Wan Po-san, Wong Siu-lun (eds) *Inequalities and Development: Social Stratification in Chinese Societies*. Hong Kong: Institute of Asia Pacific Studies, Chinese University of Hong Kong.

Ngo, Tak-Wing 1997a 'Hong Kong Under Colonial Rule: An Introduction'. *China Information* 12, 1/2: 1–11.

Ngo, Tak-Wing 1997b 'Social Values and Consensus Politics in Hong Kong', in Antlov, H., Ngo Tak-Wing (eds) *The Cultural Construction of Politics in Asia*. London: Curzon Press.

Postiglione, G. A., Tang, J. T. H. (eds) 1997 *Hong Kong's Reunion with China: The Global Dimensions*. Armonk, NY: M.E. Sharpe.

Salaff, J. W. 1998 'The Gendered Social Organization of Migration Work'. *Asian and Pacific Migration Review* 6(3–4): 295–316.

Salaff, J. W., Fong, E., Wong Siu-lun 1996 *Using Social Networks to Emigrate from Hong Kong: How Present Directions Foretell the Future*. Honolulu: paper delivered at the Annual Meeting of the Association of Asian Studies.

Salaff, J. W., Fong, E., Wong Siu-lun 1996 'Using Social Networks to Exit Hong Kong', in Barry Wellman (ed.) *Networks in the Global Village*, Boulder, Col: Westview Press.

Scott, I. 1989 *Political Change and the Crisis of Legitimacy in Hong Kong*. Hong Kong: Oxford.

Scott, I. 1995 'Political Transformation in Hong Kong: From Colony to Colony', in Kwok, R. Yin-wang, So, A. Y. (eds) *Hong Kong-Guangdong Link: Partnership in Flux*. Hong Kong: Hong Kong University Press.

Shambaugh, D. (ed.) 1995 *Greater China: The Next Superpower?*. Oxford: Oxford University Press.

Shen, S. M., Lai, Y. L. 1997 'Social Well-being During 1988–1995: An Index Approach', in Lau Siu-kai, Lee Ming-kwan, Wan Po-san, Wong Siu-lun (eds) *Indicators of Social Development: Hong Kong 1995*. Hong Kong: Hong Kong Institute of Asia-Pacific Studies, The Chinese University of Hong Kong.

Skeldon, R. 1991 'Emigration, Immigration and Fertility Decline: Demographic Integration or Disintegration?', in Sung Yun-wing, Lee Ming-kwan (eds) *The Other Hong Kong Report*. Hong Kong: The Chinese University Press.

Skeldon, R. 1997 'Hong Kong: Colonial City to Global City to Provincial City?', *Cities* 14(5): 265–271.

So, A. Y. 1997 'Hong Kong's Embattled Democracy: Perspectives from East Asian NIEs'. *Issues and Studies* 33(8): 63–80.

So, A. Y., Kwitko, L. 1992, 'The Transformation of Urban Movements in Hong Kong, 1970–90'. *Bulletin of Concerned Asian Scholars* 24(4): 32–44.

Tam, M. 1996 *Youth Culture in Hong Kong: Re-rooting of an Identity*. Honolulu: paper delivered at the 1996 Annual Meeting of the Association of Asian Studies.

Thomas, N. 1997 *Emergence of the Hong Kong Identity*. Hong Kong: paper presented to the CAS and the Department of History, University of Hong Kong.

Van Maanen, J. 1995 (ed.) *Representation in Ethnography*. Thousand Oaks: Sage.

Waters, M. C. 1990 *Ethnic Options: Choosing Identities in America*. Berkeley: University of California.

White, H. 1987 *The Content of the Form: Narrative Discourse and Historical Representation*. Baltimore: Johns Hopkins University Press.

Wong Siu-lun 1995 'Political Attitudes and Identity', in Skeldon, R. (ed.) *Emigration from Hong Kong*. Hong Kong: Chinese University Press.

Wong Siu-lun, Salaff, J. 'Network Capital'. *British Journal of Sociology* (forthcoming).

Woon, Yuen-fong 1985 'Ethnic identity and Ethnic Boundaries: the Sino-Vietnamese in Victoria, British Columbia'. *The Canadian Review of Sociology and Anthropology* 22(4): 534–558.

Yao, Souchou 1997 'The Romance of Asian Capitalism: Geography, Desire and Chinese Business', in Berger, M. T., Borer, D. A. (eds) *The Rise of East Asia: Critical Visions of the Pacific Century*. London: Routledge.

Part IV
External Relations

15

The External Relations of the Hong Kong Special Administrative Region

Miguel Santos Neves

Introduction

The post-Cold War international system has been characterized by the coexistence and interplay of contradictory centrifugal and centripetal forces both at the political level (where there are manifestations of unipolarity but at the same time the emergence of the PRC as a new global power prepared to challenge in the future the current US monopoly) and at the economic level, where the intensification and acceleration of globalization coexists with the expansion and consolidation of regionalism.

Hong Kong is an increasingly important player in this new international system, where the power of transnational actors and informal networks has been reinforced at the expense of sovereign states. The importance of Hong Kong as an international city and economic centre derives firstly from its economic power and remarkable achievements – eighth largest trading economy, fourth leading source of foreign direct investment (FDI) and third most competitive economy. Secondly though, there are the specific, complex and strategic functions it performs for the regional and global economies as:

- a centre of co-ordination of globalization operations
- a major investor at both the world and regional levels, emerging as the first foreign investor in ASEAN and APEC
- the regional headquarters for multinationals and a major financial centre
- the capital of overseas Chinese business networks which co-ordinate their world operations from Hong Kong
- a crucial trade entrepôt with China, managing more than 50 per cent of the PRC's exports and a catalyst for the modernization of China's economy (Enright, Scott and Dodwell 1997).

Since the early 1990s there has been an 'internationalization' and 'politicization' of the Hong Kong question – a trend China tried to resist – as a consequence of the high profile of Hong Kong's and China's economies after the end of the cold war, the row over Hong Kong's political reforms initiated in 1992 and the escalation of the US–China trade conflict.

Hong Kong has a unique international status, being clearly the most visible and powerful non-sovereign entity in the international system. This chapter will analyse how the transfer of sovereignty and the new HKSAR's external relations framework may affect this status. Is it likely to weaken, stabilize or reinforce it, taking into account that external relations are a fundamental dimension of the HKSAR identity and the preservation of international ties a vital condition for its survival, not only to maintain its role as an international economic centre but also to protect its autonomous status *vis-à-vis* Beijing?

The chapter is structured in three parts. The first analyses the fundamental rules and principles of the new HKSAR's framework for external relations. The second includes an assessment of this framework in an attempt to understand the main risks and constraints likely to be faced by the HKSAR. The third addresses the substantive priorities of the HKSAR's external relations at the bilateral and multilateral levels, taking into account the external actors' future strategies towards Hong Kong.

The basic framework of the HKSAR'S external relations

The new framework of the HKSAR's external relations, based on the relevant provisions of the Sino-British Joint Declaration of December 1984 and the Basic Law approved by the National People's Congress in April 1990, is one of the four key factors likely to determine the future pattern of relations with the outside world and Hong Kong's position in the international system. The other factors related to the evolution of the PRC-foreign policy, Beijing–Hong Kong relations, and the policies and strategies of foreign powers towards Hong Kong, will be analysed in the following sections.

The analysis and assessment of this new framework, developed since 1984 and formally entered into force on 1 July 1997, requires prior reference to the features of Hong Kong's international status before the handover.

Hong Kong as a 'quasi-state'

Hong Kong has been clearly recognized for some time as a non-conventional member of the international community, a unique case whose status is difficult to capture by traditional analysis of international relations and international law. In fact, the international status of Hong Kong has been characterized by tension between law and reality, between the lack of formal and juridical sovereignty on one hand, and its 'factual sovereignty' on the other, based on an increasing economic power and influence as a strategic player in the global economy and on a clear capacity to engage autonomously in international relations.[1]

The extent of this 'empirical' sovereignty, together with the fact that Hong Kong is the most autonomous and powerful non-sovereign government in the international system, was the basis for James Tang's description of Hong Kong as a 'quasi-state', a unique category for a unique case (Tang 1993, p 205). While this interesting formula seems to reflect accurately the international status of Hong Kong, its practical relevance has still to be demonstrated.

Beside the possession of an international legal personality, i.e. the ability to be a subject of international law exercising rights and bearing duties, and its characterization as a 'quasi-state', Hong Kong's international status has evolved in three other aspects. Firstly, there has been a gradual expansion and deepening of that status since the beginning of the transition period in 1985 as Hong Kong joined a considerable number of international organizations including the two priority ones – GATT (1986) and APEC (1992) – and became a party to new international agreements. This was a result both of the implementation of the Joint Declaration and the co-operation between the UK and China to promote Hong Kong's international participation and status in the context of the transition process.

Secondly, Hong Kong's international status is characterized by the dominance of informal relations as Hong Kong specialized in cultivating the more informal dimensions of international relations and promoting informal links (Yahuda 1995, p 42). In fact, Hong Kong became not only the regional headquarters for some 200 transnational corporations (TNC) but also the strategic centre for co-ordination of the activities of the informal networks of overseas Chinese business communities, the second major economic force in Asia. The absence of sovereignty seems to have worked to the advantage of Hong Kong since it enabled the territory to have more freedom to act in ways that would have been impossible for a sovereign entity.

Thirdly, there is the 'brokerage' dimension of Hong Kong's status, as the colony developed a role as broker in the conflicts between China and other countries, almost an instrument of sublimation of China's tensions with the outside world. Hong Kong has been traditionally the gateway to countries that did not recognize China, as well as the main centre for the development of indirect trade and investment between the PRC and Taiwan. In this respect, one of the most significant tasks performed between 1989 and 1984 has been mediation in the US–China trade conflict, through the diplomatic activity developed by the Hong Kong trade office in Washington, in favour of MFN status renewal with China.

It is against this background that the potential impact of the new framework of Hong Kong's external relations shall be assessed.

The framework of the HKSAR'S external relations

The new status of the HKSAR is based on two fundamental principles, the 'high degree of autonomy' (JD art. 3(2) and sec. I Annex I, BL art. 12) and 'Hong Kong people running Hong Kong' (JD art. 3(4)). These principles are embodied in an autonomous executive, and legislative and judicial powers that will enable the design and implementation of policies consistent with the preservation of Hong Kong's current social and economic systems and its life-style.

External relations as an exception

In the external relations field the main characteristic of the new framework is its qualification as an 'exception' (together with defence) to the two structural HKSAR principles mentioned above. It is clear that foreign affairs and defence, two areas lying at the heart of sovereignty, belong to the 'One Country' dimension of the 'One Country – Two Systems' formula, and therefore are subject to a different logic.

This qualification has three basic implications. First, external relations is an area where the high degree of autonomy does not apply, meaning that Hong Kong is subordinated either to the principle of 'no autonomy' or to the principle of 'a low degree of autonomy'. I would argue that both are applicable. Secondly, external relations are not run by Hong Kong people but by the Central People's Government. Thirdly, the Central Government will manage the HKSAR external relations in accordance with, and sometimes in subordination to, the principles and objectives of the PRC's global foreign policy.

The application of Chinese national laws within the HKSAR

The second characteristic of the HKSAR external relations regime relates to the possibility of applying, within the HKSAR, national laws related to foreign affairs issues, which would constitute an exception to the legislative autonomy and to the principle that 'national laws are not applicable in the HKSAR' (BL art. 18). The list of national laws applicable in the HKSAR is contained in Annex III of the Basic Law, which includes six laws of which three are related to foreign affairs (PRC Declaration on Territorial Waters, Nationality Law, PRC Regulations on Diplomatic Privileges and Immunities). Similarly, the HKSAR courts have no jurisdiction and cannot intervene in acts related to defence and foreign affairs (BL art. 19).

Degrees of autonomy

The third characteristic of the new framework involves a complex and heterogeneous status characterized by the coexistence of areas of autonomy and areas of no intervention for the HKSAR. However, a more careful analysis of the relevant provisions reveals the existence of a four-tier structure that goes beyond this simple dichotomy.

First, there is the policy formulation level involving the global definition of long-term objectives, guidelines and priorities for Hong Kong's external relations, as well as supervision. The competence is accorded to Beijing, with the HKSAR's participation being clearly indirect through regular consultations between the HKSAR government and the central government. Issues such as the HKSAR's accession to new international organizations or the extension of international treaties will also be decided at this level.

Secondly, at the policy implementation level, there is a sphere of 'conditioned autonomy' in specific areas defined as *rationae materiae*. This subsystem is structured around paragraphs 3(10), Annex I, section XI of the Joint Declaration and article 151 of the Basic Law. According to paragraph 3(10) of the Joint Declaration:

> using the name of *Hong Kong, China*, the HKSAR may on its own maintain and develop economic and cultural relations and conclude relevant agreements with states, regions and relevant international organizations in the appropriate fields, including the economic, trade, financial and monetary, shipping, communications, touristic, cultural and sports fields. (art. 151 BL added a new sector, science and technology, which was not foreseen in the JD)

The list of sectors where Hong Kong can conduct its own external relations is basically concentrated on economic and technical matters. Whilst it is not surprising that political areas have been excluded from the list, it is less obvious why social sectors were also removed, in particular when they are included in the list of sectors in which NGOs 'can maintain and develop relations with their counterparts in foreign countries and regions and with concerned international organizations' (BL art. 149). One of the interesting questions to be asked is whether the list contained in article 151 is a 'closed' or an 'open' one. The use of the words 'including' or 'namely' suggests that formally this is an open list to which other appropriate fields can be added. However, in practice the system is less flexible as the decision to qualify a sector as an 'appropriate field' is likely to be controlled by the Central Government.

It should be noted that the capacity of the HKSAR to conduct its own external relations depends upon authorization accorded by the central government, hence the term 'conditioned autonomy' (BL art. 13). As for the contents, it seems that this authorization has a general nature, is not given on a case-by-case basis, and will concern all sectors. It is possible that the authorization act includes some broad guidelines, orientations or criteria on how the competence should be exercised. In addition, the authorization system is not incompatible with the introduction by Beijing of a requirement for approval or ratification *a posteriori* of specific acts considered more structural or sensitive, performed by the HKSAR government in areas included in its sphere of autonomy.

Thirdly, there is an area of 'restrictive autonomy' involving a lower degree of autonomy than the previous level. This refers mainly to civil aviation (BL art. 128 to 135), a sector not included in the list in article 151 given its security implications, and in particular the provisions of article 133 of the Basic Law. The key question relates to the negotiation and renewal of Air Service Agreements, which can be carried out by the HKSAR on the basis of 'specific authorizations' from the Central People's Government. Contrary to general authorizations, this clearly implies a case-by-case approach and more detailed content, including the *a priori* definition of specific aspects of the negotiation. Under this system, Beijing can intervene more strongly and directly control the process, thus restricting the HKSAR's autonomy.

Fourthly, there is a 'negative sphere' of no autonomy, involving areas where HKSAR intervention is forbidden and Beijing can act alone. This includes, in principle, all the sectors not mentioned in articles 151 and 133, in particular external relations related to social and political sectors as well as external relations linked with defence. A good example is the process regarding the access of foreign warships to HKSAR ports which requires 'permission of the Central People's Government' (JD sec. VIII, Annex I; BL art. 126), already given to American warships after the handover.

In principle, the responsibility for conduct of external relations at this level is assigned to the PRC Ministry of Foreign Affairs office in Hong Kong (BL art. 13), which is also responsible for the supervision of the HKSAR's actions that fall in its sphere of autonomy. In the areas where the central government conducts the HKSAR's foreign affairs, the Region can have indirect participation and be involved through the participation of HKSAR representatives in the Chinese delegation in diplomatic negotiations directly related to Hong Kong (BL art. 150) and conducted at the national level. Violation by the HKSAR of this central government 'reserved area' of competence would lead clearly to a conflict and probably to a decision to annul the actions of the HKSAR.

Policy towards NGOs

The fourth characteristic of the external relations framework relates to the regulation of the non-governmental dimension of the HKSAR external relations, by imposing two fundamental limits to the activities of NGO:

- the definition of a positive list of sectors in which HKSAR organizations can establish relations with foreign counterparts (education, science, culture, sports, labour issues, social welfare, etc.), which automatically defines an implicit 'negative list' (art. 149 BL)

- a 'prohibition for HKSAR organizations or associations to establish relations with foreign political organizations or bodies' (art. 23 BL), a potential mechanism to control and restrict Hong Kong civil society from contacts with the international community.

It seems clear that the main objective of the Basic Law is – in the context of a policy to prevent Hong Kong from being used as a platform for 'subversion' against China – to avoid the establishment of links between Hong Kong political parties and foreign political parties. However, the formula used is too broad and affects potentially all HKSAR organizations or associations, which in principle can only establish relations with non-political foreign organizations, eventually contradicting the rules of article 149. In addition, this mechanism can easily generate an arbitrary instrument to restrict and control exchanges with the outside world given the absence of a legal definition of key concepts such as 'subversion' and 'political'.

Potential challenges to Hong Kong's international status

This new framework clearly presents opportunities for and constraints on the HKSAR. It is still uncertain whether the new system will deliver in practice a higher or lower level of autonomy in external relations, particularly when compared with the situation prevailing before the handover, and to what extent it constitutes a potential instrument to strengthen Hong Kong's international status in the future. The experience of having the new system in operation is obviously limited, and so it is still too early to have a clear and definitive assessment of performance, trends and results.

In examining the major practical obstacles to the consolidation of Hong Kong's international status and the factors that might lead to tensions and conflicts with Beijing, four main potential problems deserve attention.

The first problem relates to the 'deficit of regulation' which has two distinct dimensions:

- the Basic Law uses vague expressions and concepts that lack an accurate legal definition
- there are omissions, as some important aspects are not regulated, in particular the relations between Hong Kong and Beijing in the management of foreign affairs.

Both aspects contribute to uncertainty and fuel an over-prudent approach, which works to the disadvantage of the HKSAR since the general competence in this field belongs to the central government. In fact the boundaries between the areas of intervention of the HKSAR and Beijing have still to be clarified, and many players do not even know the new rules and therefore have no idea how to react when confronted with new situations.

A good example is the case of a group of Hong Kong businessmen who owned a factory in Indonesia. When caught in a dangerous situation during the riots in Jakarta in April 1998, they requested the protection of the Chinese Embassy in Jakarta. The Embassy's first reaction was to deny assistance and only after the intervention of the head of the Ministry of Foreign Affairs office in Hong Kong did the Embassy change its position and acknowledge the responsibilities China has regarding the protection of the life and property of Hong Kong citizens abroad.

The second problem area is related to the role of the PRC Ministry of Foreign Affairs office in Hong Kong, which is not clearly specified. It is likely that it will have a global supervisory role and intervene directly in the process of accreditation of consuls and in relations with foreign consulates. The consulates in Hong Kong (the majority covering also Macau), which used to deal directly and almost exclusively with the Hong Kong government in the past, will have to adapt to a new triangular relationship characterized by a more active role on the part of the sovereign power.

It should be noted that the problem goes beyond the status and role of the Ministry of Foreign Affairs office to involve all the offices of central government Ministries and Departments in Hong Kong, which have tended to proliferate since the handover. The division of labour between these different offices, or how much scope they have to act, is not clear, but it is possible that they will compete with each other in trying to assert positions and gain influence, which could lead to some tension. This is one of the constraining factors that could limit in practice Hong Kong's autonomy, including in the external relations field.

The third problem area concerns the difference of interests between Hong Kong and the mainland, which might in practice constrain HKSAR action. It is possible to identify three different scenarios for situations involving Hong Kong and PRC interests:

- convergence of interests – Hong Kong and the PRC share the same interests, or the interests are complementary even if they differ with regard to marginal aspects
- clear differentiation of interests with no contradiction – Hong Kong has specific interests and there is no overlap with PRC interests
- contradiction of interests.

While the first two situations do not raise a significant threat to the HKSAR's position, the emergence of conflicting interests can have a potential negative effect on the HKSAR's sphere of autonomy. In fact, it is open to question whether the HKSAR will be able to adopt in an international organization, for instance in APEC where Hong Kong is a full member, a position exactly opposite the PRC position, or vote against a PRC proposal or initiative, in particular on a subject that China considers very important or vital to her interests.

The fourth potential risk to Hong Kong with respect to external relations relates to the increasing politicization of the activities of economic and technical international organizations. The assumption behind the Basic Law is that the economic and technical dimensions of the international system are separable from the political dimension and so the HKSAR should concentrate its external action in the economic field. The problem is that the boundaries are increasingly less clear and overlapping zones emerge. A good example is trade, which became increasingly more politicized with the introduction of labour standards and social dumping issues. In this context, the HKSAR's participation in international organizations, even in the areas defined by article 151, might become more political, thereby generating tensions with Beijing and eventually a more restrictive approach to the SAR's autonomy.

Finally, the increasing visibility of politically sensitive questions, such as human rights and the development of relations with the international community, could generate a negative reaction and attempts to control international contacts. The HKSAR is a party to the International Covenants on Civil and Political Rights (ICCPR) and on Economic and Cultural Rights (ICECR) (BL art. 39, JD section XIII Annex I). An important and difficult question, which also has important implications for the protection of human rights in Hong Kong, is the periodic reporting system associated with the covenants (art. 40 of ICCPR and art. 6 of ICESCR).

Until China signed the ICCPR in October 1998, there was considerable speculation inside Hong Kong and abroad about the way in which this obligation would be observed. China's unexpected accession, however, even though it still awaits ratification, opened the way to a simple solution: the Hong Kong authorities will prepare their own report, whilst the PRC will formally present it.

This could cause Hong Kong and the PRC difficulties if Geneva criticizes possible human rights abuses in Hong Kong in the future. Beijing's representatives would be held responsible, whatever the Basic Law says about Hong Kong people running Hong Kong. Nevertheless, for the moment, this procedure offers greater reassurance about the observance of human rights than seemed possible in July 1997.

In sum, it is still too early to make a global and definitive assessment of the new framework given the short period the system has been operating. So far, the assessment tends to be positive, as the PRC has respected Hong Kong's autonomous status. The HKSAR has been able to maintain its visibility and autonomy of relations with the outside world, following the set of high-level international visits of Tung Chee-hwa to Southeast Asia, Japan, the USA and the EU, and there was a note of continuity in Hong Kong's representations to multilateral organizations.

As for long-term trends in the HKSAR's international status, two tendencies, apparently contradictory, are likely to develop:

- the reduction of Hong Kong autonomy in conducting external relations
- the stabilization of the current international status rather than its expansion.

The reduction in Hong Kong's autonomy in the foreign affairs field is a consequence of various factors. First, the new HKSAR's status, and a more formal and detailed legal framework, reduces Hong Kong's 'room for manoeuvre' and flexibility to further develop or maintain the informal dimensions of its international status. Moreover, during the transition period, Hong Kong was able to reinforce its autonomy as it took advantage of the unique position of being caught between two sovereign powers that controlled each other, but neither of which had full control over the process. The final outcome was a natural and gradual reduction in the influence and control exercised by the UK as the sovereign power as it departed, a trend which will now be reversed by the incoming sovereign power, China.

In the future, the HKSAR will be more tied and vulnerable to the evolution of the sovereign power's foreign policy. Instead of promoting, as in the past, informal links between China and countries that were in conflict with or did not recognize the PRC, Hong Kong will have to limit or even suppress the activities of such countries' representations in the HKSAR. In addition, it is neccessary to take into account that China has just recovered Hong Kong in the context of a highly emotional process of reunification of the motherland, and will have a clear motivation to demonstrate its sovereignty in the few areas that are left. On the other hand, China needs to bear in mind the effect of all that happens on the prospects for the mainland's reunification with Taiwan. To be seen to fulfil the promised high degree of autonomy will be important, and clearly a factor for moderation in China's position regarding the HKSAR's external relations.

A different but related question is the tendency for the stabilization of Hong Kong's international status rather than its expansion. In fact, it is likely to be impossible to maintain the dynamics of the transition period when Hong Kong's international status expanded very rapidly. Both China and the UK were under pressure to co-operate under the terms of the Joint Declaration to develop Hong Kong's external relations in the context of the Joint Liaison Group (annex II JD), and had a clear interest in avoiding blame for an unsuccessful outcome.

The priorities of the HKSAR's external relations

Bilateral relations

Hong Kong has a high-profile status at the level of bilateral relations, as more than 90 states have diplomatic representation in the HKSAR. In terms of its own external representation, Hong Kong has a smaller but effective network composed of 10 Economic and Trade Offices located in Washington, San Francisco, New York, Tokyo, Toronto, Brussels, London, Geneva, Sydney and Singapore, covering the most important trade partners and countries with significant Hong Kong emigrant communities. This is clearly one of the most important instruments for the promotion of external relations and the HKSAR has the possibility to expand this network through the creation of new offices (BL art. 156).

The main priorities for Hong Kong are clearly the major economic powers and the Asian NICs, which are also Hong Kong's most important trade partners: the US, Japan, the EU and Southeast Asia. It is not a coincidence that the first international visits of Chief Executive Tung Chee-hwa after the handover were to these countries, showing clearly where the HKSAR's priorities lie.

The USA became, in recent years, in particular after 1993, the most active supporter of Hong Kong in the international arena, replacing the UK. This was explained both by the size of American interests in Hong Kong and the escalation of US–China trade and political tensions, further aggravated by the ideas of a 'China threat' and 'China containment' in Washington.

The US has substantial interests in Hong Kong, which is a strategic centre for US economic interests in Asia. Hong Kong is the regional headquarters for many US multinationals (around 457 regional offices) and more than 1100 US businesses are represented in Hong Kong (employing more than 250 000 workers), with total investment stocks amounting by 1996 to US$13.8 billion. This economic presence is complemented by relatively intense political relations, clearly illustrated by the number of high-level visits. In 1996 alone, nearly 40 US Government delegations and five State delegations visited Hong Kong for discussions on topics such as trade, monetary (Federal Reserve), security (FBI) and military matters. Perhaps the most revealing aspect of the high political relevance of Hong Kong relates to the fact that nearly 100 members of the US Congress (both from the Senate and House of Representatives) visited Hong Kong between April 1996 and March 1997 (US State Department 1997).

US policy towards Hong Kong was structured and formalized in the early 1990s, and possesses a legal basis in the Hong Kong Policy Act of 1992. This is a separate and autonomous policy that tends to treat Hong Kong 'as a territory which is fully autonomous from the PRC with respect to economic and trade matters' (sec 103(3)) mirroring and reinforcing the HKSAR 'high degree of autonomy'.

The relevance of this Act derives not only from its substance but also from its procedural provisions, as it is one of the most important political instruments of the reporting mechanism, foreseen in title III section 301. The Secretary of State has to present on a regular basis a report to the Speaker of the House of Representatives and to the Chairman of the Senate

Committee on Foreign Relations, on the conditions in Hong Kong covering a wide range of topics, including the 'development of democratic institutions in Hong Kong'. This will probably be one of the most important international monitoring instruments of post-handover Hong Kong's evolution. These reports, to be produced until 31 March 2000, will probably remain a source of tension between the US and China, but at the same time one of the most effective 'soft' instruments to influence Beijing's behaviour.

Relations with the US are likely to remain Hong Kong's first priority. The visit to the US in September 1997 of Chief Executive Tung Chee-hwa showed the importance the US administration attaches to Hong Kong, as well as its commitment to reinforcing Hong Kong's autonomy and international profile. The Chief Executive's visit was given a high level status including three important meetings with President Clinton, Secretary of State Madeleine Albright and the Congress, in particular the Senate Foreign Relations Committee.

It is also interesting to note that at the same time as the Chief Executive's visit was taking place, Emily Lau Wai-hing went to the US to discuss Hong Kong human rights problems and to visit Los Angeles, San Francisco and Oregon. This was a clear message that the US will maintain its links with the democratic movement and is willing to listen to different views and talk to different players.

In conclusion, the US is the most important partner, the only one adopting a truly global and integrated approach to bilateral relations covering economic, political and social dimensions. Moreover, it is the single external actor capable of raising its voice and moderating China's position if things go wrong in the HKSAR.

For Hong Kong, the US plays diverse, important and positive roles namely:

- it is the largest external market
- at the global level it is an ally in the rules-setting debates in multilateral forums with respect to globalization
- it performs an insurance-policy role against the risk of violation of the HKSAR's high degree of autonomy by China.

However, the HKSAR is likely to have mixed feelings, as an intimate relationship with the US may also bring about potential risks. The links between the US and Hong Kong's Democratic Party, and the US pressure on political issues, if not carefully handled, might generate a negative reaction from Beijing, which would then reassert control and restrict autonomy and the international exposure of the HKSAR. In this context, the US attitude would be the cause of, not the antidote for, the violation of HKSAR autonomy. On the other hand, there is some concern that in the case of escalation of the US–China conflict, Washington could instrumentalize Hong Kong and use it as a weapon against Beijing in an attempt to hurt China's interests by hurting Hong Kong.

Japan emerges clearly as the second most important partner, being the first foreign investor in Hong Kong with total FDI stocks of US$25 billion in 1996, although it is only the third trading partner, accounting for 10.2 per cent of Hong Kong's total trade in 1996. However, while Japan is very active in the economic field, it has a very low profile and adopts an over-cautious position in relation to political issues in Hong Kong. This is clearly reflected in the statement of their Foreign Minister Yukihiko Ikeda on the reversion of Hong Kong, issued on 1 July 1997, where all references to Hong Kong's political processes were avoided, and there was only a reference to the economic role of Hong Kong, stating that the HKSAR should 'keep playing an important role as Asia's financial, information and traffic centre'. It goes on to say that 'the government of Japan expects that Hong Kong will, after the handover, develop as a centre of the Asia-Pacific economy, retaining the confidence of the international community and in particular of international economic circles'. Even more explicit was the Japanese Consul-General to Hong Kong, Hideaki Ueda, in an interview with the *Far Eastern Economic Review* in which he said '... we don't make sharp comments on every aspect, like human rights activists. Compared to the US our approach is a bit soft' (Far Eastern Economic Review, May 1997, p 28).

In this context, it seems clear that Japan's first priority is to ensure that Hong Kong remains a successful international financial centre. The Japanese government, already worried about the increasing tensions with China at both economic and security levels, is eager to avoid adding Hong Kong to the list of problems, hence its reluctance to comment on or to take a position in relation to HKSAR internal political developments. In any case, it is possible that some 'pressure in private' could be exerted on Beijing in special circumstances, in particular in a situation where a rapid degradation of the business environment and subversion of market rules could seriously affect Japanese economic interests.

From Hong Kong's point of view, Japan is basically regarded as a major regional economic partner but not as a global partner with a strategy that goes beyond Asia. In this context, Japan can play specific roles in relation to the HKSAR, in particular, monetary co-operation and joint action aimed at the stabilization of regional financial markets, and a provider of technology to support the HKSAR's re-industrialization process based on high-tech industries and the diversification of the Hong Kong economy. Given the nature and current stage of Sino–Japanese relations, it is not likely that Japan will exert public pressure on Beijing if things go wrong in the HKSAR. Nevertheless, Hong Kong may count on a discrete and 'face saving' supporting intervention by Tokyo, which will be taken seriously by Beijing.

Relations between Hong Kong and Southeast Asia are characterized by a dual logic of competition and co-operation. The intensification of relations with Southeast Asia emerged as one of the important developments in recent years, in particular with ASEAN and within it Singapore, Malaysia and Indonesia. This trend is a consequence of the interplay of different factors, namely:

- the process of regional integration of productive structures as a response to the new challenges of globalization and the necessity to preserve competitiveness
- the normalization of diplomatic relations between China and Southeast Asian countries since the early 1990s
- the increasing interest of those countries in entering the Chinese market through Hong Kong.

Asia as a whole has gradually become a much more important region for the Hong Kong economy since the late 1980s, both in terms of markets for exports, accounting for nearly 54 per cent of the total exports in 1996 (up from 49 per cent in 1992), and even more as a provider of imports, accounting for 76 per cent of the total in 1996. Trade relations with Southeast Asia followed this regional trend. The most important partners are Singapore (Hong Kong's fifth trade partner, accounting for 4.1 per cent of Hong Kong's total trade in 1996, ahead of the UK and Germany) and Malaysia (ninth trade partner, equal to France, accounting for 1.6 per cent of Hong Kong's total trade).

The investment links are even more important, as Hong Kong has emerged as a leading foreign direct investor in Asia. As mentioned earlier, Hong Kong became the leading foreign investor in ASEAN, accounting for almost 20 per cent of FDI in 1994–1995, ahead of the US, Japan or Singapore. In this period, Hong Kong was the largest foreign investor in Indonesia, the second investor in the Philippines and the third in Thailand and Taiwan. An important feature of this Hong Kong outward investment is that it is dominated by a myriad of small projects based on business networks rather than on large-scale projects.

The most important link is associated with the informal network of overseas Chinese business communities from Southeast Asia, and with the fact that Hong Kong is the capital and the centre for co-ordination of their activities, not only in Asia but also for the global economy. Among the major overseas Chinese business conglomerates are the Kuok Group from Malaysia, the Lippo Group and Salim Group from Indonesia, the Sophonpanich Group and the Charoen Pokphand Group from Thailand, and the Frank Chan Group from the Philippines. These all have a strong presence in Hong Kong and their operations in the SAR function as:

- the primary international location and base for contact with western multinationals

- a base for finance
- the primary base for investment in China and in other parts of the world.

In short, Hong Kong performs a powerful economic role that will become even more important as globalization advances.

However, it should be noted that economic ties between Hong Kong and Southeast Asia are also associated with important, though less visible, political processes, which lie at the heart of regional relations between China and its Southeast Asian neighbours. First, Southeast Asian governments and conglomerates regard relations with Hong Kong also from a political perspective. Their recent considerable investment efforts in the HKSAR have clear political objectives, as a mechanism to boost confidence in Hong Kong and to demonstrate support for China and its policies towards the HKSAR (Far Eastern Economic Review 1997, pp 30–32). The objective is for governments to gain political credit and improve relations with China, while businesses expect to gain preferential treatment and access to the mainland market in return.

Secondly, there are seeds of political tension in Southeast Asian countries as its governments and political elites, following the exit of capital to be invested in China and Hong Kong, tend to question the loyalty of the economically powerful Chinese business communities and regard them with distrust. This could not only lead to conflict and destabilization of the national economies in Southeast Asia but would also affect negatively the functioning of the Chinese overseas network, hence Hong Kong's economy and the FDI flows to the PRC. In this respect, Hong Kong plays an important stabilizing role, since it had become a dominant foreign investor in Southeast Asia and is responsible for an important inflow of capital to those countries. This partly compensates for the outflow, thus re-establishing a minimum balance and reducing the risk of conflicts.

The European Union and its member states' interests and presence in Hong Kong are, in general, less important than American or Japanese ones. Traditionally the EU maintained a low-profile, passive attitude, with the exception of the UK, being rarely involved in the row over political reforms. This was a result of the low priority status accorded to Asia, including China and Hong Kong, in the context of EU global external relations, and the inhibition effect related to the circumstance that the sovereign power in charge of Hong Kong was an EU member (which systematically opposed a common EU approach), thus leading EU partners to be over cautious in order to avoid any interference in another partner's reserved area.

While lagging behind the US and Japan, EU economic relations with Hong Kong have increased in recent years. In terms of trade flows, Hong Kong became the 10th trade partner of the EU. From a Hong Kong perspective, the EU has declined as a market for exports, accounting for 14.9 per cent of Hong Kong's total exports in 1996 (down from 15.8 per cent in 1992), but remains the second most important market after the US and ahead of Japan. As for individual EU countries, the flows are highly concentrated in three countries: Germany which accounted for 3.2 per cent of Hong Kong's total trade in 1996 (Hong Kong's seventh trading partner) followed by the United Kingdom (2.7 per cent) and France (1.6 per cent).

The EU position in terms of investment flows is far weaker when compared to the US and Japan, as the accumulated European FDI between 1980 and 1996 is estimated to be US$3.8 billion, that is to say, less than one-third of the amount invested by the US and Japan. In spite of the small amount invested, the EU has around 180 companies operating in the financial sector (basically banking and insurance), and another 100 in the manufacturing sector, while nearly 250 EU companies have their regional headquarters in Hong Kong. Hong Kong is also a relatively important investor in the EU, with a total accumulated stock of US$1.3 billion, making it the most important Asian investor after Japan (Wai 1997).

The most striking feature of the EU approach is the absence of a strategy or policy towards Hong Kong, in particular at the level of the EU member states. For most EU countries, with the exception of the UK, and to some extent Germany and France, Hong Kong is not an issue on their foreign policy agendas, and there is no distinct policy designed to deal with the HKSAR. This would be crucial not only to enhance the HKSAR autonomy in external relations, but also to consolidate the overall 'high degree of autonomy' status of Hong Kong.[2] On the contrary, Hong Kong tends to be swallowed up in the relations between each member state and China.

Only the European Commission has attempted to build a coherent and common approach to the HKSAR, especially on trade matters, the only area where the EU states act together and with a single voice. In fact, following its 1995 China strategy, the Commission presented in April 1997 a communication to the Council on relations with Hong Kong, which was endorsed by the European Council in June 1997. This communication proposes four priority areas for future EU policy towards Hong Kong.

The first area is the monitoring of the evolving situation in Hong Kong through the production of an annual report covering commerce, finance, bilateral and multilateral co-operation, and human rights. This was clearly inspired by the model of the Hong Kong Policy Act produced by the US State Department, but it is less certain that the report will cover exactly the same issues. It should be noted that there is no explicit reference in the EU proposal to monitoring the political situation and changes in the political system, which suggests a cautious approach, though references to the human rights situation will be included.

The second area is that of visa policy towards Hong Kong people. The Commission advocates a more concerted approach and the adoption of visa-free access to the EU for Hong Kong people, stressing that free access would be in the interests of the EU. This is an important question and it is clear that the restrictive policy adopted by many EU member states will remain an obstacle to the development of contacts between the EU and Hong Kong citizens, and runs contrary to the objective of greater internationalization and exposure of Hong Kong.

The third area concerns the development of more intensive and closer ties with Hong Kong as a major hub in Asia, recognizing its important regional role and the need to make more use of Hong Kong as a platform for European interests in Asia.

The fourth area relates to the formalization of EU–Hong Kong economic relations (trade, investment and co-operation) through a more permanent framework. This proposal posits the eventual signature of a Trade and Co-operation Agreement between the EU and Hong Kong, inspired by the model of the 1993 EU–Macau Agreement. This would certainly be an important instrument for reinforcing Hong Kong's international autonomy and visibility, which is a major goal for the Commission, as stated by Sir Leon Brittan:

> The best way to make a reality of the high degree of autonomy promised for Hong Kong is for us all to deal directly with Hong Kong in the wide variety of policy areas for which it has been given responsibility (Brittan 1997).

In spite of the tendency to concentrate on the economic sectors, and the failure to put more emphasis on co-operation in social areas, especially education at the tertiary level, this seems to be a promising set of proposals that could make an effective contribution to enhancing EU–Hong Kong relations.

However, even if these proposals are implemented, their effectiveness might be limited since there is no guarantee of coherence and co-ordination with bilateral policies. Moreover, the majority of member states have no distinct policy towards Hong Kong and tend to attach priority to their relations with Beijing. In general, they may not be prepared to speak out to defend autonomy and human rights if things go in the wrong direction, as they fear possible retaliation by China, which could jeopardize their economic interests and their prospects for access to the Chinese market. In short, the 'soft approach' the EU has adopted in relation to the PRC could well be extended to the Hong Kong case.

In spite of these limitations, further aggravated by the recent failure to strengthen the Common Foreign and Security Policy within the EU, it is possible that the EU could play an important and useful role in mediating disputes between China and Hong Kong, and help to reduce tension. The logic behind this reasoning is that the EU has presently a more constructive and positive relationship with China than does the US, and is regarded as a trustworthy partner given its more flexible attitudes in relation to human rights and WTO accession, for example. If tensions develop between China and Hong Kong, EU 'mediation' could be more easily accepted by Beijing and be more effective than the more radical, emotional and disruptive action likely to be taken by the US. For the EU to be able to play this role, it is important that a common and co-ordinated EU approach develops, diluting more visible UK action which would be likely to raise old tensions. It seems that following the handover, the UK (and perhaps later Portugal in relation to Macau) might be more open to the idea of 'communitarization' of the Hong Kong question, as it ceases to be a British issue and becomes a European one. Furthermore, the EU role will probably become more relevant, in the monetary area, as the Euro emerges in the future as a strong and stable international currency (probably leading to changes in HKSAR monetary policy, similar to the 'fixed peg' option with the American dollar) and in the technology area, as the EU becomes more involved in providing relevant technology. Similarly, the strong EU position in the world trade system could lead the HKSAR to regard Europe as a useful ally, in particular in the contextof the WTO, in its promotion of Hong Kong's specific interests.

Multilateral relations

The participation of Hong Kong in multilateral organizations and agreements is a fundamental part of Hong Kong´s international status. In terms of multilateral organizations, accession to the majority of international organizations in which Hong Kong participates occurred after the Joint Declaration came into force, clearly showing that the transition process had a very positive impact in boosting Hong Kong's international status.

The Joint Liaison Group has approved Hong Kong's participation in 31 international organizations at three different levels:

- full and autonomous membership, seven organizations (WTO/GATT, World Customs Organization, International Textiles and Clothing Bureau, Asian Development Bank, World Meteorological Organization, Network of Aquaculture Centres in Asia and the Pacific, World Health Organization Regional Committee for the Western Pacific)
- as part of the sovereign government's delegation, 18 organizations, the majority belonging to the UN system (FAO, ILO, IMF, WB Group, UNCTAD, IAEA) covering six major areas: economic, financial, intellectual property, telecommunications, postal and soft security
- as an associate member, six organizations, mostly regional with the exception of the International Maritime Organization, which admits exclusively sovereign states as full members.

In addition, Hong Kong currently participates, in various capacities, in 10 other organizations in relation to which JLG agreement is not required.

This group includes, among others, two very relevant organizations for Hong Kong – the Asia-Pacific Economic Cooperation Forum (APEC) and the OECD, where Hong Kong is an observer on the important Trade Committee and actively involved in the informal dialogue between OECD and the Dynamic Non-Member Economies (DNMEs).

Furthermore, a total of 203 multilateral agreements are applicable to Hong Kong as agreed by the Joint Liaison Group. These include:

- 170 multilateral agreements covering 20 different areas, most notably: human rights (15 treaties), customs (14), international labour conventions (46), merchant shipping (22), international crime (10), warfare and disarmament (8), intellectual property (5), political and diplomatic areas (8)
- 24 treaties that establish international organizations in which the HKSAR participates, and are therefore instrumental
- nine treaties related to foreign affairs and national defence, which, as a consequence of a PRC decision, began to be applicable to the HKSAR after the handover.

To complete the picture of Hong Kong multilateral relations, reference should be made to the fact that, beside international organizations, Hong Kong participated in 972 non-governmental organizations in 1995, while there were 75 organizations that situated their headquarters in Hong Kong (Yearbook of International Organizations 1995/6: 1685–1710).

The multilateral dimension of HKSAR external relations serves to:

- give the HKSAR visibility, international exposure and reinforce Hong Kong's image as a responsible member of the international community,
- provide an opportunity for Hong Kong to participate in and influence the formulation of multilateral rules, which set out fundamental standards of international behaviour,
- moderate and counterbalance bilateral pressure and the potential use of arbitrary measures by the most powerful and influential partners against the HKSAR through coalitions with other members.

At the multilateral level, while it is true that the HKSAR has an interest in participating in as many organizations as possible, it should be stressed that Hong Kong attaches priority to participation in the World Trade Organization (WTO) and the Asia-Pacific Economic Cooperation Forum (APEC). These are important links to the globalization and regionalization processes respectively.

Following completion of the Uruguay Round, the WTO became an increasingly influential organization. Hong Kong is the eighth trading nation and the fourth largest world investor, and is therefore very interested in participating in the work of the organization, which is not only a rule-making but also a rule-enforcing body in those areas.

Hong Kong, represented in Geneva by its Economic and Trade Office, is generally regarded as a very active and responsible member of the WTO. A small but efficient team of six diplomats manages, under the instructions of the Hong Kong Government Trade Department, the participation of the HKSAR in these bodies.

In this respect, the textiles sector is important. Hong Kong's major objective is the liberalization of trade in this sector, involving the effective implementation of the WTO Agreement on textiles and clothing, which will end the MFA scheme, and integrate textiles and clothing products into the WTO rules on the basis of a 10-year transition programme. Hong Kong is particularly active in this area, with the HKSAR represented in the Textiles Monitoring Body, the forum created to oversee the integration programme.

Hong Kong is also especially interested in the work of the Services Council, and in the negotiations for the liberalization of trade in services, in particular financial services.

Thirdly, there is an interest in more systemic issues, in particular anti-dumping questions, and the functioning of the Dispute Settlement Mechanism. Until now, Hong Kong has never been directly involved as a party in any dispute to be settled by WTO mechanisms, but the head of the Geneva Mission has chaired the important Banana Panel since 1996, a clear sign of Hong Kong's prestige within the organization.

The active participation of Hong Kong is also demonstrated by the numerous proposals it has put forward for discussion. In the Singapore ministerial meeting last December, Hong Kong presented three important proposals, concerning the relationship between trade and investment, trade and competition, and transparency of government procurement.

In connection with the work of the WTO, the HKSAR also participates in the OECD Trade Committee, an important forum for debate on trade policy, which not only introduces new ideas later followed up by the WTO, but also plays an important complementary role by dealing with difficult problems still blocked in the WTO. In addition, Hong Kong participates in meetings conducted by the Trade Committee and other OECD Committees on trade-related issues, such as the environment, competition, investment and labour standards.

The WTO is clearly the most important international stage for Hong Kong at the multilateral level, given the prominence of the organization in the international system, and the fact that Hong Kong is one of the freest economies in the world, thus exemplifying the free trade pursued by the WTO. The difficulty Hong Kong is likely to face within the WTO relates to the fact that many influential members are insisting on a 'fair trade' logic, somewhat different from the 'free trade' position advocated by Hong Kong.

This may lead to an increasing politicization of the trade debate, and create some inhibition on the part of the HKSAR, particularly when China joins the organization.

Participation in APEC as a full member since 1992 guarantees the active involvement of the HKSAR in the regionalization process going on in the world economy. Hong Kong participates through its Economic and Trade office in Singapore, and has taken specific responsibilities in the organization. At present the HKSAR is the Convenor of the Government Procurement Experts Group, and the Co-Vice Chair of the Committee on Trade and Investment.

Hong Kong is very interested in the APEC process, with its three pillars – trade and investment liberalization, trade and investment facilitation, and economic and technical co-operation. This interest is justified not only by the fact that the large majority of Hong Kong's external trade is concentrated in the Asia-Pacific region (in 1996 around 80 per cent of Hong Kong's total external trade was conducted with the other 17 members of APEC), but also because of the main APEC goal, that is to say, to create, according to the 1994 Bogor Declaration, a free trade area in two stages: by 2010 for developed members, and by 2020 for developing members. In addition, Hong Kong was, in 1995–1996, the number one foreign investor in the APEC area, a noteworthy and surprising development.

Since Hong Kong already has a very open and liberalized trade system, it is interested in obtaining advantages and reciprocity from Asia-Pacific partners as soon as possible. However, the global plan for the liberalization process is a long-term one and therefore does not deliver immediate results. Thus one of the main priorities of Hong Kong in APEC is to push for the early voluntary liberalization of specific sectors in advance of the above-mentioned deadlines, and along the lines of the 1996 Information Technology Agreement. In this process there is, with respect to some sectors, a convergence of interests with the US, but probably a divergence with some Asian partners, which are not yet prepared to open up their markets.

Hong Kong has put forward proposals for voluntary elimination of tariffs on toys, and for action on nuisance tariffs. Concerning toys, Hong Kong proposed to reduce progressively to zero the tariffs on certain toy items, starting the process in 1998, and aiming for it to be completed by 2000 and certainly no later than 2005.

The proposal on nuisance tariffs (those with an applied MFN rate of below 2 per cent, which damage the efficient flow of trade while generating considerable administrative procedures, and costs in general in excess of the revenue) points to the removal of those tariffs for all sectors in one go, possibly by 1999, thus allowing for a trade facilitation effect particularly helpful to small-and medium-sized enterprises.

Another area for Hong Kong is technical co-operation, where the HKSAR can be simultaneously a recipient, e.g. in science and technology, and a provider of technical advice on trade facilitation and efficiency issues for other Asian countries.

Finally, there is the matter of the links between APEC and the WTO. In the view of many specialists, the US tends to see APEC as a multilateral mechanism to soften its trade deficits with China and Japan, and above all as an instrument to enhance its leverage and bargaining position in the WTO (Calder 1997). The HKSAR will certainly adopt a different approach and is likely to value APEC on its own merits and for its potential regional impact. On the other hand, China is also a member of APEC, and Hong Kong will want to avoid being caught between the strategies for the Asia-Pacific region of the US and China. Up to now, the US interest in rapid liberalization of specific sectors has been shared by Hong Kong, but it is not likely that the HKSAR will continue to adhere in the future to the US global instrumental approach to APEC.

Conclusions

Hong Kong has a high profile and a unique international status, described by some as that of a 'quasi-state'. This status, reinforced in the last decade as a consequence of the transition process and by the end of the cold war, has been characterized by a real 'international legal personality', the pre-dominance of informal ties, and the performance of a discrete broker role in conflicts between China and the outside world.

The future evolution of the HKSAR's international status, and the pattern of its external relations, will likely be determined by the interplay of various factors, in particular:

- the implementation in practice of the new HKSAR external relations framework
- the evolution of the PRC foreign policy
- the pattern of relations between Beijing and the HKSAR
- the policies and strategies which foreign powers will adopt towards the HKSAR.

The external relations dimension of the HKSAR is an exception to the 'high degree of autonomy', and is submitted to the principle of sovereign power competence, while granting that the HKSAR has a limited sphere of auton-omy in specific matters. The new institutional framework that entered into force after the handover has a complex four-tier structure that provides for global policy formulation and overall supervision by the central govern-ment, with areas of 'conditioned autonomy', 'restrictive autonomy' and 'no autonomy' at the policy implementation level.

The main argument put forward is that this complex framework will tend to reduce the HKSAR's current level of autonomy in conducting external relations, because the freedom and flexibility Hong Kong used to possess to cultivate informal ties will diminish, and the supervision and influence exerted by the new sovereign power will intensify. However, the precise degree of autonomy the HKSAR will be allowed to exercise in practice is not yet clear.

It has been argued that this reduction in autonomy does not lead automatically, or necessarily, to a decline or weakening of Hong Kong's international status in the short and medium term, given Hong Kong's starting point of a strong and consolidated substantive status, and the interest of Beijing in preserving the HKSAR's international role in order to use it to its own advantage.

The most likely scenario for the next few years seems to be one of stabilization, not expansion, of the HKSAR's international status after an exceptional phase of rapid expansion during the transition period, the momentum of which was difficult to maintain. The challenge for Hong Kong will be to see to what extent in this scenario of stabilization it will be possible to promote qualitative improvements and the deepening of existing international ties, a crucial condition for the preservation of its identity and role as an international city, as well as a way of protecting its global autonomy *vis-à-vis* Beijing, and preventing future violations.

The US will remain the key player, the single foreign power that has an autonomous and integrated approach to its relations with Hong Kong, and which is prepared to exert pressure on Beijing if things go wrong in Hong Kong. However this relationship also presents clear risks to the HKSAR, which fears becoming caught in the middle of a major US–China conflict. In this context, the HKSAR may have a clear interest in adopting a more active diversification strategy and in reinforcing its ties with other strategic partners to balance the dominant US position. The EU is a potential candidate, also because of its strong position in the trade system, for a more active role. This would require a European effort to develop a more autonomous policy towards the HKSAR, and to promote greater co-ordination between bilateral policies and common EU policies, and would require the EU to be prepared politically to play an 'insurance policy' role.

Lastly, an issue for further study is a comparison of the processes of retrocession of Hong Kong and Macau to the PRC. The Macau transition may be more problematic, not only because the continuity of public administration is not guaranteed, but also because of an underdeveloped civil society, and political stagnation in Macau. For the Portuguese authorities, the dominant perception of future threats to the Macau Special Administrative Region (MSAR) is that they are not political, and do not come from Beijing, but tend to be more economic, and relate to the risk of Macau being absorbed by Zhuhai. Its international status is extremely fragile. In short,

Macau lacks both the internal and the external instruments to protect its future autonomy *vis-à-vis* Beijing.

The main problem is that Macau has a formal international status but, unlike Hong Kong, lacks a substantive status and an international image more adequate to its interests. Macau has anchored its international status in multilateral organizations but, unlike Hong Kong, has not invested in the bilateral dimension. In this respect, the MSAR will have much to learn from the HKSAR experience.

Analysis of the similarities and differences between the HKSAR and the MSAR will clearly emerge as an important topic in the future, and will raise questions about the extent to which the two SAR systems, subordinated to similar rules, will converge or diverge. The pattern of co-operation and co-ordination likely to develop between the two SARs, in particular in the field of foreign relations, will be important, as will the kind of relations the SARs will maintain with Taiwan. The SARs' experiences will have clear relevance for that reunification process.

Notes

1   According to Enright, Scott and Dodwell (1977), there are 'unique combinations' in Hong Kong, i.e. a special balance between government/business; local/overseas firms; entrepreneurship/management; and strategies of commitment/hustle, which are regarded as crucial factors to Hong Kong's success.
2   This was one clear conclusion of the analysis carried out in the context of the IEEI Conference on 'The EU Member States' Bilateral Policies towards China and the Future SAR', where the bilateral policies of Germany, France, the UK, Italy, the Netherlands, Portugal and Spain were analysed.

Bibliography

Brittan, Sir L. 1997 Introductory speech to the Council of the EU, 23 April.
Calder, K. 1977 *America and the Emerging Economic Community.* Paper presented in March to the Macau Conference on Regional Integration Areas: Future Relations in the XXI Century.
Enright, M., Scott, E., Dodwell, D. 1977 *The Hong Kong Advantage.* Oxford: Oxford University Press.
Far Eastern Economic Review, 29 May 1997.
Lo Shiu Hing 1995 *Political Development in Macau*, Hong Kong: Chinese University Press.
Tang, J. T. H. 1993 'Hong Kong's International Status'. *The Pacific Review* 6(3).
US State Department, Bureau of East Asian and Pacific Affairs 1997 *United States–Hong Kong Policy Act Report.* Washington D.C.
Wai Ting 1997 *Europe, China and the Future of Hong Kong*, Paper presented at the IEEI conference 'The EU Member States' Bilateral Policies towards China and the Future SAR', October (forthcoming).
Yahuda, M. 1995 *Hong Kong, China's Challenge.* London: Routledge.
Yearbook of International Organizations 1995/6, Vol. 2. Union of International Associations. Munchen: Saur.

Index